BEYOND THE SPITFIRE

BEYOND THE SPITFIRE

THE UNSEEN DESIGNS OF R.J. MITCHELL

RALPH PEGRAM

The History Press

All images herein from the author's collection unless otherwise stated.

First published 2016
Reprinted 2017

The History Press
The Mill, Brimscombe Port
Stroud, Gloucestershire, GL5 2QG
www.thehistorypress.co.uk

British Library Cataloguing in Publication Data.
A catalogue record for this book is available from the British Library.

ISBN 978 0 7509 6515 6

Typesetting and origination by The History Press
Printed in India.

CONTENTS

ACKNOWLEDGEMENTS

The aircraft types built by Supermarine during the lifetime of Chief Designer R.J. Mitchell are reasonably well known and most have been described in numerous books and articles. Likewise, a fine company history, *Supermarine Aircraft since 1914*, by Andrews and Morgan, was published in 1981 and has stood the passage of time well serving as a key reference for later works including this one. However, tantalising comments have cropped up here and there mentioning projects and designs that never saw the light of day, sufficient to demonstrate that there was a far deeper story yet to be told.

It is therefore extremely fortuitous that someone with foresight preserved a fair record of the many designs produced by Mitchell and his team; drawings salvaged after Supermarine's offices were bombed in the war and subsequently after a fire in their new premises. In time, these drawings were donated to the Royal Air Force Museum, where they are now available for viewing. Among them are a large number of previously undescribed projects that outnumber the aircraft types built by the company by a factor of around three to one. They provide fascinating insight into the workings of Mitchell's team, filling gaps in the narrative, throwing a light on competition from rivals and adding context to the company's products.

Other pertinent material continues to surface as archives and libraries place catalogues on their websites, and the advent of online auction sites has served to unearth many more documents, photographs and ephemera of relevance. The availability of back issues of *Flight*, *The Aeroplane* and similar aviation magazines in digital formats has also facilitated research. As a consequence, it is now possible to piece together a far more complete story of how Mitchell matured both as a designer and leader, how key members of his team contributed to projects and how the technical expertise of the team as a whole grew over a period of two decades. It is particularly rewarding to be able to highlight the contribution made by less well-known members of Mitchell's team and to correct a long-standing error as to the identity of his predecessor. Their work needs to be recognised. Nevertheless, this story remains work-in-progress and there will, of course, be many gaps that others hopefully may fill in the future.

I have been fortunate to tap into the knowledge of several people while assembling this book, people who are mostly anonymous and known only through their user names on various forums, and this has proven extremely helpful. There is an awful lot of expertise out there and much is shared freely. I thank you, whoever you may be.

Finally, special thanks go to Matt Painter whose exceptional talent as a computer graphics artist has produced the cover montage and several of the wonderful aircraft models for colour illustrations in this book. The realisation of these unbuilt aircraft projects is a tricky business: not only is the quality of many of the Supermarine layout drawings variable, with problems translating them into three dimensions, but it is also debatable what modifications may have been made to these aircraft prior to construction. In general, Matt and I have chosen to stay true to the original designs, minimising adjustments and only adding detail where it is obvious that it should be applied.

INTRODUCTION

Despite its undoubted fame, Supermarine in the 1920s and early 1930s was a second-tier aircraft company that specialised in an eclectic range of flying boats and seaplanes that sold in very small numbers. They occupied a motley collection of sheds on a cramped triangular site hemmed in by the river Itchen, a railway line and a small housing estate, yet had managed to build the fastest aircraft in the world and one of the first truly practical service flying boats. However, sustained commercial success largely eluded them and they were never financially secure until a lifeline was thrown when they were purchased by Vickers. This saved the company from collapse in the early years of the Depression, a period when they were desperately short of orders and their latest prototypes had proven disappointing. The company began to claw its way back slowly but appeared to have lost its way somewhat, building biplane flying boats in an era when monoplanes were coming to the fore. Then came the Spitfire.

Throughout this period, Supermarine's Design Department was led by one man, Reginald Joseph Mitchell, and to him and his team can be attributed all the commercial and technical successes, and the disappointments of lacklustre aircraft, among the twenty-two or so types the company constructed. There is no doubt that the successes were great and as a consequence Mitchell is unquestionably Britain's most revered aircraft designer; the man who created the formidable Spitfire, the majestic Southampton, the hard-working Walrus and the exotic Schneider Trophy-winning racing seaplanes. His reputation with the general public was assured by the exploits of the Spitfire in the Battle of Britain, and, through numerous articles, books and films he has been elevated to the status of national hero and genius.

Popular history, however, does have a tendency to be rather simplified and selective, and accounts of Mitchell's life and career are no exception. Books on the subject of Mitchell as a designer are dominated by the Spitfire and otherwise focus heavily on those aircraft types that proved successful. His failures and disappointments, of which there were a significant number, are pushed to the background and all but a handful of the aircraft projects on which he devoted much energy yet failed to win production contracts are ignored. There were more than eighty of these projects, ranging from early concepts through to complete detailed designs that were tendered to potential customers.

Mitchell worked within an industry where numerous companies pursued relatively limited opportunities in a world struggling to recover from the economic burden of the First World War. The financial state of Supermarine, as with many of its peers, was fragile on a number of occasions. The two men who served as Managing Director during Mitchell's tenure, Hubert Scott-Paine and James Bird, were both strong personalities and well connected with key people within the Air Ministry and industry. They devoted a great deal of time and energy to promote the company's products and endeavoured to stimulate growth. They gave Mitchell every support and encouragement in his work, and he was rewarded with a position on the Board. Within the Design Department many of the key staff had been selected and recruited by Mitchell personally and under his benign leadership they developed to become perhaps one of the best integrated team of designers and technicians in the industry. From a small company specialising in flying boats constructed along traditional yacht-building lines they blossomed in just ten years to build the fastest aeroplane in the world, an all-metal seaplane. Within another half dozen years they were busy putting the finishing touches to the world's fastest fighter monoplane: the Spitfire. Along the way it had been a roller coaster ride of highs and lows.

1

SUPERMARINE – ORIGIN AND THE EARLY YEARS

The Supermarine works were not yet three years old when Mitchell was recruited, but these had been event-packed years that set in place a firm foundation for the company's future character and thus helped to shape his career.

NOEL PEMBERTON BILLING

The town of Woolston is located on the eastern bank of the river Itchen facing Southampton docks and at the close of the nineteenth century it was linked to the city by a pontoon ferry known as the Floating Bridge. Immediately upstream of the ferry landing there was a small boat yard and ship's chandlers known as Oakbank (previously Oak Bank) Wharf comprised of a collection of sheds and workshops, a slipway and a small tidal basin. In 1913 this yard was purchased by Noel Pemberton Billing as the base for his new aircraft business.

Billing was born in Hampstead, north London, in 1881. He was a man rich in ideas, overwhelmed with self-confidence, abrasive, quixotic and with a huge capacity for self-promotion. As such, it is difficult to disentangle the truth from the self-created myth. It is self-evident that he was determined to make a success of his life through his own initiative and, looking for opportunities, he dabbled in a wide variety of endeavours, including farming, property speculation and publishing. He recounts that he began to experiment with simple man-carrying gliders launched from his bungalow roof at his farm in Sussex.

By 1909, after six years casting around for a fulfilling, and lucrative, career, Billing had managed to accumulate sufficient funds to purchase a group of engineering workshops standing in 3,000 acres of flat marshy land adjacent to the river Crouch at South Fambridge in Essex, where he hoped to develop a flying ground for pioneer aviators. To help promote this venture, which he termed a 'Colony of British Aerocraft' he founded and edited his own magazine, *Aerocraft*, and also managed to induce *Flight* magazine to publish a three-page article on the project. In the short period while living at Fambridge, Billing says that he designed, built and tested two or three crude monoplane aircraft that all proved to be unsuccessful, although one may possibly have achieved brief hops. Despite enjoying a measure of early success after the arrival of a small number of fledgling aircraft builders, the airfield venture failed within a year. Billing sold his interest in *Aerocraft* at the same time. Not disheartened and apparently still solvent, Billing indulged in property speculation at Shoreham on the Sussex coast, set out to study law, abandoned that after a few weeks and decided instead to trade in motor launches and yachts.

In late 1911, Billing purchased facilities at White's Yard, a wharf on the Itchen just upstream from Woolston, as a base for his yacht and motor launch business. There he employed Hubert Scott-Paine as manager. Billing had met Scott-Paine a few years earlier while both were living in Shoreham and found they shared a somewhat wild and adventurous spirit and a love of the sea. Billing, his wife and Scott-Paine all lived on board his yacht *Utopia*, which was moored at the yard. With this business established, and under Scott-Paine's astute guidance turning in a profit, his thoughts returned to aircraft, in particular flying boats. He conceived the idea of a flying boat in which the wings and propeller could be detached so that the hull, with engine and water propeller, could function independently as a motor launch. This was considered as both a safety feature in case of a forced landing on water or as a way in which the aircraft could serve a dual purpose. Assisted by Scott-Paine, who was fascinated by the idea of flying boats, he drew up a number of designs to show various configurations of aircraft and quick release mechanisms for the flying surfaces. These were drawn together into a patent application, which he submitted at the end of October 1913. In this application he described himself as an aviator-constructor. He was, indeed, an aviator by this time having obtained his flying certificate in somewhat bizarre circumstances on the morning of 17 September that year, but the claim to be a constructor was a little premature.

With his renewed interest in aircraft Billing had visited Hendon, a prominent centre for early aviation in Britain, in the summer of 1913 in order to meet up with some of the pioneer aviators of the era who were based on the airfield. He got into a discussion with Fred Handley Page regarding how much time would be required for a competent person to learn to fly and obtain their aviator's certificate, Handley Page asserting that a pupil learning on his latest machine, the monoplane Yellow Peril, which he deemed to be inherently stable, could do so within a 24-hour period. Billing replied that this could be achieved on any machine and made a wager of £500 that he would obtain his certificate in this way before Handley Page. Handley Page accepted the bet; he would make the attempt on the Yellow Peril and Billing on a machine of his own choosing. Billing elected to train at Brooklands, another centre for early aviators where his brother ran the Blue Bird cafe, but none of the schools there was willing to risk their machines on what they considered to be a foolish venture. He was obliged to make an on-the-spot purchase of an ageing Farman biplane fitted with a 50hp Gnome engine. Robert Barnwell, chief instructor at the Vickers school, agreed to provide tuition and the pair set out at 5.45 a.m. on 17 September. The weather was cool and drizzly but nevertheless the lessons proceeded, with Billing at the controls and Barnwell sitting behind and shouting instructions over his shoulder. After a couple of flights, Billing set out on his own, flying erratically, but somehow safely, until around eight o'clock. He then sent a runner to locate Mr Rance, the official Royal Aero Club (RAeC) observer, so that he could make an attempt at the specified flights and landings required to obtain his certificate. Reluctantly, Rance agreed to observe and Billing made his flights, not without incident, and Rance, quite possibly against his better judgement, awarded him his certificate in time for breakfast. Barnwell is quoted as commenting later that his pupil had shown some aptitude 'but if he thinks he knows anything about flying – God help him'. Handley Page, who had barely commenced his lessons, paid up. Billing, always seeking publicity, ensured that *Flight* magazine published the full story.

On his return to Woolston, Billing set about preparations to launch a new company in order to construct his first true aircraft. He had acquired the premises at Oakbank Wharf for this purpose and renamed the sheds there as the Supermarine works. The new company was funded jointly by Billing and Alfred Delves de Broughton, a minor aristocrat and sportsman, who were named as directors. The nominal capital of the company was £20,000. Billing held 6,800 shares and a Rolls-Royce limousine, while de Broughton had 3,700 and the works engineer, Lorenz Hans Herkomer, received 500. Herkomer's father, Hubert, was a highly regarded artist and member of the Royal Academy who was both a 'von' and a 'sir'. He had died in March 1914 so it is not impossible that Lorenz had invested part of his inheritance in the new business. Billing employed Hubert Scott-Paine as Works Manager. The official date for the foundation of Pemberton-Billing Ltd was 27 June 1914, although subsequent company advertising material chose frequently to backdate this to 1912.

While details of the launch of the company were being finalised, the works, staffed by experienced local boat builders, had commenced construction of Billing's first flying boat, the Supermarine P.B.1. Billing had adopted the name Supermarine to 'convey to the mind a craft capable of navigating the surface of the sea as also the air above' and for some time thereafter the company used variations on the slogan, 'boats that fly, rather than aeroplanes that float' to stress the marine heritage of their products. The P.B.1 was a small single-seat biplane flying boat featuring a cigar-shaped hull built on a racing yacht hull principle, which, in a letter to *Flight* in the 1930s, Scott-Paine claimed had been designed by him. The aircraft was powered by Billing's 50hp Gnome from his Farman biplane, which drove a custom-built three-bladed propeller mounted as a tractor unit in an egg-shaped nacelle positioned between the wings. The aircraft was completed in time to be displayed at the Olympia Aero, Motor Boat, Marine and Stationary Engine Exhibition in March, although it lacked its engine and had yet to be tested.

A smart silk-bound brochure was issued by Billing to accompany the start of his business, which included a description of the factory, somewhat short of reality; a history of Billing's earlier aviation ventures, a little embellished; and details of the first three P.B. designs to be built by the company. Advertisements in *Flight* and *The Aeroplane* featured artwork showing a Supermarine P.B.7 'flying lifeboat' with detachable wings. Billing's patent application was updated in April 1914 with additional examples of the slip-wing principle and in this he gave his address as the Supermarine Works, Southampton. The hulls for the first two P.B.7 aircraft were under construction alongside the P.B.1 and are said to have been ordered by the German military.

When the P.B.1 returned from Olympia, the Gnome engine was installed but despite numerous attempts it failed to become airborne. The aircraft was taken back into the workshop where the nacelle was removed and the engine remounted on the top of the hull within the wing centre section, from where it drove twin pusher propellers via chains and sprockets. The cockpit was relocated ahead of the wings. However, these changes made little difference and the aircraft still failed to fly: there is a limit to what can be achieved with an aging and tired engine producing less than 50hp.

Billing and Scott-Paine had been busy stocking the workshop with useful material and parts, mainly from defunct companies, and all this expenditure took its toll so Billing was forced to sell one of his yachts in order to meet the wages bill and other costs. In mid-year, part of the works was leased to Tom Sopwith for the assembly and testing of his Bat Boat.

As war approached, Billing abandoned any further thoughts of flying boats and commenced design and construction of a simple scout-type, designated P.B.9. Only minimal design work was required as Billing is said to have been able to use a set of biplane wings that he had acquired from Radley-England. The sole drawing to have survived from this time is signed by Carol Vasilesco, the company's Rumanian draughtsman and detail designer, who worked from Billing's and Scott-Paine's sketches. The biplane wings had full span spars and were connected by four pairs of interplane struts. This assembled and rigged biplane unit was slid along the fuselage and the spars of the lower wing secured to the bottom fuselage longerons by 'U' bolts. A simple cowl was constructed to be large enough to accommodate an 80hp Gnome rotary but the aircraft was fitted with the now-ageing 50hp engine taken from the P.B.1. The P.B.9 flew reasonably well but was not deemed sufficiently worthy to justify production. From initial design to first flight it had taken nine days, but for dramatic effect Billing liked to refer to the aircraft as 'the seven-day bus'.

Shortly after the declaration of war, Billing enlisted in the Royal Naval Volunteer Reserve (RNVR) and was no longer involved in the day-to-day running of the works. Without any production orders and with Billing absent, the business effectively collapsed. Eighty per cent of the staff had to be laid off, leaving just fourteen employees, whose wages were then halved. As a consequence, eight more left before the end of the year. In early September, his Farman biplane and a second aircraft, with their engines, were advertised for sale but in early November the company's solicitors reported that 'it was impossible to get on at all, consequent upon the war and the inability to obtain funds to pay any fees whatever'. However, on 18 November an agreement was reached whereby de Broughton dug deep into his pocket and agreed to pay all debts. Worse was to come when Carol Vasilesco died

suddenly of heart failure, which left the company without a designer. Billing effectively handed the business over to Scott-Paine, who somehow managed to keep the small workforce active with one-off aircraft repair work.

In the early months of 1915, the company was barely limping along undertaking small repair jobs for Sopwith and other menial tasks. It was steered by Scott-Paine on his own as de Broughton, too, had signed up for military service. He managed to secure a contract to build twelve Short S.38 seaplanes under licence, which enabled the company to keep its remaining skilled workshop staff employed gainfully while the fledgling Design Department was restructured.

In-house design had continued on a small scale and the next Pemberton-Billing aircraft to leave the works was the P.B.23E, a single-seater biplane pusher scout. The prototype was delivered to Hendon for trials in September 1915 and these indicated that the aircraft could be of some interest but was in need of modification. As a result, a slightly revised version was built in early 1916 with a lighter central nacelle-fuselage and wings with small sweepback: the P.B.25E. The company was awarded a production contract for twenty of these machines for the Royal Naval Air Service (RNAS) but none saw service. It is not known who was responsible for the detail design of these aircraft although they were almost certainly conceived by Billing.

By the end of 1915 Billing was back on the scene having served for around a year in the RNVR and RNAS. In his words, he had conceived of, planned and participated in the attack on the Zeppelin works at Friedrichshafen and, as a consequence, had risen to the rank of squadron commander. During his time in the services Billing had reached two conclusions; firstly, that the squadrons were being provided with woefully poor equipment and incompetent tactical leadership, and secondly that Britain was effectively defenceless against attack by Zeppelins. He determined that the best place from which to make his case, free from the risk of writs for slander and libel, was within the House of Commons and set about plans to get himself elected. However, he first set in motion the design and construction of a quadruplane anti-Zeppelin patrol fighter, the P.B.29E, to his own specifications.

In January 1916 Billing stood as an independent parliamentary candidate for the constituency of Mile End in the East End of London but was unsuccessful despite a vigorous campaign within the constituency and the vocal support of Horatio Bottomley in his right-wing newspaper, *John Bull*. However, he was not deterred and in March managed to get elected in the constituency of East Hertfordshire. He prepared to take his seat in the House while at the same time publishing his first book, *Air War: How To Wage It*, in which he promoted aircraft of the P.B.25 and P.B.29E type as defenders of the air over London.

By this time Scott-Paine had forged good relations with the Air Department of the Admiralty and the company came under their jurisdiction for wartime production. The Air Department were a small group headed by Harris Booth, an early expert in aerodynamics who had worked at the National Physical Laboratory (NPL) and on the Research Committee of the Royal Aeronautical Society (RAeS). Harold Bolas, formerly at the Royal Aircraft Factory, and Linton Hope, a marine architect, were the lead designers for aircraft to serve with the RNAS. The regional overseer appointed by the Navy to supervise aircraft construction by the various companies in the Solent area was James Bird, a qualified marine architect then serving with the RNAS. Pemberton-Billing Ltd was awarded a contract in May 1916 to build the flying surfaces for the patrol and reconnaissance A.D. Flying Boat and to carry out the detailed design and construction of the A.D. Patrol Seaplane, a large pusher biplane on flat-bottomed pontoon floats to fulfil much the same role. The hulls for the first A.D. Flying Boats were to be built by specialist boat builders May, Harden and May.

As Billing was about to embark on a rampage against the Government, the military high command, and the quality of aircraft and engines produced at the Royal Aircraft Factory at Farnborough, he was obliged to distance himself from the company in order to avoid any accusations of conflict of interest. Therefore, he negotiated to sell his holding to Scott-Paine and the other directors. Agreement was reached in June, setting the price at around £12,500. From this point he played no further role in the company's affairs and left the scene to create widespread indignation through his venomous and unsubstantiated attacks on prominent people, gaining a degree of popular support in the short term and condemnation thereafter.

HUBERT SCOTT-PAINE

Hubert Scott-Paine was born in 1890 at Shoreham on the Sussex coast. His father died while Hubert was still young and he, his sister and two brothers were brought up by their mother. Hubert and his brothers shared a passion for boating and mechanics, and had built their own motorcycles and powered boats.

Scott-Paine met Billing during the brief period when Billing was dabbling in property speculation in Shoreham and they became friends, so when Billing moved on to Southampton at the end of 1911 to start his steam-yacht trading business he asked Scott-Paine to join him. Throughout 1912 Scott-Paine was deeply involved in overhauling and maintaining Billing's

yachts, organising cruises, recruiting crews and delivering the vessels to clients. He was hard working and organised so Billing was content to leave much of the day-to-day running of the business in his hands. He also found time to customise a small number of cars for Billing's use. It is certainly possible, given later events, that it was Scott-Paine who had convinced Billing that he should channel his growing interest in aircraft towards flying boats.

When Billing established Pemberton-Billing Ltd, Scott-Paine was in his element, contributing to the detail design of the aircraft, the engine installations and hull construction. He nursed the fledgling company through the tough winter of 1914 and grew into the role of leader and canny businessman as he negotiated contracts to build aircraft for the RNAS under licence. He was thus well positioned when the opportunity arose to buy out Billing's share in the company and to launch Supermarine Aviation Works Ltd. His early robust and somewhat wayward tendencies, so useful when running Billing's yachts, had matured considerably and he was now an astute co-owner, director and general manager of a thriving aircraft company.

SUPERMARINE AVIATION WORKS LTD

Supermarine Aviation Works Ltd were registered officially on 27 June 1916. Hubert Scott-Paine was all too aware that the Pemberton-Billing name could prove detrimental to the future success of the company following Billing's outspoken attacks in Parliament and in the press, hence the company was renamed. Despite their earlier friendship the relationship had soured considerably and Scott-Paine was anxious to distance himself from his increasingly erratic former mentor.

Billing had been an energetic maverick in the world of aircraft constructors and some element of this adventurous spirit, tempered by practical business sense, could be found in Scott-Paine and hence in the character of the company that he now ran. Under Scott-Paine's firm leadership, and free from Billing's more wayward influence, Supermarine were soon placed on a stable footing with plenty of work in hand and a competent workforce of woodworking craftsman. It is hard to say for certain how Scott-Paine had viewed the design work they had undertaken on Billing's pet wartime projects but it had at least provided the fledgling Design Department with useful experience. He had aspirations to capitalise on this expertise as soon as possible, but focussed on more practical aircraft. While the ground war was mired on the Western Front with no end in sight, aerial warfare was coming to the fore and aircraft of diverse types were in demand for both the RNAS and Royal Flying Corps (RFC), providing many opportunities to exploit. Notwithstanding the ongoing work on the P.B.29E and P.B.31E quadruplanes and P.B.25E scouts, Supermarine remained at heart a specialist in marine aircraft. Its location on the banks of the Itchen, the lack of an airfield and the predominantly boat-building training of much of the workforce were testimony to that.

Scott-Paine saw the A.D. Flying Boat as an excellent example of the type of aircraft on which his company should specialise and took a keen interest in the design, construction and performance of their hulls and floats. When the contract had been awarded the Air Department had set up a small design office at the Woolston works and sent Harold Bolas and his deputies Clifford Tinson and Harold Yandall to oversee Supermarine's work. However, both this aircraft and the A.D. Patrol Seaplane had been passed to Supermarine with their designs substantially complete, leaving Scott-Paine's staff to handle the details. Frustratingly, the first contract for construction of the hulls had been awarded to May, Harden and May and Scott-Paine resolved to remedy this apparent slight and to ensure that his woodworkers acquired the skills to undertake this work in short order. Surviving drawings indicate that Supermarine did indeed construct some hulls for the later production batches.

The prototype A.D. Flying Boat was found to suffer from poor performance on the water and a considerable amount of testing and experimentation had to be undertaken to rectify the problems. Eventually, modifications to the planing bottom and step led to more satisfactory behaviour, although the aircraft continued to be prone to porpoising and instability in yaw. A total of thirty-four were constructed but none saw service with the Navy and most went straight into storage. The episode had been a valuable lesson for a company aiming to compete for future contracts for flying boats.

In order to drive the company forward, Scott-Paine saw that he needed to strengthen the capabilities of his technical team, so, among other positions, he advertised for a qualified engineer to act as his personal assistant. Reginald Mitchell applied.

REGINALD MITCHELL ARRIVES

Reginald Joseph Mitchell was born in Stoke-on-Trent in 1895, the son of a schoolmaster-turned-printer and the eldest of five children. Mitchell, like so many of his generation, developed a boyhood interest in engineering and aircraft, and built a few flying models for fun. However, there were no flying grounds or aircraft constructors in the immediate area of Stoke and he is not known to have had any contact with aviators or even to have seen any aircraft flying. After completing school, he undertook an engineering apprenticeship at the nearby railway locomotive manufacturer Kerr, Stuart & Co at Fenton while attending night school to obtain qualifications in engineering drawing and mathematics. His enthusiasm for aircraft, however it had arisen, had not diminished and must have been foremost in his mind when he sought employment. He joined Supermarine fresh from completing his apprenticeship.

How or why Mitchell came to apply for the job at Supermarine is, sadly, not recorded. As a qualified engineer, his skills were much in demand in a time of war and hence he was denied the option to enlist in the armed forces. He sought employment but whether he pursued a job within the aircraft business exclusively is, alas, also unknown. Stoke-on-Trent is about as far from the sea as it is possible to be in Britain so it does seem a little curious that he would have had a particular interest in marine aircraft, of which there had been precious few in the pre-war years. Pemberton-Billing Ltd was mentioned rarely in the press, had not placed any company advertisements since the summer of 1914, and hence was largely anonymous to the general public. The launch of Supermarine in the summer of 1916 was noted, but only in the context of Billing having sold his interest, and there was no mention of their activities, as was to be expected in wartime. It is therefore a little unlikely that Mitchell would have had any knowledge of the company and equally unlikely that he would have contacted them on spec seeking a job. Advertisements for job vacancies within the aircraft industry placed in *Flight* and *The Aeroplane* magazines through 1916 included many each week for engineers, engineering draughtsmen and qualified aircraft designers. However, and largely due to official restrictions imposed by the war, these rarely mentioned either the name or location of the employer and applicants were instructed to apply at their local labour exchange quoting a PO box number. It does appear reasonable to assume that Supermarine would have advertised in one or both of these magazines and that one of these published vacancies was therefore the job for which Mitchell applied. Regardless of how he became aware of the opportunity, Mitchell applied and travelled to Woolston, where he was interviewed by Scott-Paine. He was impressed sufficiently to offer him the job on the spot.

The earliest record of Mitchell's work at Supermarine are his initials, R.J.M., as draughtsman on at least fifteen of the over 500 surviving drawings for the P.B.31E quadruplane, which date from July to November 1916. This is rather curious as he does not appear to have produced drawings for any other design under way at this time, or, indeed, over the following three years. In addition to this conundrum there is also uncertainty as to the actual date on which Mitchell's employment commenced. Several published accounts, including those of Supermarine's public relations department in the 1920s, a presentation by his close friend and successor Joe Smith and the biography written by his son record that he had joined Supermarine in 1917, while on the other hand his obituaries in both *Flight* and *The Aeroplane* magazine stated 1916. As the evidence of the drawings is irrefutable, perhaps we can surmise that he served a probationary period of six months, working in a variety of roles, before his employment contract was confirmed.

In common with so many people working in aircraft design in these early years, Mitchell had to expand upon his basic engineering skills to match the requirements of a growing industry within which new technology and ideas arose at an astounding pace. His experience of workshop engineering was restricted to that acquired during his apprenticeship, the construction of small steam engines, which had nothing in common with the woodworking skills necessary for hull and wing design. In his first two years with the company Scott-Paine had Mitchell work in a variety of roles, broadening his experience and learning every aspect of the aircraft building business. He worked alongside Supermarine's Chief Designer, William Hargreaves, and head draughtsman, Cecil Richardson, and would have been of great assistance to both given his knowledge of engineering theory. For a while he served as Deputy Works Manager and through that became familiar with the methods of the skilled woodworkers and boat builders in the factory.

At the time of Mitchell's arrival, in addition to the aircraft production mentioned previously, Supermarine completed and tested the large P.B.31E quadruplane, which failed to win a production order, were awarded contracts to build both Short 184 torpedo bomber seaplanes and Norman Thompson NT2B trainer flying boats under licence, and they were selected to build a single-seat fighter flying boat to Navy specification N.1(b). This last aircraft, named Baby, was the first wholly Supermarine-designed flying boat to be built since the original P.B.1 back in 1914 and was destined to play a significant role in Mitchell's subsequent career.

THE SUPERMARINE BABY

Navy Air Board Specification N.1(b), issued in early 1917, requested designs for a single-seat flying boat or seaplane naval fighter to counter the German seaplanes that were flying reconnaissance patrols over the southern North Sea.

The specification called for a top speed of at least 95kt at 10,000ft and a service ceiling of 20,000ft. Scott-Paine placed Hargreaves in charge of the design.

William Abraham Hargreaves, one year older than Mitchell, was a trained engineer who had joined Supermarine as Chief Designer in early 1916 after completing an engineering apprenticeship in Wakefield. His initials can be seen on the majority of drawings from this date; either as original draughtsman or signing official approval on drawings made by others, including the aforementioned P.B.31E drawings produced by Mitchell. The earliest example of a new Hargreaves design to have survived dates from February 1917 when he suggested a version of the A.D. Flying Boat with refined wings. Hargreaves built upon the valuable knowledge Supermarine had gained while working with the Air Department designers developing and constructing the A.D. Flying Boats, and hence it is no great surprise that the layout for the N.1B Baby was broadly similar. The small 24ft hull was designed in detail by Lieut Linton Hope, now freelance after leaving the Air Department, to Supermarine's specifications. It was barely 3ft in maximum diameter with the cylindrical fuel tank located mid-hull beneath the wings in order to keep the centre of gravity low. As in the A.D. Flying Boat, the engine, a 200hp Hispano-Suiza, drove a pusher propeller, and was mounted above the hull on twin 'N' struts within the fixed centre section of the biplane wings. This layout for the engine and propeller was favoured by most flying boat designers at the time as the forward hull and lower wing shielded the propeller from the worst effects of spray during take-off and placed it well clear of the pilot. Supermarine fitted fore-and-aft canvas screens, which they referred to as stabilisers, between the innermost inter-wing struts and these also served to further reduce the impact of spray. It was a feature carried through on to several of their subsequent flying boats. The outer wings were designed to fold rearwards to facilitate storage on board ships; those on the A.D. Flying Boat had folded forwards. A small single fin and rudder was fitted on the rear of the hull with the tailplane mounted on the top, and both were braced by struts to the hull. The design was completed by the late summer of 1917 and the Navy ordered three aircraft for evaluation. It is worth noting in passing that the claim made by Cecil Richardson's son in *Aeroplane* in October 2004, that his father, as head of the draughting department, was responsible for the design of the Baby, does not stand up to scrutiny. It is Hargreaves who signed to approve the Baby drawings, although it is fair to say that Richardson's initials have been added outside the legend box, as supplementary, on a few. While he was clearly deeply involved in the design, as any on the small team would have been, it would be stretching the point to attribute the Baby to him.

→ The Supermarine N.1B Baby was a fast and nimble fighting scout. It proved to be a fine aircraft and may well have won a production contract had the war continued.

The first Baby, registered N59, was completed in February 1918 and proved to be amongst the smallest and neatest flying boats of its time. Early testing at the works showed that it was very slightly above design weight and had a tendency to ship a lot of water into the cockpit while accelerating, so the prow was revised to reduce spray from the bow wave. However, the Supermarine team clearly felt that there was room for further improvement so Hargreaves drew up a series of alternative hull profiles, at least six and all of the same basic size, in an attempt to address the problem. One of these new designs was selected for the third aircraft, N61, and construction may have commenced before the programme was cancelled.

Pilots reported that N59 handled well in the air and was stable on all axes. It was said in *The Aeroplane*, some years later, that the aircraft had been looped. Evaluation of the Baby was virtually complete by the autumn of 1918 and it may well have attracted a modest production contract had not the Armistice been signed.

Mitchell was by now an invaluable member of Scott-Paine's team and settled into his new life in Woolston. In the autumn of 1918, just before the end of the war, he married Florence Dayson, the headmistress at a primary school in his old home town of Stoke and eleven years his senior. The newly-wed couple moved into a rented house in Itchen and Mitchell bought a motorcycle so he could drive to work.

2

1919 – SUPERMARINE MEETS THE CHALLENGE OF PEACE

SECURING THE BUSINESS

Once the Armistice had been signed the British Government moved swiftly to terminate the vast majority of military construction contracts, and those held by Supermarine were no exception. Supermarine was still a relatively small business when compared with many other British aircraft constructors and they did not hold production contracts for significant numbers of aircraft. Nevertheless, the cancellations hit hard. Workmen were laid off and all construction work ceased.

Although faced with the potential collapse of his business, Hubert Scott-Paine was not a man to give up easily and, while keeping the works ticking over with menial woodworking tasks, he formulated a plan to keep Supermarine active as an aircraft constructor. As an indication of this intent, Supermarine joined the Society of British Aircraft Constructors in late 1918. Although the company's wartime production had included land-based aircraft and seaplanes alongside flying boats, Scott-Paine resolved to return to the roots of the business as he and Billing had envisaged it before the war and hence to specialise exclusively on flying boats. He would be able to capitalise on the hull-building expertise of his workforce, and the works, of course, were laid out to build and test marine aircraft. Scott-Paine's plan was accepted by his fellow directors: de Broughton and the solicitor Charles Cecil Dominy.

Even before the Treaty of Versailles had been signed to end the war officially the government placed a vast quantity of surplus aircraft, engines and related material up for sale at knock-down prices. Scott-Paine's first action was to negotiate the purchase of about sixteen unused A.D. Flying Boats from storage and the two completed Baby fighters, along with engines, spare parts, unfinished components and other useful material. The A.D. Flying Boats he

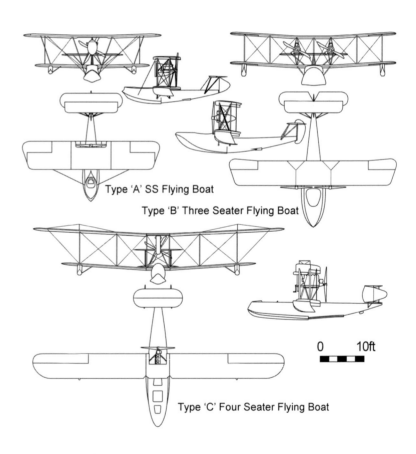

Type 'A' SS Flying Boat

Type 'B' Three Seater Flying Boat

Type 'C' Four Seater Flying Boat

0   10ft

↑ In 1919 Supermarine issued a brochure featuring a variety of flying boat designs.

intended to convert for commercial use, renamed the Type 'C' Channel, while the Baby would form the basis for a new high performance machine for use as either a military scout or for private flying. He also moved quickly with the aim to secure the company's rights to several key design features of both these aircraft by submitting a number of patent applications in the joint names of himself and Supermarine. Quick though he was, he slightly overstepped the mark as some features infringed patents taken out shortly before by Linton Hope and Harold Bolas. Nevertheless, with suitable phrases added to acknowledge these prior claims, they were all accepted by mid-1919.

In common with many aircraft constructors aiming to survive and, hopefully, prosper in the post-war world, Supermarine issued a new brochure to advertise their business. This featured the Channel and Baby plus designs for a new single-seat flying boat, the Type 'A', derived from the Baby, and a three-seat, twin-engined flying boat, the Type 'B', powered by 100hp, three-cylinder Cosmos Lucifer air-cooled radials. Both of these last two featured revised hull designs covered by Scott-Paine's patents.

STAFF CHANGES

Cecil Richardson had left the company in mid-1918 and William Hargreaves chose to follow suit in the summer of 1919. Hargreaves went to work for Vospers, the shipbuilders in Portsmouth, before joining Blackburn Aircraft as assistant designer of flying boats in 1927. In the 1930s he held the post of Chief Draughtsman and subsequently Assistant Works Manager. He did sterling work, especially during the Second World War when he oversaw the construction of Sunderland flying boats, for which he was awarded the MBE. He rose to become a director of the company in 1951.

Mitchell, recently married and settled in Southampton, was keen to remain with Supermarine, and Scott-Paine, fully aware of his competence and enthusiasm, promoted him to the position of Chief Designer in the second half of the year following Hargreaves' departure.

On the cessation of hostilities, James Bird at the Air Department of the Navy was promoted to the rank of squadron commander and promptly demobbed. However, he continued to work for the Admiralty in much the same role as before as a civilian overseer of the Solent-based aircraft constructors. When this job wound down in 1919 he was invited by Scott-Paine to join him on the Board at Supermarine.

Scott-Paine also employed six pilots for his commercial flying operations; Basil Hobbs, Francis Bailey, Philip Brend, John Hoare, Herbert Horsey

and Henri Biard, all ex-RNAS. Biard, the most experienced member of the group having acquired his aviator's certificate way back in 1912, was destined to fill the role of company test pilot for many years.

THE FIRST CHANNELS

The wartime ban on civilian flying in Britain was lifted in May 1919 and Supermarine moved swiftly to obtain their first civil certificates of airworthiness for ten of the refurbished Channel flying boats, which were granted in July. They were now ready to start commercial operations flying passengers and light freight. These aircraft were advertised under the name of the Supermarine Transport Company, initially for private charter and pleasure flights, and flown by the company's small group of experienced pilots.

The Channel was a simple adaptation of the A.D. Flying Boat where the cockpits had been modified to carry three passengers seated ahead of the pilot; two squeezed in side-by-side and one in the nose. They sat on simple cushioned seats that were spring-loaded to fold away when not in use to facilitate boarding and to keep them relatively dry. Attached to the hull sides were an anchor and a boathook, with a patented Supermarine latching hook, for the pilot to use when mooring. The cockpit also featured a hand operated bilge pump. Operations commenced in earnest in August with the inauguration of regular services from Southampton Docks to Bournemouth and the Isle of Wight, supplemented by ad hoc charter flights along the south coast. The company obtained several contracts ferrying newspapers and other small loads during the rail strikes that autumn. In general, three of the Channels were kept reasonably busy with the others held in reserve.

Scott-Paine sought customers for the remaining Channels and delegations from Japan, the Netherlands, Norway, Chile and others visited the works over the coming year.

RACING

In 1914 Howard Pixton, flying a Sopwith HS Tabloid seaplane, won the Schneider Trophy for Britain at the second annual contest, held in Monaco; the first success by a British aircraft in international competition. The RAeC thus had the responsibility to be the hosts for the following contest, scheduled for 1915 but postponed on account of the war. As early as February 1919 they had been contacted by the Fédération Aéronautique Internationale (FAI) requesting a date and location for the contest and it was agreed that it would take place in September on the south coast at Bournemouth. There was considerable interest from the British aircraft industry, who saw this as an excellent opportunity to showcase the capabilities of their designers and construction works in what was clearly destined to be a tough market for sales. Scott-Paine, always with an eye towards speed and competition, was keen for Supermarine to participate and had a suitable aircraft, albeit in pieces, readily available.

The RNAS contract for three N.1B Baby fighters was near to completion at the time of the Armistice. The prototype, registered N59, had proven to be a fine pilot's aircraft and had carried out a full test programme. The second machine, N60, was complete but remained unflown, while the components for the third, N61, which included a variety of design changes, were largely finished but yet to be assembled. This last aircraft featured a revised hull design, from the series evolved by Hargreaves in 1918 and covered by one of Scott-Paine's 1919 patents, and new flying and control surfaces. It was

this heavily revised Baby design, in the 1919 brochure as the type 'A' S.S. (Single Seat) Flying Boat, which was now prepared by the works to compete for the Schneider Trophy.

The Baby is acknowledged to have been designed by William Hargreaves, influenced heavily by the work of Harris Booth, Harold Bolas, and Linton Hope in the Air Department of the Navy, while the proposed S.S. Flying Boat, with its substantial changes, could be construed to suggest the input of another hand, although the surviving drawings, dating from July 1919, bear the initials of Hargreaves alone. The hull was of almost identical size to that on the first Baby but had been redesigned so that the cross section aft of the rear hull, egg-shaped on both aircraft, was pointed end up rather than down and the nose around the cockpit featured a flared decking designed to deflect spray. The wings were also completely new with increased chord and unequal span, ailerons with large horn balances on both wings, and outward-raked interplane struts. To adapt this aircraft for racing the wings were decreased in chord and fitted with reverse-tapered ailerons on the top wing only, while both the rudder and elevators were enlarged. The aircraft

← The Sea Lion was adapted from the third Baby scout and fitted with a 450hp Napier Lion engine.

was then re-engined with one of the first Napier Lion, twelve-cylinder, broad-arrow engines, loaned by the manufacturer, who were also keen to promote their products, and the aircraft was named Sea Lion. It is highly likely that Mitchell would have played a key role in the design changes and preparation of the aircraft for the contest.

By the rules of the Schneider Trophy competition each national aero club could enter a team of up to three aircraft. As Avro, Sopwith, Fairey and Supermarine had all notified the RAeC that they wished to participate it was necessary to hold elimination trials. The club selected the Sopwith and Fairey biplane seaplanes for the team on spec while the new Avro racer, also a biplane seaplane, was required to fly-off against the Sea Lion. Presumably the club considered that Sopwith had earned the right to be in the team as they had won in 1914 and there was every expectation that their new machine, the Schneider, would be the fastest of the British entrants. It was small, no larger than the 1914 Sopwith HS Tabloid, and powered by the new Cosmos Jupiter nine-cylinder air-cooled radial engine. Fairey's entry, the N.10, was a less obvious selection for the team. The N.10 was a modified version of a 1918 prototype two-seat torpedo bomber that Fairey had purchased back from the Air Ministry at the end of the war, cut the wingspan drastically and re-engined it with a Napier Lion. It was large and robust but no racer. The Sea Lion, therefore, faced off against Avro's Type 539, a small aircraft tailored tightly around its Siddeley Puma six-cylinder inline engine. The trials were delayed briefly when the Avro was damaged by debris in the Solent, which gave Supermarine time to install a new racing propeller that had only just been delivered due to industrial action at the manufacturers. The two aircraft then ran seaworthiness and air speed trials.

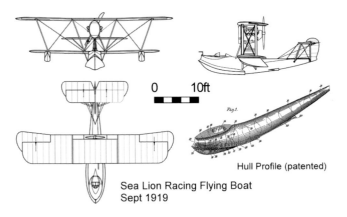

0   10ft

Fig.1.

Hull Profile (patented)

Sea Lion Racing Flying Boat
Sept 1919

The Avro proved to be marginally the faster of the two but in the end the decision was made in favour of the Sea Lion on the basis of its superior performance on the water. It was indeed wise not to select three seaplanes for the team as should the sea conditions on the day of the contest prove poor a flying boat would definitely have the edge.

On the day of the contest Scott-Paine and Bird flew to Bournemouth in one of the company's Channel flying boats. Once there, Supermarine's pilot Henri Biard took spectators out for joyrides around the bay for three guineas (£3.15) each, a huge sum at the time but a rare experience for those who could afford it. The company's small launch, *Tiddlywinks*, allegedly built using one of Pemberton Billing's discarded P.B.7 hulls, was also in attendance to assist.

Notwithstanding all their careful preparations, the race was to prove a disaster for Supermarine. Confusion had characterised the preamble as no facilities had been provided for the participating aircraft in the area of the race course start line. The overseas visitors had been based at first at Saunders' palatial and well-equipped workshop premises at Cowes on the Isle of Wight, so they were somewhat stunned when they arrived at Bournemouth to find that they were expected to simply moor offshore or pull up on to the pebble-strewn beach. Sadi Lecointe, in the SPAD S20, headed for the beach, thereby damaging its floats, while the Nieuport NiD 29, piloted by Lieut Casale, stayed offshore before noting that one float was leaking and he, too, took to the beach. Fortuitously, the more robust Savoia S.13 flying boat was pulled on to the beach without incident but was then besieged by spectators. The British, with local knowledge, were better off. Fairey sent a team on to the beach to secure a landing point for Vincent Nichol in the N.10 by clearing the foreshore and erecting a fence to keep the curious spectators at bay. Supermarine, with their sturdy hull, elected to stay afloat with *Tiddlywinks* keeping watch. Sopwith, however, suffered similar problems to the French and also sustained damage on the beach.

The weather was still and a fog bank hung offshore for much of the day, but, after a long delay, the club officials, who were based on the yacht *Ombra* at anchor beyond Bournemouth pier, decided to take a chance and start the race. The lengthy delay, dithering over rescheduled start times, poor communication with the participants and numerous misunderstandings meant that when the contest started some were caught unprepared and others confused as to when and how they were expected to start. While confusion reigned, Vincent Nichols in the Fairey N.10 took matters into his own hands and set off, followed soon after by Basil Hobbs flying the Sea Lion. However, it soon became apparent to them both that the fog in Swanage Bay completely obscured the turn marker located on a boat moored near the beach and Hobbs, having come close to colliding with the Fairey, decided to land in order to regain his bearings. On his take-off run he snagged a floating object and heard a loud bang but, as the aircraft flew without problem he carried on, only to discover when he touched down for the obligatory landing and taxy near Bournemouth Pier that the aircraft's planing bottom and hull had both been ripped and holed. The aircraft filled with water rapidly and tipped on to its nose, but luckily Hobbs was uninjured and swam free. The Sea Lion floated inverted and was towed ashore to be recovered later; it was wrecked beyond repair.

Neither French contender was in a fit state to participate and both withdrew. Nichols landed in the Fairey and declared the conditions to be unfit for the race to continue while Harry Hawker in the Sopwith Schneider took-off, had one look at the fog bank and promptly returned and also withdrew. Yet Janello bided his time, watched and then took off in the Savoia. The spectators waited and at around the expected time he reappeared having completed a lap, which he then repeated ten times and most assumed that he had won. However, some more knowledgeable observers, including Savoia's manager, felt that his lap times appeared to be too quick and so he was sent off to fly one more to be sure. He then ran out of fuel and it was some time before he was recovered, only to discover that he had failed to round the first marker in fog-filled Swanage Bay and had in error been flying around a ship moored in the adjacent bay. Although he could not be awarded the trophy, having failed to complete the course, the Italians were offered the chance to host the next contest.

Representatives of the British aircraft constructors were incensed by the conduct of the contest and protest was made to the RAeC and via letters in the press. Bird was one of the more outspoken. The club had organised a substantial buffet lunch on the *Ombra* for 170 invited guests, which prompted C.G. Grey, editor of *Aeroplane*, to remark: 'The committee of the RAeC may not be great as organisers of flying events, but it certainly is astonishingly competent in arranging for the social side of the sport of aviation.'

The Savoia S.13 was a small single-seat scout flying boat of similar size to Supermarine's Baby and powered by an engine of comparable power. It was produced in various forms, most as two-seaters, sold moderately well in Italy and achieved limited success in the export market. Its success at Bournemouth and the loss of the Sea Lion was a major blow for Scott-Paine, who had hoped to capitalise on the event to promote Supermarine's products.

SPECULATIVE DESIGNS

In 1919, Supermarine also drew up schematic plans for two large commercial triplane flying boats. The first, Type 'D', which emerged in February, was designed to be powered by three engines, either Napier Lion or Cosmos Jupiter, and carried a crew of five, twenty-four passengers in seats facing inwards to the centre, and more than a ton of mail. This was a very large aircraft for the time with a total loaded weight of 21,400lb and has been referred to as the 'Dolphin'. The hull does not appear to have been of the Linton Hope type familiar to the workforce as it was relatively slab-sided. The cockpit, which was enclosed fully, was placed high in the bows with three seats facing forward for the pilots and, presumably, the navigator, and

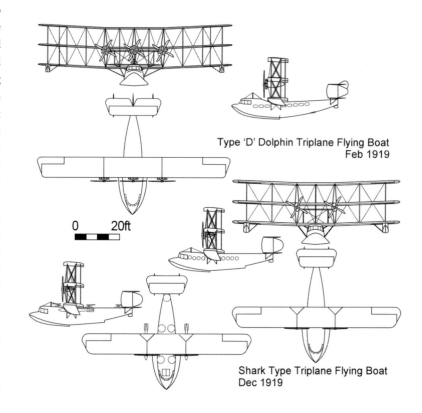

Type 'D' Dolphin Triplane Flying Boat
Feb 1919

0   20ft

Shark Type Triplane Flying Boat
Dec 1919

↑ The Shark was the first project to be 'signed off' by Mitchell in his new role as Chief Designer.

two facing outwards. The centre section was braced in four bays with the three engines in nacelles mounted just below the middle wing. The outer wings were braced in three bays and designed to fold to the rear. There were ailerons on each plane. The tailplane was of biplane form with triple fins and rudders. The wire bracing of the wing followed the simplified pattern established for the P.B.29E and 31E quadruplanes, which had been the subject of a 1915 Billing patent.

At the end of the year a second flying boat was drawn. This aircraft was clearly a derivative of the early machine but reduced in size to carry three crew, eighteen passengers and a ton and a half of freight. It was known as the Shark type and was to be powered by two Rolls-Royce Eagles. A torpedo-carrier version had a mount for a single torpedo on either side and no less than five gun rings on the top of the hull; one in the tail just ahead of the tailplane and side-by-side pairs just behind of and ahead of the wings.

Although both aircraft appeared in the Supermarine catalogue, neither was promoted with much effort; the company, like many of their competitors, sketched out large commercial aircraft of various types at this time more to promote the capabilities of their designers than with any real prospect to obtain orders.

The drawing of the Shark type was signed off by Mitchell in his new role as Chief Designer but it does seem a little doubtful that he was actually responsible for the design. Even by the standards of 1919, these aircraft looked rather dated and are reminiscent of Pemberton Billing ideas, so they may have been based on concepts dating from that pre-Supermarine era.

Thus ended 1919, a mixture of success and disappointment. Mitchell was now in charge of the Design Department and drawings signed off in the last month of the year bear his initials.

3

MITCHELL'S FIRST FLYING BOATS

OLYMPIA – NEW VARIATIONS ON OLD THEMES

The brief commercial operations and subsequent sales of Channel flying boats provided Supermarine with a modest income but their financial state, like that of so many of their competitors, remained fragile. The participation of the Sea Lion in the Schneider Trophy had gone some way to raise the profile of the company, previously barely known to the public, and Scott-Paine aimed to capitalise on this before the memory faded. Two events in 1920 dominated the company's work plans; the Aero Show at Olympia would open in July while the Air Ministry was sponsoring a competition

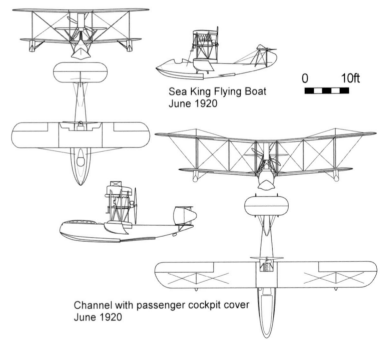

Sea King Flying Boat
June 1920

0   10ft

Channel with passenger cockpit cover
June 1920

← At the Olympia Aero Show in June 1920 Supermarine exhibited a cleaned up version of the Baby renamed the Sea King.

↑ Supermarine's exhibits at the Olympia Aero Show in 1920.

for commercial amphibian aircraft in September. The Supermarine stand at the former would just need some existing aircraft to be prepared to display standard while to participate in the latter would require a totally new aircraft to be designed and built within the period of a few months.

On their stand at Olympia, Supermarine presented two aircraft: an example of the Channel and an aircraft named Sea King that was derived from the Baby. Supermarine had provided descriptions and drawings of the latter aircraft to the press prior to the event and these showed a standard Baby hull and tail fitted with new wings of unequal span braced by outwardly raked struts, similar to those on the ill-fated Sea Lion and the S.S. Flying Boat design from the 1919 brochure. However, photos taken at the Olympia show are of a very different machine. From these it is quite clear that the Sea King was actually fitted with standard Baby-type wings with vertical struts, and that the hull featured an enlarged and raised cockpit fairing. Perhaps the cash-strapped company with its reduced workforce were unable to justify the expense of building new parts. It is almost certain that the aircraft they displayed was simply the second Baby, N60, revised slightly by Mitchell. The Sea King, which was powered by one of Supermarine's stock of 160hp Beardsmore engines, was described as a fighting scout but, hedging their bets, the company were also keen to recommend it for sports purposes. The Channel exhibit was a standard commercial version seating three passengers and fitted with a cabin canopy. The display also included an alternative dual-control cockpit structure with which to convert the aircraft into a trainer.

SELLING THE CHANNEL

Passenger and freight operations using the first of the Channel flying boats had drawn to a close as winter approached in late 1919. Schedules on all the routes were often disrupted by poor weather over the autumn but a reasonable level of activity was achieved and there were no accidents while carrying passengers or freight, neither on the established routes nor on charter and joyriding flights. However, one Channel, G-EAEE, had been wrecked on a return flight from France after a forced landing south of the Isle of Wight but the pilot, Capt. Bailey, was uninjured.

The focus now turned to selling the Channel. All the cockpit seats, controls and fixtures in the Channel were mounted on a triangular steel tube subframe that bolted on to strong points in the hull, and this detachable control unit was covered by one of Supermarine's 1919 patents.

The flexibility of this system allowed Mitchell's team to design a set of alternative and interchangeable interiors: the four-seat version for passenger operations, a dual-control three-seater for flight training, and a two-seat fighter. The cockpit types could be exchanged in less than half an hour. For the passenger carrier Mitchell also provided the option of a two-piece removable canopy.

Scott-Paine was a shrewd businessman and open to explore partnerships and joint ventures to keep the works active. He struck a deal with Colonel Alan Burgoyne, an MP and entrepreneurial businessman with his fingers in many pies. After the war, Burgoyne sought partners in a new corporation covering automobile, marine and aeronautical industries. Scott-Paine became associated with this organisation in early 1920 and was thus able to benefit from Burgoyne's network of subsidiaries and contacts throughout the world. They undertook marketing of all Supermarine's products: aircraft of all types and marine vessels of less than 350 tons. The Supermarine workers were skilled in all aspects of woodwork and could turn their hands to boats just as readily as to flying boat hulls, so he set them to design and build a variety of launches. A number of vessels were prepared for the Motor Boat and Marine Stationary Engine Exhibition held at Olympia in June 1920, including a luxurious 25ft launch built as a tender for the HM Royal Yacht *Victoria and Albert III*. In July, the works were visited by representatives of the Port of London Authority to assess the navigability and handiness of small flying boats with a view to authorising operations from the Thames in central London. Despite the successful demonstration of the Channel in the hands of Capt. Hoare with members of the delegation on board, nothing became of the opportunity.

Notwithstanding the dire financial state of the global economy in the immediate post-war years, Supermarine were quite successful in attracting customers for the Channel. The first sales were made to the Norwegian military, who ordered four examples, one a dual control trainer, in early 1920. These entered service in May that year but one was lost in a crash in July. The Norwegians, although satisfied with the aircraft, thought it to be rather underpowered so the 160hp Beardsmore engines were replaced by 240hp Siddeley Pumas. This was a modification undertaken in association with Supermarine, who produced the parts necessary to complete the conversion. Norway proved to be a good market as a new airline, Det Norske Luftfartrederi, which had been launched in early 1920 to provide a service along the coast from Stavanger to Bergen, was to be Supermarine's second customer. This was envisaged as a scheduled mixed passenger, mail and freight service for which three Channels were purchased, all from the batch of ten registered in Britain in 1919. Operations commenced in August 1920 supported by a government contract to carry mail. However, both passenger numbers and the quantity of mail carried were lower than hoped, largely the result of high ticket and mail prices, and when the service shut down for the winter the airline ceased operations. At least two of the airline's aircraft were subsequently transferred to the Norwegian military, one as a replacement for the crashed aircraft and the others to be cannibalised for spares.

Three of Supermarine's original batch of civil Channels were sent to Bermuda in 1920 to join the Bermuda and West Atlantic Aviation Company, a joint venture between Avro, Supermarine and Beardsmore. The small airline ran a private charter and joyriding service and flights between the islands. One of the airline's aircraft was sent to Trinidad in March 1921 where it was joined by two new Channels to participate in an aerial survey of the area of the oilfields within the Orinoco delta in Venezuela. These aircraft were powered by the Puma engine and incorporated revisions to the cockpit, main step, wing floats and the method for mounting and bracing the lower wing, patented and similar to that of the Baby. These revised aircraft were known as Channel IIs. For survey work they were also fitted with glazed camera ports in the nose of the planing bottom.

A single dual-control Channel was shipped to Auckland in New Zealand where it was used for training by the New Zealand Flying School, who also ran ad hoc passenger, mail and freight services between Auckland and Whangerei. During its life the aircraft was upgraded by fitting a Puma engine and undertook a flight to Fiji where it carried out survey flights around the coast. The aircraft was scrapped in 1924 after the flying school ceased operations.

In March 1921 a delegation of Japanese Government and military officials visited Woolston and were taken out in a Channel by Henri Biard in poor weather. The aircraft performed well in the blustery conditions and an order was placed for three Channel II aircraft.

A single Channel II was purchased by the Royal Swedish Navy in 1921 for evaluation but was lost in a fatal crash in Sweden before tests had taken place. It is said that the Channel had been selected in preference to Vickers' Viking amphibian as Supermarine intended to supply interchangeable wheel and ski undercarriages. No such system was actually constructed for the Channel, although Mitchell was working on the idea for other designs.

A final sale was made in 1922 when the Chilean Naval Air Service purchased a three-seat Channel II for use as an armed reconnaissance aircraft. By this time Mitchell was working on several new flying boat designs and

elements of these are seen in the revision to the hull nose and planing bottom of the Chilean machine.

In total Supermarine sold eighteen Channels overseas. Twelve aircraft had been registered in Britain, of which one had been wrecked, and at least eight of these had been refurbished and subsequently exported. The remainder of the aircraft may well have included a significant number of parts taken from stock purchased from the Air Ministry or cannibalised from other aircraft. It therefore remains very uncertain how many new hulls or wing sets Supermarine may have constructed.

COMMERCIAL AMPHIBIAN COMPETITION

By the summer of 1920 Reginald Mitchell had been working at Supermarine for approaching four years, he was twenty-five years old and had been married for two years. Florence was pregnant and would give birth to their son, Gordon, in November. Mitchell had been able to observe the construction or repair in the works of aircraft designed by Supermarine, the Air Department of the Navy, Shorts, Sopwith and Norman Thompson, and in 1918 he had no doubt shared in the design of the successful Baby fighter working under Hargreaves. It is clear that Mitchell was qualified adequately to step into his shoes as Chief Designer in mid-1919 and in 1920 Scott-Paine decided to expand his role to include that of Chief Engineer.

In these early years Mitchell's Design Department was, by necessity, quite moderate in size and as Chief Engineer and Designer, he was able to manage the team personally. In time, as the department grew, an increasing amount of routine work was deputised. Frank Holroyd had joined the company in the mid years of the war and held the post of Chief Draughtsman, replacing Richardson. He undertook the role of Mitchell's deputy. Joe Smith, who had been employed previously in the aircraft division of Austin Motors, was to be recruited in 1921 and joined the Drawing Office as a senior draughtsman. Their initials can be seen on a great many of the company's project drawings throughout the decade. Other notable recruits in these early years included Arthur Shirvall in 1918 and George Kettlewell in 1920, who rose through the ranks to lead the hull and wing design sections respectively by the late 1920s.

In the tight financial conditions at Supermarine Mitchell was distinctly restricted in the amount of innovation he could apply to new designs and he may, perhaps, have been a little grateful that this allowed him time to learn his craft in careful steps. The 1919 Supermarine patents, and aspects of the structure of the Channel and Baby, defined a 'box of parts' from which Mitchell could select and adapt; component types with which the workforce were familiar and could construct swiftly and with ease. Foremost in this list was the cigar-shaped wooden hull with separate planing surfaces that had been the key feature of the Supermarine flying boats produced up to this date.

The hull profiles and structure for both the A.D. Flying Boat and Baby had been designed in detail by Lieut Linton Hope, a marine architect who had specialised in racing yachts in the pre-war years and who had been employed by the Admiralty Air Department on the outbreak of war to work on flying boats. He had moved quickly to patent his aircraft hull structure techniques in 1918, securing approval just before Scott-Paine's attempt to patent aspects of his methods. Linton Hope's hulls were built around an internal keelson and a framework of closely spaced, lightweight, longitudinal stringers secured between equally lightweight concentric hoop pairs of circular, elliptical or ovoid shape. This semi-flexible framework was then covered by layers of diagonal and longitudinal planking, with a waterproof fabric layer interleaved. Supermarine's workforce would become highly skilled in this form of construction and it was reported that a work team of three skilled woodworkers supported by two helpers could build a 31ft Channel-type hull in five and half weeks.

Supermarine hulls were built with two robust internal hoops to which the lower wings were attached; at the top via metal brackets and by bracing struts to similar brackets on each side. Scott-Paine liked to demonstrate the merits of this construction method by pushing his fist into the hull side to show the flexibility and by hanging his full weight off the rear of the tailplane to prove the strength. The patents held by Supermarine covered the design of the attachment systems for the wings and tailplane, details of waterproof coverings for the flight surfaces, inverted section tailplanes to stabilise the aircraft in pitch and the metal support framework for the pilot's seat and controls. This was such a comprehensive and flexible tool kit that Mitchell's wooden flying boats designed and built throughout the 1920s shared all or at least most of these features.

In the immediate post-war years, the Air Ministry aimed to maintain the design and technical capability of the aircraft industry at a time when military orders were few and far between and commercial airline businesses were struggling to get started in a harsh economic climate. To do so they awarded contracts for prototype aircraft on a piecemeal basis and sponsored competitions to try to stimulate private flying and airline businesses. The policy was far from perfect, not always proactive, at times rather wasteful and under constant attack from various quarters, but overall it did much as intended and managed to keep British aircraft and engines competitive. In early 1920, the Ministry announced a series of competitions for civil aircraft types: small aircraft in June 1920, amphibians in August and large aircraft in September. In each case substantial prize money would be awarded.

For the 1920 Commercial Amphibian competition Mitchell, with limited time, chose to adapt the basic hull design of the Channel for Supermarine's entrant. To address the issue of bow wave spray he incorporated a boat-like nose profile and a raised planing surface prow. The forward cockpit was arranged to carry three: two passengers, the minimum number stipulated under the contest rules, in tandem at the front under glazed and hinged canopies, and the pilot to their rear. To save further time the design of the wings and the tail surfaces were essentially scaled-up versions of those fitted to the Sea Lion, which lends credence to the idea that these may have been designed, or at least influenced, by Mitchell. The wings were thus of unequal span in two bays with outward-raked struts. Large ailerons with overhanging horn balances were fitted on both upper and lower planes and incorporated another new Mitchell idea, a mechanism that allowed all to be lowered together to operate in the manner of flaps, a variation of the system used on various Fairey aircraft and patented by them. Unlike the Channel, this new aircraft had a monoplane tailplane and single fin and rudder, which was fitted with a small horn balance. An essential feature designed by Mitchell was the partially retractable main undercarriage. This attached to the same strong points on the hull and lower wing centre section that served to secure the wing bracing struts. The wheels were raised clear of the water by a rather untidy system of external cables and pulleys that swung them upwards and outwards around a hinge on the point of attachment on the wing. A catch on the hull side locked them in place when lowered. A small combined water rudder and tail skid was fitted just to the rear of the secondary step of the planing bottom. The aircraft was powered by a single 350hp Rolls-Royce Eagle, an engine available cheaply from war-surplus stock, mounted as a pusher. Mitchell also sketched out a speculative design for a fixed ski undercarriage. The aircraft is commonly referred to as the Commercial Amphibian, although this name does not appear on any of the company drawings and at the time it was called simply the Supermarine Amphibian. The initial layout drawings for the Amphibian were produced by Mitchell himself; it would be many years before he was to do so again. Scott-Paine, ever eager to promote the company, had 'Supermarine' painted in huge letters along the side, as he had done for the Sea Lion and the Channel in 1919.

↑ Mitchell's first completely new design was the Amphibian.

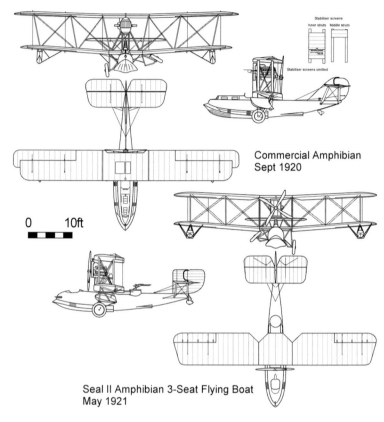

Commercial Amphibian
Sept 1920

0   10ft

Seal II Amphibian 3-Seat Flying Boat
May 1921

Although five aircraft were entered for the competition, only three made it to Martlesham Heath in Suffolk in time. Those present were the Vickers Viking III amphibian, a Fairey III on floats fitted with auxiliary wheels and Supermarine's Amphibian. Beardsmore's WB 1X had remained on the drawing board while Saunders' Kittiwake had been wrecked after hitting a submerged rock.

The trials had been well thought out to evaluate aircraft intended to enter the commercial airline business. In addition to measurements of high and low speed, take-off and landing performance, and stability in the air, on the ground and on water, the judges assessed the overall standard of construction, cockpit layout and equipment, and passenger comfort. The Supermarine team was headed by pilot Herbert Hoare, dressed in nautical gear complete with boots, and they soon became known to the others as the Supermen. The Amphibian was the heaviest of the three contenders by a wide margin and also the lowest powered; the other two having been fitted with 450hp Napier Lions. As a consequence, it exhibited the lowest overall performance but gained marks for its strength, reliability and quality of construction. The advantages of the Linton Hope hull were very apparent, the inherent flexibility proving its worth both on water and on land. The aircraft was landed in a ploughed field, where it tipped on to its nose but

remained undamaged. Further tests, where it was stalled deliberately while several feet up to induce a heavy landing, also failed to break the hull. Overall the Amphibian performed extremely well at the competition; the only real criticisms raised were regarding lateral control, which may have been influenced adversely by the 'stabiliser' screens on the inner wing struts, the ineffective performance of the drooping ailerons, and the untidy design of the undercarriage retraction mechanism. As expected, it was judged to be rather underpowered and a tad heavy compared to its competitors, and it lost out for first place to the Vickers Viking III. However, it had proven to be so impressive in terms of handling, strength and construction that the Ministry doubled the second place prize money to £8,000. Positive reports in the aviation press were most helpful to the company but Supermarine's success was to prove short lived as the aircraft was wrecked in October after a bad landing.

MILITARY DESIGNS

Although Scott-Paine exhibited a distinct preference to pursue opportunities in the sphere of commercial aviation, which dated back to the pre-war Pemberton-Billing era, he certainly did not intend to neglect the military market, small as it may be in the immediate post-war years. The Baby had proven to be a welcome success with performance on a par with many land-based fighter aircraft and it was hoped that straightforward derivatives of this type would find customers both in Britain and overseas. Flying boat fighters had served well enough around the alpine lakes and coast of northern Italy and a few other countries with similar terrain had shown an interest in adding this type of aircraft to their air forces.

As he settled into his new roles, Mitchell developed four military projects in 1920, all based closely on the 1919 S.S. Flying Boat concept. In this time of uncertainty and flux it was not yet apparent how the Air Ministry would choose to structure its naval air forces and it was quite plausible that a variety of smaller flying boat types could be required. The first project drawn up by Mitchell, the Single Seater Flying Boat dating from March 1920, was in essence just the Sea King design as originally intended for the Olympia show. It was to be powered by a 160hp Beardsmore engine and would probably therefore have had a performance slightly inferior to that of the Baby, which had been powered by a 200hp engine. The second was named as the S.S. Fighting Scout and Bomber and followed immediately after the Commercial Amphibian in the Supermarine drawing number system. A fixed Lewis gun was mounted in the upper nose ahead of the cockpit, beneath a fairing, and bomb racks to carry a single 100lb bomb on each side were mounted under the lower wings between the struts. It was to be powered by a 240hp Siddeley Puma that would give a top speed of 120mph. The third design, the S.S. Ship's Flying Boat, was essentially the same aircraft but re-engined with either a Napier Lion or Hispano-Suiza V8 engine. There is little, if anything, that was new in these early Mitchell designs; they were all an amalgam of the Baby, Sea Lion and Sea King with just minor variations in armament and power.

The final 1920 project, described as an Amphibian Flying Boat for Ship Work, took the basic design a step further and incorporated ideas developed for the last of the Channel IIs built for Chile and from the Commercial Amphibian. The hull forward of the wings was extended ahead of the pilot to allow for the inclusion of a second cockpit fitted with a Lewis gun on a ring mounting. The unequal span wings of the earlier designs were discarded in favour of simpler equal span in two bays with vertical struts, and the tail

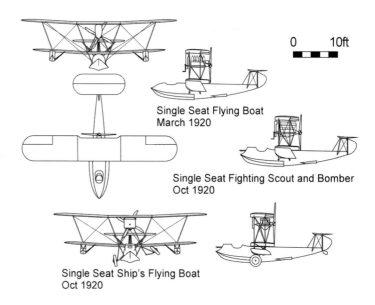

Single Seat Flying Boat
March 1920

Single Seat Fighting Scout and Bomber
Oct 1920

Single Seat Ship's Flying Boat
Oct 1920

0   10ft

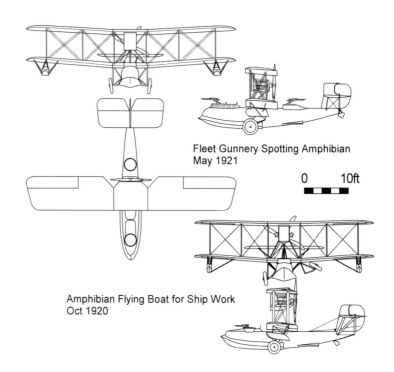

Fleet Gunnery Spotting Amphibian
May 1921

0   10ft

Amphibian Flying Boat for Ship Work
Oct 1920

was a modified version of that fitted to the Commercial Amphibian. This aircraft was also fitted with a retractable undercarriage that operated in the same manner as that on the Commercial Amphibian. It was to be powered by a 450hp Napier Lion and would have had a top speed of 120mph.

None of these projects progressed beyond basic layout but they were shown to the Air Ministry to demonstrate the flexibility of Supermarine's flying boat design and construction techniques. As a result, and supported by the good performance demonstrated by the Commercial Amphibian, the company won an order for a prototype three-seat Fleet Spotter Amphibian around which the Ministry wrote Specification 7/20. Mitchell used his previous project as the basis for this aircraft but moved the second cockpit behind the wing so that the ring-mounted gun could provide defence to attack from the vulnerable rear quarters. The Napier Lion was flipped around to the tractor position, presumably in order to increase the clearance between the propeller and the gunner/observer and wireless operator in the rear cockpit, and to rebalance the aircraft. The wings folded to the rear for storage on board ship. A fixed but retractable Lewis gun could be mounted on the hull nose ahead of the pilot. Mitchell took the opportunity to redesign his undercarriage retraction system completely so that the wheel units pivoted around the hull attachment points rather than those on the wing, with a screw-jack set into the lower wing to draw the top mounts of the main leg inwards to raise the wheels. This system was considerably tidier than the earlier cable activated design. The combined tail skid and water rudder was also moved to the sternpost of the hull; previously it had been located just to the rear of the secondary planing surface step. The location on the sternpost avoided the need to provide a pivot passing through the hull. Scott-Paine named this aircraft as the Seal II. It was to be one of the quirks of Supermarine in the early years that they would occasionally name aircraft in a manner to suggest that there had been an earlier model in the series, presumably to imply continuity and that the company was more productive than was actually the case. In this instance it has to be assumed that he chose to rename the Commercial Amphibian, or perhaps the unbuilt amphibian project, retrospectively as the Seal.

The Seal II is often described as a direct military derivative of the Commercial Amphibian but this is demonstrably not the case; the two aircraft sharing no common parts and only a superficial similarity in design; Mitchell had started with a clean sheet. The aircraft was given experimental Navy registration N146 and first flew in May 1921 for brief manufacturer's tests, after which it was transferred to the Isle of Grain for assessment by the Royal Air Force (RAF), about which more will be said later.

Mitchell also drew up a variant of this aircraft to meet Air Ministry requirement 198783/20, dated March 1921, for which the engine was returned to the pusher position. The rear cockpit was then reduced in size to house just the gunner and an extra cockpit was added ahead of the pilot for the observer and for the wireless operator, who also manned the Scarff-mounted Lewis gun in the nose. This project was designated as a Fleet Gunnery Spotting Amphibian.

For his next military project Mitchell went out completely on a limb. The aircraft he drew up in June 1921 was a Torpedo Carrier armed with two 21in torpedoes and appears to have been aimed at fulfilling an early Air Ministry requirement, DofR Type 10, the precise details of which are a little obscure. It was a large twin-engined, triplane flying boat, reviving a layout and aircraft type that had first been considered in late 1919 as the Shark type. It is not at all clear why he chose to resurrect the idea but he took the opportunity to update the aircraft with all the knowledge he had acquired over two years as Chief Designer. The hull now followed the standard Linton Hope pattern, scaled up considerably, and incorporated the raised foredeck, as tested on the Sea Lion, which was intended to reduce spray. On top of the hull between the wings Mitchell added a separate cabin structure, streamlined in plan and with vertical sides, which enclosed the pilot's cockpit, seating for the other crew, and a Lewis gun on a ring mount at the rear. A second gun position was built into the hull bow and a downward-firing gun was added on a swivel mount in the rear hull, firing through a hatch located to the rear of the second planing bottom step. Additional seating and rest quarters for the crew was provided in the bows, while to the rear there was a small petrol motor that drove a water propeller, the perceived need for which is rather unclear. The triplane wings were anachronistic. The top two were of equal span and rigged in three bays while the span of the bottom was reduced and extended for just two bays. The wire bracing followed the simplified system patented by Billing in 1916 for his quadruplanes. A large single-surface tailplane was mounted halfway up the main central fin with twin auxiliary fins attached outboard. The aircraft was to be powered by two Rolls-Royce Condor V12 engines driving tractor propellers. The two torpedo racks sat under each lower wing root. Despite its distinctly clumsy design and the lack of a need for such an aircraft there must have been something about it that did attract the attention of the Air Ministry as it was to reappear in modified form a couple of years later.

The naval division of the RAF fared particularly badly in the immediate post-war years and was able to field only a minimal force, comprised mainly of reconnaissance aircraft and torpedo bombers, numbering fewer than 100

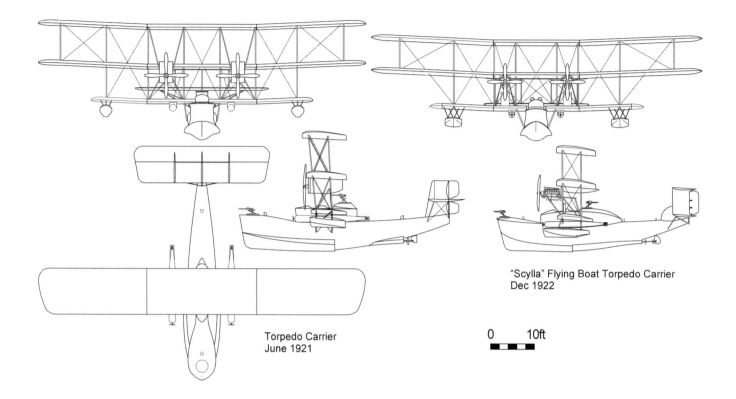

"Scylla" Flying Boat Torpedo Carrier
Dec 1922

Torpedo Carrier
June 1921

0   10ft

in total. Only one aircraft carrier, HMS *Argus*, had been kept operational and its consignment of fighters, of which there were few, were rotary-engined relics from the closing days of the war. Even in an era of tough austerity it was clearly necessary to upgrade the force. In June 1921, the Air Ministry issued DofR Type 6 (64928/21) for a single-seat fleet fighter. This could be either an amphibian or capable of quick conversion from a wheeled undercarriage to floats. Supermarine realised that their Baby-based designs would probably no longer suffice yet still wished to promote the advantages of the flying boat, so Mitchell prepared a completely new amphibian design to meet the requirement. As was to be expected, this project deviated considerably from the earlier fighter types although it still retained a form of Linton Hope hull as its basis. The cockpit was moved from the nose to behind the wings, raised slightly and enclosed within a large aerodynamic blister fairing. Twin Vickers machine guns were mounted on top of the lower wing centre section with their breaches adjacent to the pilot. The usual elliptical cross section of the hull terminated just ahead of the wing from where the top surface curved downwards steeply and the hull extended forward to form a sharp, low profile boat prow. It was fitted with Supermarine's standard external planing surface and secondary rear step. The biplane wings were braced in single bays by 'I' struts, both for the centre section and outboard, and the air-cooled radial Bristol Jupiter or a Siddeley Jaguar engine, was mounted mid-gap in the centre section as a tractor unit within an egg-shaped nacelle. The cylinder heads of the engine were exposed outside of the nacelle while the barrels were inside, with a cooling airstream drawn in through an opening in the nose of the propeller spinner and vented through apertures to the rear. The engine was positioned well ahead of the wings supported by forward canted 'N' struts. An unusual feature on an aircraft of this size was the small tailplane, which was of biplane form with twin fins, similar to that on the Channel. Finally, the fighter was fitted with Mitchell's revised retractable wheels and a rear-mounted combined skid and water rudder. Lowering the undercarriage also lowered a set of hooks located on the hull that were designed to engage the longitudinal wire system that had been tested recently on the carrier. These wires ensured that the aircraft did not veer to the side on landing and hence were quite different in operation to the transverse arrestor wire system adopted by the Navy in later years. The view for the pilot would have been distinctly limited; the cockpit sat over the rear portion of the lower wing and restricted his view downward to the sides, essential for landing on a carrier, and the nacelle partially blocked the forward and upward view. Its utility as a fighter would have been questionable. Surprisingly, Supermarine noted 'Pilot Vision' as one of the aircraft's special features, suggesting that it had a good all-round view.

It is this aircraft, rather than the Commercial Amphibian and earlier military projects, which gives the first true indication of Mitchell's thoughts as a designer and his desire to move away from the restrictions of the templates established by the Channel and Baby that formed the basis of so many of his earlier projects. Although it still incorporated a deal of established Supermarine techniques, it was a bold step sideways to try to envisage a new

form of fighter for the Navy. However, nothing became of this proposal and the RAF requirement was eventually filled by the conventional biplane Fairey Flycatcher, an excellent aircraft, and, to a lesser extent, the Parnall Plover, but only after the Air Ministry specification had been revised and reissued in 1922.

While working on this project, Mitchell also designed an aircraft that was a mixture of the Channel and the new fighter. It may well have been intended that this would be employed as a trainer for the pilots destined to fly the new aircraft. The hull, wings and tail surfaces were clearly based on the Channel while the raised cockpit structure positioned over the lower wing for the pupil and instructor, the retractable undercarriage and the single radial engine in an egg-shaped nacelle, are features shared with the fighter. The wings folded rearwards for stowage on board ship. It is notable that the fuel tank, fitted within the hull on all Mitchell's previous designs, was now mounted on the upper wing centre section. As with the fighter, no orders were received.

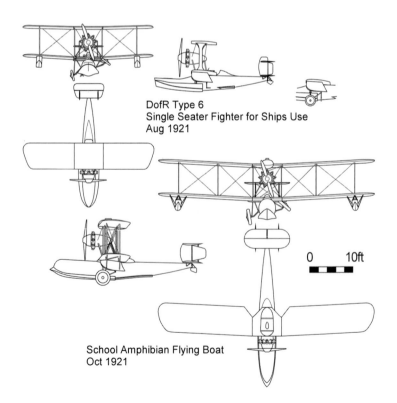

DofR Type 6
Single Seater Fighter for Ships Use
Aug 1921

School Amphibian Flying Boat
Oct 1921

0   10ft

RACING AGAIN

In late 1921, the Sea King, about which little had been heard since it had been exhibited at Olympia the previous year, had been resurrected. The hull was given new wings and tail surfaces designed by Mitchell and re-engined with a 300hp Hispano-Suiza engine to become the Sea King II. The aircraft was now fitted with Mitchell's retractable undercarriage and a combined tailskid and water rudder. In this form it had a top speed of 125mph and could climb to 10,000ft in 12 minutes. In its original guise as the Sea King the aircraft had remained unregistered and may, therefore, never have flown, but as the Sea King II it was registered as G-EBAH in December 1921 and described on the documents as the Supermarine Amphibian Scout. The aircraft received favourable comment in the press but once again failed to attract any production orders. As a class, the single-seat fighter flying boat, even in amphibian form, found little favour with most of the world's armed forces. However, Scott-Paine had a small task for the aircraft; he would enter it for the 1922 Schneider Trophy contest.

After the debacle of the 1919 contest at Bournemouth, declared null and void after fog had caused confusion and several aircraft had been damaged, the subsequent contests had failed to attract international competition. The event was just one of several similar competitions held in this era and was yet to acquire special status. The Italians, to whom the FAI awarded the

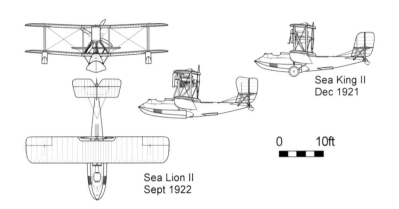

Sea King II
Dec 1921

Sea Lion II
Sept 1922

0   10ft

opportunity to host the contest in 1920 after their entrant in 1919 had been the only aircraft to come close to completing the course, had organised both the 1920 and 1921 contests at their naval air station near Venice and in both cases they alone had entered a team. As a consequence, Italy had won the trophy twice uncontested. Under the rules of the competition they now needed just a single win from any of the next three contests to hold the trophy outright. Although the Italians had designed and built dedicated racing aircraft to compete in both of these contests, due to a series of problems none had actually made it to the start line. Hence, from the perspective of outside observers, Italy had won twice using standard service aircraft of indifferent racing prowess. There was nothing to suggest that they had made any effort to develop specialised racers. Scott-Paine was aware that the Sea King II would have proven a match for any of the aircraft the

← Sea King II.

Italians had fielded and that if it were to be re-engined with the latest Napier Lion it could be a good racer. He therefore decided to give Mitchell the task of preparing the Sea King II to become the Sea Lion II, the successor to the Sea Lion of 1919. As the Sea King II had been adapted from the Sea King and this aircraft was simply the second of the Baby fighters revamped, the hull of the Sea Lion II thus dated from 1918 but had seen little use. Contrary to some reports, the rest of the aircraft was barely changed at all by Mitchell. A 450hp Napier Lion was substituted for the Hispano-Suiza, giving a 50 per cent increase in power, and the fin and rudder were increased in size, which required a further strengthening of the tail of the hull, achieved by applying an additional layer of varnished outer fabric covering. Finally, the wheels were removed; a simple operation as they were designed from the outset to be detachable. Scott-Paine sought co-sponsors for the venture and obtained support from Napier, who supplied the engine, and from Shell and Castrol, who provided fuel and lubricants respectively. Fortuitously, he also had business contacts within the General Steam Navigation Company through his earlier cross-Channel flying boat services and was able to negotiate passage for the team and crated aircraft on the SS *Philomel*, which was diverted to Naples, the location for the contest. Even better, this was made available free of charge.

Unknown to Scott-Paine, the Italians had built a sleek new racer for the contest, the Savoia S.51, which was likely to prove faster than the Sea Lion II. The small team from Supermarine saw this aircraft for the first time when it was brought out for the preliminary trials that preceded the main contest. The S.51 had a very small and slender hull and was of sesquiplane form. The span of the lower wing was actually less than half that of the upper and of small chord, in essence little more than stubs on which to mount the wing floats and to brace the upper wing. The Hispano-Suiza engine was mounted close under the top wing in a tight-fitting nacelle that was faired into the wing. It was every inch a racer but visibly top heavy, and indeed it paid the price when it capsized during the preliminary trials and had to be dried out hastily prior to the main contest. In truth, it should have been disqualified for this under the rules of the contest but nobody lodged any objection when it lined up to start the race the following day.

Henri Biard, Supermarine's race pilot, has left a full account of the contest in his autobiography *Wings*, in which he describes the hectic start-line

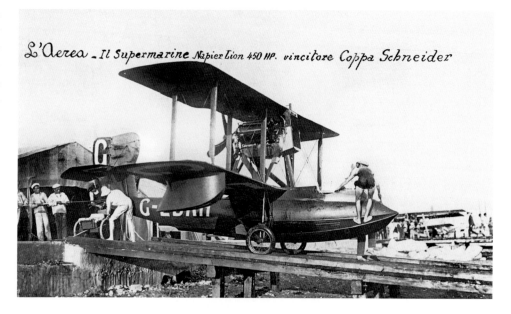

↑ The Sea Lion II at Naples.

take-off of the contestants and the ensuing game of cat and mouse that he and the Italians played with each other flying in close formation, dodging and blocking around the course until he was able to zoom up rounding a turn to break free and win the race. Unfortunately, when this story is reviewed against the official timekeeper's sheets it proves to be a work of pure fiction. None of the incidents mentioned in the text actually occurred and the aircraft were never grouped together around the course. In truth, the Schneider contest was always run as a time trial, never a race where all participants started together, and in this case the contest was entirely uneventful as the S.51 was unable to achieve its promised speed, crippled by a vibrating and de-laminating propeller, and the other two Italian aircraft, a standard Macchi M.7 and the small, rather lower powered, Macchi M.17 racer, were no match for the Sea Lion II. Biard was able to win with relative ease and to establish a number of speed-over-distance records.

The attention of the press consequent upon this win, the first post-war success by a British aircraft in an international competition, brought much needed publicity to Supermarine and they featured the success in their advertisements: 'We claim these facts: world's fastest flying boat'.

4

COMMERCIAL AIRCRAFT AND AIRLINES

DIVERSIFICATION AND EXPANSION

Scott-Paine had long held a particular interest in the development of commercial air routes and the marine aircraft with which to service them. They were ideas he had incorporated into the brochure for the original Pemberton-Billing company in 1914, noting their intention to inaugurate an aerial marine navigation service flying daily between Southampton and Cowes on the Isle of Wight. The very first business venture of the Supermarine company in 1919 had been to use the refurbished Channel flying boats for commercial work, which proved to be quite lucrative for a brief period when the country was hit by a series of strikes and train services were disrupted. Scott-Paine now looked at opportunities to expand this side of the business and instructed Mitchell to draw up designs for commercial flying boats and amphibians with an eye to securing orders from the fledgling airlines.

The first of Mitchell's concepts for a new passenger carrying aircraft, dating from June 1921, was a seven-seater Amphibian Flying Boat powered by a 450hp Napier Lion in a pusher configuration. Although the Amphibian entered for the Air Ministry competition the previous year had been judged to be a success, he chose not to use this as the basis, preferring to start again from scratch, a trait that continued throughout his design career whenever possible. The hull was once again a standard Linton Hope structure with a diameter of 4ft 6in, about 9in greater than that of the Commercial Amphibian, with accommodation for five passengers within the nose section in a fully enclosed cabin with porthole windows. The two-seat pilot's cockpit sat on top of the main hull in a raised fairing, similar to that proposed for the triplane torpedo carrier. There was a monoplane tailplane and single

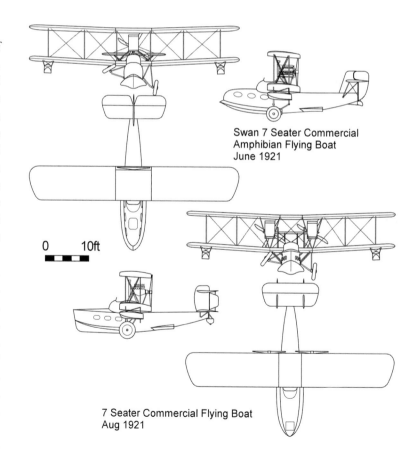

Swan 7 Seater Commercial
Amphibian Flying Boat
June 1921

0   10ft

7 Seater Commercial Flying Boat
Aug 1921

fin, similar to that on the Commercial Amphibian but with reduced rake on the leading edge. The equal-span biplane wings were braced in two bays outboard of the centre section. This design was named as the Swan, a name to be reused for a completely different project a couple of years later. A second design, dating from August, also carried five passengers but was powered by twin engines; either Rolls-Royce Falcons or Eagles, both readily available and relatively cheap. This aircraft had a range of 380 miles. The hull was of similar dimensions to the earlier design but incorporated a revised raised boat prow. The passengers entered the cabin via a top hatch, which was reached via a fixed ladder on the side of the nose. The biplane wings were braced in two bays outboard of the engine mounts and the tail surfaces comprised a biplane tailplane with twin fins. On both aircraft the usual combined skid and water rudder was fitted at the rear and Mitchell's standard retractable undercarriage, with large wheels, completed the design.

The third commercial amphibian project, also dating from August 1921, was designed specifically for S. Instone and Co. Ltd, a shipping company that had established a small pioneer airline subsidiary, Instone Air Line,

in 1919. The company operated a service between London and Paris and aimed to expand to serve Brussels and Cologne. British airlines were coming under growing pressure from their Continental rivals, most of whom were now receiving substantial financial support from their respective governments, and a conference had been held between the Air Ministry and representatives of the airlines and aircraft constructors to draw up a strategy with which to respond. The allocation of new routes, some of which may have favoured flying boats, formed part of the discussions. Supermarine were responding to a request received from Instone, but it is a little hard to understand why the airline would have wished to add an amphibian to their fleet as, with the exception of the Channel crossing, their routes were dominantly overland.

Mitchell drew up a design for a large Commercial Amphibian Flying Boat powered by two Napier Lions and providing cabin space capable of holding twenty-one passengers along the full length of the hull. Substantial additional space had been made available as Mitchell had moved the main fuel tank from the hull to the upper wing centre section. Not only did this allow

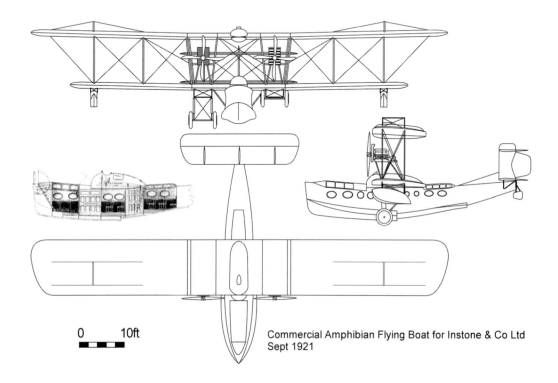

0   10ft

Commercial Amphibian Flying Boat for Instone & Co Ltd
Sept 1921

unimpeded access along the length of the hull, it also dramatically reduced the possibility of fire in the cabin. The routing of fuel pipes through the cabin of the 1920 Commercial Amphibian had been one of the criticisms levelled at this machine. Wing-mounted tanks also provided simple gravity fuel feed to the engines, but at the expense of a heavier wing structure, a higher centre of gravity, and more inconvenient refuelling procedure. As in the previous designs, the pilot's cockpit sat above the main hull within a separate streamlined housing. The flying surfaces were basically enlarged versions of those on the smaller machines but with an extended span upper wing and the addition of a third, central, fin and rudder. A new form of retractable undercarriage was proposed for this aircraft that had two-wheel units on each side with a supporting strut framework that attached to the wing beneath the engine mounts. The wheels swung upwards and forwards to retract clear of the water using the same screw-jack mechanism as before but rotated through 90 degrees. Instone did not order the aircraft but two of its new features were carried over to many future Supermarine flying boat designs; the placement of the fuel tanks on the top wing and the inclusion of an extended rear planing surface to replace the separate step structure used previously.

BRITISH MARINE AIR NAVIGATION

From the outset, Scott-Paine was not content to rely solely on the small number of existing airlines as a market for his aircraft and looked to incorporate the operation of a scheduled air service within Supermarine's business. The government were expected to approve new routes to the French Channel ports and there was a perceived need for a service to the Channel Islands. As he required support for the venture he commenced negotiation with London and South Western Railways, the owners and operators of part of Southampton Docks, as a potential partner to connect their network to the new destinations. This company was in the throes of amalgamation with several other operators in southern England to form Southern Railways under the government's 1921 Railways Act. By late 1922, Scott-Paine's negotiations had proven successful and substantial government subsidies were approved, amounting to 25 per cent of the gross earnings from passengers, freight and mail plus £1 10s (£1.50) per passenger and 1½d (0.6p) per pound of goods. Additional funding was also secured from the Asiatic Petroleum Company, a subsidiary of Shell. The British Marine Air Navigation Co. Ltd was established as a joint venture in 1923.

Naturally, the company's fleet of aircraft would be provided by Supermarine, paid for from government grants.

In early 1922, Mitchell designed a new eight-seat Commercial Amphibian Flying Boat powered by a single 360hp Rolls-Royce Eagle with the airline venture in mind, and no doubt Scott-Paine used his layout drawings and projected performance figures during negotiations. The aircraft carried six passengers in an enclosed cabin in the nose and had a slightly raised cockpit for two pilots positioned just behind. In an improvement to the layout used on the seven-seater projects, the fairing around the cockpit was extended forward over the cabin and incorporated the passengers' portholes. The wings were designed to fold rearwards and there was a biplane tail with twin fins and rudders. Twin fuel tanks were fitted on the centre section of the top wing. An artist's rendition of this aircraft was used in Supermarine's advertisements. Mitchell refined the project at the end of the year, substituting a monoplane tailplane and single fin and modifying the wings so that they folded forwards, and the updated aircraft eventually saw the light of day as the Sea Eagle in 1923. Three Sea Eagles were built to fly on the Southampton to Guernsey route.

The Sea Eagle was a familiar Mitchell-Supermarine design; a Linton Hope hull with a boat prow and propelled by a single engine in pusher configuration. The cabin roof hinged sideways in two portions for access and had windows both in the sides and top. After early test flights with the first aircraft the wing floats were increased in size and the rudder profile was revised to add height and area. Performance in the air was clearly not a high priority as the hull was more akin to a small cabin cruiser rather than an aircraft and the Sea Eagle represented the epitome of Billing's doctrine that the company's products would be 'boats that fly, rather than aeroplanes that float', or 'a seaworthy hull that will fly' as Scott-Paine expressed it in Supermarine's advertisements. In common with the preceding Channel and Amphibian, the Sea Eagle carried an anchor and boathook on the hull side within reach of the pilot, and mooring ropes trailed from the prominent bow bollards through cleats to the cockpit. Early in development a second fuel tank was placed on the top, then long grab-rails were added running the full length of the passenger cabin, both on the roof and along the top edge of the hull. Two fixed ladders, one at either end of the cabin, completed the un-aerodynamic paraphernalia.

The scheduled daily service to Guernsey commenced on 25 September 1923 but the routes to France were not implemented. Flights to Guernsey from Southampton took between 1½ and 2½ hours, depending on the

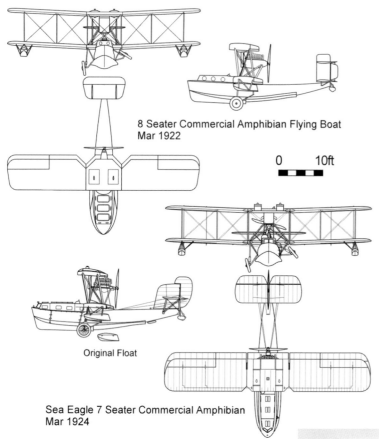

8 Seater Commercial Amphibian Flying Boat
Mar 1922

0   10ft

Original Float

Sea Eagle 7 Seater Commercial Amphibian
Mar 1924

→ The Sea Eagle was ordered to serve with British Marine Air Navigation Co. Ltd, in which Supermarine was a major shareholder.

prevailing wind, and were generally flown by Supermarine's pilots Horsey and Bailey. In March 1924, the government formed Imperial Airways by merging the assets and routes of a number of airlines, including British Marine Air Navigation, and the Channel Islands operation was taken over along with the aircraft and pilots. One Sea Eagle was lost in a crash in May and was not replaced and the whole service was suspended in mid-1925, which suggests that the route may have struggled to be commercially viable. It was reopened in the spring of 1926 but a second Sea Eagle was wrecked in January 1927 when hit by a boat in St Peter Port harbour. It, too, was not replaced. The sole remaining aircraft continued to operate, on and off, until 1928. Although in no sense a ground-breaking aircraft, the Sea Eagle carried six passengers in reasonable comfort, was stable in the air, tractable on its wheeled undercarriage and eminently seaworthy. However, although proven to be a reliable and robust aircraft, no other orders were secured.

In early 1922 Sir Ross and Sir Keith Smith, brothers famous for their pioneering flight from Britain to Australia in 1919 in a Vickers Vimy, announced that they planned to make a round-the-world trip in a Vickers Viking IV amphibian. Unfortunately, Sir Ross was killed while test flying the Viking at Brooklands and the plans were abandoned. However, the lure of being the first to make such a trip remained and others looked into the opportunity. Mitchell was aware of this and so a variant of the Sea Eagle was

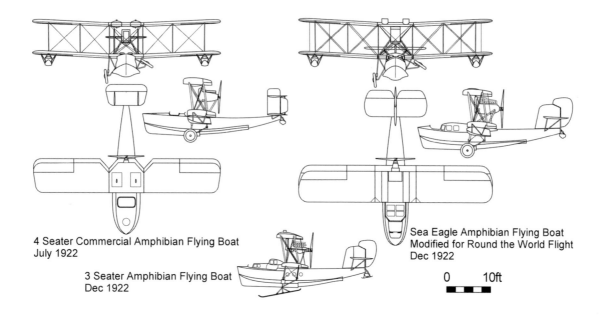

4 Seater Commercial Amphibian Flying Boat
July 1922

3 Seater Amphibian Flying Boat
Dec 1922

Sea Eagle Amphibian Flying Boat
Modified for Round the World Flight
Dec 1922

0   10ft

drawn up at the end of 1922 reconfigured for a possible round-the-world flight. The basic aircraft was modified to carry a crew of three with the pilot's cockpit moved to the nose and a shortened enclosed cabin directly behind. However, the aircraft failed to attract an order and it was to be another Vickers amphibian, the Vulture, which embarked eventually on an ultimately unsuccessful attempt in 1924.

Smaller versions of the basic Sea Eagle design were also toyed with: a four-seater with open cockpits for both pilot and passengers and a three-seater with both cockpits enclosed and an optional ski undercarriage, presumably targeted at markets with a cold climate such as Canada and the Scandinavian countries. Neither drew any interest and Mitchell moved on to consider an altogether larger aircraft.

5

PRODUCTION AT LAST

THE STRUGGLE TO SURVIVE

The Seal II was considered to have performed reasonably well during evaluation by the RAF at the Isle of Grain and once the test programme had been completed the Air Ministry requested that a small number of modifications be made. Most important of all, the fuel tank was removed from the hull and replaced by twin tanks attached to the upper wing centre section. The fin and rudder were both increased in size.

In early 1922 two prototypes were ordered of a slightly updated design to specification 21/21. These aircraft incorporated all the modifications that were to be applied to N146 but also had larger hulls that added 2ft to the length with a corresponding small increase in beam. The 30ft hull had been one of Supermarine's standard sizes inherited from Linton Hope and dating back to the A.D. Flying Boat but this was now perceived to be rather too small. A small amount of sweep was added to the wings, presumably to correct balance. Mitchell made modifications to the bracing of the tail surfaces, enlarged once more, by adding three extra struts each side, a somewhat inelegant and drag-inducing arrangement. Both of these aircraft, registered N158 and N159, were referred to at first as Seals but they were renamed Seagulls prior to delivery. Trials of these aircraft commenced in March 1922.

N158 ended its days at the Royal Aircraft Establishment (RAE) in early 1923. The hull was inverted in a sand bath and weights were added progressively to the planing bottom to measure the crushing strength of a Linton Hope hull for comparison with a theoretical method on which they were working. The maximum load the structure could bear was 25,819lb,

→ Seagull amphibians N158 and N159 under construction at Woolston.

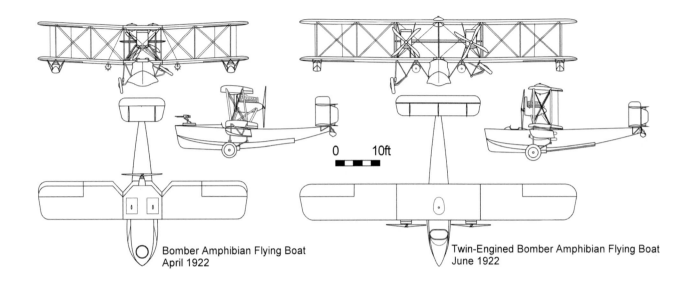

0   10ft

Bomber Amphibian Flying Boat
April 1922

Twin-Engined Bomber Amphibian Flying Boat
June 1922

very close to the calculated value of 24,280lb. For comparison, a similar test on an A.D. Flying Boat resulted in collapse at a load of 13,000lb. Nevertheless, the report was rather critical of some details of the Seagull structure, considering several of the hoops and stringers to be superfluous and others to be weakened by the method of clinching applied.

A derivative of the Seagull, named as the Bomber Amphibian Flying Boat, was drawn in April 1922. This featured a revised hull with a boat prow, the biplane tail from the Channel and the engine installed as a pusher. Elements of this project would reappear two years later. A slightly larger twin-engined version was also proposed in July.

Supermarine had managed to survive for nearly four years since the end of the war and had remained solvent mainly on the strength of orders for the Channel and from commercial charters, but by mid-1922 this work was practically at an end. Once the two Seagulls had been completed the situation looked dire as the order books were empty and the directors gave serious consideration to laying off the bulk of the construction staff and closing large parts of the works. James Bird visited the Air Ministry to appraise them of the situation and to urge them to bring forward a production order for the Seagull that the company believed to be in the offing. While the response he received was encouraging, no contract was forthcoming immediately. However, on the strength of this and the imminent conclusion of Scott-Paine's negotiations for the launch of British Marine Air Navigation Co. Ltd, and their order for three Sea Eagles, the works were kept open.

In 1923, Supermarine also expanded their office in London as Southampton was beginning to feel rather remote from many of their potential customers.

SEAGULLS

The Seagull had been designed to fulfil much the same reconnaissance role as intended for the A.D. Flying Boat and was similarly sized, crewed and armed. However, the Napier Lion engine provided more than twice the power of the earlier aircraft's 200hp engine, which made the Seagull a far more tractable machine. The most important improvement, however, was the addition of the retractable undercarriage, which enabled the aircraft to operate from the fleet's carriers, from where it was able to carry out gunnery spotting duties. The A.D. Flying Boats had never seen active service and no similar aircraft were in service with the RAF at this time, although a variety of single flying boat, amphibian and floatplane prototypes had been evaluated. As a result, the service had no experience in operating an aircraft of the class represented by the Seagull upon which to draw.

A production contract for just five Seagulls was awarded late in 1922 but this was soon followed by two further contracts for batches of five and thirteen respectively in the first half of 1923. The production machines were given the name Seagull II, although they differed only in some minor respects from the two prototypes. Scott-Paine was playing his renaming game again.

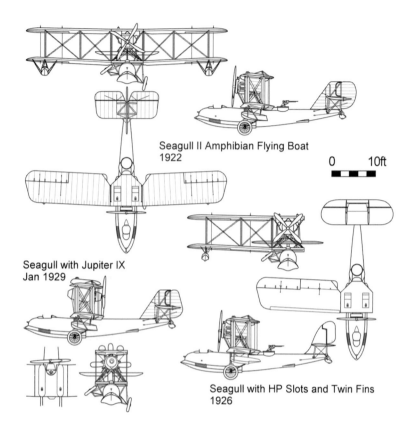

Seagull II Amphibian Flying Boat
1922

0   10ft

Seagull with Jupiter IX
Jan 1929

Seagull with HP Slots and Twin Fins
1926

In the early summer of 1924, six Seagull IIs, forming 440 (RAF) Fleet Reconnaissance Flight, embarked on the recently commissioned aircraft carrier HMS *Eagle*, which sailed for Malta to serve with the Mediterranean Fleet. Unfortunately, under service conditions the aircraft were not found to be particularly successful. Their pilots found the water handling poor with a tendency both to porpoise and yaw and with a protracted take-off run. Despite the removal of the hull fuel tank, it was still considered difficult to communicate between the front and rear cockpits; the outside diameter was several inches less than 4ft and the internal keelson, strong-point bulkhead formers and the undercarriage retraction mechanism all served to restrict passage. The official assessment stated starkly that the Seagull II had 'no potential naval use' and they found the rugged Fairey III, which could be fitted with either wheels or floats, to be a more flexible and convenient aircraft for the spotter and reconnaissance role. These aircraft replaced all the Seagulls in early 1925. This was a considerable blow to Supermarine, which

had grown their business around production of aircraft of this size and class and would struggle without the ability to sell to the RAF.

The Seagull II remained in RAF service for coastal patrol, although little used, until 1928, after which several were sold for civil use, others were returned to Supermarine to be used for test purposes and three were sold to the Royal Australian Air Force.

In 1927 one Seagull II was used in an experiment to assess the effects of moving the step on porpoising characteristics. It is interesting to note that the assessors judged the performance of the unmodified aircraft to be good, with only a slight tendency to porpoise at 36kt regardless of the position of the elevators. This is contrary to the experience of the RAF squadrons, suggesting that the performance of the aircraft on the water may have been sensitive to load or sea state.

Supermarine re-engined one Seagull II with a Bristol Jupiter radial installed as a pusher. This required the centre section of the wing to be deepened and the fuel tanks moved to the top of the upper wing. The aircraft also had a revised fin and rudder profile. A second aircraft was used to evaluate full-span Handley Page slats on the upper wing and this also tested a new tailplane design with twin fins. It has been suggested that one or other of these aircraft was unofficially designated as the Seagull IV, but this is considered unlikely as a more plausible candidate for this name was designed a few years later.

Three ex-RAF Seagull IIs were sold to commercial operators and joined the civil register. Aircraft N9605 was registered as G-AAIZ on 13 February 1930 in the name of George Higgs and described as a six-seater. N9653 and N954 became G-EBXH and G-EBXI respectively on 3 April 1928, both registered to Frank Winn, but G-EBXI lasted just two months before it was withdrawn. Winn established a small airline, Coastal Flying-Boat Services, to operate out of Brighton and serve the south coast towns, with a bi-weekly flight to Dieppe and Le Touquet to ferry passengers to the ocean liners using these ports.

Despite the distinctly negative views expressed by the RAF, the Seagull design was not without merit and it continued to be used by Mitchell as the basis for a number of new projects. Several were drawn up from the spring of 1922 onwards and by the end of 1923 he was focussed on a design that had a boat prow and continuous planing bottom derived from that of the Sea Eagle. For reasons that remain somewhat obscure, but presumably for comparison with the service Seagull II, the Air Ministry ordered a single example of this aircraft in 1923. It was named Sheldrake and issued registration N-180. However, both the Air Ministry and Supermarine

→ The unwanted
Sheldrake made just
two public appearances.
(Chris Michell)

lost interest in the project after the RAF's assessment of the Seagull II proved to be disappointing and priorities in naval requirements moved on. Construction of the aircraft was very much delayed and it flew for the first time only in 1927, by which date it was both unwanted and obsolete. The Sheldrake made only a single public appearance, at the Hampshire Air Pageant held at Hamble in May 1927.

A passenger-carrying derivative of the Sheldrake, the Commercial and General Service Amphibian, was also considered, with the rear cockpit, housing three passengers, enclosed by a fairing with windows.

In January 1924 the Sheldrake design was reconfigured as the Amphibian Service Bomber. This aircraft was a bomber-reconnaissance amphibian aimed at meeting a requirement of the Spanish Navy. As it was designed for offensive operations against marine and land targets, the crew of three, comprising a pilot, gunner and navigator, were all housed in cockpits ahead

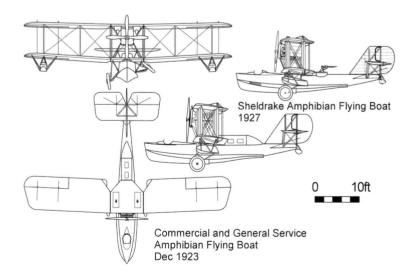

Sheldrake Amphibian Flying Boat
1927

Commercial and General Service
Amphibian Flying Boat
Dec 1923

0   10ft

of the wing. As a consequence, the aircraft was configured as a pusher and was offered powered by either a Napier Lion or Rolls-Royce Eagle. A bomb load of 1,000lb has been suggested, which would be high for an aircraft of this size. Part of the load was carried internally and a mechanism that may have been installed had been included in the Bomber Amphibian Flying Boat design from early 1922. This comprised a revolving drum rack for twelve 50lb bombs, suspended by their tails, which dropped them through a hatch in the planing bottom located just ahead of the main step. The aperture could also be used as a mount for a camera, allowing the aircraft to undertake photo-reconnaissance missions. The additional bombs were carried under the lower wings on racks capable of carrying two bombs each; on photographs one 230lb and one 112lb.

Twelve of these aircraft, named Scarab and fitted with Rolls-Royce Eagle IXs, and hence perhaps a little underpowered for its role as a bomber, were sold to the Spanish Navy in 1924. The Spanish were engaged in subduing a Rif rebellion in their protectorate territories in Morocco and were planning an amphibious landing and assault on the rebel stronghold. The Scarabs were built rapidly and flight trials took place even as the Spanish were preparing to take delivery. The first flight, with Biard at the controls, was on 21 May 1924 and full-load tests, with both Spanish and Air Ministry officials present, took place a week later, both on land and at sea. The Air Ministry's experienced flying boat pilot, Flying Officer Paull-Smith, flew the Scarab back from Worthy Down airfield, where it had been inspected by the Spanish representatives, to Woolston and carried out the official airworthiness tests, which it passed. His official report, which may not have been shared with the Spanish, was not uncritical and he stated 'with the present engine and full load this aircraft is not suitable as a Service type'.

The Spanish had acquired an old British-built German cargo vessel that they had impounded during the war as reparation for losses to German U-boats. They carried out extensive modifications in 1922 to turn this into a flying boat and balloon tender, and it was then renamed *Dédalo*. It was sent to Southampton in July 1924 to collect the consignment of Scarabs. One machine is believed to have been damaged in a take-off accident in the hands of a Spanish pilot and its subsequent fate is unknown. The aircraft were loaded on to the *Dédalo*, covered by tarpaulins and lashed down. There is an anecdotal story that the ship's lift was too small to accommodate the Scarab and that this was why the aircraft were carried on the deck, but in truth the amount of internal hangarage on the vessel was very restricted and could never have held twelve aircraft. Whether the lift was actually too small is not known. On the return voyage to Spain, the *Dédalo* was caught in a gale and several Scarabs were badly damaged. As many as five may have been wrecked.

In 1925 the *Dédalo* and its flight of Scarabs participated in the joint Franco-Spanish assault and amphibious landings at Alhucemas in Morocco. This was the first time that aircraft had participated in a marine landing,

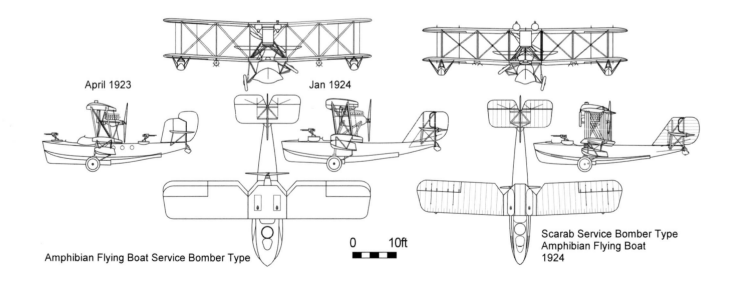

April 1923

Jan 1924

Amphibian Flying Boat Service Bomber Type

0   10ft

Scarab Service Bomber Type
Amphibian Flying Boat
1924

→ The Scarab
came as a welcome
export success for
Supermarine.

itself the first major offensive of this type since Gallipoli in 1915. It was a large-scale operation that involved thousands of troops, armoured divisions with tanks, and the entirety of Spain's naval force. However, the precise contribution made by the Scarabs is not known. The last Scarabs were retired from Spanish service in 1928.

The Royal Australian Air Force ordered six Seagulls in 1925 to form a flight tasked with photographic air reconnaissance of the Australian coastline and Great Barrier Reef. This was a combined operation between the Royal Australian Navy and Air Force to provide a detailed hydrographic survey of their territorial waters. The Seagulls replaced a number of Fairey IIIDs that had been found to have limitations for this work, a complete reversal of the RAF's appraisal of the two aircraft types and possibly reflecting the greater emphasis on operations from the water in the absence of an aircraft carrier.

These Australian aircraft differed little from those in RAF service other than the fitment of larger radiators suitable for tropical areas but nevertheless they were renamed Seagull III. The first aircraft arrived in Australia in June 1926. In mid-1927, the Australians purchased three ex-RAF Seagull IIs at scrap price with the intention to use them as a source for spare parts but they were found to be in such good condition that all were refurbished to join the flight of Seagull IIIs.

In 1929, after the survey had been completed, the aircraft were assigned to HMAS *Albatross*, a newly built seaplane tender that had been designed with the Fairey III in mind and for which the Seagull III was not ideal as it could not be launched by catapult and was too tall to be manoeuvred within the small hangars on its wheels. In 1930, eight of the aircraft were stripped down and given a thorough overhaul before resuming service. Notwithstanding

the problems encountered operating from HMAS *Albatross*, the Seagull III served with distinction and they were well-liked by their pilots, in contrast to the more negative views of their RAF counterparts. They soldiered on until the last was retired in 1938, when they were all replaced by another of Mitchell's aircraft, as will be related later.

Mitchell had designed the Seal II very much in the style of the Channel. Through time, and influenced by the parallel work that led to the Sea Eagle, the basic aircraft design evolved and improved. Reworking the tail surfaces improved stability and control, and the relocation of the fuel tanks enabled better use of the internal space. The Scarab demonstrated that both tractor and pusher engine installations were equally viable. Mitchell had learned a great deal through the life of the extended project and, although the production contracts had been for modest numbers of aircraft, he had set the company on the course to prosperity.

6

MORE RACING AND SCOTT-PAINE DEPARTS

DEFENDING THE SCHNEIDER TROPHY

After the Sea Lion II won the Schneider Trophy contest in 1922 it had returned to the Woolston works, where it was dismantled and put into storage over the winter. The Air Ministry had a mind to purchase the aircraft for evaluation but before the sale was complete Scott-Paine was induced by the RAeC to enter it for the 1923 contest, for which they were the hosts.

By the summer of 1923 no constructor had yet come forward to participate in the British team and the club were a little desperate that the trophy would be undefended by Britain and won by a foreign team. It had been known for some time that the US would be sending a full team of three aircraft manned by navy personnel and equipped with seaplane adaptations of the Curtiss and Wright racers that both companies had built for the Pulitzer Prize races, which were held annually in the US. The performance of these aircraft had been well covered in both the aviation and popular press and it was readily apparent that they would provide formidable and extremely well-funded competition, which goes a long way to explain the reticence of any British company to spend their own meagre funds to enter against them. On top of that, the Italians now held the world air speed record for marine aircraft as their Savoia S.51 flying boat, the accident prone runner-up in the 1922 contest, had been thoroughly refurbished and was now showing its true potential. So, giving in to pressure to uphold British prestige, Scott-Paine agreed to enter the Sea Lion II but was all too aware that it would be thoroughly outclassed. There was always the outside hope that the newer and faster aircraft could suffer mishaps and allow the more seasoned and reliable Sea Lion II to prevail. Mitchell was given the brief to do what he could to improve the performance of the aircraft while keeping

expenditure to the absolute minimum as Supermarine's finances were in dire straits. Mitchell designed new wings of reduced span, smaller wing tip floats of novel shape and an enlarged fin and rudder. The aircraft also underwent a rudimentary aerodynamic clean-up comprising a reshaped nose cover, streamlined 'glove' fittings around the strut attachment points and improved fairings to the rear of the main and secondary planing surface steps. Napier provided an upgraded Lion engine and this was housed in a new nacelle with a neat circular cowl around the radiator. In this form the aircraft was renamed the Sea Lion III just prior to the contest.

Saunders had once more provided his extensive hangar space at Cowes for the visiting teams and as the contest course lay in the Solent it was ideally located. The US Navy turned up early with their team of three racers, two Curtiss CR-3s and one Wright NW-2, aboard the SS *Leviathan* accompanied by the cruiser USS *Pittsburgh*. The first contingent of the French team, two CAMS racing flying boats, arrived on board the *Verdun* while their remaining team aircraft were expected to fly over. The Italians withdrew their entry of two aircraft at the last moment. It is believed that they were unable to acquire the higher-powered Hispano-Suiza engines they had planned for the upgraded Savoia S.51. Meanwhile, the British were struggling to fill the remaining two places in their team. Hawker were planning to enter the 1919 Sopwith Schneider, now renamed Rainbow and in landplane form, if a deal could be struck with the receivers of the former Sopwith company, and Blackburn were working feverishly to fit their old 1918 N.1b hull with new wings and a Napier Lion engine to produce the Pellet racer.

All in all it appeared that the quick reworking of the Sea Lion II would face stiff opposition from all quarters in the contest, but then the Schneider curse took effect. One of the French Latham L1 flying boats got blown off course on the flight over the Channel and was badly damaged on the beach at Littlehampton as a result of overzealous handling by locals helping to pull it ashore, while the Blanchard C1 flying boat was suffering from engine problems during testing and never left France. On a high-speed practice flight around the Schneider course, the propeller on the US Wright NW-2 disintegrated and the aircraft was wrecked after making a hasty touchdown. Hawker lost the Rainbow in a crash before they had even started to reconfigure it as a seaplane and Blackburn's Pellet had overturned while being launched for the first time and required a thorough overhaul. The field was thinning rapidly.

The day allocated for the contest's preliminary trials was fine and all the remaining aircraft went through the process without incident until the Pellet, fresh from a rapid rebuild and the last-minute installation of an additional radiator but woefully short of flight testing, accelerated away to take off. In a slight chop, the top heavy aircraft wallowed as it accelerated and started to porpoise. As the oscillations built up it eventually dipped a wing and cartwheeled. Pilot Kenworthy was recovered after a worrying time underwater but the aircraft was beyond repair.

On race day further woes beset the teams. The engines of the US Navy's reserve TR-3 and the French Latham could not be coaxed to start and both aircraft retired. The CAMS 36bis taxied neatly into a launch and it, too, had to retire. On its take-off run the CAMS 38 badly damaged an elevator but soldiered on only to suffer engine misfires that ended its race after a single lap. That left the two Curtiss CR-3s to fly lap after lap at high speed with Biard in the Sea Lion III manfully flying flat out. To no one's great surprise he was unable to match their speed and he came a distant third. What did

← Scott-Paine was pressured to defend the Schneider Trophy in 1923 and gave Mitchell the task of upgrading the Sea Lion II as the Sea Lion III.

come as a surprise was that the Curtiss, with a fastest lap of 181mph, was fully 20mph faster than the Sea Lion.

After the contest the Air Ministry purchased the Sea Lion III, re-registered as N170, and took it to Felixstowe for evaluation. The modifications that Mitchell had made to the planing bottom in order to reduce drag, combined with the high power of the engine and decrease in wing area, had resulted in rather unpredictable handling on the water and Biard had warned the RAF pilots that the aircraft was prone to leave the water before flight speed had been reached. Unfortunately, on one test flight experienced pilot Flt Lieut Paull-Smith encountered just this problem and was unable to control the aircraft. In the ensuing crash the Sea Lion III was wrecked and he lost his life.

In the autumn of 1923 Mitchell commenced early design work on a radically new aircraft for the 1924 Schneider Trophy contest and, despite the emphatic win by the Curtiss seaplanes, this was to be another flying boat. Supermarine were not yet prepared to venture away from their area of expertise. The hull was a standard Supermarine wooden construction but with a slightly upturned tail incorporating an integral fin, an interesting feature

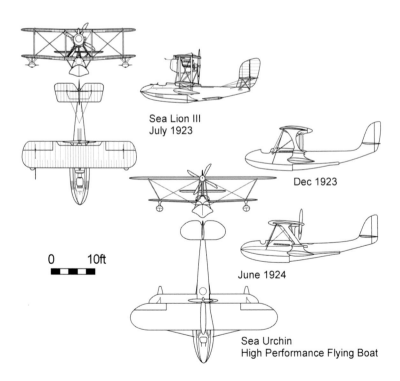

Sea Lion III
July 1923

Dec 1923

0   10ft

June 1924

Sea Urchin
High Performance Flying Boat

that he would return to later. In an attempt to achieve a drastic reduction in drag the engine was to be housed within the central hull and to drive a pusher propeller via two right-angle gear drives and a vertical extension staff. The aircraft was a biplane of sesquiplane type and the wings were connected by single 'I' struts outboard, and in the centre section by light struts and a central pillar that also served as the housing for the driveshaft. The four-blade pusher propeller was fitted at the rear edge of the upper wing with the shaft and gearbox enclosed in a full-chord bullet fairing. It was planned that the engine would be a specially modified Rolls-Royce Condor VII, producing 800hp according to some technical reports. Supermarine named the new racer the Sea Urchin and a top speed of 215mph was envisaged. The project was approved for construction under Air Ministry Specification 40/23 with the understanding that they would purchase the aircraft after it had participated in the contest. The RAeC submitted the Sea Urchin as one of the British team entrants for the contest in the US.

Once Supermarine and Rolls-Royce embarked on the detailed design of engine, transmission and aircraft both companies ran into problems. Rolls-Royce, whose Board at this point included a significant number who were less than enthusiastic about the company participating in racing and competition in general, soon discovered the design of the two right-angle gearboxes to be unexpectedly complex and the engineers no doubt found that both the extra funds and support required from management were lacking. Not only did these gears have to handle the high power output of the engine but they had to do so while severely constrained by size; the upper gearbox in the bullet housing being particularly restricted. Mitchell, too, found that he had run into serious structural problems. With the large engine occupying the central section of the hull, the spar attachment for the small lower wing, which was on the strengthened frame behind the engine, was pushed some distance to the rear. Also, the position of the upper wing was constrained by the location of the engine driveshaft and the relationship of centre of gravity and centre of lift. The biplane wings thus exhibited extreme stagger with inevitable dire consequences for the bracing and general structural strength. The rearward shift of the lower wing also placed the wing tip floats in a poor position relative to the main hull step and hence water performance would have been affected adversely. In addition, there were unresolved questions about the best means by which to provide low-drag cooling for the engine as surface radiators of the type pioneered by Curtiss had yet to be constructed with success in Britain and Mitchell was unsure whether to commit to this means of cooling. Consideration was given to the use of ethylene glycol as the coolant in order to enable conventional tube matrix radiators of small size to be used but there were concerns about the impact of higher fluid temperatures on both the engine lubrication and the solder joints in the radiators. Time moved on, the date of the contest grew ever closer, and by the summer of 1924 the project was quietly dropped and Supermarine's entry withdrawn.

JAMES BIRD TAKES OVER

The relationship between Hubert Scott-Paine and James Bird began to get fractious in 1923, possibly due in part to Scott-Paine's preoccupation with establishing the airline business, and towards the end of the year Bird resolved to take action. He sought funds with which to buy out Scott-Paine's share in Supermarine and was able to secure sufficient money to make an offer. How he managed to do so and whether Scott-Paine was aware of the move in advance is unknown. However, on 16 November Bird confronted him and made an offer which, presumably after some negotiation, was accepted and Scott-Paine left with £192,000 in his pocket; a huge sum at the time.

Scott-Paine continued to manage British Marine Air Navigation Co. Ltd and in 1924 he was appointed as a director of Imperial Airways when his company was bought out and merged with rival airlines Handley Page Transport, Instone Air Lines and Daimler Airway. A few years later he went on to establish British Powerboats Ltd at Hythe where he built high-speed motor boats for racing and military use. Scott-Paine had been both an effective manager and dynamic leader who had guided Pemberton-Billing

Ltd and subsequently Supermarine Aviation through difficult times and put the company on a firm footing for growth. His management skills were to secure equal success at British Powerboats. Curiously, it appears that there were some among the Supermarine workforce who believed he had run the company more as a personal hobby than as a commercial venture, or at least this was the view expressed by Denis Webb, who was to join Supermarine as an apprentice a full three years after Scott-Paine had left. However, this is completely unjust in the light of his achievements.

Mitchell had been recruited by Scott-Paine personally and worked very closely with him through the difficult immediate post-war years. There are no indications that their relationship was anything other than positive so it must have come as something of a surprise, to say the least, when he left abruptly. After his departure, Mitchell negotiated a new employment contract with Supermarine and, as this was drawn up by his family solicitors in Stoke, improved his position significantly and increased his influence, it can be inferred that the negotiation was most probably instigated by himself rather than by Bird. The negotiation process ran through until the end of 1924 but the effective date of the contract was backdated to December 1923 and tied Mitchell to Supermarine for ten years. In addition to agreeing details of salary escalation, annual leave and annuity rights, the contract obliged the company to offer Mitchell a technical directorship at the end of 1927. It is also important to note that it included a clause stipulating that Mitchell was committed to stay with the company in the event that it was subject to merger or takeover, should the new management request him to do so. This became most significant a few years later.

7

THE MOVE TO BIG 'BOATS

MULTI-ENGINED FLYING BOATS

Despite the modest success of the Sea Eagle and the good sales that had been achieved with the Seagull and its derivatives, the market for smaller flying boats and amphibians was proving to be quite restricted and subject to considerable competition. Hence, to enable them to explore other markets Supermarine began to concentrate a greater part of their effort on a number of larger, multi-engined designs targeting both civilian and military customers. Mitchell had commenced design work on aircraft in this class back in 1921 with the cumbersome triplane Torpedo Carrier and a derivative of this project was now under development in parallel with a commercial amphibian with a similar hull size and design. The triplane was to be powered by two Rolls-Royce Condors and the civil machine by Rolls-Royce Eagle engines, while the military machine also had a Green auxiliary petrol engine fitted in the hull to drive a marine propeller located just to the rear of the second step. Both projects were covered by Air Ministry specifications; 14/21 for the Torpedo Carrier Flying Boat and 21/22 for the Commercial Amphibian Flying Boat. Supermarine received a contract in October 1923 to construct one example of the commercial amphibian, now named the Swan, but unrelated to the earlier project with the same name.

Immediately after the war there had been considerable debate regarding the strengths and weaknesses, literally, of the various forms of hull construction employed by aircraft companies. Perhaps unsurprisingly two of the most outspoken critics were qualified marine architects, Linton Hope and David Nicolson, both of whom advocated the necessity of following the best practices of their discipline. They did have a point, the basic box-like construction of some of the early hulls, for example the Curtiss flying boats and those built under licence at Felixstowe, had proven quite inappropriate and the vessels were prone to be damaged with ease in anything other than a light sea and leaked badly. Under the watchful eye of Col John Porte and his deputy Lieut J.D. Rennie the situation with later aircraft improved somewhat over time but the structures remained rather weak, albeit that they were simple to construct by a relatively unskilled labour force. For smaller aircraft the situation was not so bad and the pros and cons of Supermarine's Linton Hope hulls and Vickers' Saunders-built squarer section hulls were finely balanced. Large Linton Hope hulls had been ordered in the last year of the war for the experimental P.5 coastal patrol aircraft and had met with the approval of the NPL and Air Ministry, who ordered further flying boats of similar size and design as the N4 series in 1918, although construction was much delayed. This apparent preference for Linton Hope hulls for larger aircraft may well have influenced their decision to issue contracts to Supermarine for their two designs.

The story of the commercial aircraft is well recorded but that of the Torpedo Carrier, now named Scylla, remains enigmatic. It is unclear why the Air Ministry would have been interested in a distinctly archaic design for a large torpedo bomber flying boat, a class of aircraft that did not appear to find favour either then or later. A brief paragraph in *Aeroplane* in May 1922 stated that Supermarine were working under instruction from the Air Ministry on 'a really large sea-going machine, intended to operate with the Fleet at sea under the most difficult of weather conditions', which may well relate to the Scylla. There is no indication from the surviving drawings that Mitchell carried out much new work of significance on the Torpedo Carrier design other than to revise the hull profile in line with his latest types.

Supermarine are known to have commenced construction of a hull for this aircraft at about the same time that they began work on the Swan. The basic size and shape was similar to that for the Swan although it was slightly longer and had an upturned prow. Why two hull designs so similar in most respects would have been thought worthwhile is curious.

Photographs show two, possibly three, hulls under construction in adjacent bays in the works that Mitchell had decided to construct in slightly different ways, which may give a clue. For the Swan the hull was built in the usual manner; the basic framework was constructed, planked and fabric covered, after which the planing surfaces were attached. On the alternative hull, of Scylla shape, the flared and curved framework for the planing surfaces were part of the main hull former structure, which was also built with fewer longitudinal stringers, and the whole thing was then planked and covered as one unit. There could have been a small weight saving but at the expense of the added safety and buoyancy inherent in the separate structure method.

A large hull, which appears to have been constructed in the conventional manner, was photographed in late 1922 or early 1923 outside the works alongside those of the Sea Lion II and a Seagull. This hull may be that for the Scylla but the evidence is circumstantial and leaves open the question of what happened to the alternative hull.

↓ The hull of the Scylla outside the Woolston works.

The Scylla was purchased by the Air Ministry under a contract in March 1924. On the whole it does seem unlikely that they ever intended for the aircraft to be completed and in the end the project was stripped back to just the hull, stub wings and a basic framework to carry a couple of Rolls-Royce Eagle engines and balance floats, sufficient to allow the aircraft to be taxied. It did, however, retain the small engine and water propeller and it may have been just this feature that the Ministry wished to assess. The Scylla was registered N174 and taken by truck to the Marine Aircraft Experimental Establishment (MAEE) at Felixstowe but there do not appear to be any surviving records of any test work undertaken there, nor of its fate.

The Swan was in many ways a more viable and somewhat cleaner aircraft, conceived as a commercial amphibian biplane to carry twelve passengers. The earliest project drawings for this aircraft date from July 1922 when it was referred to simply as the Twin-engined Commercial Flying Boat, and Mitchell made only minor detail changes to the design prior to construction. An artist's impression of the aircraft was included in Supermarine's press advertisements through late 1922 and 1923. The engines were to be 360hp Rolls-Royce Eagle IXs mounted angled slightly inwards.

The hull had a maximum width of 6ft, 6in less than the Scylla, which provided internal space for a substantial cabin with sufficient headroom to enable the passengers to stand up. At the back of this cabin a ladder led up to the rear of the pilot's cockpit fairing where there was a door to the outside and a fixed ladder for embarkation from attending launches. A hatch in the nose decking also gave access to the passenger cabin and baggage hold.

The structure of the centre section of the biplane wing followed standard Supermarine practice but was of significantly greater span on account of the need to provide mounts for two engines. It was braced as a Warren girder with the front and rear struts forming two large 'W's when viewed from the front. The engine mount struts formed inverted and canted pyramids above the strong point on the lower wing, which also served as the attachment point for the hull-to-wing bracing struts. The engines, driving tractor propellers, were located well forward over the wing leading edge. Unusually, the wing was rigged with a small degree of reverse stagger. The outer wings were given slight sweep and were designed to fold forward, although the reduction in total span achieved by this was quite small. The rear of the hull was canted upwards compared to the fore part in order to bring the monoplane tail and triple fins with balanced rudders in line with the slipstream from the engines.

Mitchell's usual retractable undercarriage system, with its hinge on the hull side, had to be modified to provide a wider track for the large aircraft. The mechanism remained unchanged but the hinge points were moved outboard and suspended beneath the engine mounts on a structure of triangulated struts; untidy but practical. As the wheel units were of considerable weight a manual retraction system was not appropriate so a small wind-driven propeller unit was fitted on the lower starboard wing to drive the screw-jacks via a gearbox. The mount pillar could be rotated through 180 degrees on its vertical axis so that the propeller's direction of rotation could be reversed in order to either raise or lower the undercarriage. It would face sideways when not in use. A combined tail skid and water rudder was positioned a little to the rear of the second planing bottom step.

Although intended as a commercial passenger carrier, the aircraft was constructed with neither cabin fittings nor hull portholes and in this form the Swan flew for the first time on 25 March 1924 carrying the military registration N175. Supermarine presented the aircraft to the press and declared it to be the world's largest amphibian, and it may well have been. After brief company flight trials the aircraft was taken back into the works for modification. It is not recorded whether any take-offs and landings had been made from land and, if so, what was learnt, but the undercarriage was removed. The opportunity was also taken to disable the wing fold, which was probably an unnecessary complication. It is perhaps no surprise that the two Eagles were replaced by 450hp Napier Lions. The three-seat Commercial Amphibian had proven to be underpowered when fitted with a single Eagle engine and the Swan was substantially larger and more than twice the weight. If it were to fulfil its role as a commercial carrier the additional power would be essential. When the Swan next left the works it was as a conventional flying boat with 25 per cent more power, this change and removal of the undercarriage serving to raise the top speed from a lacklustre 92mph to 105mph. It was displayed in this form, the centrepiece of the exhibits on the hardstand outside the sheds, when the Prince of Wales made a brief visit to the works on 27 June.

After testing at the MAEE over the following weeks the Swan was returned to Supermarine and transferred to the civil register as G-EBJY on 23 August 1924. On the certificate it was still referred to as an amphibian. Little is known about the life of the aircraft over the next two years but in time the cabin was modified to fulfil its original purpose as a passenger carrier, with ten seats rather than twelve, and an additional ladder was fitted on the starboard side of the bow to reach the front hatch. In this form the aircraft was re-certified for commercial work on 30 June 1926 and loaned by the Air Council to Imperial Airways to augment the one remaining Sea Eagle on the service to the Channel Islands and the French Channel ports.

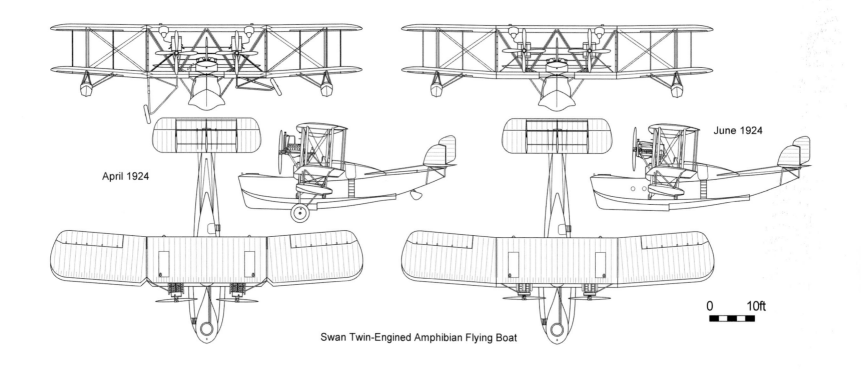

April 1924

June 1924

0   10ft

Swan Twin-Engined Amphibian Flying Boat

By mid-1927 it was no longer required and the aircraft was scrapped in 1928. Although the Swan failed to find a market as a commercial flying boat or amphibian it had proven to be a rugged aircraft with good performance both on the water and in the air. As will be seen later, the Air Ministry were sufficiently impressed that they took the unusual step of ordering a military derivative for production straight off the drawing board without the need for a prototype.

While Mitchell was finalising the design work on the Swan, the Air Ministry issued specification 9/23 for a large three-engined patrol flying boat to replace the aging Porte/Felixstowe aircraft then in service, whose designs, and in some cases construction, dated back to the war years.

Specification 9/23 called for a large, long-range, armed, three-engined reconnaissance flying boat and bomber. The nominal crew was five; pilot, navigator and three observer/gunners. Mitchell chose to design his aircraft from scratch rather than to adapt the layouts of either the Swan or Scylla. The new design had a hull that was slightly longer but of similar width, within which the pilot and navigator sat in tandem cockpits in the fore part surrounded by a moderately raised decking to shoulder height. A Lewis gun

on a ring mount was fitted in the nose. The external planing surfaces had a sharp boat prow and a water rudder was fitted just aft of the second step.

Mitchell proposed to place two Lewis guns within large streamlined barbette or 'fighting top' fairings outboard on the upper wings from where the gunner would have a clear field of fire to both the front and rear. The Air Ministry had recently awarded a contract to Vickers to test this type of gun mount on a Virginia bomber and it appears that a conceptual flying boat project by Vickers to meet 9/23 also placed gun positions here, so it may possibly have formed part of the specification. The placement of these large and heavy structures outboard on the top wing necessitated an unusual design for the wings and their bracing arrangement. The centre section of the lower wing was of parallel chord, mounted on top of the hull and braced to its side by struts in the usual Supermarine manner. The outer wing panels had elegant curved taper and carried wing tip floats that in some drawings are shown with streamlined fairings. The upper wing was more complex and, while it shared the general plan of the lower wing, the thickness varied considerably with span. The parallel chord section extended as far out as the barbettes, just short of half-span, but the aerofoil thickness doubled from the

↑ The Swan was the main exhibit when the Prince of Wales inspected the works in June 1924.

centre line to the fairings. Outboard the wings tapered in the same manner as the lower units. The whole wing structure was braced by struts that slanted span-wise to form a Warren girder system, similar to that used for the central section on the Swan but extended to include the outboard struts. Bomb racks for either a 500lb or 250lb bomb were fitted under the wings on either side. The tailplane was a biplane unit with quadruple fins and rudders.

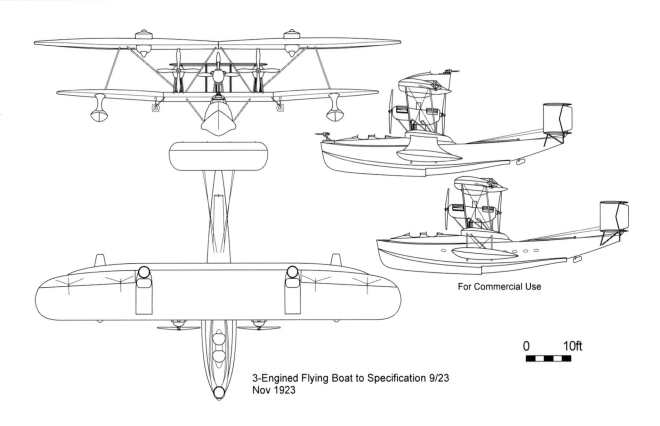

For Commercial Use

0   10ft

3-Engined Flying Boat to Specification 9/23
Nov 1923

The support structures for the engine nacelles sat on the lower wing centre section; unusually the outer two were installed as tractor units while the central unit was a pusher. All three engines had their radiators installed immediately below the nacelles and resting on the wing, an arrangement originally considered for the Swan but in this case enclosed in aerodynamic cowls with roller shutters to control the airflow. Mitchell selected Napier Lions to power the aircraft. The design was signed off in November 1923 and a commercial civil version capable of carrying up to twenty passengers was also considered.

It does not appear to be recorded why but the Air Ministry chose to cancel specification 9/23, partly re-thought the requirement and issued new replacement specifications in 1924. Two of these, 14/24 and 22/24, were again for three-engined flying boats, for which contacts were issued to Blackburn for the Iris and Saunders for the Valkyrie respectively. Two further specifications called for twin-engined flying boats; 13/24 was issued to Shorts for the metal-hulled Singapore and 18/24 went to Supermarine.

THE SOUTHAMPTON

The Air Ministry assessment of the Swan had been largely favourable and on the strength of this they awarded Supermarine a contract to build six twin-engined marine reconnaissance flying boats to specification 18/24 without first ordering and testing a prototype, an unusual procedure for the time. Although this new aircraft was to be based broadly on the Swan it was a completely new design combining elements of the Swan and the 9/23 project plus many new features. The aircraft would be named Southampton.

In early March 1924, Mitchell first considered a quick and simple conversion of the Swan for armed reconnaissance. This aircraft had 9/23-style gun positions; two barbettes on the top wing and a gun ring in the nose. After the draughtsman had completed this drawing it was amended in pencil, presumably by Mitchell, with sketches for an improved layout. The undercarriage and water rudder/skid were deleted and the raised cockpit fairing was scribbled out and the pilot's and navigator's positions moved forward to the fore part of the hull. The barbettes were also to be removed and replaced by a single gun position in the rear of the hull. However, this revised design was soon dropped in favour of a completely new approach.

The Southampton started life as the Service Type Twin-engine Flying Boat, a project dated 27 March 1924, just two days after the first flight of the Swan. It was drawn up in two forms, one with a side-by-side cockpit, the second with tandem cockpits. The hull was based closely on that of the Swan; of similar length and profile but reduced slightly in width and depth. Mitchell selected the tandem cockpit version for further development.

By July, the definitive Southampton featured a completely redrawn hull of far greater refinement than had been achieved before. The upward angled rear hull was discarded and replaced by a more aesthetically pleasing curve with an upswept tail terminating in an integral aerodynamic-section stub pylon to which the tailplane was attached. This addressed neatly one of the weaknesses of the standard Linton Hope hull where the inherent flexibility of the structure resulted in a sub-optimal mount for the tailplane, which was prone to vibration and twisting. In the smaller flying boats this flexibility could be reduced to an acceptable level by winding additional layers of

doped fabric around the stern section but for larger tailplanes this would be inadequate. The wider upturned tail on the Southampton went a long way to solve this issue while at the same time ensuring that the tailplane was positioned within the slipstream from the engines. The rear hull also incorporated twin gun ring mountings in staggered positions, one offset to the left and one to the right. A third gun ring was fitted in the nose of the hull with the tandem pilots' cockpits immediately behind. This gun position was lowered so that it did not impede the forward view of the pilot as the cockpits were not raised as high as in the earlier projects. The whole hull showed a refinement of design and minimalist elegance that had largely eluded Mitchell's previous flying boats and, in part, this is believed to reflect the input of Arthur Shirval, who was now Mitchell's hull and hydrodynamics specialist.

The layout of the wings was based closely on those of the Swan although the chord was reduced, span increased and there was no stagger or sweep on the outer panels. Mitchell selected the A.D.64 aerofoil. The tail surfaces were also refined from those fitted on the Swan but all the control lines ran within the hull rather than externally, a far neater arrangement. Power

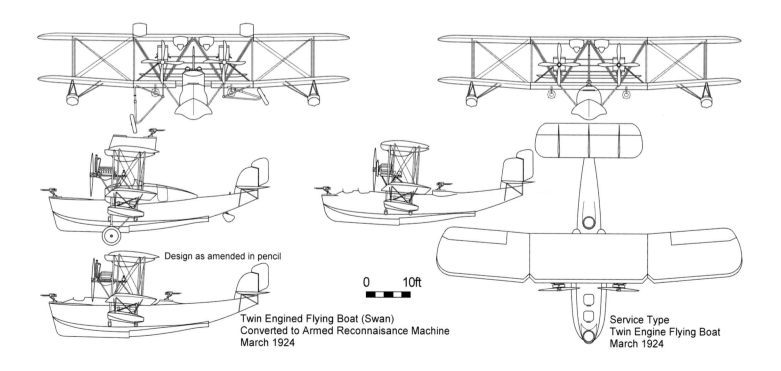

Design as amended in pencil

Twin Engined Flying Boat (Swan)
Converted to Armed Reconnaisance Machine
March 1924

0   10ft

Service Type
Twin Engine Flying Boat
March 1924

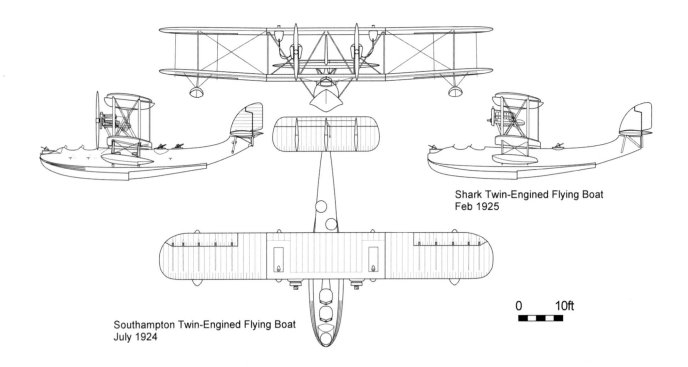

Shark Twin-Engined Flying Boat
Feb 1925

Southampton Twin-Engined Flying Boat
July 1924

0   10ft

was provided by two Napier Lions which, somewhat curiously on what was otherwise a relatively clean aircraft for its time, were left completely uncowled with basic flat panel radiators in front.

The first Southampton was flown on 10 March 1925, almost exactly a year after that of the Swan. Early tests showed that the wing floats had a tendency to dig in under certain conditions so these were adjusted to raise their noses as a temporary measure and subsequently replaced by an improved design. Just four days later the aircraft was taken for acceptance trials in Felixstowe, where flying commenced on 2 May.

Models of flying boat hulls were tested as a matter of routine in the tanks at the NPL but the results were not yet totally reliable as scale effects were large and it was difficult to simulate the appropriate variable loading and changes in angle of attack to represent an aircraft accelerating to flight speed. Consequently, the design of planing bottoms remained to a large extent a matter of experience blended with a degree of luck. In the case of the Southampton, Mitchell and his team had managed to get it spot on and the aircraft was renowned for its clean running. Their design would, however, have benefited to some extent from the tests that had been run at

the NPL on a model of the Swan and confirmed by the aircraft itself. In the air, too, the Southampton proved to be a benign machine to fly and could maintain altitude on a single engine. Its faults were few, perhaps the most notable being that spray thrown out by the fore part of the hull tended to impact upon the large twin-blade propellers and tip damage was common even when sheaved with copper. As smaller diameter three or four blade propellers proved to be less efficient for take-off the RAF accepted the need to replace propellers at regular intervals. With open cockpits at the front and gun ports at the rear the interior was also extremely draughty.

Such was the confidence in the aircraft that after only brief familiarisation flights the Southampton was sent on a three-day cruise to the Firth of Forth, then a fortnight flying in and around the Scilly Isles and topped it off with a week touring the English coast. The Southampton was cleared to enter service and Supermarine received a contract for twelve additional aircraft in July 1925.

The first Southamptons entered service with No 480 (Coastal Reconnaissance) Flight at Calshot from 25 August 1925. Shortly after, four of the aircraft undertook a twenty-day, 10,000-mile, cruise along the west

↑ The Southampton proved to be an instant success in service.

coast of Britain and the Irish Sea and a single aircraft flew from Felixstowe on a round-Britain trip carrying various Coastal Area Command officers. These demonstrations of the aircraft's ability to operate away from base for extended periods was a fundamental requirement for a type that was intended for service overseas as well as in Britain. As a further demonstration of this capability, two aircraft flew out to Egypt in 1926 and returned, all without problems, which gave the RAF confidence to consider further orders for the type. This would, however, be dependent upon Supermarine developing the capability to construct hulls in metal, as will be discussed later.

The success of the Southampton and the publicity that surrounded its long-distance tours caught the attention of several foreign air forces. The Argentine Navy ordered six examples powered by 450hp Lorraine 12E engines, an engine very similar in layout and power to the Napier Lion. Five of these aircraft were delivered with wooden hulls while the sixth and a subsequent order for two further examples had the later metal hull. Two Southamptons were sold to the Royal Australian Air Force and are believed to have been refurbished aircraft previously in RAF service.

The potential of the Southampton to form the basis for a commercial passenger carrier was not overlooked and a design was sketched out in a drawing dated February 1925 and named as the Swan Mk II. The aircraft had the flying surfaces of the Southampton mounted on an enlarged hull akin to that of the project that had immediately preceded it. This, plus the fact that it lacked the tailplane, fins and rudders adopted for the Southampton, may suggest that the origin of the design was probably somewhat earlier than the drawing indicates. Once again Mitchell offered the commercial aircraft as an amphibian although he reverted to the hull-mounted undercarriage hinge attachments rather than the ungainly strut system used on the Swan, which gave it a rather narrow track for an aircraft of this size. In October 1925, a true civil version of the Southampton was proposed. This featured a hull similar to that of the Southampton but of slightly increased width and depth to accommodate fourteen passengers and a side-by-side pilot's cockpit.

The production contracts for the relatively large Southampton flying boats necessitated an expansion of the works at Woolston, which was still centred on the sheds constructed in the Pemberton Billing era and during the war. New fabrication workshops were constructed in 1924 and a large erection hangar was added in 1926. In early 1927 the company acquired a lease on the Air Ministry's large wartime flying boat assembly and test sheds located at Hythe on the opposite side of the Solent from their Woolston works. Supermarine used these facilities for final erection and testing of the Southamptons.

For the first time in many years the company were granted a number of patents, all relating to various features of the Southampton design. Mitchell submitted four in 1924. The first covered an adaptation of his undercarriage system to function as beaching gear for flying boats. Mitchell also wrote a short paper describing its use on the Southampton that was published in

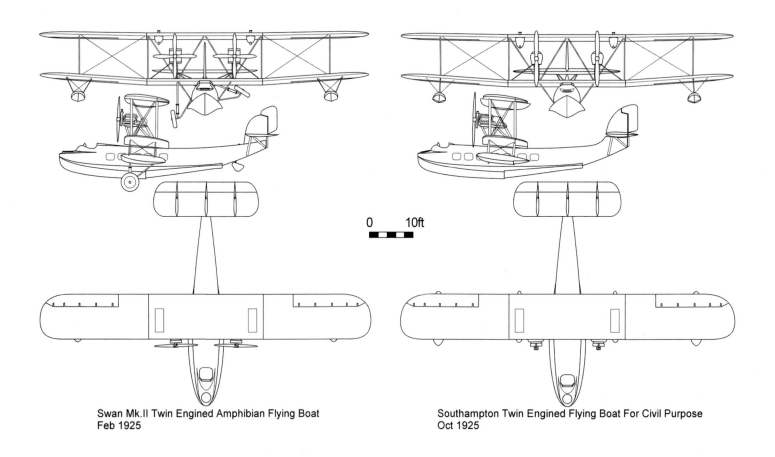

0   10ft

Swan Mk.II Twin Engined Amphibian Flying Boat
Feb 1925

Southampton Twin Engined Flying Boat For Civil Purpose
Oct 1925

the *Aircraft Engineer* supplement to *Flight* magazine in March 1926. The second patent was for the inverted pyramid engine mounts on the Swan and Southampton. The third was illustrated with drawings of the Southampton and relates to a number of design features of the aircraft; the construction of the tailplane, the disposition of the rudders and the upswept hull rear. The fourth concerned the design of the wing tip floats and their support struts. In 1925, a further patent described the control actuator mechanisms for the elevators and rudders.

The first Southampton, registered N9896, appears to have been retained by the MAEE to undertake experimental work. To reduce drag the twin fuel tanks under the top wing were removed and replaced by a conformable tank within the wing centre section and additional tanks in the fuselage to make up the volumes. At one stage the aircraft was fitted with a 'fighting top' on the upper central section that had gun rings both fore and aft. One valuable study was the fitting of ground-adjustable variable pitch Leitner-Watts metal propellers. An increase in top speed of 5mph was achieved with the added advantage that the low frequency beat note, which was wearing for the crew, was eliminated. Although these propellers were never fitted as standard they were used on some long-distance flights.

Apparently Supermarine were issued a contract to convert N9896 to become the prototype for a radial engine powered Southampton III. No drawings exist that are so designated although there are several alternative layouts for a Southampton with radial engines. Later, the prototype Southampton II was re-engined with Bristol Jupiter radials but showed no significant improvement in performance.

NANOK

New projects based on the Southampton soon followed. In September 1924, when the Southampton design was being finalised, it was redrawn powered by two 600hp Rolls-Royce Condors. By February 1925 this project was referred to as the Shark-type. Shortly thereafter Mitchell reviewed alternative ways to increase the Southampton's capabilities by modifying the aircraft to accommodate three engines. Denmark had expressed an interest in purchasing a Southampton adapted as a long-range torpedo bomber and component drawings labelled Nanok, the Danish name chosen for the aircraft, begin to appear in the drawing lists as early as the last months of 1924 for a standard two-engined Southampton adapted for the new role. The first drawings for a three-engined derivative date from May 1926 when

two proposals were suggested, one powered by Bristol Jupiters and the other by Armstrong Siddeley Jaguars. The Jaguar-powered project was given the name Solent and this became the basis for the aircraft offered to the Danes, who then ordered one aircraft in June. Drawings for the definitive Nanok were finalised in October. Mitchell patented the underwing torpedo racks designed for this aircraft in June 1927 and they were tested by the MAEE fitted to Southampton N9901, but the Air Ministry considered the aircraft to be too large to be used for the torpedo bomber role with the RAF.

The Nanok's wooden hull was virtually identical to that of the Southampton, the only visible difference being the change to a single gun position behind the wings. The tailplane was also identical. The wings, however, were revised with a 1ft increase in chord and a thicker SA12 aerofoil section to increase wing area and lift to handle the heavy payload. The centre section was a completely new design to take the three engine mounts for the 420hp Armstrong Siddeley Jaguar radial engines, and the

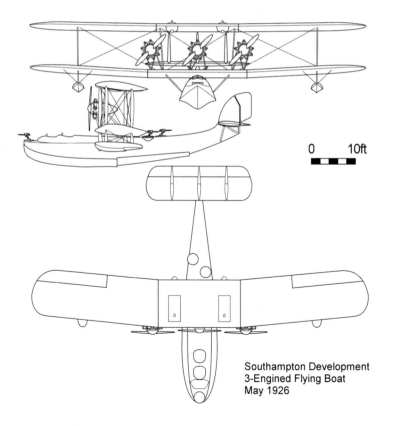

0   10ft

Southampton Development
3-Engined Flying Boat
May 1926

support struts for the engines doubled to brace the wing structure. The outer wing panels were swept back by 5 degrees and the interplane struts sloped slightly inwards. There was a rack under each lower wing to carry a 1,500lb torpedo. As a result of the many design changes required to carry the torpedoes the unladen Nanok was significantly heavier than the Southampton, it could carry a larger payload and had nearly 50 per cent greater power.

Early flight testing in the summer of 1927 established that both top speed and range were marginally higher than the Southampton but the rate of climb was reduced and overall performance failed to meet specification. When the aircraft was tested at Felixstowe, manoeuvrability, essential for a torpedo carrier, was considered to be inadequate and any remaining possibility of the RAF adopting a version of the Nanok/Solent evaporated. Flight tests had also shown that the aircraft was nose heavy and the problem was shown to be caused by the slipstream from the propellers interacting

adversely on the tailplane. This was solved by reducing its span and by fitting free-flying auxiliary elevators between the fins. In view of the lower than expected performance the Danes cancelled the contract and purchased a single standard Southampton fitted with Jaguar engines instead. Supermarine were left with an unwanted aircraft.

In 1928 the Nanok reverted to the name Solent and Supermarine advertised it for sale as a torpedo bomber, but without success. The name Solent was also applied to a planned fourteen-seat civil passenger carrier version that would have been fitted with the hull designed earlier for the civil Southampton. Although this new civil design did not find a market, the Nanok/Solent itself had all the military equipment removed and was refitted as a luxurious nine-seater air yacht. In this form it was sold to the Hon. A.E. Guinness, the brewery magnate, so that he could commute on a regular basis between Britain and his estates in the Irish Republic. It was registered G-AAAB in August 1928. One of the problems with civil adaptations of the Southampton was that the hull was a little restricted in height and passengers were unable to stand up. Guinness may well have found this a problem too as he requested a new air yacht design from Supermarine almost as soon as he took delivery of the Solent. The Solent was deleted from the civil register in 1934.

Nanok FB VII Torpedo Bomber
Aug 1927

0   10ft

↑ The Nanok had wings of greater area and thicker section than the Southampton in order to handle the weight of two torpedoes.

8

EXPANDING THE DESIGN TEAM, LIGHT AIRCRAFT AND MORE AMPHIBIANS

THE DESIGN DEPARTMENT

Southampton production contracts and design work on derivatives dominated Supermarine's business in the mid-1920s and occupied a large percentage of the Design Department's time, with much of the remainder being taken up by the succession of new Schneider racing seaplanes. In order to handle the increasing workload and expand the technical capabilities of his team, Mitchell sought new talent and recruited two important new members.

Alan Clifton was born in 1901. He studied engineering at the Northampton Engineering College where he became a student member of the Royal Aeronautical Society. On graduation, Clifton sought employment in the aircraft business and wrote to many major aircraft construction companies. He was invited to an interview with Mitchell in April 1923 and received an offer to work in the fledgling technical group to carry out stress calculations for £3 10s (£3.50) per week, which he was grateful to accept.

Although he was only a couple of years younger than Mitchell, Oliver Simmonds was one of the new generation of university-trained graduate engineers now seeking to enter the aviation business. Immediately prior to the war he had won a scholarship to study history at Magdalene College, Cambridge, but put this on hold when he signed up for service with the Royal Flying Corps. After obtaining his aviator's certificate in 1916 he was posted to France, where he flew F.E.2b fighters. On leaving the service in 1919 he took up his scholarship but requested to be allowed to change to study for a mechanic science tripos as he was by now determined to pursue a career in aviation. While at Magdalene he held the post of honorary secretary to the Cambridge University Aeronautical Society, a prestigious group affiliated to the RAeC. After graduating with honours in 1921 Simmonds was employed at the RAE at Farnborough, where he worked first as an aerodynamicist and subsequently in aircraft certification. While at the RAE he was elected to be honorary secretary of their Aero Club, an organisation notable for designing and building their own light aircraft. Simmonds was approached by Mitchell in mid-1924 and recruited to join his technical group to provide much-needed aerodynamic expertise, especially as Supermarine were about to embark on the design of a radical racing aircraft to compete for the Schneider Trophy. This was also the year in which the Air Ministry instigated the 'Approved Firms Scheme', which transferred a large element of the responsibility for airworthiness testing from the RAE to the aircraft construction companies. Simmonds' prior experience in this regard would have proven most advantageous.

It is clear that Simmonds was regarded as a senior member of the technical team, perhaps even to the extent of deputising for Mitchell in some respects, as within a year he was permitted to present a paper on flying boat design to the engineering section of the British Association. One year later he presented a second paper at the Institution of Aeronautical Engineers on the subject of the development of civil marine aircraft. In this paper he included a wealth of technical data pertaining to marine passenger aircraft and made the case that such aircraft were capable of being the equal of their land counterparts on a pound payload per horsepower basis. Not everyone was convinced by his conclusions and when he attempted to provide additional explanation via the correspondence page of *Flight* magazine he managed to provoke an argument with the Fokker company that was carried out through an exchange of letters in the magazine over several weeks. It is not known how Mitchell regarded Simmonds' responses but it is clear that he chose not to curb him. Simmonds played a major role in the design of Supermarine aircraft over the following four years.

Other important recruits during this period included Harold Tremmeling in 1922 and Ernest Mansbridge and Eric Lovell-Cooper in 1924, all destined for senior positions in later years.

The area around the Solent had long been one of the country's main hubs for aircraft construction. The likes of Saunders, Fairey, Avro and Sopwith had established facilities there prior to the war and by the mid-1920s the industry still employed a significant number of people, yet there was no local flying club to cater for them. So, in early 1926, Simmonds and Clifton were instrumental in establishing the Hampshire Aeroplane Club, based on Avro's airfield at Hamble. This was a prestigious club with Lord Louis Mountbatten as president and several notable vice presidents including A.V. Roe, S. Saunders, Lord Montague of Beaulieu, Sir Charles Wakefield and their own employer, James Bird. As directors of the club, Simmonds and Clifton held the positions of chairman and honorary secretary respectively. Mitchell was one of the founder members. In the same year, Clifton wrote to the Royal Aeronautical Society to suggest that a satellite branch should be established in Southampton in amalgamation with the Institution of Aeronautical Engineers. The society approved the idea in principle but it failed to receive support from James Bird and so foundered. Clifton resurrected the idea in 1935, supported by a large number of society members in the area, and this time was successful.

Mitchell also took on a small number of apprentices, among whom was Roger Savernake Dickson, taken on at the age of 19 in October 1925. The practice in these years was for the parents of an apprentice to pay the employer an annual fee for this education and there was no guarantee of a job once the apprenticeship had been completed. Indeed many employers, including Supermarine, encouraged their apprentices to seek employment elsewhere on completion of their term in order to broaden their experience, with the expectation that they would be re-employed at some future date. Dickson worked at first in the erection and fitting department, then the inspection department before moving to the Drawing Office in May 1927, where he completed his apprenticeship. He was employed at £1 10s (£1.50) per week as a junior draughtsman, an interesting contrast to Clifton's initial salary of £3 10s (£3.50) as a graduate recruit, and, indeed, Mitchell's salary of £25 per week. In 1926 he considered starting a gliding club in Southampton but was talked out of it by Simmonds, who encouraged him to join the newly founded Hampshire Aeroplane Club. As a member of this club he learned to fly gliders, of which more will be said later.

Sometime around mid-1926, Mitchell reorganised the expanding Design Department into two parts: the Drawing Office and the Technical Office. Design work was carried out in both but aerodynamics, stress calculations and weight estimates were the responsibility of the Technical Office. Joe Smith was named as the Chief Draughtsman and Frank Holroyd as Assistant Chief Engineer, a formalisation of the roles they had filled for several years.

MITCHELL'S FIRST LAND AEROPLANE

One area of aviation that was proving slow to grow in the 1920s was that of private flying. Despite the availability of cheap ex-military aircraft, the cost of buying and maintaining them remained well out of reach of most people and as many of the available aircraft were formerly scouts and light bombers they were less than ideal for general civilian use. The concept of a light 'plane, a reasonably cheap and low-powered machine with docile flying characteristics capable of being flown by novice pilots, did not appeal to many of the aircraft companies who saw little profit in such a venture. Some form of stimulus was thought to be required in order to encourage new designs to be produced. The first attempt came in 1923 when a competition for single-seat aircraft powered by modified motorcycle engines of 750cc or less, referred to as motor-gliders, was held at Lympne near Dover and administered by the RAeC. Prizes were offered by, among others, the Duke of Sutherland, the *Daily Mail* and Sir Charles Wakefield, of Castrol. Although this competition was judged to have been a reasonable success, as twenty-eight aircraft had entered, it was all too apparent that aircraft with such low power were not really appropriate for general use. The Air Ministry then agreed to become involved and offered prizes for a similar competition the following year.

The 1924 Light Aeroplane Competition was for two-seat dual-control aircraft suitable for use as trainers, which were to be powered by engines not exceeding 1,100cc in capacity. Both the aircraft and engine had to have been designed and manufactured within Britain or the Empire. A prize of £2,000 would be awarded to the winner and £1,000 to the runner-up. As the prize was worthwhile many companies agreed to enter, although there was still some concern regarding both the cost to build a new aircraft for the competition, estimated at around £1,000, and the commercial value. It was felt that the sales price for such a machine, £700–£800 when produced in modest numbers, would still remain out of reach for most potential buyers.

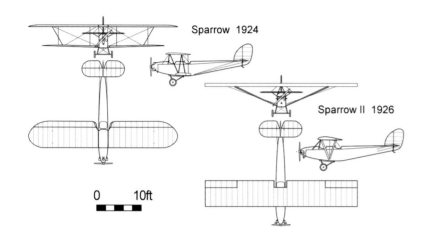

Sparrow 1924

Sparrow II 1926

0   10ft

A set of performance tests was drawn up to measure low and high speeds, and landing and take-off distance, but first there were elimination trials involving dismantling, towing and re-erection to assess the practical aspects of each aircraft. Supermarine decided to enter the competition and Mitchell and his team embarked on the design of their first land aircraft.

The Supermarine Sparrow was of all-wooden construction and for simplicity the fuselage was covered with thin ply panels. The high aspect ratio sesquiplane wings were braced in single bays. Mitchell gave careful thought to the requirement for short take-off and landing runs and designed the rear fuselage with slight upward kink so that when the aircraft was resting on the ground the wings were set at a higher angle of attack. He also fitted the full-span ailerons on both top and bottom planes with a mechanism that allowed them to be drooped to act as flaps, as he had on the Commercial Amphibian in 1920. Mitchell selected different aerofoils for the top and bottom planes. He chose Sloane for the top and A.D.1 for the bottom, a system aimed at providing high lift for take-off and lower drag for cruising, an idea that had been the subject of a patent by Folland and Preston at the Gloucester Aircraft Co. in 1923. The chosen engine was the three-cylinder Blackburne Thrush, a new and untried 1,096cc air-cooled unit intended to provide about 38hp.

Fifteen aircraft passed the elimination trials at Lympne, of which seven were monoplanes and eight biplanes. All but one were of wooden construction. The Sparrow had the lowest power and wing loading of the group. The Air Ministry assessment of the Sparrow was not especially favourable, with typical comments of 'normal' and 'conventional'. The cleanliness was ranked

as good except for attention to detail; criticism was aimed at the unclean landing gear design and profusion of external controls. The cockpits were considered to be acceptable although the view from the front cockpit was poor as it was positioned under the top wing and the centre section bracing wires were dangerously close to the pilot's face. The bracing of the sesquiplane wings was also singled out for comment as the single bays were felt to be rather wide. Top speed of the aircraft was just 63mph and stall speed estimated at 36mph, placing it towards the bottom of the group. In the end it all became rather academic as the engine threw a connecting rod through the crankcase and its replacement could not be induced to run reliably. As a result the Sparrow was eliminated from the competition before completion of the flight test phase. Although the Sparrow could not be judged as a success, and was demonstrably inferior to the majority of the other aircraft, the competition demonstrated once again that very low powered aircraft were not acceptable for club flying and training. None of the competing aircraft was considered worthy of production. The nominal winner was the Beardmore Wee Bee I powered by a Bristol Cherub engine, which, although its ranking was high, it achieved this primarily as a result of actually having completed all the tests that had defeated most, generally through engine failure.

↑ Mitchell's first venture into the design of landplanes was the Sparrow.

In 1926 a second competition was arranged by the RAeC for two-seat aircraft with engines weighing less than 176lb. This, too, was held at Lympne with prizes offered by the *Daily Mail*, the first prize to go to the machine that achieved the greatest useful load carried per pound of fuel consumed over a series of courses totalling around 2,000 miles. Supermarine had the Sparrow rebuilt as a parasol monoplane, re-engined with a 32hp Bristol Cherub III, and renamed Sparrow II. The new wing was a simple rectangular one-piece unit of some 20 per cent less area than the biplane wings it replaced. The reconfigured aircraft was 130lb heavier and 7mph slower.

This competition attracted a field of far more efficient and potentially commercial aircraft designs, for example the de Havilland Moth and Avro Avian, and totalled twelve in number after three had failed to arrive for the elimination trials. The Sparrow II looked to be on the small side and outclassed. Although it passed the elimination trial, it was a slow process to demonstrate the practicality of the machine for storage or towing as this required the entire wing to be removed and lashed to the side of the fuselage.

This time around biplanes predominated and only three other monoplanes joined the Sparrow in the line-up. However, Supermarine's luck was against them and the Sparrow's performance became academic as Henri Biard failed to cross the start line correctly after taking off in gusty conditions and then suffered a forced landing away from Lympne when a strut worked loose. As a consequence, the Sparrow II was unable to compete in the flying trials, which were won by the Hawker Cygnet. The result, however, meant little as Hawker did not follow up on the win and it was developed versions of the Avro and de Havilland machines that went on to commercial success.

After the competition, Mitchell used the Sparrow II to evaluate the performance of various aerofoils; Clark Y, RAF 30, T64 and SA12, an experimental programme run in conjunction with the Air Ministry to compare full size performance with results obtained from wind tunnel experiments. On completion of these tests the aircraft was sold to the Halton Aero Club in 1929, where it continued to fly until scrapped in 1933.

← The Sparrow was rebuilt as a monoplane in 1926.

THE NEXT GENERATION OF AMPHIBIANS

Although the Design Department was focussed heavily on development of the Southampton, new projects continued to receive some attention, mostly military amphibians of the Seagull type and no doubt considered as potential successors to the Seagull II with the carrier fleet. Despite the distinct lack of enthusiasm shown by the Fleet Air Arm for this class of aircraft, Mitchell and Bird still saw merit in continuing to develop new designs, not least because the workforce were trained to build aircraft of this style. The Fleet Spotter Amphibian Flying Boat project dates from March 1924, the same as the original Southampton project, and incorporated a number of ideas gleaned from Mitchell's work on the Schneider racing flying boats. The hull was essentially a cleaned up version of that used on the Scarab with a fine boat prow and faired wing tip floats. The aircraft was a pusher with gun positions both ahead of and behind the wing, which necessitated the design of an aerodynamic slipstream shroud for the rear gunner who was located just feet away from the propeller. In a clever move, this shroud doubled as the radiator for the engine. The pilot sat in the extreme nose with the second gunner to his rear. The tall single fin and egg-shaped nacelle for the

Rolls-Royce Condor engine suggest that Mitchell had been inspired by the French CAMS 30, a flying boat first exhibited at the Paris Aero Salon at the end of 1922 that was the work of Rafaele Conflenti, formerly the Chief Designer at the Italian firm SIAI Savoia. CAMS also sent two new Conflenti-designed racing flying boats to the Schneider Trophy contest at Cowes in 1923, where they were on open view at Saunders' works. Mitchell updated this spotter aircraft design in September 1924, changing the engine to a Napier Lion and refining the rear hull to incorporate a tall integral fin, as on the Sea Urchin. The wing plan and tailplane are also reminiscent of this aircraft. A further refinement, one year later, named as the Condor Flying Boat Amphibian, saw the hull redesigned to resemble a scaled-down Southampton and the single-fin tail replaced by a twin-finned version. The rear cockpit was no longer fitted with a gun. This aircraft was powered by a single tractor Napier Lion.

In 1924 Mitchell's dogged promotion of small amphibians seemed to have borne fruit when the Air Ministry issued specification 29/24 drawn up around a further project by Supermarine. The first drawings for the aircraft date from October 1924 and it was formalised in January 1925. The specification was for a twin-engined amphibian flying boat powered by a

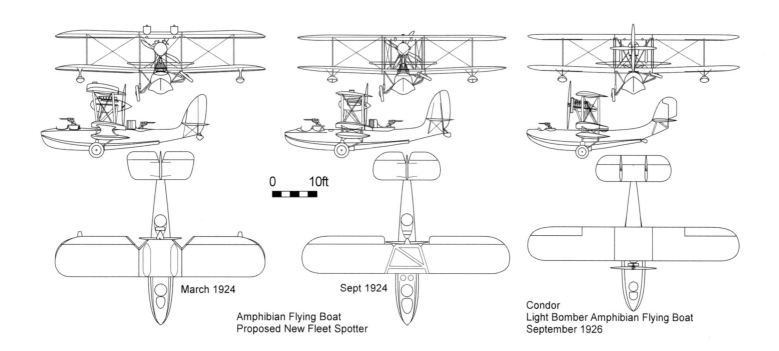

0   10ft

March 1924

Sept 1924

Amphibian Flying Boat
Proposed New Fleet Spotter

Condor
Light Bomber Amphibian Flying Boat
September 1926

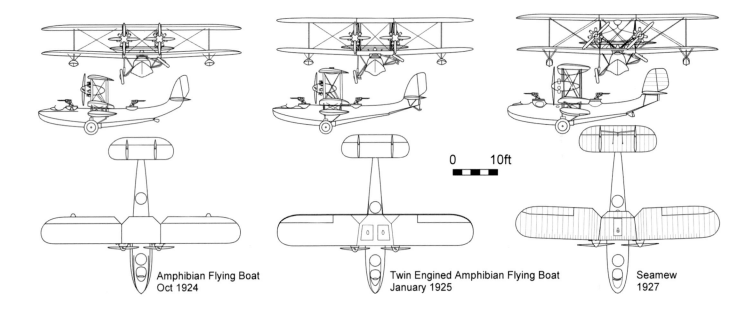

Amphibian Flying Boat
Oct 1924

Twin Engined Amphibian Flying Boat
January 1925

Seamew
1927

0   10ft

238hp Armstrong Siddeley Lynx air-cooled radial. Supermarine received a contract in 1925 to construct two prototypes and the aircraft was allocated the name Seamew. The contract was clearly not a high priority while work on the Southampton and Schneider racers occupied most of the design team's time so the Seamew remained substantially unchanged over the following year before final detailed drawings commenced in February 1926. The Seamew was very close in size, weight and engine power to the Seagull II and in many ways can be described as a scaled-down Southampton; the wooden hull had much the same lines with one gunner to the rear of the wings, the gunner/observer to the front and the wireless operator/navigator between him and the pilot's cockpit in the nose. The wings were designed to fold rearwards for storage on ships and had a conventional centre section as the smaller size of the aircraft did not warrant using the Warren-girder system developed for the Southampton. The spars, however, were fabricated from Duralumin, the first use of metal wing structural components by Supermarine, while the ribs were wood. The aerofoil section selected by Mitchell was the high-lift Goetingen 387. The tail was reminiscent of that on the Southampton but fitted with twin fins and rudders rather than three. Mitchell's usual retractable undercarriage mechanism was installed and there was a tailskid just behind the rear step. The mounts for the Lynx engines were enclosed within neat aerodynamic nacelles.

While the works were in the throes of producing Southamptons, establishing new metal fabrication facilities, and working on the complex design of the next Schneider racer, building the Seamew had to wait so detailed design and construction proceeded slowly through 1927. As a result, the aircraft became something of a joke among the Design Department staff. The first flight finally took place in January 1928, by which point it was all but obsolete. Early testing showed that the propellers were affected badly by spray, a problem also encountered on the Southampton but exacerbated on the Seamew as they were that much closer to the water. An attempt to reduce the problem by fitting smaller diameter four-blade propellers was not entirely successful as this resulted in a marked reduction in both climb rate and speed. The aircraft also proved to be slightly nose heavy. After only a small number of hours of testing at Felixstowe some of the Staybrite cast stainless steel wing fittings failed, a problem also encountered with similar castings on the Southamptons, and considerable time was spent by the new metallurgy department to find a solution. It was obvious that, as it stood, the Seamew would not attract any orders.

Mitchell's team sketched out a number of aircraft projects based around the Seamew to try to breathe new life into the project. The first was a simple civil commercial version to carry six passengers, first proposed in September 1927 before the Seamew had flown. The disappointing performance high-

lighted by early test flights led to consideration of three re-engined versions in March 1928. Two had single engines; a pusher Napier Lion or tractor Bristol Jupiter, while the third was to see the Lynx engines replaced by two Bristol Jupiters, which would have more than doubled the power of the aircraft and made it comparable to that of the far larger Southampton. The commercial conversion idea was resurrected in 1929 and *Flight* reported that the hull was constructed of Duralumin and the wings of wood. Whether this was an error or an indication that Supermarine was considering reconfiguring the aircraft is not known.

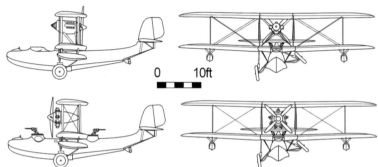

Seamew Flying Boat Napier Lion or Bristol Jupiter March 1928

← Construction of the Seamew was much delayed. It flew at last in January 1928 and proved to be a poor performer.

9

RACING: A NEW DIRECTION AND A DEAD END

MITCHELL'S FIRST MONOPLANE

The Sea Urchin project, intended to compete for the Schneider Trophy in 1924, had proven a damp squib; an interesting concept but fundamentally flawed and, hence, aborted. Fortuitously for Supermarine, and indeed Britain, at the eleventh hour the contest had been postponed and rescheduled for 1925 when, in an act of great sportsmanship, the National Aeronautic Association (NAA), the US aero club, decided against flying the contest unopposed after the Italian team had withdrawn and the sole remaining British entrant, the Gloster II, had been wrecked during early testing at Felixstowe.

The driving force behind Supermarine's involvement in racing and record breaking had always been Scott-Paine, a speed fanatic and man with a strong competitive streak, yet after his departure Bird was quite prepared to follow his example. Despite the failure of the Sea Urchin, neither he nor Mitchell were deterred and resolved to come up with something radically new with which to compete in 1925. It was abundantly clear that competition from the US team, still supported fully by Army and Navy funds, would be formidable. The Curtiss CR3 that had won in 1923 had been adapted from a land-racer originally built in 1921, yet it had totally eclipsed all the aircraft the Europeans had ranged against it. In the meantime the US had not stood still and new Curtiss and Wright landplane racers had been produced each year to compete for the Pulitzer Trophy and their performance had risen relentlessly. The Curtiss R2C-1 had taken the absolute air speed record in 1923 immediately after winning that year's Pulitzer race and this aircraft had then been put on floats to compete for the Schneider Trophy in 1924 as the R2C-2 where, barring accidents, it would have far exceeded the capabilities

of the Gloster II, and no doubt that of the Sea Urchin too. Mitchell knew well enough that he had to surpass himself with his next design if he was to produce a credible competitor and fortuitously the British had one great asset when it came to air racing; the Napier Lion. The Lion had powered the majority of the best British racing aircraft in the early 1920s and had established a number of national and world records, although up until 1924 these engines had been little more than just well-tuned versions of the standard production models. However, in 1924 Napier had invested in the development of a dedicated racing variant on which they had rearranged the layout of the carburettors, magnetos and coolant pipes to enable the aircraft designers to tailor tighter and more aerodynamic cowlings, and the Gloster II had been the first racer to benefit from these improvements. For 1925 Napier decided that this engine would be cleaned up further and boosted in power to produce 700hp. It was given a new designation, the Mk VII. Mitchell would use this engine for his racer.

By late 1924 it seemed pretty clear that the day of the conventional racing flying boat was drawing to a close and as a consequence many designers now looked upon the seaplane as the best way forward. The Curtiss racers cast a long shadow. They had dominated American racing for several years, were at the leading edge of construction and aerodynamic refinement for their time, and were in every way the gold standard for racing aircraft design. There was, therefore, a strong temptation for other companies to emulate their style; Wright did so in the US and Folland surely cast a glance in that direction too when designing the Gloster racers. Nevertheless, Curtiss did not have the field entirely to themselves and the French in particular had experimented with a variety of sesquiplane and monoplane designs. Having abandoned the Sea Urchin it appears that Mitchell was thinking along similar lines.

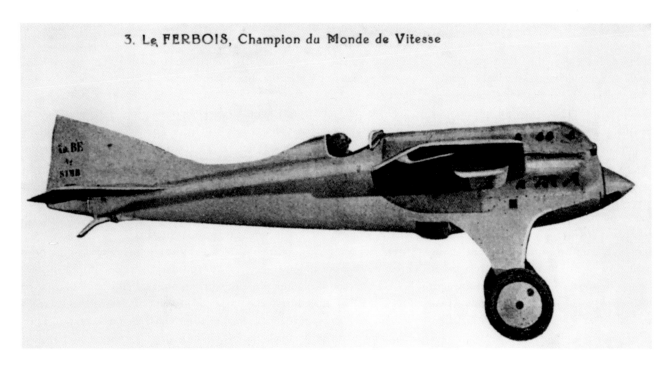

3. Le FERBOIS, Champion du Monde de Vitesse

← The Bernard V2 brought the absolute airspeed record back to France. Its sleek monoplane design with the engine carefully cowled to merge with the lines of the fuselage and wings was mirrored by Mitchell's design for the S.4 racer.

In late 1924 the French regained the world air speed record from the US with the S.I.M.B (Ferbois) V2, an aircraft now known more commonly as the Bernard V2. The V2 was a radical mid-wing cantilever monoplane designed by M.J. Hubert, and one of two similar aircraft, the other being the V1, which he had designed to participate in the Beaumont Cup race in 1924. The V2 was powered by a twelve-cylinder Hispano-Suiza 12Gb engine that had the same 'broad arrow' configuration as the Napier Lion and was cooled by two finned Lamblin radiators that fitted into recesses in the lower surface of the wings. Lamblin had patented and produced radiators where the water passed through a large number of narrow flattened tubes arranged as fins. For the V2 the input and output pipes, which ran spanwise, were recessed into the lower wing and the fins projected downwards below the surface aligned with the airflow. The main fuselage was a wooden monocoque with integral fin and the wing was of cellular construction built around twin main spars. The wings and undercarriage struts were carefully faired to the body and the engine was enclosed in a cowling that blended the lateral cylinder banks into the wing leading edge.

After one failed attempt and extensive modifications, the V2 took the world air speed record at 448km/h (279mph) on 11 December. A replica was displayed at the Paris Aero Salon in early December and was widely reported in the press. However, this replica was not an accurate representation of the actual record-breaking aircraft. The nose, in particular, was foreshortened significantly, which made it appear less refined than was the case.

In his relatively short career as Chief Engineer and Designer Mitchell had been given just one opportunity to build an aircraft other than a flying boat; the diminutive, underpowered Sparrow biplane for the Light Aeroplane Trials in 1924. Now he was presented with a blank sheet of paper, no preconceived ideas, no catalogue of company parts and techniques on which to draw, and the task to build the world's fastest seaplane racer. No records survive to indicate how Mitchell approached this project but there can be little doubt that he would have studied photographs and articles in the aviation press regarding all the contemporary racers and speed record contenders, including the V2. He would, of course, have been almost negligent not to have taken note of the world's fastest aircraft when he was in the process of designing a seaplane with much the same intent and powered by an engine with the same geometry as the Hispano-Suiza. Mitchell's first drawings for his new racer, named the S.4, date from 26 January 1925 and show that it shared many characteristics with the V2. Both were mid-wing cantilever monoplanes with the outer engine cylinder banks faired into the wings, and both had a monocoque rear fuselage with integral fin. Furthermore, both featured ailerons extending out to the wing tips with the hinge line at an angle to the span. Mitchell's design is noticeably sleeker overall but the similarities are still quite marked. However, whether Mitchell adopted this layout independently or was inspired by the V2 remains uncertain. Incidentally, this preliminary drawing is often misidentified as a later refinement of the S.4 but the date on the drawing, and the annotation indicating the fitment of a 600hp Lion, shows this interpretation to be incorrect.

During detailed design and development the S.4 lost a little of its initial rakish elegance. The fuselage was constructed in two pieces; a wooden semi-monocoque with integral fin that included the cockpit and a forward section constructed of steel tubes. The rear fuselage was built up in a similar way to a Linton Hope hull. There were transverse formers spaced about a foot apart and multiple longitudinal stringers around which two layers of thin mahogany planks were wound diagonally. The completed fuselage was covered in doped fabric. The forward structure was built upon two 'A' frames, the legs of which formed the float support struts, and included the engine mounts, the wing attachment brackets and fitments for the fuel and coolant water tanks. It was covered by shaped Duralumin panels. On the original design the float chassis had been fully cantilevered but there was some concern about the possibility of resonance developing in the

long struts so lightweight cross members were added between them. The framework was functional, although rather complex and a trifle clumsy with numerous cross-bracing members, and Mitchell decided to patent the idea. A second patent covered the internal rudder and elevator activators within the tail.

The wings were tapered with skewed elliptical curved outer portions and built as a single unit on multiple full-span spars. They were skinned with ply. Unique for a racer in this era, the S.4 was fitted with flaps and a mechanism that allowed the ailerons to droop in unison with them.

The floats were built in much the same manner as the fuselage around a central longitudinal keel and transverse bulkheads. An alternative set of floats of the same shape and size were produced by Shorts in Duralumin but it is unclear whether these were ever fitted to the aircraft.

The S.4 was built in relative secrecy and it was only revealed to the press a few weeks prior to the contest. *Flight* reported: 'The Supermarine-Napier S.4 is an exceptionally fine piece of work from every point of view, and at first sight one cannot help feeling a certain amount of surprise that a British designer has had sufficient imagination to produce such a machine.' They went on to praise Mitchell for his abilities and his courage in pursuing such a bold design. Shortly thereafter, Henri Biard took the S.4 over a measured speed course and set a new world air speed record for seaplanes at 364.9km/h (226.7mph); all seemed to be going well.

Once in the US, the problems started. First, the facilities for visiting teams had yet to be completed when Mitchell and the S.4 arrived and his small team were unable to unpack and erect the aircraft. After several days' wait, and housed in an aging canvas tent hangar, the S.4 was erected only to be damaged by a falling tent pole during a violent storm. Repairs were made and Biard took the aircraft out for a test flight. The bare facts of what happened next are that the aircraft oscillated violently while making a tight turn at high speed, lost height rapidly and pancaked into the water. The S.4 was wrecked but fortuitously Biard was not badly hurt. He reported that the wings had developed flutter while many observers on the ground felt that he had induced a high-speed stall while turning. In all probability both interpretations are correct in part, with flutter having either induced the stall or the stall provoking flutter. Either way, loss of control during high-speed turns was one of the more common reasons for the crashes of racing aircraft at that time and had resulted in several deaths, so Biard was rather fortunate. Mitchell made no comment on the cause of the crash but it is notable that hardly any features of the S.4 design were carried forward into any further aircraft project.

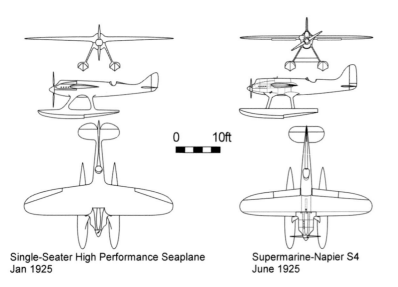

Single-Seater High Performance Seaplane
Jan 1925

0   10ft

Supermarine-Napier S4
June 1925

→ Supermarine's triumph at having taken the world airspeed record for seaplanes was to be short-lived; the US reclaimed the record just weeks later with their Curtiss R3C-2.

The Schneider contest went ahead with just a single British aircraft, a Gloster Napier III, able to compete. A second Gloster had been left in its packing cases and had to be assembled rapidly when the S.4 was wrecked. Bert Hinkler, the team's reserve pilot, took it out in very choppy conditions but his undoubted skill enabled him to get the aircraft into the air to carry out the requisite flight. Choosing his moment carefully, he touched down among the waves and appeared to have landed successfully but then the aircraft crashed down from a wave crest and the float chassis collapsed on impact, causing the propeller to chop into the float noses. The British were down to a single aircraft.

US team comprised three US Curtiss R3C-2 seaplanes, two raced by the Navy and one by the Army. They came fresh from a barnstorming display of speed and dominance at the Pulitzer races. The Italians fielded two Macchi M33s, a cantilever monoplane flying boat with a pylon-mounted Curtiss engine. They were clearly outclassed by all the seaplanes. On race day the engine of the second M33 could not be induced to start and so just five aircraft made it to the start line.

In the race the Curtiss racers strode away, all three aircraft setting lap speeds of 220mph or higher while Hubert Broad in the Gloster Napier III could just exceed 200mph and de Briganti in the Macchi M.33 was stuck lapping at just over 170mph. But then Lieut Offstie's Curtiss engine expired, followed just one lap later by that in Lieut Cuddihy's machine, leaving only Lieut Jimmy Doolittle in the running. However, he went on to win convincingly with Broad second and de Briganti bringing up the rear.

The S.4 was a highly significant aircraft with which Mitchell made a solid statement about his ability and aspiration. The contrast between this racer and all his prior designs was truly dramatic and, although its triumph was short-lived, it demonstrated his desire, and indeed James Bird's desire, to move Supermarine into the premier league of aircraft constructors. This was, of course, easier said than done in a country still struggling under financial austerity but home to a vibrant and competitive aviation industry all chasing the few available contracts. Nevertheless, with cash flowing in from the Southampton production contract, the company embarked on a programme of expansion.

10

COMPETITION AND THE INTRODUCTION OF FABRICATION IN METAL

THE RISE OF THE FLYING BOATS

In 1924 the Air Ministry took its first significant steps to foster the development of flying boats since the war. With the Navy now firmly committed to expanding its fleet of carriers their interest in small flying boat amphibians, never notably high, had waned, and for the foreseeable future their requirements focussed on a range of offensive and defensive conventional aircraft that could be fitted with floats if so required. However, for coastal patrol, both in Britain and overseas, the larger type of flying boat was still favoured. Moreover, commercial aviation was now centralised in the government-supported Imperial Airways and there was a growing perception that there would be a need for similar sized aircraft to fly some of their longer distance routes.

By the end of 1919 Supermarine had emerged from the war years as the sole manufacturer in Britain dedicated to flying boats. Their competitors, of which there were relatively few, had either been liquidated or had land-based aircraft or boats as their primary business. Although this allowed Mitchell to concentrate his efforts on a single class of aircraft, it did leave the company in a relatively poor position to pursue contracts for other types and it soon became apparent that the market for flying boats was really quite restricted. Then, as the 1920s progressed, other companies began to eye the few opportunities that did arise and Supermarine began to feel the competitive pressure increasing. Initially it was the aviation department of Vickers that provided direct competition; their Viking III amphibian flying boat had beaten the Commercial Amphibian in the Air Ministry competition in 1920 and they had pushed ahead with further development of this type with enthusiasm and some commercial success. The hulls for Vickers'

flying boats were constructed at first by Saunders, the boat-builders based at Cowes on the Isle of Wight. Saunders had constructed several types of marine aircraft under licence during the war in a co-venture with Vickers and had continued this alliance into the 1920s. However, Sam Saunders had now bought out Vickers' holdings in order to establish his own Design Department. English Electric, formed in 1918 through the merger of a number of companies, continued in a minor way to develop the flying boat range built during the war by one of their divisions, Phoenix Dynamo, but their interest in aircraft was in decline. The Gosport company, launched to market flying boat designs by John Porte, had faltered on his death. Fairey, after completing the long-delayed Atalanta, chose to withdraw from building flying boats in order to concentrate on the lucrative market for their Fairey III family of biplanes and others. However, of greatest concern to Supermarine, the two large aircraft companies Blackburn Aircraft and Short Bros had decided to enter the market and each had significant resources upon which to draw.

Blackburn Aircraft was founded by Robert Blackburn in 1908 to build aircraft of his own design and to supply components for other aviation pioneers. The company had expanded during the war years, building B.E.2c and Sopwith aircraft under licence and their own large twin-engined Kangaroo torpedo bomber. They also began a small flying boat fighter to specification N.1B designed by former Admiralty Air Department Designer Harris Booth, although this was never completed. Blackburn saved his company from financial failure in the tough post-war years through the design and construction of the Swift, a Napier Lion-powered torpedo bomber for use on carriers. The company's long association first with the RNAS and subsequently the RAF Navy division and Fleet Air Arm led, somewhat inevitably, to an interest in the production of flying boats. Indeed, their works at Brough were on the banks of the river Humber. Blackburn's first foray in this direction came about in 1923 when the old N.1B hull was recovered from storage and used as the basis for a Schneider Trophy contender; the Pellet. This unfortunately ended in disaster when the aircraft bounced badly on take-off and was wrecked when it nosed into the Solent. However, around the same time the company was seeking an opportunity to build a large flying boat.

Short Bros was the oldest of the British aircraft manufacturers, established by the three brothers Oswald, Eustace and Horace in around 1897 to fabricate balloons. The company had grown rapidly over the years and they had been one of the main suppliers of aircraft to the Navy through the war. Pemberton-Billing Ltd, and subsequently Supermarine, had been one of several companies contracted to build seaplanes of Shorts design. Shorts' first flying boat, the Cromarty, was designed in 1918 to wartime specification N.3 but construction was delayed due to post-war austerity until 1921. More important though was Oswald Short's commitment to construction using metal. The sensation of the 1920 Olympia Aero Show had been the Silver Streak biplane, which was built entirely of metal, including all the wing and fuselage skins. The rear fuselage was a stressed skin monocoque. Oswald Short was well aware that his patented metal construction techniques were ideally suited to flying boat hulls and obtained a contract from the Air Ministry to fit a prototype hull to the flying surfaces of a Felixstowe F.5 flying boat. This aircraft, the S.2, was flown in 1924 and although slightly heavier than a service F.5 the advantages of metal were soon established during testing; the hull withstood heavy landings, never leaked and was free from the problems of water soakage that could add several hundred pounds to the weight of a wooden hull over its life. In the same year they built a small, single-seat, monoplane flying boat, the S.1 Cockle, of similar construction that they used for research purposes.

Metal components had been used in the construction of aircraft from the very early years for fixtures and fittings, but when used for the primary structure this was generally limited to engine mounts, undercarriage and struts. Weight was a major barrier against more widespread usage, steel being the most readily available stock, as was the relative cheapness of wood and the ready availability of a skilled workforce to work with it. However, in the immediate pre-war years metallurgy had progressed to the point where strong yet light aluminium alloys had begun to reach the market. Post-war, the shortage of high quality timber, a direct result of the huge demand generated by the war, had caused the price to rocket to a point

that brought it in line with that of the new metals. At first a shortage of advanced metalworking skills among the workforce acted as a disincentive to most aircraft manufacturers to make the move away from wood, but in time the situation would change. The Air Ministry were not blind to these new developments and had purchased the Silver Streak from Shorts in 1921 for extensive testing. The scepticism voiced in some quarters regarding the durability and anti-corrosion properties of aluminium alloys was soon dispelled, backed by materials research carried out at the RAE and NPL. On the strength of this they sanctioned Shorts' fabrication of the first metal hull for a flying boat and even before this had flown they made the decision that the aircraft industry as a whole had to be encouraged to move towards metal construction. The manufacturers of flying boats were, perhaps, the first to come up against, and benefit from, this policy.

Not surprisingly, Shorts were awarded a contract to build a new all-metal flying boat prototype under specification 13/24, as they had proven their capability to work with alloy construction. The hull was constructed from Duralumin plate while the flight surfaces were fabric covered on Duralumin spars and ribs. Duralumin is an alloy of aluminium mixed with around 4 per cent copper and minor amounts of magnesium and manganese that

↑ The proven capabilities of Shorts' S.2 metal hull resulted in a contract to build a new all-metal flying boat. The large twin-engined Singapore flew in 1927.

combines many of the strength characteristics of steel with the lower density advantages of aluminium. Shorts named their flying boat Singapore; it was designed by Arthur Gouge and C.P. Liscombe, was powered by two 650hp Rolls-Royce Condors and first flew in August 1926. The Singapore enjoyed an eventful career surveying potential air routes into and around Africa and was an outstanding success.

Blackburn received a contract for an even larger aircraft to specification 14/24, the Iris, powered by three Condors, and this flew just one month after the Short Singapore. The Iris, designed by Major J.D. Rennie, was built with a wooden hull but the contract stipulated that a metal hull should also be constructed to replace it and this was ready by early 1927, when the revised aircraft was renamed Iris II. This aircraft, too, was successful.

THE METALLURGY DEPARTMENT

Supermarine, as we have seen, received a production contract to produce wooden-hulled Southampton flying boats, but the Air Ministry specified that any future orders would require the aircraft to be equipped with metal hulls and the contract included an order for one such prototype. Supermarine took immediate steps to add metal testing and production facilities at the Woolston works and to recruit staff to work there. The new metallurgy department was headed by Arthur Black, who joined the company towards the end of 1925, aged twenty-five, from Brown Firth Research Laboratories, a Sheffield-based steel development company.

Although the construction techniques for metal hulls were poles apart from the yacht builders' woodworking methods required for a Linton Hope-type, Mitchell was not totally free in the way he designed the new hull for the Southampton. The greatest restriction was that the Air Ministry contract was solely for the construction of a replacement hull; all other aspects of the aircraft were to remain unchanged. Therefore there was a need to provide the same crew positions and equipment as in the wooden hull and to ensure appropriate balance and flying and water handling characteristics as on the original aircraft. Although it would certainly have proven possible

to undertake a degree of new design, Mitchell took the pragmatic approach and elected to emulate the entire shape of the wooden hull in metal, with the sole exception of the planing bottom, which was now built as an integral part of the main structure rather than as a separate construction attached to the hull. This resulted in a small increase in the internal width of the fore-hull as the flare of the sides down to the chines added marginally to the internal space.

The design for the metal hull was largely complete by the autumn of 1925 but the time required to construct new workshop buildings and to install all the tools, heat and anodic treatment tanks extended well into 1926 and it was only by the second half of the year that everything had been tested and new workers employed and trained so that construction of the first experimental hull could commence. This was completed in the early days of December after which it was moved to the erection building to be mated with standard

↓ The prototype metal-hulled Southampton II, N218, was flown in the early weeks of 1927 and was an immediate success.

Southampton flying surfaces and engines. The aircraft was registered N218 and test flown in early 1927. Mitchell's rather conservative approach with the design was vindicated as the aircraft performed extremely well and the hull weighed in 500lb lighter than a wooden hull. The only negative point was that the complex double-curvature of many of the hull plates, so easy to form in thin and narrow wood planks, took quite some time to produce and required a high level of skill from the metal workers. Nevertheless, the design was considered to be a total success and production contracts were received for around twenty-six new aircraft, named as the Southampton II, in three batches plus a number of additional hulls with which to replace the wooden hulls on the original Southamptons.

With the introduction of the Southampton II the full potential of the design was met. None of the strengths of the original Southampton had been sacrificed and the aircraft was now both lighter and more durable. The installation of the latest Napier Lion V, of slightly increased power, added to

the benefits. The RAF immediately ordered four modified aircraft optimised for extended service within the topics. When these were delivered in the summer of 1927 they were allocated to a special unit as the Far East Flight.

As the 1920s progressed aircraft had reached the point where they were capable of undertaking long-distance flights and looked poised to provide a reliable high-speed link throughout the Empire, for both the military and civil airlines. Extensive surveys for air routes had commenced to link Egypt through the mandated Middle East territories and on to India, and moves were afoot to do the same across Africa down to Cape Town. The Air Ministry drew up an ambitious plan to fly a group of flying boats out to Singapore via Karachi and Bombay to assess the feasibility of using aircraft to provide reinforcements and supplies to distant garrisons; surveying the route, seeking safe harbours and other facilities,. The survey would then be extended to Australia and Hong Kong. Four aircraft were assigned to the flight, which was placed under the command of Gp Capt. Henry Cave-Brown-Cave.

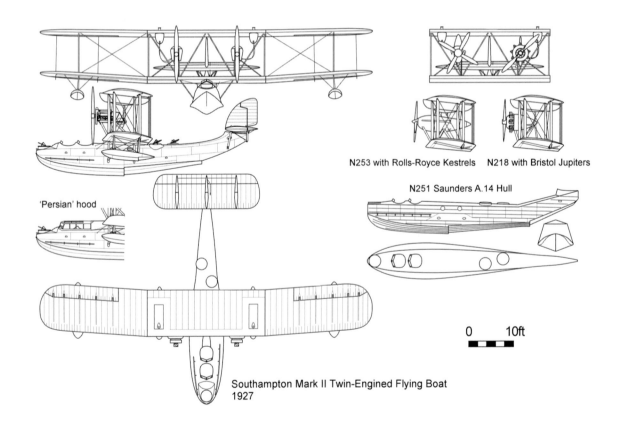

'Persian' hood

N253 with Rolls-Royce Kestrels   N218 with Bristol Jupiters

N251 Saunders A.14 Hull

0   10ft

Southampton Mark II Twin-Engined Flying Boat
1927

← In late 1927 four
Southampton IIs were
prepared to undertake
an extended tour
of the Far East and
Australia.

For Mitchell and Supermarine, this was an exacting challenge. While the Southampton had been proven in service, including long flights to the Mediterranean, the metal hull of the Southampton II was new, as yet unproven except in short flights and no flying boat of any type had spent significant time in tropical climes. The four aircraft that had been ordered were standard Southampton IIs, the only modifications being larger fuel tanks constructed of tinned steel for ease of repair, larger oil tanks, and radiators providing 50 per cent greater cooling area. The hull and wing floats were finished in a special white enamel varnish. No armament was installed and the hulls were kitted out for extended missions that would require the crew to remain on board.

The four aircraft, registered S-1149 to 1152, were delivered to Felixstowe in September 1927. Cave-Brown-Cave would lead the flight in S-1152. The other three aircraft were painted with vertical identification stripes on the front and rear hull; one stripe for S-1149, two for S-1150 and three for S-1151. The flight departed Felixstowe on 14 October and arrived in Karachi on 18 November without incident. They departed after a three-week stay and reached Singapore on 28 February 1928. It was probably at this point that the aircraft had their propellers replaced by the variable pitch Leitner-Watts units as tested on the first Southampton. The flight received permission to continue the trip and to make a circumnavigation of Australia, departing on 21 May and arriving back on 15 September. There was then a brief pause to allow a replacement aircraft, S-1127, to replace S-1149 before resuming the trip out to Hong Kong on 1 November and arriving back on 11 December 1928.

The flight had proven to be an outstanding success. There were, of course, numerous minor problems but all had been overcome. The majority related to corrosion of one form or another; encrustation by barnacles and other

← N218 was used to evaluate the installation of Bristol Jupiter radials.

marine life proved a particular nuisance, paint broke down rapidly in the intense sun and heat, and many of the alloy rivets deteriorated and had to be replaced with stainless steel ones by the crew. This was all to be expected and did not reflect adversely on Supermarine, who were rightly hailed for having provided an outstanding aircraft. A great deal had been learned about operations in the tropics that was of immense value for the future.

On 8 January the flight was officially disbanded and reformed as No 205 Squadron based at RAF Seletar in Singapore, still under the command of Cave-Brown-Cave.

The prototype Southampton II, N218, was retained for research purposes. Early on it was used to trial new wings with a small amount of sweepback designed to rebalance the aircraft. After a successful outcome these became the standard for production. It also tested metal wings with leading edge slots on the upper planes, but the slots were not judged to be worthwhile. The metal wings had been designed in 1928 and an example was exhibited at Olympia in 1929. Finally, N218 was used to test the installation of two

Bristol Jupiter XIF radials, as Type 189, and subsequently Jupiter XFBMs. These did not prove to be particularly satisfactory as the engines induced resonance in the structure.

Southampton II S-1122 was taken out of service and used as a test bed for Rolls-Royce Kestrel engines, initially, it would appear, Kestrel XIIs. It seems likely that it was this aircraft that was later fitted with metal wings with Frise ailerons, and evaporatively cooled Kestrels, in which form it was redesignated Type 184 and re-registered N253.

Some Southampton IIs that would serve with 203 Squadron in the area of the Persian Gulf were fitted with enclosed cockpit canopies, a test example had been trialled on a Southampton, S1059.

Over the years the wooden hulls of the Southamptons were gradually replaced by metal hulls and the straight wings replaced by swept. Metal wings replaced wooden and the Napier Lion Vs were replaced by Vbs. In this way the distinction between a Southampton and a Southampton II became completely blurred.

11

A MOVE AWAY FROM MARINE AIRCRAFT

MITCHELL'S FIRST TRUE FIGHTER

By the mid-1920s the Navy's aircraft carrier fleet was in the process of increasing to five. The fighters based on the ships were mainly Fairey Flycatchers, a worthy and generally well-liked aircraft but soon to be in need of replacement. To address the requirement the Air Ministry issued specification 21/26 in late 1926 to solicit designs for its next generation of fighters, stipulating all-metal structure, interchangeable wheel and float undercarriage, provision for deck-landing equipment, including wheel brakes, and a preference for the use of the new 450hp Bristol Mercury air-cooled radial engine. At the time the Mercury engine had only run on the test bench. Earlier that same year the Ministry had issued specification 9/26 for a fighter for the RAF to replace their Armstrong Whitworth Siskins and Gloster Gamecocks, and this too stipulated an all-metal aircraft with an air-cooled engine. There was thus a fair degree of similarity between the two requirements and the potential for quite large production contracts. Consequently they drew a great deal of interest from the aircraft constructors and all the major firms embarked upon designs. Both specifications were amended and adjusted after release and alternative engine types were allowed.

Mitchell saw 21/26 as an ideal opportunity for Supermarine to expand its business beyond their traditional flying boat market and to capitalise on some of the research and development work he had undertaken on small racers for the Schneider Trophy. His team drew up a number of closely related designs to fulfil the requirements.

Despite the Air Ministry's initial preference for the Bristol Mercury, Mitchell selected the latest Rolls-Royce water-cooled V-12 engine for the first of his designs. This engine, initially designated the Falcon X, later the

'F' and finally the Kestrel, was as untried as the Mercury as it, too, had only run on the bench by the end of 1926. Rolls-Royce had designed this engine with strong support from the Air Ministry as a British response to the Curtiss D-12, the engine that had proven so successful in the Curtiss racing aircraft and which now powered several service aircraft in the US. Mitchell gave the nose of his fighter fine aerodynamic lines with the engine enclosed within tight-fitting cowls and fitted zero-drag surface radiators on the upper wing centre section. He gave special attention to providing a clear field of view for the pilot and, hence, the cockpit was raised slightly to improve the line of sight over the nose. The single bay biplane wings were of conventional twin-spar construction and connected by outboard 'N' struts. The lower wing had no sweep while the upper wing centre section, mounted on short struts above the fuselage, had a large cut-out at the rear in order to provide excellent upward view, and the outer wing panels had a small amount of sweep. Ailerons were fitted on the upper wings only. Twin Vickers machine guns were mounted on either side of the nose and four small bombs could be carried under the lower left wing.

A second design, with the same basic layout as the first, was to be powered by the Ministry's preferred Mercury engine. Overall, this aircraft was slightly smaller than the Rolls-Royce-powered version and had been drawn with a completely new main fuselage in which the fin appears as if it were intended to be an integral part of the structure, which could just suggest, although rather unlikely at this time, that the rear fuselage was to be of metal monocoque construction. The span of the upper wing centre section had been reduced in the absence of the radiator and there was less stagger between the planes. A final re-draw of this project saw some minor adjustments to the size of the fin and rudder and the replacement of the outboard wing 'N' struts with single

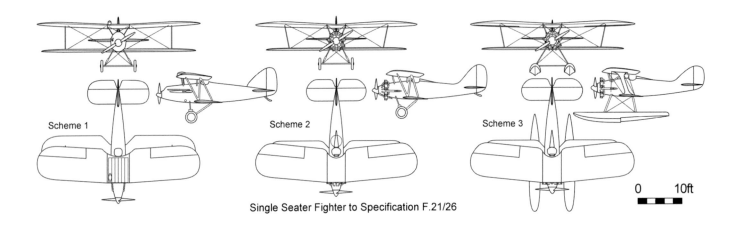

Scheme 1   Scheme 2   Scheme 3

Single Seater Fighter to Specification F.21/26

0   10ft

'I' struts, a type that was not normally considered acceptable on a military aircraft for reasons of structural redundancy.

As the requirements of 21/26 had placed quite tight constraints on the aircraft designers, it was somewhat inevitable that their proposed fighters would be similar, at least superficially, and Mitchell's were no different in this regard. His designs do not stand out from the crowd and they share many features with those submitted by Gloster, Hawker, Bristol and the others. Indeed, it does seem possible given the absence of documentation that Supermarine decided against making a formal tender to the specification, maybe acknowledging that they had no track record in either metal frame construction or in fighter design and hence would be unlikely to be favoured for a contract.

At least eight companies submitted tenders to 21/26, with several choosing to enter more than one design, and the Air Ministry issued contracts for eleven aircraft to be built as prototypes. As the selection process was run in parallel with that for specification 9/26 and was delayed due to concerns over the Mercury engine and then by the partial rewrite of the specification, it was some time before all the aircraft had been constructed and prepared for assessment. In the end no production contract was awarded, a reflection of the specification providing little challenge and the submissions lacking much in the way of innovation, although some of the prototypes did provide the basis for new designs in the coming years.

In 1927 the Air Ministry issued specification 20/27 for a high-performance interceptor fighter which, once again, drew submissions from almost all the aircraft companies, including some who had never before tendered for this market. Curiously, Supermarine was not among them and there are no drawings in the records to suggest that Mitchell spent any time considering the opportunity. It would be some time before he considered a further attempt to enter the arena for fighters.

12

SCHNEIDER TROPHY RACERS – A TRIUMPH AND A DISTRACTION

SUCCESS IN VENICE

The 1925 Schneider Trophy race had proven to be a dismal affair for the British team. Their greatest hope, the Supermarine Napier S.4, had been wrecked in early practice and one of the two Gloster IIIs had been badly damaged when the float chassis collapsed and had to be withdrawn. The sole remaining Gloster III had soldiered on through the race and managed to finish a valiant second, but its performance was eclipsed by that of the winning Curtiss R3C-2 and it placed high only as a consequence of mechanical failure of the other two US aircraft and not through competitive speed. More depressing still was the realisation that Doolittle's aircraft was more than a match for the S.4, a point rubbed in when he took back the world air speed record for seaplanes shortly after the contest.

When the team arrived back in Britain the atmosphere was a trifle acrimonious with Gloster blaming Fairey for having produced inferior propellers, mumbled comments about the cause of Biard's crash in the S.4 and a general air of gloom around the competitive state of Britain's aircraft industry. Presentations by Buchanan from the Air Ministry and by Richard Fairey threw a spotlight on the shortcomings of the British aircraft, especially their size compared to the Curtiss racers, and on the lack of practice flying undertaken by the British pilots. Just about the only matter on which there was general agreement and praise concerned the power and reliability of the Napier Lion engines.

Mitchell was in the audience at these presentations and participated in the discussions. He had reached much the same conclusion as both speakers and saw that any future racer would need to be significantly smaller than the S.4, most especially in terms of frontal cross section area, with particular attention

paid to all drag-inducing components. A $^1/_8$-scale model of the S.4 had been sent to the RAE in mid-1925 for testing in their 7ft wind tunnel and Mitchell had seen the conclusions just prior to the contest. It is almost certain that this was the first time that one of Mitchell's designs had been tested in this way, Supermarine had no such facilities at their works and there had been no particular reason for any of his earlier aircraft to be investigated. The wind tunnel tests measured lift, drag and pitch moments for the aircraft as a whole and then for the floats separately before investigation focussed on the impact of the Lamblin radiators on lift and drag. These results proved to be rather inconclusive as it was not possible to represent the radiators accurately on the model and scale effects inherent in the tests made interpretation of the measurements difficult. However, it was readily apparent that this type of radiator, although developed especially for high performance aircraft, was responsible for a significant amount of the total drag. The Curtiss racers had long-since employed finely corrugated brass radiators on both the upper and lower surfaces of the wings and these had a minimal impact on aircraft drag. As yet, no British manufacturer had managed to perfect a similar radiator.

Discussions took place between the Air Ministry, representatives from the aircraft industry and the RAeC to establish a policy for any future participation in the Schneider Trophy contest. Industry was adamant that they would be unable to field truly competitive aircraft without substantial support from the government, both in terms of funding and access to research facilities. The government were reluctant at first to commit money for what was just a sporting event but the Air Ministry saw, as their US service counterparts had done several years previously, that research into high-speed aircraft for military application could be stimulated in this way and supported the idea. It was agreed that a government-sponsored programme would be set up in

1926 to investigate various aspects of high-speed aircraft design and that this could involve participation in future Schneider Trophy contests if it were deemed to be beneficial, and if there were a reasonable prospect of winning. By the end of 1925 Mitchell had a new aircraft design in mind already and this bore no relation at all to the S.4.

While the details of government sponsorship were finalised, Mitchell and his team pushed ahead with the design for his next racer, the S.5. He had been advised that the Air Ministry were to fund the development of a specialised version of the Napier Lion and that this engine should power his next racing aircraft. For the new engine Napier continued the external clean-up process that had been applied to the series VII and also undertook a major revision of the main engine components. They designed shortened pistons and conrods so that the cylinder banks could be reduced in height without affecting the stroke and this also allowed the engine to be run at higher revs. The cylinder head camshaft covers were to be shaped to the contours of the aircraft so that they would not require cowling and could remain open to the airflow. This helped reduce the cross section of the aircraft and aided the cooling of the engine. It was also to be constructed in both geared and ungeared forms that shared the same dimensions, and hence were interchangeable in the aircraft.

It must be understood that the Air Ministry's programme was not aimed specifically at winning the Schneider Trophy, although this was implicit in the specifications for the aircraft as seaplanes, and there was a genuine intent to compare alternative approaches to the design and construction of high-speed aircraft and engines. To this end they also sponsored development of the Bristol Mercury air-cooled racing engine for comparison with the Napier Lion and issued contracts for more than one type of racing aircraft. By the end of 1925 it was known, but not yet confirmed officially, that both Supermarine and Gloster would be awarded contracts for aircraft to be powered by the Napier Lion while the engine division of Bristol were working with Major Bristow, a private consultant, to design a racer for their Mercury engine.

Despite the loss of the S.4, Mitchell remained committed to the monoplane layout, although he stepped back from a second full cantilever design both to avoid any possibility of wing flutter and to enable the use of a reasonably light wing. In a very bold move he also intended to construct both fuselage and floats from metal, a gamble as Supermarine had yet to commission their metalworking department and had no expertise in this area. However, this was exactly what the Air Ministry wished to see as the S.5 would provide a useful comparison to the Gloster design, which was a biplane of wooden monocoque structure. Both companies were granted full access to the facilities at both the NPL and the RAE where their competing designs would be subjected to an extensive range of wind tunnel and structural tests before contracts were issued for the full-scale aircraft. These investigations commenced in the spring of 1926, which left too little time for aircraft to be built to compete in the Schneider Trophy contest that year and the RAeC declined to enter.

For the wind tunnel programme Supermarine constructed a ¼-scale model of the S.5 with several interchangeable parts. This enabled Mitchell to compare a number of alternative configurations; most notably a comparison of strut-braced and wire-braced wings, and an assessment of the impact of moving the wing from mid-fuselage to bottom fuselage position. It was known that a low wing was less desirable from the perspective of interference drag but that in this position the wing root structure could be made lighter and the bracing angles for the wires would be more optimal. Models of the floats were tested both in the wind tunnel and in the Froude water tank at the NPL. All these tests confirmed that Mitchell's design was sound, in contrast to those of both Gloster and Short-Bristow which underwent a number of significant design changes as a result of the evaluation.

While the British research programme was in full flow, the 1926 Schneider Trophy contest took place between teams from the US and Italy. The US Navy and Army were both beginning to question the value of continuing to fund an expensive programme of racing aircraft and engines but agreed to pool resources to field a team one last time as a third contest win would secure the Schneider Trophy in perpetuity. Italy was by now firmly under the control of Mussolini, who was determined to raise Italy to a position of power. Mussolini and his deputy in the air ministry, Balbo, decided that a win in the Schneider Trophy would provide just the prestige they sought. Full government funding and air force support was put in place.

The US wished to minimise cost. They knew that the Italians were the only team they would face and as they had raced uncompetitive monoplane flying boats at the 1925 contest the likelihood was that they would struggle to equal, let alone beat, the US aircraft. However, an increase in performance was going to be required to set the bar higher so they spread their bets by fielding three revised versions of the 1925 Curtiss racers each with a different engine type. Curtiss prepared two of the aircraft: the R3C-4 with a new Curtiss V-1550 engine and the R3C-2 little changed from 1925. The Navy Aircraft Factory undertook the conversion of the third aircraft, R3C-3, to fit a new Packard 2A-1500.

However, unknown to the US, the Italian programme had been intense and their team, placing all their eggs in one basket, comprised three all-new

↑ The Macchi M.39 introduced a new era for low-wing monoplane racers and there were accusations that Mitchell had copied Castoldi's design for the S.5.

Macchi M.39 seaplanes fitted with equally new Fiat A.S.2 racing engines. The M.39, designed by Mario Castoldi, was a major step forward for Macchi, as dramatic as the S.4 had been for Supermarine. It was a low-wing, wire-braced monoplane constructed in wood with a sleek finish. The wings were fitted with corrugated surface radiators similar to those perfected by Curtiss.

Both teams suffered fatalities during testing and numerous serious engine failures in the preliminary trials and then in the contest itself. In an intense contest the Italian team captain, de Bernardi, brought his Macchi through to win, thereby depriving the US of the chance to secure the trophy outright and bring the contest to an end. As a result, the next contest would take place in Italy in 1927 and provided a strong incentive for the British programme to proceed.

As a result of the positive reports from the NPL and RAE model tests Supermarine received a contract to build two aircraft and commenced construction of the first S.5 late in 1926, at much the same time as the first Southampton II metal hull was being finalised. A contract for a third example was issued in early 1927. The contrast in the new metalworking department must have been profound; on the one hand a large and somewhat conservative hull and on the other a fuselage so slim that it presented considerable difficulty for the riveters to gain access to the inside.

Mitchell had concluded that one key route by which to achieve a significant decrease in drag was to minimise frontal cross-section area. With the S.4 he had contoured the fuselage to approximate an ideal aerodynamic shape, often referred to as 'airship' or 'fish', in which the depth and width increased smoothly back from the nose to reach a maximum at somewhere around 30 per cent of the fuselage length before tapering to the tail. As a consequence, the engine cowl panels did not conform tightly to the shape of the engine, the cockpit was larger than necessary, and maximum cross section area was dictated by the contouring formula rather than the size of the engine or pilot. Castoldi at Macchi adhered closely to this approach and Folland at Gloster had done the same for his new racer, the Gloster IV. However, for the S.5 Mitchell chose to take an alternative approach and to tailor the fuselage to fit as tightly as possible around the engine and pilot, so the pilot was not provided with a proper seat, just a small cushioned pad on the floor of the cockpit, and his shoulders were close to the fuselage sides. Napier had done a superb job in repackaging the Lion engine and now all the coolant and fuel induction pipes were placed close to the cylinder banks while the magnetos, carburettors and pumps were clustered at the rear and sat within the frontal silhouette of the engine. Mitchell was able to sculpt the nose of the S.5 to the bare minimum to enclose the Lion and he had the rocker covers reduced to the smallest possible size. Those that Folland designed for the Gloster IV were noticeably taller. The cockpit was positioned just behind the firewall bulkhead so the size was more or less dictated by the height and width of the engine in front. It was very compact indeed and almost too tight as some pilots had difficulty lowering themselves into the cockpit and had to twist sideways in order to get their shoulders through the narrow aperture. The fuselage then tapered to the rear and included the integral fin.

The fuselage was built as a single stressed structure from nose to tail. Twin longitudinal members ran for almost the whole length, lightweight at the rear and strengthened at the front where they formed the engine mounts. Two other light members ran at shoulder height from the cockpit to the integral tail fin. Transverse formers were spaced at approximately every 9in and then the whole structure was skinned with Duralumin plates. The fore section was strengthened with doubled plates to act as a cantilevered mount

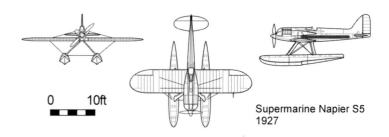

0   10ft

Supermarine Napier S5
1927

for the engine. In addition to the drastic reduction in cross section area, the two other key means by which Mitchell achieved a considerable decrease in the size of the fuselage compared to the S.4 was by moving the main fuel tanks to the floats and by adopting a low wing, which allowed the cockpit to be moved forward to sit directly behind the engine and over the wing roots.

The metal floats were constructed around a central longitudinal keel frame and transverse bulkheads, stabilised by thin stringers. These, too, were skinned with Duralumin. To save weight the fuel tank was not a separate component but formed by sealing the central portion of the float and fitting tinned steel skins. Mindful that the torque load from the high-power engine could prove to be severe on the small airframe, the fuel tank was placed in the starboard float and this was rigged to be 6in further from the centre line than the port in order to provide an offset load. Concern that this would have an adverse effect on the aileron loads was raised by a short study based on analogue data in a report dated May 1927 but flight tests showed this to be unfounded. For the wings of the S.5 Mitchell selected the RAF30 symmetrical section aerofoil, at 12.5 per cent thickness-to-chord ratio a relatively thin section for a monoplane wing of this era. They were built of, and skinned with, wood as it may have been considered a step too far to attempt to fabricate metal spars and ribs at this stage and it would be a year or two before Mitchell's team completed the design of a metal-framed wing and the works was able to fabricate them. Flat-surface, zero-drag copper radiator panels were attached to both the upper and lower surfaces of the wing, and corrugated oil coolers ran along the fuselage sides.

The first S.5 was registered N219, next in the experimental aircraft sequence after the metal-hulled Southampton II, N218, and launched in early June 1927. It was tested by Flt Lieut Worsley of the newly formed RAF High Speed Flight, who was based at nearby Calshot rather than Felixstowe in order to be close to Supermarine's works. No serious problems arose but it did prove necessary to enlarge the oil coolers and to add extra cooling

← The second S.5, registered N220, differed from the first, N219, in detail, most especially in the use of flush riveting for the fuselage.

vents around the engine. Various propellers were tested, all fabricated by Fairey under their licence agreement with Curtiss-Reed, to find the best compromise between maximising speed and ensuring a safe take-off. The second S.5, N220, was flown in mid-July. This was a more refined aircraft than the first as Supermarine had been able to apply flush riveting to a greater part of the fuselage and floats. Both aircraft were dismantled, crated and shipped to Venice to participate in the Schneider Trophy contest.

The Italians provided excellent facilities for the team at their seaplane base at Sant'Andrea in Venice lagoon and there was more than ample hangar space for all the team's aircraft. Preparation and test flights of the race aircraft proceeded without a hitch for both the Supermarine and Gloster teams, but the Short-Bristow Crusader was lost as a result of the aileron control cables having been connected incorrectly, thankfully without serious harm to the pilot.

The Italian team had elected to follow the same strategy they had employed in 1926, placing all their eggs in one basket and fielding three Macchi M.52s, the same basic design as the previous year's M.39 but fitted with new wings and tail of reduced area. The engines were Fiat AS.3 racing engines, an upgraded version of the AS.2.

The US Navy and Army had by now lost interest in the Schneider Trophy contest and would no longer agree to fund development of racing aircraft. However, the US still only required a win in 1927 to take the trophy outright and there was a groundswell of irritation expressed in the press. Navy test pilot Lieut Al Williams, who had competed in several air races and held the world air speed record in 1923, stepped forward and found backers to finance the construction of a new racing seaplane, designed by a number of former Curtiss staff and built by Kirkham Industries. Williams persuaded the Navy to allow him to use the experimental Packard

1A-2775 engine. Much was expected of this Kirkham–Williams aircraft in the USA, not least because Williams was good at selling a story to the press, but it failed to come close to expectations in early tests as a result of poor float and chassis design and a recalcitrant engine. When the NAA was unable to persuade their Italian counterparts to delay the contest, due in no small part to Britain, whose team was already in Venice, refusing to agree, the US entry was withdrawn.

In the days preceding the contest it became very apparent that the Macchi M.52 was a fast competitor but plagued by serious engine problems. For a while it looked possible that they would not be able to compete but all three aircraft were made ready for the preliminary trials and passed without incident. The British fielded the two Supermarine S.5s, one with a geared

Napier Lion VIIB and the other with an ungeared Lion VIIA, and the Gloster IVB with a geared Lion.

On the day of the contest all of Venice was in a state of high anticipation with the majority of the crowd convinced that Italy was heading for a second stirring victory after Mussolini and the press had stoked the fires. But it was not to be as all three Macchis failed to complete the course; one barely managing to cross the starting line before its engine burst. The two that managed to fly a few laps were seen to be slower than the British aircraft, which dominated the race. The two S.5s finished first and second, the only two aircraft to complete the course as the Gloster IVB was forced to pull out on the last lap due to severe vibrations caused by a cracked propeller shaft. Flt Lieut Webster won in the geared S.5 with Flt Lieut Worsley close behind in the ungeared aircraft.

→ The third S.5, N221, being prepared for an attempt on the air speed record in March 1928.

In January the following year Mitchell, Capt. Wilkinson of Napier and Ralli from Fairey read brief papers at a meeting of the Royal Aeronautical Society and each was presented with the society's silver medal. Mitchell's paper, *Schneider Trophy Machine Design, 1927*, concerned the construction of the S.5 and the design decisions that had led to it, without divulging too much about the research programme that was still classified as secret. The paper concluded with a short section on further developments in which Mitchell indicated how an increase in engine power of 10 per cent could affect weight and speed, an insight into how he was thinking in preparation for the 1928 contest.

During the contest, Webster's S.5 had set several speed-over-distance records but as the High Speed Flight were ordered home immediately after the award ceremony they were unable to set a new absolute air speed record while in Venice, which was well within the capabilities of the S.5. So back in Britain the third aircraft, which had not yet flown, was prepared for an attempt. This S.5 had the most refined finish of the three and was therefore potentially the fastest. The High Speed Flight had been disbanded immediately on their return but in early 1928 Flt Lieut Kinkhead, who had been the pilot of the Gloster Napier IVB for the Schneider contest, was brought back to Calshot in order to make the attempt. A small team was assigned to the project and the aircraft made ready in wintery conditions in March. Poor weather led to many delays and Kinkhead managed just one practice flight, which was actually the first flight of N221 and the first that he had made in any S.5. Unfortunately, his attempt at the record ended in a crash into the Solent and Kinkhead was killed. The cause was not determined, or at least the conclusions of the official enquiry have never been disclosed, and there are serious discrepancies in the accounts of observers who could not even agree on whether the aircraft was travelling at high or low speed immediately prior to hitting the water. However, it is generally accepted that the crash was the result of pilot error, misjudging his height above the water in poor weather conditions, although some form of unspecified structural failure has been suggested as an alternative. A second attempt at setting the record late in 1928 missed out by the narrowest of margins as Flt Lieut D'Arcy Greig failed to exceed the current record, now held by Macchi's much-modified M.52R, by the required minimum amount.

The two surviving S.5s continued in service until late 1931, carrying out a programme of high-speed flight research, serving as trainers for the 1929 and 1931 Schneider Trophy teams and even participating as the third entrant for the 1929 contest. They behaved without fault, failure or accident throughout. Mitchell's racer, expected to have a useful life of less than a year, continued to earn its keep for more than four.

The workload within the Design Department associated with development of the S.5 had been intense for more than a year, possibly at the expense of focus on more commercial work, but the rewards were high.

The S.5 was a remarkably successful aircraft, standing among the very best of competitive racers. Not only did Mitchell's design require no reworking after the wind tunnel research programme but it also proved to handle well both on the water and in the air from the outset. No effort had to be expended to undertake last-minute modifications. It was essentially vice-free, by the standards of racing aircraft of that era, and an excellent pilot's machine. The Napier Lion VIIA and VIIB, around which the aircraft had been built, was without doubt one of the all-time greats of racing engine design; light, powerful and, above all else, reliable. Mitchell had designed an aircraft with which to get the very best from this engine.

13

1927 – NEW IDEAS

SUPERMARINE RELAUNCHED

At the end of 1926 James Bird sought additional funds with which to expand the business and Supermarine Aviation Works Ltd underwent a recapitalisation. The original company was wound up, with all creditors paid in full, and a new company established, with the same name, to take on all the assets and liabilities with shares issued on the Stock Exchange. Capitalisation rose from £13,500 to £250,000 but this has been reported as largely an accounting process to enable access to credit and that little new cash was actually invested in the business.

As they moved into 1927 Supermarine were totally committed to metal construction, for both hulls and wing structures, and, while the old woodworking department remained as an essential part of the business and continued to be reasonably busy fulfilling existing contracts for the Southampton flying surfaces, the quantity of work requiring their skills was in terminal decline. Despite Mitchell drawing up numerous designs for single-engined amphibian flying boats, all, it has to be said, basically the same but fulfilling a variety of roles, sales had proven elusive and this class of aircraft was put to one side, at least for a few years, while the company concentrated on larger, multi-engined flying boats.

Production of the Southampton II was in full swing and would provide a healthy income for some time, yet the aircraft was already beginning to look dated so both the Air Ministry and Supermarine were considering a replacement. Despite the high workload as Southampton upgrades, derivatives and experimental versions received high priority, the staff were keen to push forward with new ideas and the first opportunity to develop an entirely new type of aircraft came when the Air Ministry notified industry of a requirement for a three-engined patrol flying boat; essentially the role fulfilled by the Southampton but with greater range and internal space. The move in policy to specify three engines was prompted by the need to ensure the ability to undertake extended patrols in safety. While the Southampton could maintain level flight with one engine out, if not at full load, it was marginal. A third engine would allow them to be run at lower throttle during the cruise or even for one to be shut down if necessary. This requirement eventually gelled into a number of separate but related specifications but started as R.4/27. Mitchell set the team to work on two designs, one a conventional biplane, as a safe option, and the other a monoplane.

DORNIER

Since the war the majority of flying boat manufacturers had gravitated towards the same formula; a biplane with the engine or engines mounted mid-gap above the hull and wing tip balance floats. Vickers, Shorts, Blackburn, Macchi, Savoia, CAMS, FBA Schreck and many others all built this way. One company, however, had chosen to take a completely different approach.

Claudius Dornier had worked for Zeppelin during the war and took over some of that company's facilities after the Armistice, then moved design to Pisa in Italy and construction to Lake Constance in Switzerland to avoid the restrictions imposed on German aviation by the Treaty of Versailles. He had conceived a new type of flying boat in the closing months of the war constructed of metal with fabric covered wings. The hull was of basic rectangular section with a single-step planing bottom, and the simple,

→ The Dornier Wal series of flying boats were all-metal parasol monoplanes with lateral sponsons in a world where most of their rivals were wooden biplanes with wing floats.

rectangular plan monoplane wing was mounted above, parasol fashion, on struts. Lateral stability on the water was provided by aerofoil section stubs from the lower hull sides that became known as sponsons. The wing was braced to these sponsons by substantial outward-raked struts. Dornier's early aircraft were almost all twin-engined and these were mounted in tandem as tractor and pusher in a nacelle resting on the wing. The first example of this type of flying boat was built in mid-1919 and flew briefly with the Swiss airline Ad Astra until Dornier is said to have had the aircraft scuttled in the Baltic to avoid having to hand it over to the Allies as part of the punitive clauses of the Treaty of Versailles. However, the design had proven successful so an improved version was introduced in late 1922 and named as the Wal. The rugged simplicity and flexibility of this flying boat attracted a lot of customers and, in addition to Dornier's production, licences for manufacture were sold to the Netherlands, Spain and Japan. Wals established a number of class records and reports of the aircraft featured frequently in the press.

A German registered Wal with Rolls-Royce Eagle engines visited Southampton in 1925 and was photographed, and possibly examined, by Oliver Simmonds. In 1927 the British test pilot Capt. Frank Courtney acquired a Wal fitted with twin Napier Lion engines in order to make an attempt at a double crossing of the Atlantic. The aircraft was purchased in Norway from Roald Amundsen, the famous explorer, and delivered in April, when it was registered as G-EBQO. Courtney established his base at Calshot and undertook test flights from there. It is obviously no coincidence that Calshot, Britain's principal base for military flying boats, was made available for this purely civil venture as it provided an excellent opportunity for the Air Ministry to assess the merits of the Wal design. An earlier and smaller Dornier aircraft, the single-engined, 185hp Delfin, had been purchased by them a few years earlier and had been evaluated at the MAEE in Felixstowe and at Calshot. It has to be quite likely that Mitchell or his design staff had the opportunity to examine the Wal in detail at Calshot, they had good relations with the RAF staff there and were frequent visitors as they carried out the early test flights of the S.5 racer. Dornier influence was very apparent in Supermarine's new monoplane design.

THE BIG 'BOAT DESIGNS

Two Supermarine flying boat projects to meet specification R.4/27, a biplane and monoplane, were developed in parallel in the closing months of 1927 and shared several features. In both cases the metal hulls were derived from that of the Southampton II with the same upswept tail, staggered rear gun positions and triple-finned tailplane. However, the hull top was broader and the sides reduced in curvature for simplicity and in order that a side-by-side cockpit could be accommodated in the nose. The wings for the biplane were also derived from work carried out as part of the Southampton development programme, in this case the three-engined version that became the Nanok, and the aircraft was powered by three unspecified single-row radials, almost certainly Bristol Jupiters, mounted in a mid-gap position. For

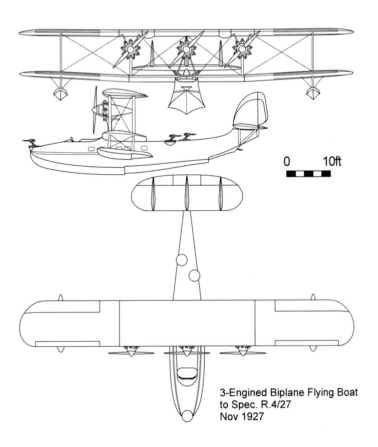

3-Engined Biplane Flying Boat
to Spec. R.4/27
Nov 1927

the monoplane Mitchell adopted the Dornier system. The hull, which was a lengthened version of the design drawn up for the biplane, was fitted with tapered sponsons similar to those on the Wal. The parasol wing, mounted above the hull on a cabane of struts, had a parallel chord centre section and tapered outer panels with a straight leading edge, fitted with Handley Page slots, and curved tips. The wing was braced to the sponson by twin struts. The three engines, once again probably Jupiters, were installed in neat aerodynamic nacelles that rested on the top surface of the wing centre section. The aircraft was large, the span was 92ft, and it was expected that the top speed would be 130mph.

As with his previous large flying boat designs, Mitchell proposed a civil version but in this case he decided against aiming for a commercial airline application and suggested instead that the aircraft could be configured as a luxury cruiser for the super-rich, a concept described as an air yacht. The aircraft carried a dinghy, upturned, on the top of the hull under the wing and it was suggested that the sponsons could be used as lounging decks when the air yacht was at its moorings.

At this point it is worthwhile clearing up a couple of misconceptions that have surrounded the Supermarine R.4/27 monoplane design. Firstly, the version adapted for civil use as an air yacht is not the same design as the aircraft Supermarine named officially as the Air Yacht, which flew in 1930. This will be described later. The two designs share a common layout, size and purpose but are otherwise completely different aircraft. Secondly, the R.4/27 monoplane air yacht was used in Supermarine marketing material in 1929 and has been erroneously described by some authors as a refined version of the Air Yacht. This is not the case as it is demonstrably the earlier of the two designs.

It is not certain whether Supermarine made a formal tender of either R.4/27 design to the Air Ministry but it is apparent that discussions had taken place with several aircraft constructors, following which the Ministry reviewed their requirements and issued additional specifications shortly after.

The Air Ministry strategy behind the revised flying boat specifications appears to have been aimed at assessing a variety of new designs and techniques for three-engined aircraft. A contract to R.4/27 was issued to Saunders for the A.7 Severn to trial their corrugated metal hull plating system, a method to simplify construction and reduce structural weight that Saunders patented in November 1927. R.5/27 was allocated to Blackburn for the RB.2 Sydney, a three-engined parasol monoplane powered by Rolls-Royce F engines. The Sydney, incidentally, was very similar to

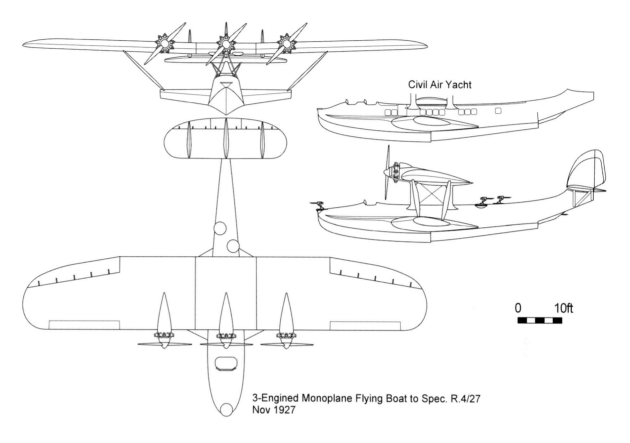

Civil Air Yacht

0   10ft

3-Engined Monoplane Flying Boat to Spec. R.4/27
Nov 1927

→ Saunders' A.7 Severn prototype
introduced an innovative corrugated
metal skin for the hull to save
weight and space by eliminating
the need for stringers between the
bulkheads and formers.

↑ Blackburn's Sydney monoplane was remarkably similar in layout to Supermarine's proposed monoplane, with the exception of the use of wing floats rather than sponsons.

Mitchell's R.4/27 monoplane except that it employed wing floats rather than sponsons.

Supermarine were issued specification R.6/27 for a three-engined biplane flying boat that was in all probability either their initial R.4/27 biplane or a design derived from it. The aircraft, which became known as the Southampton X, was much delayed in detailed design and construction and strayed significantly from the R.4/27 project, a trait that became quite distinctive of much of Mitchell's work in the coming years. The Southampton X will be described in more detail later.

MITCHELL JOINS THE BOARD

At the end of 1927, in accordance with the terms of his contract, Mitchell was offered the position of Technical Director with Supermarine, which he accepted. His Design Department at this point was growing but was still relatively modest in size and employed around thirty-eight staff in the Drawing Office, reporting to Joe Smith, twelve or so reporting to Frank Holroyd in the Technical Office, another fifteen tracers under Sadie Duggan, and a handful of 'boys' as assistants (see Appendix 3).

14

VICKERS

TAKEOVER

In 1928 the vast industrial empire of Vickers Ltd celebrated its 100th anniversary. In their century of operation the company had grown almost exponentially and now had subsidiaries involved in just about every aspect of engineering, including aviation. Vickers Ltd (Aviation Department) had been established in 1911 based at Erin in Kent and at Brooklands, the motor racing and flying centre outside of Weybridge, and had proven an almost immediate success. At Brooklands they established one of the first professionally organised flying schools and it was here that Pemberton Billing had taken his flying lessons and obtained his aviator's certificate back in 1913. The company designed and produced a number of scouts and bombers during the war of which their most famous product was undoubtedly the Vimy bomber, designed by Rex Pierson and developed in the closing year. A slightly modified version of the Vimy succeeded in making the first non-stop crossing of the Atlantic by air in 1919 in the hands of Alcock and Brown. The Vimy had formed the basis for a series of civil and bomber aircraft produced after the war and the business had remained profitable.

In the tough economic climate of the late 1920s Vickers' management embarked upon a series of mergers and divestments, and instigated a thorough reorganisation of the whole company. The largest and most complex change, in 1927, involved a merger with their principal shipbuilding and armaments competitor, Armstrong Whitworth (excluding that company's aviation division) to form Vickers-Armstrong Ltd. Then, in 1928, the aviation department was restructured as Vickers (Aviation) Ltd, a semi-independent subsidiary with Robert McLean at the helm. Although he had no background in aviation, McLean was tasked to expand Vickers' aircraft business both from within, using the capabilities of the existing factory at Brooklands (Weybridge), and through the purchase of additional facilities. McLean and the Board decided that they wished to add the manufacture of flying boats and seaplanes to their portfolio and set about a review of the few companies who specialised in their design and construction; namely Short Bros, Blackburn Aircraft, Saunders and Supermarine. It is understood that they concluded that Shorts' business was too large and diverse, Blackburn's was in poor shape and Saunders' was potentially too costly as they were already engaged in the process of negotiating a rival bid from a consortium headed by A.V. Roe. Supermarine, however, appeared reasonably attractive, despite some reservations regarding the disorganisation in the Woolston works and their high labour costs. Vickers went ahead and purchased the entire share capital of Supermarine Aviation Works Ltd in mid-year and by the end of 1928 the company was renamed the Supermarine Aviation Works (Vickers) Ltd.

It was said, many years later, that one of the terms of the purchase stipulated that Reginald Mitchell should continue to lead the Design Department. It was a sensible provision to ensure stability and continuity of design capability, and, of course, he was bound by the terms of his contract with Supermarine to stay with the new company should they wish to retain his services. It has also been said that acquiring Mitchell's expertise was the main reason for purchasing Supermarine, but there is no evidence that this would have been the case. While Mitchell was to become one of Britain's more accomplished designers, his portfolio of work by 1928 was not so astounding as to suggest that an entire company should be bought in order to secure his services. Neither, on completion of the takeover, did Vickers choose to involve Mitchell in any design activity at Vickers (Aviation) Ltd, which continued with their own design and production programme as before. It should also be made clear that Vickers purchased Supermarine outright. It was not in any way a merger, as some writers have stated.

REORGANISATION

After the takeover was complete, reorganisation began. James Bird retained his position as Managing Director and also became a director of Vickers (Aviation) Limited. Mitchell continued as Technical Director while all the other Supermarine directors were replaced by Vickers appointees. Under the new administration, Supermarine preserved a fair degree of independence although all major decisions had to be referred to McLean for approval. Regular meetings were held between Supermarine and Vickers management and liaison between the two Design Departments was formalised in late 1931 by the setting up of a joint design committee, which met monthly to share ideas and agree strategy. The members of this committee were McLean, Bird, Mitchell and the two Vickers designers, Reginald 'Rex' Pierson and Barnes Wallis. However, there was to be only a limited amount of shared project design work between the two companies over the coming years, in the main mostly Supermarine float designs for Vickers aircraft.

McLean moved to deal with the perceived shortcomings of the company and dispatched key Vickers personnel to Woolston to oversee the instigation of Vickers' business control procedures and work practices. Foremost in this was the placement of Trevor Westbrook, a forceful, blunt and somewhat abrasive young man of just twenty-eight, as Works Superintendent. It was a move that was not at all well received on the shop floor, nor, indeed, with many at management level. Wilf Elliot, Supermarine's Works Manager since the war years, was now obliged to report to him. Westbrook came directly from Vickers' Brooklands factory at Weybridge, where he had been employed in a similar role and despite the inevitable friction with the Supermarine staff his presence would in time lead to significant improvements.

More controversial still was the arrival of Barnes Wallis in late 1930, fresh from his role with the Airship Guarantee Company, a Vickers subsidiary, where he had been designing structural elements of the R.100. He was instructed by McLean to help improve the efficiency of Supermarine's technical department. As this was the domain of Mitchell himself, who was absent on leave when Wallis arrived, his input was distinctly unwelcome and he was recalled after a very brief time due to an irresolvable clash of

personalities. While Wallis was older than Mitchell and technically highly skilled he lacked Mitchell's experience of the aircraft construction business, and Mitchell was now, of course, a director of the company. McLean's move had been distinctly tactless. Shortly thereafter, Maj. Harold Payn, a former First World War pilot, test pilot and engineer within Vickers' design team, was assigned as Mitchell's technical deputy, as McLean was adamant that Vickers' work practices would be introduced into Supermarine as a matter of urgency.

The Vickers team confirmed their earlier impression that Supermarine's business was in dire need of an overhaul if it were to remain viable. Records management and stock control procedures were considered to be rudimentary and highly inefficient. The original sheds at Woolston, many dating from the Pemberton-Billing era, were cramped and not of the best quality while the additional buildings that had been added piecemeal along the river frontage over the years were little better. Houses in the adjacent streets had been acquired for use as offices and additional construction space had been leased at Hythe on the opposite side of Southampton Water, so activity and manpower was spread over a wide area with the risk that communication and co-ordination was compromised. The workforce was dominated by skilled craftsman, many in the woodworking section, with just 25 per cent being general labourers, the inverse of the situation at Vickers, and the newly installed metalworking department was struggling to make good progress within a business still rooted in a heritage of boatbuilding with wood. Despite this the potential for future growth was self-evident and at the time of Vickers' decision to purchase the company Supermarine was turning in a good profit.

One early change imposed upon Supermarine's Design Department was the introduction of Vickers' project and drawing numbering system. Early Supermarine drawings followed a simple sequential system that numbered drawings as they were produced regardless of to which aircraft they related. Similarly, projects were not numbered and there was no pattern to the way they were named. Immediately prior to Vickers' takeover the department had introduced a more structured lettered and numbered system but this was now discarded. Under Vickers' system each new project, once approved for further work, was allocated a Type number that was then used as the prefix for the subsequent drawings. The next group of numbers identified the major part of the aircraft structure to which the drawing referred, for example 08 for the wings, followed by the component drawing number itself. Letters were added sequentially if the drawing was revised. Vickers assigned a block of Type numbers to Supermarine in order to get the transition started, the initial batch running from 178 to 190. Type 178 was used as a convenient holding place for various Supermarine projects in progress at the merger or shortly thereafter were deemed to be of interest but which had not as yet developed to the point where they warranted their own project number.

NEW RECRUITS

In 1929 Vickers-Armstrong injected £250,000 into the combined Vickers and Supermarine aviation business to support integration and to stimulate expansion. One important decision taken at this time was to increase the capabilities of Supermarine's Design Department through the recruitment of new technical staff with a diverse range of external experience. While it is not clear whether this was instigated by Vickers or by Supermarine, the former appears to be the more likely in the light of the dismissal of several long-serving Supermarine employees around the same time, which is unlikely to have been the initiative of either Mitchell or Bird. Regardless of how the decision was made, Mitchell used the opportunity to recruit people who had experience working in more than one company and, in some cases, experience of working overseas. The most notable among the new recruits, all taken on in or shortly after 1930, were Alfred Faddy, William Munro and Beverley Shenstone.

Alfred Faddy joined the Drawing Office reporting to Joe Smith before moving later to the Technical Office and reporting to Alan Clifton. He had served with the RNAS during the war and was employed subsequently as a design draughtsman at Parnall, where he had worked on their various fighter projects. He became known to some of the younger staff at Supermarine as 'Old Fadd' as they considered him to be rather backward-looking, but his strength was to be found in his attention to detail and capable management of projects.

William Munro was an expert in hydrodynamics and metal hull construction. He had been employed previously by Gloster to work on the design of floats for their Schneider racers and in late 1928 moved to Canada where he was employed by Canadian Vickers and the Towle Aircraft Company in the USA. In mid-1930 he returned to Britain.

Beverley Shenstone was a Canadian who had qualified with a masters degree in aerodynamics from the University of Toronto in 1928. He was exceptionally talented both as an engineer and as a mathematician. Upon graduation he moved to Germany where he had been employed in the Junkers works and also collaborated with innovative German designer Alexander Lippisch, who was building advanced tailless gliders. Mitchell interviewed Shenstone in early 1931 and offered him a job in the Technical Office, which he accepted. Shenstone was the first academically trained aerodynamicist to work for Supermarine.

Frank Holroyd, Mitchell's deputy from the earliest days, was dismissed shortly after the new recruits came on board and he joined Fairey and, at a later date, Fokker before returning on the outbreak of war to work for the Admiralty.

Henri Biard, the company's test pilot from 1919 onwards, was demoted in mid-1930 and test flying of all new Supermarine aircraft was carried out thereafter by Vickers pilots. Biard was famous for his practical jokes and somewhat irreverent attitude, which probably did not sit well with the Vickers management style. He continued with the company for a few more years carrying out test flights of Vickers aircraft fitted with Supermarine floats, one of which, the Vildebeest, he took on a demonstration tour of the Baltic in 1931. The amount of work requiring his services declined rapidly and he left Supermarine in 1933.

The other senior stalwarts of the Technical and Drawing Offices, Joe Smith, Arthur Shirvall, George Kettlewell and Alan Clifton, all retained their positions. Towards the end of 1931 Alan Clifton was promoted to head the Technical Office, replacing Holroyd.

In mid-1928 Supermarine had lost the services of Oliver Simmonds, one of the more talented of their design staff. Simmonds was a dynamic personality, keen to become involved in many ventures, and he had continued along this route after he had been employed by Mitchell. He was ready and willing to present papers on aviation subjects to external bodies, something that Mitchell was noticeably reticent to do. Despite the workload at Supermarine, Simmonds found time to carry out some personal work on aircraft design and conceived the idea of a basic light biplane where all the wings were identical and interchangeable as a way to drastically reduce production costs. The tail surfaces were treated in the same way. He patented the concept in February 1928 and commenced the construction of an airframe at his home in Southampton. At least some of his colleagues were aware of this work and it has to be likely that Mitchell was too. This was a very open department and word would have spread with ease. By June all was out in the open when the aircraft was registered G-EBYU, named as the Spartan, and Simmonds entered it for the King's Cup in July flown by Flt Lieut Sidney Webster, the pilot of the Schneider Trophy-winning S.5 in the previous year. Clearly Simmonds was adept at obtaining favours from notable friends and acquaintances. Simmonds resigned from Supermarine in order to establish two companies: Simmonds Interchangeable Wing Co. Ltd, to manage his patents rights, and Simmonds Aircraft Ltd to build the Spartan. He was, of course, Chairman and Managing Director of both companies. His co-director in the new businesses was Col Strange, a former commandant of the Central Flying School. Simmonds was able to ensure that both his move from Supermarine and the establishment of his new businesses were reported in *Flight* magazine, and when his new factory in Woolston was opened formally at the end of the year by the mayor of Southampton this was covered by a two-page spread in the magazine. His business looked to be in good shape, he had orders for twelve aircraft, including orders from overseas, and a staff of seventy. It is, perhaps, notable that in his opening speech Simmonds thanked those in the aviation business who had assisted him, mentioning A.V. Roe and Co. and Fairey Aviation Co. Of Supermarine there was not a word, which could be taken to suggest that Mitchell was less than happy about the manner in which Simmonds had worked on aviation projects outside the office. If so, the problem must have been related to the way in which Simmonds had chosen to inform, or not inform, Mitchell of this work, as Mitchell was not concerned, per se, with staff pursuing aviation-related activities outside of the works. He was well aware, for instance, that Roger Dickson was moving along a similar path and, being far more junior and younger than Simmonds, would most surely have incurred Mitchell's wrath should he have disapproved of these activities.

Dickson had joined Supermarine as an apprentice in 1925. In early 1926 he had been involved in a serious road accident while riding his motorcycle and this left him deaf and nearly cost him his job, but he was allowed to carry on and moved into the Drawing Office in 1927 as a junior draughtsman. Shortly after, he completed his apprenticeship and in 1928 was transferred to the Technical Office.

Dickson's outside interests are first seen when he submitted a paper to the *Aircraft Engineer* supplement to *Flight* magazine in December 1928 in which he described a cheap all-metal single-seat aircraft design that he called the Beetle. Although he wrote that he was working on detailed construction drawings, nothing more became of the project.

As a consequence of his deafness, Dickson was unable to obtain a pilot's licence and so transferred his interests to gliding, where, apparently, no such restriction applied. He had followed his colleagues Oliver Simmonds and Alan Clifford into the newly formed Hampshire Aero Club and in 1929 set about designing a simple primary training glider for their use. This design drew a lot of praise, especially from the correspondent from *Flight*. *Flight* magazine had long held an interest in gliding and had taken steps to stimulate greater awareness of the sport among its readership, most notably by holding a glider design competition in 1923. However, the level of interest had remained markedly lower than on the Continent but by the late 1920s the situation was changing and an increasing number of gliding clubs were appearing. The rise of advanced sailplane designs made the sport considerably more attractive. The magazine was very impressed by Dickson's simple training glider and decided to publish a series of articles detailing the design and construction methods aimed at encouraging readers to build their own machine. Plans for the glider were printed in the magazine over a number of weeks from late 1929. *Flight* also sold copy blueprints for the glider for 30s (£1.50). It was expected that the construction costs for a home-built glider would be in the order of £20.

Capitalising on this success, in 1930 Dickson established his own business, Cloudcraft Glider Company, which he ran on a part-time basis while still employed by Supermarine. Cloudcraft built examples of his training glider for £35 to £45 apiece, and later the more advanced sailplanes, Junior and Phantom.

None of this appears to have caused Mitchell any concern; he was, quite clearly, very broadminded and flexible when it came to the personal ambitions and activities of his staff, which was a most refreshing and unusual attitude for that time.

By the end of 1931, after the reorganisation of Supermarine's business was substantially complete, the Design Department had been revitalised and the key senior members were notably young. The two department heads, Joe Smith in the Drawing Office and Alan Clifton in the Technical Office, were 33 and 30 respectively. Many in their teams were younger; Dickson and Shenstone were both just 25, Shirval and Mansbridge, 29. Alfred Faddy, at 38 and older than Mitchell, was indeed 'Old Fadd' in comparison.

The impact of the takeover was felt across all levels of the company and resulted in a considerable degree of uncertainty and resentment. Despite Mitchell retaining his position as Technical Director, it is readily apparent that McLean had stamped his authority on Mitchell's organisation, casting out long standing members of staff, inserting Vickers management personnel into key positions and introducing new blood. For Mitchell this must have been uncomfortable at the very least but nevertheless the relationship between himself and McLean appears to have been good and the newly recruited staff were welcomed into the Design Department.

15

HARD TIMES

It is a quirk of fate that the years immediately after the takeover by Vickers were among the leanest experienced by Supermarine, who were short of production work and failing to achieve commercial success with their new designs. By 1929 fabrication of the replacement metal hulls for the Southampton flying boats was beginning to run down and the company had failed to secure production contracts for any new aircraft types. The shop floor staff were looking distinctly underemployed. To provide a measure of continuity for the workforce, Vickers transferred responsibility for the construction of wings and final completion for two of their Viastra small airliners to Woolston, although the first fuselage was fabricated at Weybridge. In 1932 Supermarine constructed a special version, the Viastra X, for the personal use of the Prince of Wales. This was fitted with a luxurious interior, the company having developed some skill in this regard through their work on Guinness' Solent and the Air Yacht.

The Design Department continued to develop new ideas but a general lack of opportunities to tender meant that much of this remained at the concept level with little detailed aircraft design under way. There is a degree of randomness apparent in the work they carried out and a notable lack of a clear direction, and as a consequence the narrative of Mitchell and the department becomes a little disjointed. On the positive side, they were working hard to develop the next racer for the 1929 Schneider Trophy contest.

SCHNEIDER SUCCESS AND THE AIR SPEED RECORD

After the win by the British team at Venice in 1927 the RAeC pushed hard to have the annual schedule of Schneider Trophy races modified to biennial in order to allow sufficient time for new aircraft to be developed, but as this idea had failed to gain the support of other nations in previous years they were uncertain that they would be successful this time. The government had also stated that they would not fund a team to compete in 1928, so there was real concern that it would not prove possible to field a competitive team. As a consequence, at the turn of the year the quick-fix solution tabled was simply to re-engine the Supermarine S.5 with an uprated Napier Lion; at first the higher-revving VIIc design and later the supercharged VIId. Gloster would do the same but in their case the idea was to build a new aircraft based on the 1927 Gloster IVB with reduced wing area. However, in January 1928 the RAeC's view was supported unanimously by the other nations and the race was rescheduled for 1929. Shortly after, the Air Ministry reversed their position and agreed to fund the development of new engines and aircraft.

Mitchell commenced work on the revised S.5 while he was also in consultation with the Air Ministry and Rolls-Royce to see whether an alternative, and more powerful, engine could be produced. By the autumn of 1928 it did indeed appear possible that a new, large racing engine could be developed from the Rolls-Royce 'H', later Buzzard, supercharged engine and so Mitchell and his team began work on a completely new aircraft, named the S.6.

Once more Mitchell was provided with full access to the facilities at the NPL and RAE so a ¼-scale model of the aircraft was constructed for testing in the wind tunnel while a variety of floats were sent to the Froude tank to assess their hydrodynamic performance. Only one float design had been tested for the S.5 and, although this was acceptable, it had been judged inferior to both the Gloster and Shorts designs. As a consequence, Mitchell and the team decided to employ an iterative approach and to start with an ideal 'airship' shape, which they then modified progressively until a reasonable compromise was reached between low aerodynamic drag and sound hydrodynamic stability. At least six alternative designs were assessed. Meanwhile, the smaller wind tunnel at the RAE was used to measure the heat dissipation capabilities of the oil coolers and wing radiators.

Although superficially similar to the S.5, the S.6 was actually a total redesign from the ground up. It was all-metal, the first, and indeed the only, Schneider racer to be built this way, and was designated as project C under Supermarine's revised naming system. The S.6 was considerably larger and heavier than its predecessor in order to handle the far greater power and weight of the Rolls-Royce 'R' engine and Mitchell took great care to optimise the strut and wire bracing angles to minimise stress. Cooling was expected to be a major issue so from the outset the wings were designed with zero-drag surface radiators that formed the entire skin of the wing. Contingency plans were in place to fit additional radiator surfaces to the floats should initial testing indicate that cooling was insufficient.

The fuselage was of elliptical section and lacked the 'shoulders' of the S.5. There were just two longeron members running from nose to tail; heavily reinforced at the nose to form the engine bearers, mount points for the front float struts and wing main spar, and becoming progressively lighter to the rear. The bulkhead to the rear of the engine formed the front wall of the cockpit and was heavily insulated and reinforced where the rear wing spar and rear float struts attached to it. The former frames were spaced between 6in and 7in apart and the whole structure was then plated with Duralumin sheet, flush-riveted throughout and doubled or tripled in regions of high stress. Large corrugated oil radiators extended along the entire length of the fuselage on both sides and bottom, and the fin was skinned in tin steel and sealed to form the oil tank.

The floats were constructed around a central keel frame, transverse bulkheads with stabilising stringers, and skinned with Duralumin. The central section of each float was sealed and skinned with tinned steel to serve as the main fuel tanks. It was intended that all, or most, of the race fuel would be carried in just one float in order to provide an offset load to aid

in counteracting engine torque. Unlike on the S.5, the floats were rigged symmetrically and were of equal length.

Mitchell selected the symmetrical RAF27 aerofoil of 9.8 per cent thickness for the wings as this had better low speed characteristics than the RAF30 used on the S.5, which adopted a very nose up attitude when landing. The wing plan remained the same as on the S.5. The structure was all Duralumin built on twin spars but was not skinned in the conventional way as the water radiators formed the entirety of the wing's top and bottom surfaces. These radiators were constructed of flat Duralumin sheets separated by $\frac{1}{16}$in thick spacers to form fore and aft pathways for the water. Feeder input and output channels were embossed in the sheeting at front and rear.

Mitchell's team worked closely with the engineers at Rolls-Royce, neither group compromised by the need for the 'R' racing engine to be tailored to fit any other aircraft as Folland had elected to power his Gloster VI monoplane racer with the Napier Lion VIId. Rolls-Royce, as was their tried and tested way, developed the engine in careful steps; modifying one component at a time and then running the engine to failure until a point was reached where the required power and one hour running at full throttle had been achieved. They designed a sophisticated forward-facing air intake and divergent trunking to decelerate the airflow and raise the air pressure before it entered the supercharger. This reduced the turbulence of the air at the intake eye and increased pressure to add appreciably to the boost of the engine. A special test facility was constructed with large engine-driven fans to simulate the airflow into the air intakes at full race speed. Fuel expert Frank Rodwell Banks acted as a consultant to help formulate a fuel mixture to meet the demands of the high compression engine.

Once more Fairey were contracted to supply the propellers, milled and twisted from huge alloy blocks.

While the British engine and aircraft constructors embarked on their development programmes, the RAeC received official entries from the French and Italians, both with full teams of three, and the USA, with a single aircraft. After the failure of all three Macchi M.52s and their Fiat AS3 engines in 1927 the Italians had embarked on a huge research and development programme and were constructing four racing aircraft of wildly different types, each with its own specialised engine. The French, too, after several years of indifference to the contest, had decided to field at least two new aircraft types and had three racing engines under development. The team from the USA was a private venture, on paper at least. Al Williams, whose Kirkham-Williams racer had been a no-show at Venice, had sought further backing and was developing a new monoplane racer. This was to be built at the Naval Air Factory at Annapolis and was powered by an improved version of the Navy's Packard 1A-2775 engine; there was more Navy support for this venture than government accountants may have been aware. Construction of two S.6 racers commenced in the early summer and time was beginning to look a little tight. Rolls-Royce were also rather slow to get their programme under way and the first runs of the new engine only started in April. Early runs resulted in frequent component failures, as expected, all of which underwent redesign and manufacture in turn, a painstaking process but one that worked well. Reliability and power slowly increased but the airframes were ready and waiting some time before an engine cleared for flight was available. Power output rose from a promised value of 1,500hp to 1,800hp, at which point Mitchell became seriously concerned about the ability of his cooling system to deal with the heat. With just a couple of weeks remaining before the contest the first engine was delivered and the S.6 was prepared for flight.

Folland's Gloster Napier VI was ready and looked to be a fine racer, but unfortunately Napier were taking their time to get the Lion VIId through its certification tests and there was practically no time remaining to get it installed in the aircraft for flight tests.

Although it was unknown to the British, the French preparations had stalled. In truth, their official entry was wishful thinking as they had barely started their research programme. The Italians were having a torrid time as all their aircraft had been built but only two flight tested. The Fiat C.29 had been first but crashed on an early flight and once rebuilt proved to be a nightmare to control, both on the water and in the air. The Macchi M.67 had also flown but the team suffered a severe blow when their team leader, Capitano Motta, suffered a fatal crash just weeks before the contest. The Savoia-Marchetti M.65 had made a brief flight but required extensive modification, while the quirky Pegna P.c.7, a flying boat fitted with hydrofoils, had yet to take to the water. Meanwhile, in the USA Al Williams had taken the Williams Mercury out on to the water where it steadfastly refused to take off.

The work on the S.6 and its Rolls-Royce engine was intense and continued right through until the contest on 7 September as the results of the initial flight tests confirmed that heat dissipation and torque were both serious issues. Mitchell had anticipated both and had started construction of slightly enlarged floats to provide an increased offset load and additional radiators that could be attached to them. Extra cooling vents were added to the engine cowls and small air scoops fitted to each wing tip provided an airflow through the interior of the wing to cool the inner surfaces of

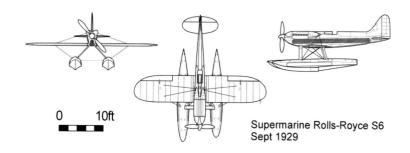

0   10ft

Supermarine Rolls-Royce S6
Sept 1929

the radiators. At one point ethylene glycol was tested as a coolant but this proved to cause problems with the engine and radiator joints and had to be abandoned. The new measures improved the situation but it was never possible to run the engine at full throttle for extended periods and the pilots had to adjust the throttle to maintain a water temperature just below boiling rather than to fly at maximum speed.

Just days before the contest, the Italians contacted the RAeC and pleaded for a delay of a month as the loss of Motta and the Macchi M.67 had left them in disarray and without a full team. Naturally, the British were sympathetic but the contest was by now a huge event involving government, military and civilian organisations and considerable expense. Special trains and ships had been contracted to bring spectators and distinguished guests to the event, and accommodation for thousands had been booked around the course. A postponement for a day would cause a plethora of problems but several weeks had to be out of the question. The request was refused, with deep regret. At this point the French and USA withdrew officially but in an act of great sportsmanship the Italians agreed to compete and arrived with their team of three; two Macchi M.67s and the current holder of the air speed record, the Macchi M.52R. They also brought the Fiat C.29 and the Savoia-Marchetti S.65 simply for display.

At the eleventh hour, Gloster were forced to withdraw as the Lion VIId simply refused to run evenly, the result of poor supercharger intake design and positioning on the aircraft. Its place in the team was taken by one of the Supermarine Napier S.5s that had been used for training. The two S.6 aircraft were completed, tested and modified just in time to participate in the contest.

The large crowd that had gathered along the Solent coastline, the largest that Britain had ever seen for a single event, were largely unaware of the pre-contest drama and were expecting a fiercely fought battle between the British and Italian teams. Unfortunately, it was not to be as the Macchi

← The second Supermarine Rolls-Royce S.6 racer, N248, is manoeuvred into position by the handling crew of the RAF High Speed Flight. This aircraft is now preserved in the Solent Sky Museum in Southampton.

M.67 and its Isotta Fraschini 'Asso Due' engine were far from race-prepared. The flight development programme had barely started when Motta had his fatal crash and no time remained to iron out the substantial problems with the aircraft. The second M.67 had not even flown before being packed up for the contest. Neither aircraft, flown by Tenente Cadringher and Tenente Monti, managed more than a single lap before retiring with engine problems. The last-minute back-up aircraft in each team, the Supermarine Napier S.5 and Macchi M.52R, were very evenly matched and fought a neck-and-neck battle before the Macchi edged ahead, but they were both eclipsed by the two Supermarine Rolls-Royce S.6s, which dominated the race. Had Flg Off. Atcherley not cut inside one of the turn markers and been disqualified after losing his goggles during a lurid, porpoising, take-off run, they would have taken both top positions. Fg Off. Waghorn brought his S.6 home in first place with Tenente Dal Molin bagging second in the M.52R and Flt Lieut D'Arcy Greig close behind in the S.5.

Speed-over-distance records were established during the contest and subsequently the absolute air speed record was secured in the winning S.6 by the High Speed Flight's team leader, Sqn Ldr Orlebar, only the second time a British aircraft had achieved this distinction following that set by Fg Off. Stainforth in the stuttering Gloster Napier VI one day earlier.

While the success in the contest was due more to the superb work of the Rolls-Royce engineers, this would have counted for little had not the S.6

proven to be a fine racer with vice-free characteristics in the air. The flight test programme had raised a host of issues but Mitchell and his team had been up to the task and addressed each one in good time.

In December Mitchell wrote an article for *The Aeroplane* on the subject of 'Racing Seaplanes and their influence on Design' and the following February Holroyd presented a paper entitled *Racing Seaplanes* to the Yeovil branch of the Royal Aeronautical Society. These provide an interesting insight into the research and development process that led to the S.6.

SOUTHAMPTON X AND THE AIR YACHT

Work was progressing, albeit in fits and starts, on the design of a very large six-engined flying boat, of which more later, and three experimental flying boat prototypes.

In 1928 the Air Ministry issued Supermarine with contracts for three experimental aircraft, to be registered N251, N252 and N253.

The first, N251, was of no value to Supermarine as it only involved the fitment of Southampton flying surfaces to an experimental corrugated metal hull designed and built by Saunders-Roe. This would be a simple way to assess the merits of Saunders' patented construction system in direct comparison with Supermarine's standard hull. It was ordered in April 1928 and is believed to have been completed late that year but the aircraft was not launched until 13 March 1930. The hull proved to be both lighter and of greater interior volume than the standard Southampton II metal hull and to have slightly superior performance on the water at full load. It was an ominous result from Supermarine's perspective, although more extensive testing revealed weaknesses in the hull construction. The aircraft was retained by the MAEE who fitted the planing bottom with a series of pressure sensors and ran extensive tests to measure load distribution during take-offs and landings.

→ Experimental Southampton N251 mated standard Southampton flying surfaces to a new corrugated metal hull designed and fabricated by Saunders.

The third aircraft, N253, started life as Southampton II S1122 powered by two Rolls-Royce Kestrel engines, later the experimental evaporatively cooled model. As Type 184, it trialled new wings with metal spars and ribs and Frise ailerons. This aircraft also flew in 1930 and appears to have been judged as successful as it formed the basis for Supermarine's later Southampton IV project.

N252, however, was an all-new aircraft design, designated the Southampton X. Under Vickers management, all Supermarine's construction methods and Mitchell's designs were subjected to detailed scrutiny in an endeavour to identify opportunities to cut costs; Mitchell had actually instigated moves in this direction immediately prior to the takeover. Many Vickers designs of this era were notable for their stark simplicity; constant

← One Southampton II was fitted with Rolls-Royce Kestrel engines to test an experimental evaporative cooling system and re-registered N253. Mitchell was highly impressed with the concept and for several years he specified this type of engine for many of his new designs.

↑ The Southampton X was Mitchell's next generation flying boat designed to replace the Southampton II and to serve as the basis for a new family of military and civil aircraft. It proved to be big a disappointment.

chord, square tipped wings, minimal use of complex curvature and so on, and McLean hoped to bring a degree of this kind of cost-conscious thinking to Supermarine. Vickers Chief Designer, Reginald 'Rex' Pierson, had provided the company with a solid foundation through his work on the many civil and military projects derived from his excellent Vimy bomber. He was four years older than Mitchell. The company had also established a licence partnership with the French designer Marcel Wibault, who specialised in functional all-metal aircraft employing corrugated skins. As a consequence of Vickers' takeover, a number of projects were delayed while changes were introduced, including the Southampton X and the Air Yacht.

The Southampton X, which had nothing at all in common with the Southampton and Southampton II and is another example of Supermarine simply reusing names to imply continuity, was a completely new design for a three-engined flying boat that Mitchell proposed in both military and civilian versions.

It seems very likely that in the earliest stages of design this project had been based on Mitchell's R.4/27 biplane project and some work on detailed

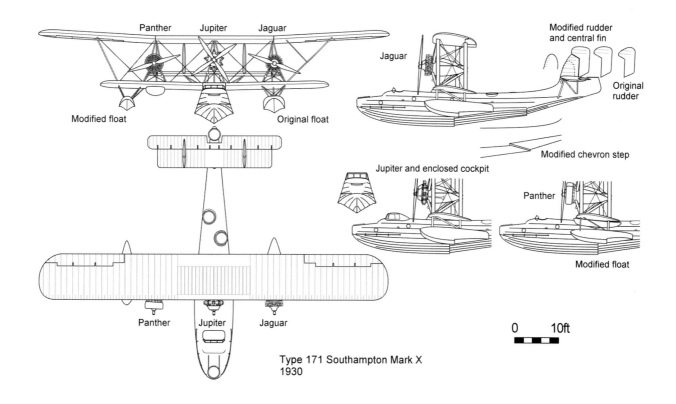

Panther   Jupiter   Jaguar

Modified float   Original float

Jaguar

Modified rudder and central fin

Original rudder

Modified chevron step

Jupiter and enclosed cockpit

Panther

Modified float

Panther   Jupiter   Jaguar

0   10ft

Type 171 Southampton Mark X
1930

design had begun in late 1927. The Southampton Mark X, ordered in June 1928 to Air Ministry specification R.6/27, was the first project to use Supermarine's new alphanumeric drawing numbering system, starting, logically, as project A, and was well in hand just prior to the takeover by Vickers. At this point work appears to have been suspended. When they restarted in 1929 the decision had been taken to split detail design and construction between Vickers' Brooklands works and Woolston, with Vickers responsible for the wings and engine mounts. The Southampton X was redesignated as Type 171, as Supermarine adopted Vickers' project number for convenience. Further delays meant that construction did not commence until late 1929.

For the Southampton X Mitchell abandoned most of the metal construction methods used for the Southampton II and devised a new style of hull built of Duralumin with a stainless steel planing bottom. The curvaceous metal hull of the Southampton II had proven to be time consuming to construct as it involved shaping many hull plates into complex three-dimensional curves, so a simpler approach was devised. The main hull frames now had straight sides, which gave the aircraft a rather slab-sided profile, and Mitchell adopted a variation of the corrugated plating system patented by Saunders in 1927. The hull plates were strengthened by longitudinal corrugations so it was possible to do away with internal stringers and eliminate weakening notches in the bulkheads. The system was anticipated to provide a lighter structure and be to be easier to construct. The rear of the hull, however, was curved and quite similar to the Southampton II.

The Duralumin wing structure, of sesquiplane layout, was built by Vickers at Weybridge employing construction techniques similar to those developed for their later Virginia bombers and other large aircraft. The aerofoil was Clark YH, a general purpose section much in favour at the time. The main inter-plane strut structure incorporated the three engine mounts and their nacelles while the outer wings were braced by large diagonal struts with

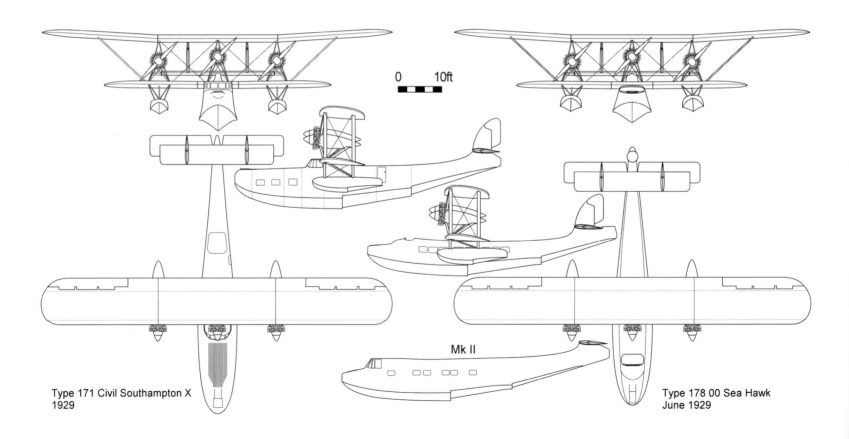

0   10ft

Type 171 Civil Southampton X
1929

Mk II

Type 178 00 Sea Hawk
June 1929

subsidiary bracing. The result was not tidy. The engines were Armstrong Siddeley Jaguar IV air-cooled radials mounted mid-gap driving two-blade propellers. Mitchell designed very large balance floats positioned well inboard below the outer engines and these also held the main fuel tanks. The tailplane was rectangular in plan with an elevator of greater span, while the twin fins and rudders were of similar shape to those on the Southampton. In the early stage of design a civil airline version was drawn up that featured a longer and deeper hull with an enclosed cockpit positioned just ahead of the lower wing. However, this design was soon superseded by a revised version named Sea Hawk. This, along with a number of modifications instigated after early flight tests, were pulled together under Type 178.

Mitchell's Air Yacht underwent a similar redesign. The original concept had been a simple civil conversion of the R.4/27 monoplane but, while the basic layout of this project was retained, the design had been subjected to a thorough overhaul to reduce construction costs. Work commenced in the second half of 1928 under the revised drawing number system as project B and pre-dates Vickers' takeover. Mitchell's redesign was radical as every part of the aircraft was simplified dramatically and redrawn so that it became a completely different aircraft. Gone were any curved parts; the wings, tailplane, fins and rudders were reduced down to simple constant-chord rectangular components and the sponsons, which contained the fuel tanks, lost their taper, as described below. The hull followed the philosophy applied to that of the Southampton X and was slab sided with some corrugated panels. Two separate open cockpits for the pilots were located in the nose with a central gangway in-between to provide access to the nose hatch. Two further open cockpits were located directly behind for the use of other crew members or passengers. The main cabin was fully enclosed with porthole windows along either side.

The normal crew was three and the cabin was designed with substantial accommodation for the owner and facilities for five guests, including up to 600lb of luggage.

The simple rectangular plan wing was a very large structure built in three parts. The centre section was mounted above the fuselage in parasol fashion on struts and the outer panels were braced to the sponsons by two substantial diagonal struts in V formation.

The tail was fitted with free-flying supplementary elevators between the triple fins similar to those devised to cure the stability problems on the Nanok/Solent.

Mitchell tested four alternative sponson types in Vickers' tank at St Albans; three tapered and one straight. These sponsons, which Mitchell referred to as stub stabilisers, were attached to the hull model in a manner that allowed their angle of incidence and fore-and-aft position to be changed. Variation in chord and span was also catered for. After completion of a series of tests at simulated maximum overload weight, the parallel chord design with full span vented step provided the best results. The step was aligned with the main step of the hull and the span was calculated to minimise adverse interaction with the bow wave. After wind tunnel tests, the depth of the sponson was reduced.

→ The Air Yacht was derived from Mitchell's monoplane designed to spec. R.4/27 but had undergone a total redesign to simplify the structure. The result was an angular and inelegant aircraft with indifferent performance.

Mitchell also took the opportunity to review the position of the engines in the wind tunnel. Their position, ahead of the upper leading edge of the wing, had been inherited from the R.4/27 design and was now compared to alternative layouts placing them in line with the wing or just below. No change was considered necessary. The chosen engines were 490hp geared Armstrong Siddeley Jaguar VIs enclosed in Townend rings and fitted with long exhaust pipes that passed above the wing to keep fumes well clear of the passenger cabin.

The finished design was distinctly boxy, an origami simplification of the initial concept, and made the utilitarian Dornier Wal look almost sleek by comparison. Construction of one aircraft, named Air Yacht, commenced at Woolston in the spring of 1929 after a conditional order had been placed by the Hon. A.E. Guinness to replace his Solent (ex-Nanok) aircraft.

Work continued through 1929 at a distinctly cautious pace. One reason for the protracted build was that the aircraft's wing structure employed metal spars and ribs, one of Supermarine's earliest such designs, preceded only by the replacement wings for the Southampton II.

In the autumn of 1929 the US stock market crashed and precipitated a worldwide slide into depression, which compounded Supermarine's problems in endeavouring to keep the works active. As a consequence, nearly a third of the construction workers had to be laid off over the winter and the prospects for the future appeared deeply uncertain. Unfortunately 1930 was destined to be a most difficult year for Supermarine and had they not been part of the Vickers empire it is quite possible that their business would have collapsed.

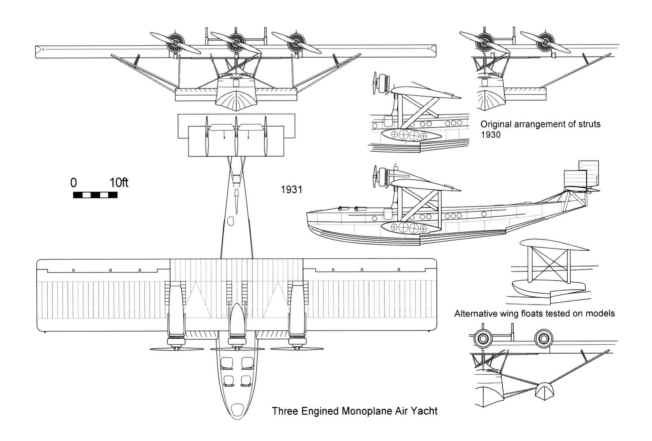

0   10ft

1931

Original arrangement of struts 1930

Alternative wing floats tested on models

Three Engined Monoplane Air Yacht

The Air Yacht made its first flight, lacking the luxurious cabin fittings, in February 1930 in the hands of Henri Biard, the last new prototype that he would fly. It proved to be underpowered with a worryingly long take-off run, poor climb and indifferent performance in the air. The sponsons were also found to provide inadequate lateral stability if the aircraft heeled by more than a couple of degrees, as could happen in a crosswind or swell. This had not been noted during testing of scale models at Vickers' water tank facility at St Albans as the cradle to which the model was attached only allowed for full freedom of movement in the vertical and pitch direction, not roll or yaw. Further testing commenced using a modified cradle.

The aircraft was returned to the erection shed at Hythe for the interior to be installed and the Jaguar engines were replaced by more powerful 525hp Panther IIs. The contract price had been set at £34,888 but Supermarine's costs had climbed to more than £52,000 when Guinness declined to complete the deal and looked elsewhere for an aircraft with which to replace his Solent.

The Air Yacht remained at Hythe until May 1931, when it was prepared to receive its certificate of airworthiness. Over the summer a series of flights were made at a total weight of 24,000lb and the report issued in October was indifferent. The aircraft tended to swing to starboard on the take-off run but could be controlled by the rudders. Handling in the air was generally good although it was found to be impossible to maintain height with one engine throttled back. At moorings it was found to be stable on the water, even in high winds. Overall the performance of the Air Yacht was judged to be inferior to other types under test and they concluded that a major factor was the high drag from the sponsons.

During the trials the starboard sponson suffered structural failure and the port sponson was found to be similarly fatigued. Supermarine were advised to redesign these but the company declined and simply repaired the damage. They did, however, fit two small wedges on the outer edge behind the step that on photographs look like a second step, and constructed hydrovanes that could be fitted to the tips. They also bolstered the bracing by fitting three extra struts each side, but whether this was to improve stability of the wing, sponsons, or both is unclear. All these modifications are believed to have been paid for by the Air Ministry. No significant improvement in performance was achieved but the aircraft was granted its certificate by the end of the year.

The Air Yacht spent a significant amount of time at the MAEE in Felixstowe, far more than would have been required to gain its certificate, which could suggest that the Air Ministry took the opportunity to assess for the first time a large flying boat built to what could be called the Dornier formula. Blackburn's Sydney flying boat, with wing floats, was also at Felixstowe at this time, which gave the MAEE an excellent opportunity to compare two surprisingly similar aircraft; similar in layout, weight, dimensions, power and, as it turned out, performance. The aircraft was then returned to Supermarine, who were left with the problem of what to do with it.

After languishing for some time at Hythe, the Air Yacht was purchased in October 1932 by a rich American woman, Mrs June James, who lived locally and was looking for an aircraft to use for a Mediterranean cruise. She contracted Biard as pilot for the voyage and an account appears in his autobiography. No doubt there is an element of truth in the story of adventure and eccentricity that he tells but Biard certainly liked to spin a yarn, embellishing the narrative if it served to improve the truth, so it should be taken with a degree of caution. Halfway through the trip Biard had to return to Britain for an operation on the stomach injury he had incurred when the S.4 crashed prior to the 1925 Schneider Trophy race and his place was taken by Tommy Rose. The Air Yacht ended its days in Capri on 25 January 1933 when an engine failed on take-off and it stalled back on to the water. In the ensuing impact the cabane structure failed and the wing centre section buckled. Fortunately no one was badly hurt, although Mrs James suffered a broken leg. The aircraft was damaged beyond economic repair and scrapped.

Somewhat perversely, an alternative version of the Air Yacht, called simply the Three-engined Monoplane Flying Boat, was advertised for sale in 1930. It was powered by Bristol Jupiters, was marginally lighter than the Air Yacht and the structural design had reverted to the more elegant hull, sponsons and flight surfaces of the original R.4/27 aircraft, but this too failed to attract any interest. The story then came full circle as a militarised version of the angular Air Yacht, returning to the original R.4/27 patrol flying boat specification, was included within Type 178.

The Southampton X was completed in March 1930 and turned out to be considerably overweight, a staggering 30 per cent over design specification by some accounts, despite the intent to simplify construction. Both the hull and wings contributed to the problem. The wing and engine mounts were festooned with struts while the weight of the robust hull frames and stainless steel plating had been underestimated. The maiden flight was made by Vickers' test pilot Joseph 'Mutt' Summers, which probably indicates that Henri Biard had relinquished his role as Supermarine's chief test pilot shortly after making the first flights in the Air Yacht a few weeks earlier.

Performance, not surprisingly, was well below specification. Top speed was 15mph below the estimate of 135mph, climb was woeful and the maximum height achieved just 6,400ft against a specified maximum of 15,000ft; drastic action was required.

Supermarine embarked on a long series of modifications to address the problems, a near repeat of the work under way to rectify the deficiencies of the Air Yacht. The need for more power was obvious so the Jaguar engines were quickly exchanged for Armstrong Siddeley Panthers, which gave around a 50 per cent increase. Lateral control must have been an issue as the rudders were increased in size by adding a horn balance extension to the top leading edge. However, these changes did not suffice and the Panthers were discarded and replaced by Bristol Jupiters driving four-blade propellers, first XFBMs and then XIFs. A small fixed central fin was added and the rudder horn balances enlarged again. The modifications for the Bristol engines were allocated Type numbers 185 and 188 respectively in February 1931. Type 188 also included a fixed cockpit cover that was fitted for a while but removed later. Despite all this work, the Southampton X still underperformed so an attempt was made to reduce drag. The large floats were discarded and substituted by smaller units mounted further outboard, which required a revision to the outer wing bracing struts. Interestingly, the engines were changed back to Panthers, now enclosed within Townend rings, and two-bladed propellers. Slipper tanks could be hung below the lower wings to replace those that had previously been enclosed in the large floats. Prior to these final modifications the aircraft had still failed to meet specification; it was 5mph down on speed and more than 3,000ft on ceiling. Records of the performance after the final changes do not appear to have survived but whatever improvements were achieved were probably inadequate.

The Southampton X was under evaluation by the MAEE at much the same time as the Saunders A.7 Severn, the prototype ordered to specification R.4/27. This aircraft shared many features with the Southampton X but was larger overall. Both aircraft were sesquiplanes powered by three Bristol Jupiter radials: 460hp XIFP for the Severn and 570hp XFBMs for the X at the time. The Southampton X was considerably overweight against design specification but nevertheless about 900lb lighter than the Severn when empty and a similar amount heavier carrying a standard load. It was also some 4mph faster. On this simple numerical basis the aircraft appears marginally superior to the Severn but the MAEE assessment suggests the contrary. The Severn received a positive report, although it was considered too stable in pitch. It was sent out to undertake full service trials, including

a cruise around the Mediterranean, and on return it served with No. 209 squadron for a brief period undertaking maritime patrol. During these extended service trials it suffered from a plethora of component failures, in many cases the consequence of excessive weight saving, and the corrugated planing bottom ahead of the step distorted on several occasions. Although no production contract was awarded for the aircraft it was well regarded and Saunders would receive a contract for a later aircraft that built upon the Severn's key design features. The Southampton X, however, was abandoned after the initial series of tests, most likely as it had failed to come close to its original specification and had only achieved modest performance after significant modification and upgrades. This effectively put pay to any prospects for production orders for the aircraft and, perhaps more importantly, for any civil version.

SMALL CIVIL FLYING BOATS

Mitchell had not neglected totally the market for smaller civil flying boats and oversaw the design of a small, single-engined pusher biplane amphibian, a version of the Type 181 military amphibian that will be described later. This had a Duralumin hull, with the option of stainless steel for the planing bottom, metal-framed, fabric covered flying surfaces and a new design of retractable undercarriage where the narrow track wheels swung to the rear to sit alongside the hull sides, the method employed earlier by Vickers for their Viking amphibians. In the retracted position the wheels sat within slots in the lower wing, protruding both above and below. The wings and tailplane appear to have been based broadly upon those of the Seamew, which was of similar size. The aircraft carried a crew of two in an open cockpit in the nose and up to six passengers in the cabin just behind. It could be powered by either a Bristol Mercury VI or an Armstrong Siddeley Panther II and would have had a range of 400 miles and a cruising speed of 95mph carrying six passengers, or 600 miles if the load were reduced to four passengers. Operating the aircraft as a flying boat by removing the undercarriage allowed the payload to be increased by 175lb or for one more passenger to be squeezed in.

The civil Type 181 was offered to Imperial Airways in April 1930 at a price of £9,495 for a single aircraft reducing to £8,910 each if ten were ordered. The company committed to deliver the first machine within eight months of receipt of order, five within fifteen months and ten within eighteen months. With the works seriously short of work at this time they

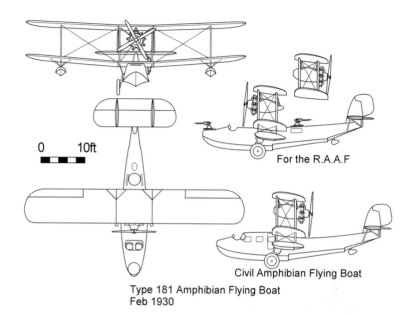

Type 181 Amphibian Flying Boat
Feb 1930

For the R.A.A.F

Civil Amphibian Flying Boat

0   10ft

were coming to the fore. To make matters worse, in 1929 Saunders-Roe had launched their latest flying boat amphibian, the metal, twin-engined, enclosed cockpit, cantilever monoplane Cutty Sark, to critical acclaim. The aircraft had been flown around the Solent on numerous occasions during the weekend of the Schneider Trophy contest, which must have proven quite irritating for the company. Saunders-Roe followed this in the following year with the introduction of the similar, but larger, Cloud. Still worse was to follow when Guinness chose to purchase one of these aircraft in preference to the Air Yacht. Mitchell and Supermarine, who had no similar aircraft on the drawing board or under development, had been comprehensively outflanked in the small to medium-sized civil flying boat and amphibian market by their neighbour and rival.

There is no doubt that 1930 had proven to be a very bad year for Mitchell. Two large flying boats upon which much depended had made their first flights and both had proven to be, at best, distinctly disappointing, thereby scuppering any prospect of attracting orders from the Air Ministry, Imperial Airways or other airlines. Much had been invested in their development and expectations had been high. Supermarine had no small flying boats of any type in development and Mitchell's only project design in this class was clearly inferior to aircraft already in production elsewhere. The Woolston works were seriously short of work with no new aircraft under construction and kept active only through the fabrication of replacement wings and other parts for the RAF Southampton IIs, modifications to the Southampton X and Air Yacht and other piecemeal parts. However, there was one more project to deal with over in the Hythe works: the largest British flying boat yet built.

would have been able to give any order a very high priority. Unfortunately, no orders were forthcoming.

Although the aircraft was a sound design it was by now distinctly dated in style, looking back to the Sea Eagle rather than forward, and most airlines by now favoured twin-engined aircraft for safety and enclosed cockpits

16

THE SAGA OF THE SIX-ENGINED FLYING BOATS

DORNIER AGAIN

Towards the end of 1927 rumours began to circulate in the British aeronautical press regarding a new giant flying boat designed to carry fifty passengers on transatlantic routes that was under construction at the Dornier works. As has been mentioned before, Dornier's parasol monoplane, sponson-stabilised flying boats had proven to be most successful and were held in high regard by many in the industry, but these latest rumours were greeted in some quarters with scepticism. Brigadier General Groves, secretary general of the Air League of the British Empire, obtained and published some basic weight and dimension data for the aircraft that prompted an editorial in *Flight* magazine which, for want of a better term, scoffed at the possibility and 'proved', with some back-of-the-envelope calculations, that such an aircraft would either prove incapable of take-off due to excessive wing loading or if it did manage to do so would be unable to cross the Atlantic. Nevertheless, the potential for such a large flying boat was intriguing and drew the attention of Oswald Short at Short Bros, who had under consideration an aircraft with broadly similar capabilities. The suggestion that Short had the idea only after first viewing the Dornier flying boat is clearly inaccurate as Dornier would not present his aircraft to the world until the summer of 1929. Short instructed his Chief Designer, Arthur Gouge, to submit a concept based on a fairly straightforward up-scaling of the Short Singapore II, which was on his drawing board at the time, and powered by six of the latest Rolls-Royce 'H' engines, which was about to make its first runs on the test bench. At first the Air Ministry were not especially interested as they saw no use for an aircraft of this size but Shorts managed to talk Hugh Trenchard, Chief of the Air Staff, into providing funds. In the meantime,

Dornier had made a visit to Britain in May 1928 and presented a paper to the Royal Aeronautical Society on the subject of flying boat design that confirmed the existence of the giant flying boat project and substantiated the data previously quoted by Groves. The Air Ministry issued specification R.6/28 for a Large Multi-engined Boat Seaplane to cover the contract for Shorts' Sarafand and this, as required, was circulated to other companies.

↑ The mighty Dornier Do X drew a lot of attention from the press yet it was not a success and never entered commercial service.

CONCEPTS FOR VERY LARGE FLYING BOATS

Supermarine reviewed the specification and decided to prepare a tender. At this point the largest aircraft that they had built and flown was the three-engined Nanok, which was only marginally larger than the Southampton and classed as a medium-sized flying boat. The Southampton X and Air Yacht were both on the drawing board but still more than a year from the commencement of construction and nearly two years before they would be flown. The task was, therefore, considerable so Mitchell and his team started work by drawing up a series of concept aircraft, all powered by six Napier Lion XI engines. Sketches of four of these designs have survived.

The simplest proposal was an enlarged version of the monoplane layout recently adopted for Mitchell's R.4/27 submission and hence had distinct Dornier-style overtones. The monoplane wing was mounted above the flat-sided hull on cabane struts and braced to the tapered stabiliser sponsons. The engines were installed in three nacelles resting on the wing upper surface of the parallel chord centre section with a tractor unit at the front and a pusher at the rear in each. The outer wing panels were straight-tapered with curved tips. The tail unit comprised a large main central fin to which the tailplane was attached halfway up. Additional fins were fitted outboard on the tailplane.

The second aircraft of the series was a sesquiplane of unusual form. The thick-section upper wing was mounted high above the hull on a central pylon and braced to the lower wing by outward-raked struts. The lower wing was attached low on the deep-section hull and had marked dihedral to keep the tips well clear of the water, a layout that had been adopted, without success, for the small experimental English Electric Ayr in 1923. The balance floats were positioned well inboard and attached directly to the lower wing. The six Napier Lions were mounted as tracker and pusher pairs in three nacelles mounted just below the top wing, the central nacelle forming part of the wing attachment central pylon. The tailplane was strut-braced to the hull and carried twin fins.

The third design was the more conventional of the proposals and reminiscent of an enlarged Southampton. The three nacelles, tractor and pusher as before, were mounted mid-gap in the centre section of the equal span biplane wings. There were standard wing tip floats, a strut-braced tailplane and twin fins.

The final design was quite adventurous and unlike any prior concept produced by Mitchell for a flying boat, so it is interesting to speculate

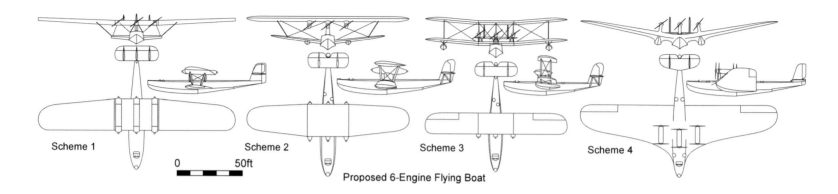

Scheme 1   Scheme 2   Scheme 3   Scheme 4

0   50ft

Proposed 6-Engine Flying Boat

whether this came from his pen or one of the members of his team. The hull was little different from that of the previous three designs and the twin-finned tailplane was also similar except that it rested directly on the hull and did without strut bracing. The 140ft-span cantilever monoplane wing, however, was radical. The trailing edge was straight while the leading edge was swept and gently curved to an ogival profile. The wing section was thick, almost as deep as the hull sides at the root, and blended carefully into the hull shape by extensive fillets. The wings had 11 degrees of dihedral to keep the tips well clear of the water and the balance floats were attached directly to the underside and blended into the wing shape. The three twin-engine nacelles were mounted on pylons above the wing. The advanced blended form of the wing was rather at odds with the otherwise conventional style of the hull and tailplane. There is nothing on the sketch drawings to indicate why a wing of such a large area and thick section had been suggested.

Notwithstanding all this preliminary work, none of these concepts was developed further and instead Mitchell instigated work on a totally new design. This proposal, prepared at the very end of 1928 as project D, was to be powered by the new Rolls-Royce 'H' in evaporatively cooled form. In this system cooling water passed through the engine under pressure and was allowed to boil around the cylinders. The steam was separated from any remaining water, depressurised and cooled in condensers before returning to the engine. This system was expected to be both lighter and more compact than a conventional water-cooled arrangement. Mitchell saw the potential merits and, mindful of his Schneider racer's zero-drag wing radiators, proposed to use the interior of the wing itself as the condenser, thereby providing a very large cooling surface without incurring any drag penalty. He submitted a patent application for such a system at the end of February 1929, illustrated with drawings of the project D aircraft wing design. The

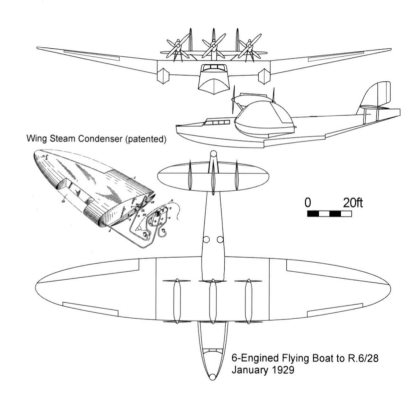

Wing Steam Condenser (patented)

0   20ft

6-Engined Flying Boat to R.6/28
January 1929

interior of the large metal-skinned wing was to be sealed in order that the entire outer surface could act as the condenser, then drainage channels on the lower surface collected the water and the wing dihedral angle caused it to drain back to a sump for recirculation.

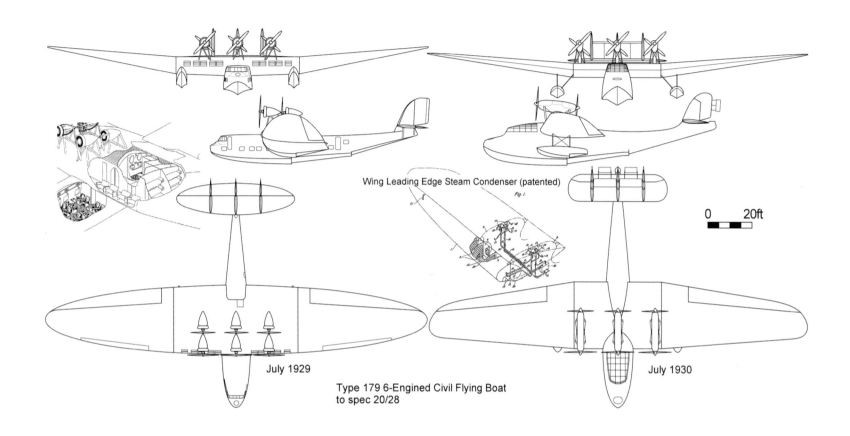

Wing Leading Edge Steam Condenser (patented)

Fig. I.

0   20ft

July 1929

July 1930

Type 179 6-Engined Civil Flying Boat
to spec 20/28

Layout drawings of an aircraft employing this cooling system were completed by the end of January 1929. It was to be all-metal with a cantilever monoplane wing. The flat-sided hull was little different from that proposed for the earlier concept designs, akin to the simple structure types adopted for the Southampton X and Air Yacht, except that the cockpit was now enclosed completely. The tail unit was broadly similar to that on the Southampton, a strut-braced tailplane carrying three fins, but the tailplane was elliptical in plan. The elevators and rudders were fitted with large trim tabs. For the 160ft-span wing Mitchell proposed using a moderately thick section and an elliptical plan form. The centre section had no dihedral and the wing balance floats were mounted flush with the lower surface at the outboard extremity. The outer wing panels had 9 degrees of dihedral, very large ailerons and leading edge slats. The three twin-engined nacelles were mounted above the wing, the centre unit on a pylon and the outer units on struts. This proposal was rejected by the Air Ministry but all was

not lost as they drew up a further specification, 20/28, for a civilian flying boat of similar size and Mitchell's design was reconfigured to meet these requirements. The specification was drawn up on the basis of the aircraft flying routes into the Mediterranean region, although there is nothing to suggest that Imperial Airways were contemplating adding a flying boat of such size to their fleet at the time. Supermarine received this specification in May 1929.

THE GIANT AWAKES

Mitchell's initial design for 20/28 was based on the earlier submission to R.6/28 but with substantial changes. The hull was deepened to increase the interior space and the cockpit was moved forward now that the nose gun position had been removed. The tailplane was once again strut braced. The wing centre section was deepened substantially and passenger accommodation, sleeping quarters with bunk beds and washrooms, was included within it. The leading edge of this part of the wing was fitted with windows and configured as an observation deck with a panoramic forward view. The six Rolls-Royce 'H' were replaced by six Bristol Jupiter radials on individual mounts in tandem pairs and so the elaborate steam condensation system was deleted. Layout drawings of this aircraft were completed by July 1929 and the design became the first new Supermarine project to bear a type number under the Vickers drawing system, Type 179. In a most unusual move, artwork featuring this project was used by Supermarine for publicity purposes.

Mitchell's Type 179 design was accepted by the Air Ministry in principle and in preference to Blackburn's Oceanic project, but they requested a number of modifications, of which the most significant was the reversion to Rolls-Royce 'H', Buzzard, engines to replace the Jupiters. These were the same engines as specified for Shorts' large Sarafand biplane that they had ordered to specification R.6/28 but in an evaporatively cooled version. The engines were installed, as in the R.6/28 design, as tractor and pusher pairs in three pylon-mounted and strut-braced nacelles. Mitchell cleaned up the lines of the hull a little around the nose and the flush-mounted balance floats were replaced by standard types on struts and moved slightly outboard. The tailplane strut bracing was removed and the rudders were revised to incorporate large aerodynamic balances. In this form the Air Ministry approved the design and a contract was issued to Supermarine in the summer of 1930. This revised design was also used by Supermarine in their advertisements in late 1930, especially at the Paris Aero Salon in December where an artist's representation and model of the aircraft were accompanied by size and weight data and performance estimates.

In March 1931 Mitchell submitted a further patent application to cover an improved steam condenser system designed for the Buzzard-powered Type 179. For this reconfigured aircraft he had adopted a new structure for the wing in which the main spar and the thick metal skin of the wing leading edge formed a 'D' section torsion box, a strong yet relatively light structure that had found much favour among builders of gliders. However, it was not this form of structure that was the subject of the patent, as this had been in general use for some time, but the method of construction and its use as a condenser for the steam cooling system. However, this, too, was not entirely an original idea as the use of the leading edge as the ideal location for a steam condenser had been suggested by Wg Cdr Cave-Brown-Cave in 1928 and the RAE had built a test rig to evaluate the system in 1929.

Although the revised Type 179 had been approved by the Air Ministry, in a move that was to become increasingly characteristic of Mitchell, he had his team undertake what can only be described as a complete redesign before construction commenced. In fact, some preliminary work had started even before the contract had been awarded. A layout design dated July 1930 features a substantially deeper hull with stainless steel plating, a thinner wing also constructed of stainless steel with simple straight tapered outer panels and no passenger accommodation in the centre section, a parallel chord tailplane and tail controls fitted with large Flettner-style servo tabs and an auxiliary elevator. The glazing for the cockpit extended back as far as the wing and included substantial panels in the roof, possibly an observation cabin for the passengers. The rear of the hull was upswept, in the manner of the Southampton, to raise the height of the tailplane. However, company advertising continued to show the older elliptical wing version of the aircraft through until at least January 1931.

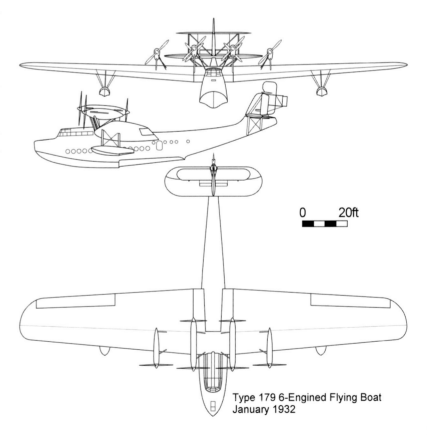

0   20ft

Type 179 6-Engined Flying Boat
January 1932

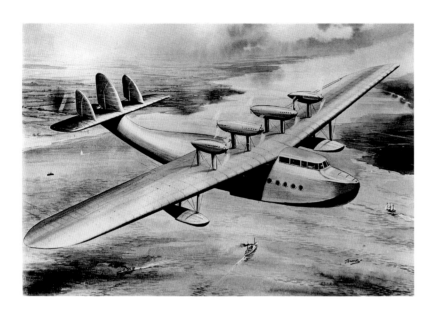

↑ The final Type 179 design looked quite conventional compared to some of the earlier work and the tail controls had sprouted an array of auxiliary and servo surfaces (not shown in artwork). However, it remained a relatively clean aircraft.

Reworking the design continued throughout 1931 until a final configuration was signed off at the very end of the year. The aircraft would carry forty passengers and a crew of seven, top speed was 145mph and range 700 miles. The hull planing bottom had been refined, removing the rear second step and replacing it with a knife-edge termination. The wing had been completely redesigned once again to a conventional straight-tapered plan. The wing floats had been decreased in size and moved even further outboard. The tailplane, cantilever on the previous design, was strut braced to the hull and the control surfaces had sprouted yet more auxiliary units, added area and servos so that overall it was a rather messy and inelegant structure. The six engines were also rearranged; two twin-engined nacelles were mounted on the wing centre section while the remaining two engines were housed in individual nacelles positioned further outboard. Somewhere along the line the aircraft had acquired the name, probably unofficial, of Giant. After three years of continual design, rethinking and redesign Mitchell had produced an aircraft that had grown substantially and lost much of its

initial elegance and style. Although notably cleaner than the Dornier Do X, it was broadly similar in form and lacked any of the innovative ideas of Mitchell's original concept.

THE GIANT'S DEMISE

Construction of the hull frame commenced in the second half of 1931 and was well under way at Hythe when the Air Ministry cancelled the contract in the early days of 1932.

Shorts' Sarafand biplane had also been delayed in construction and finally made its first flight in June that same year. It performed well enough and met the contract requirements but the RAF had no real use for it and consequently it spent most of its days at the MAEE at Felixstowe. No production contract for further aircraft was awarded. Supermarine's Type 179 Giant would no doubt have shared much the same fate as Imperial Airways had no identified use for an aircraft of this size and performance in the early 1930s, and it is questionable whether they would have placed it in service. Dornier faced the same problem as only three examples of the Do X were constructed and none actually achieved full operational status despite the aircraft making a number of high-profile overseas flights and gaining substantial press coverage. The Giant was indeed a giant. With a wingspan of 174ft, over 50ft more than the Sarafand and nearly 20ft more than the Dornier Do X, it could have proven a tricky aircraft to manoeuvre in many harbours and restricted waterways and would hence have been of limited use to Imperial Airways or other airlines. The number of routes over which it could have operated would have been small. In terms of innovation and new ideas there was little, if anything, in the design of the aircraft that would have provided useful information for any of Mitchell's future projects, and monoplane flying boats were destined to evolve in a completely different direction within just a few years.

The loss of the work on the Type 179 was a serious concern to Supermarine at the time but the loss of the aircraft itself was, in all probability, of lesser importance. There are reports that another purge of the Design Department took place shortly after the contract for the Type 179 Giant was cancelled and that a further twenty jobs were lost. In the workshops the situation remained grim with little more than three months' work in hand at times. Wages were cut by 5 per cent in early 1932.

17

THE TYPE 178 PROJECTS

RANDOM IDEAS, EMBRYO PROJECTS, NONE OF THE ABOVE

As mentioned earlier, a number of Supermarine concepts and projects were collected together under the single project Type 178 while the new organisation deliberated on whether they should be developed further. From preceding chapters it can be seen that a fair amount of the design work undertaken by Mitchell around this time was speculative and many ideas did not advance much beyond basic layout. These were difficult times for the aircraft industry in general with production contracts few and far between.

There were fourteen Type 178 project subdivisions in all, numbered 00 to 14, omitting 13, although some contain more than one design. They were an eclectic mix and ended up being catalogued as Miscellaneous Drawings.

Type 178 00 covered a selection of civil and military aircraft projects: a civil variant of the Southampton X in three distinct forms, an unrelated three-engined amphibian, a Kestrel-powered version of the Southampton X, and a Jupiter-powered version of the Southampton II.

Mitchell clearly held high hopes for the Southampton X as he used the aircraft as the basis for a large number of civil projects. In early 1929 his team worked on two flying boat versions of the aircraft, which were given the name Sea Hawk. One was a simple adaptation of the Southampton X and the other featured a lengthened and deepened hull with an enclosed cockpit, which they named the Sea Hawk MkII.

The Sea Hawk was shown in two forms, one with the large inboard balance floats from the original Southampton X and the other, drawn in 1930, with smaller wing floats moved further outboard and revised inter-plane struts as trialled on the Southampton X. The aircraft were powered by twin-row

Armstrong Siddeley radials, either Jaguars or Panthers. On both of these designs the hull of the Southampton X was to be retained unchanged apart from the incorporation of passenger windows.

The Sea Hawk MkII was to be powered by three Armstrong Siddeley Panther or Bristol Jupiter radial engines. The new hull and interior was designed to conform to the current requirements of Imperial Airways with the cabin volume split equally between passengers and a cargo compartment for carrying mail. There was to be a crew of four: the pilot and co-pilot in a fully enclosed side-by-side cockpit, and the navigator and radio operator in the cabin behind. The main cabin had accommodation for ten passengers and 185 cubic feet of mail. Maximum range was 1,000 miles at a cruising speed of 110mph, and top speed was estimated at 140mph, although the test programme of the Southampton X shows that this was wildly optimistic and later specifications were modified accordingly. The project was developed to the point where it was tendered to the airlines, so it is curious that it was never allocated its own type number.

In March 1930 Mitchell added an amphibian version of the Sea Hawk. Shallow blister fairings were added to the hull sides to cover the retraction mechanism for the cantilevered single-leg undercarriage units. These retracted by rotating to the rear and in the up position the wheels sat within slots in the lower wing roots, as on the Type 181. A combined skid and water rudder was fitted behind the rear planing bottom step.

Also included under Type 178 00 was a project for a three-engined civil amphibian drawn by William Munro, who we will meet again later. Two versions were proposed, one powered by Bristol Jupiters, the other by Rolls-Royce Kestrels. The design style was unrelated to any prior Supermarine project and may well be Munro's first design for the company,

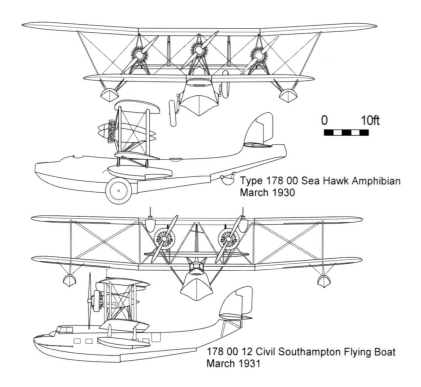

Type 178 00 Sea Hawk Amphibian
March 1930

178 00 12 Civil Southampton Flying Boat
March 1931

a retractable skid. This was a neat and clean design and, on paper at least, superior to the various concurrent Southampton X-based projects. Some of the main features would reappear later in the Scapa and Stranraer.

The twin-Jupiter-powered civil Southampton II had a deepened metal hull with an enclosed side-by-side cockpit and the engines were fitted with Townend rings. Jupiter engines had been tested in the prototype Southampton II, N218. None of the various proposals for civil versions of the Southampton proved to be of interest to the airlines, although one standard military Southampton II was modified with eighteen seats for civilian use in Japan and an RAF machine was loaned to Imperial Airways for carrying mail between Alexandria and Salonika in the winter of 1929.

In 1928 Imperial Airways had introduced the three-engined Short Calcutta flying boat into service and the Sea Hawk would presumably have been

an independent piece of work. The flying boat had a deep, straight-sided flared hull with a stub upturned stern to which the strut-braced tailplane was attached. There were twin fins and rudders with Flettner servo surfaces, a feature shared with other Munro designs. The lower wing was mounted in the shoulder position, the root section tapering in chord and thickness in order to accommodate the retracting undercarriage, and the outer sections straight with small balance floats. The upper wing comprised a centre section, to which the three engine mounts and nacelles were attached, and outer panels featured dihedral, leading edge slats and large ailerons. The engine nacelles were supported by single struts from the lower wing and faired into the under surface of the top wing. On the Kestrel-powered version there were no indications of radiators so it is assumed that they were to be evaporatively cooled and that the steam condensers were housed in the wings. On the Jupiter-powered version the engines were enclosed in broad Townend rings. The main undercarriage comprised a single oleo leg braced by a radius strut and the wheels retracted into wells within the lower wing, a system that was used later on the Seagull V. At the rear there was

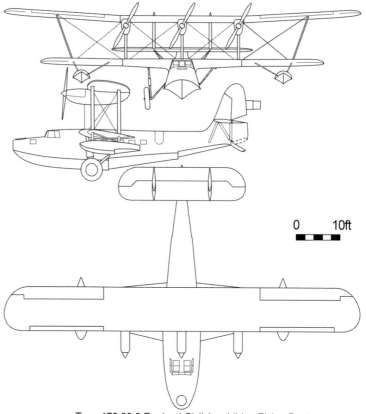

Type 178 00 3 Engined Civil Amphibian Flying Boat

broadly comparable. However, as the airline had expressed no requirement for further flying boats in this class the Sea Hawk would have had to look elsewhere for a market. Only a few major airlines chose to add larger flying boats to their fleet at this time and it seems most unlikely that any of Mitchell's big flying boats or amphibians would have found a buyer.

A re-engined version of the Southampton X, drawn in 1931, incorporated a revised planing surface featuring a chevron rear step, and Kestrel engines that may have been intended for evaporative cooling. Presumably this was intended as a means to breathe new life into the ailing Southampton X project.

Type 178 01 was a fast monoplane Civil Mail Carrier with a retractable undercarriage powered by two Rolls-Royce Kestrel III engines. The drawings date from early 1931. The aircraft was a fairly advanced concept and almost certainly intended to be of metal construction, in keeping with Supermarine policy at this time, with a fully enclosed cockpit and a cantilever tapered wing of moderate thickness. The engines were mounted on the wing leading edge and their sleek nacelles enclosed the undercarriage retraction mechanism. The wheels were retracted by pivoting the legs rearwards, and a curious feature was that in the retracted position a substantial part of the wheel protruded through the upper surface of the nacelle. Amendments in pencil indicate that a revised mechanism was under consideration that allowed the wheels to be stowed within the nacelles. The absence of any obvious radiators suggests that evaporative cooling was to be employed, using the wing leading edge as the condensers.

This aircraft project almost certainly originated in response to specification 21/28, issued in early 1929, which called for a Mail Carrying Aircraft capable of carrying 1,000lb of mail over 1,000 miles at an average speed of 150mph, and able to fly on one engine at full load. At this time there was growing concern in some quarters about the provision of an efficient mail service throughout the overseas territories as carrying mail as cargo on Imperial Airways passenger aircraft was considered to be too slow and of limited capacity. The solution was seen to be a fleet of dedicated cargo aircraft optimised for range and speed. The specification was quite flexible as it set no preference for the type or, in a later amendment, the number of engines, or for the layout of the aircraft. However, the requirement was not pursued with any great priority and tenders were not submitted until 1931. A wide variety of single and twin-engined biplane and monoplane designs were received by the Air Ministry, who selected the P.64 project from Boulton Paul to be built as a prototype. This aircraft was a biplane with fixed undercarriage, powered by twin Bristol Pegasus air-cooled radial engines in

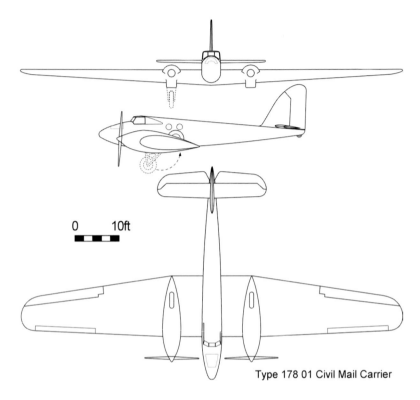

0   10ft

Type 178 01 Civil Mail Carrier

Townend rings. It was not particularly advanced in design but nevertheless achieved a top speed of 185mph. Had the Supermarine monoplane been built it would no doubt have proven to be fast for its era and capable of fulfilling a variety of civil and military roles. It could have been comparable to the US ten-seat commercial Boeing 247, first flown in 1933, or the Lockheed model 10 Electra, flown in 1934. However, the concept was not pursued further and a potentially interesting design was abandoned.

The Type 178 02 drawing dates from April 1931 but would not have looked out of place among Mitchell's designs from 1924. It was a single-engined pusher biplane amphibian of the Seagull type intended as a naval bomber and reconnaissance aircraft. It had open cockpits, partially retractable undercarriage and, judging from the profile, a wooden hull. The wings folded to the rear and the engine appears to be a Rolls-Royce Kestrel. The tailplane and twin fins were derived from the experimental Seagull II. It is not at all clear why this design was included in Type 178 or for what

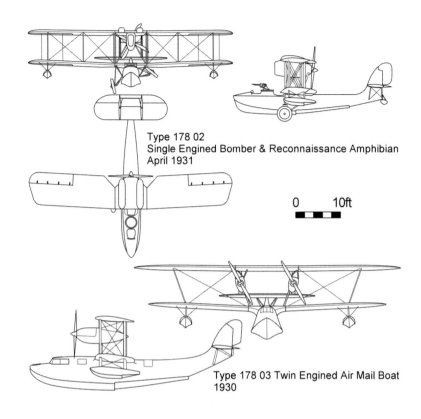

Type 178 02
Single Engined Bomber & Reconnaissance Amphibian
April 1931

0   10ft

Type 178 03 Twin Engined Air Mail Boat
1930

radiators were identical to those designed for experimental Southampton II N253. It is possible that this aircraft was submitted as an alternative design to fulfil specification 21/28 alongside the Type 178 01 monoplane.

Types 178 04, 178 05 and 178 07 were all alternative designs for the intended Southampton II replacement, an aircraft named eventually as the Southampton IV, which will be described in a later chapter.

Type 178 06 was a militarised version of the Sea Hawk powered by Jupiter XF.B.M engines. It appears to be just a re-engined version of the aircraft drawn as Type 178 00 sheet 11.

Type 78 08 was drawn in November 1931 and titled Proposals to Reduce Landing Speed. It shows the Schneider racing S.6b seaplane adapted to a biplane configuration by fitting an upper plane. Two versions were shown, one with a large upper wing, tailplane of increased size and lengthened floats, and the other with a smaller upper wing. The anticipated landing speeds were 80mph and 90mph respectively. The landing speed for the standard S.6b, fully loaded, was of the order of 110mph. There is no apparent reason why Supermarine undertook this study after the 1931 contest had been won as the Air Ministry had stated categorically that they had no intention to continue the programme of high-speed research and the High Speed Flight had been disbanded. The contest-winning S.6b was destined for an extended tour around the country and overseas and then to be displayed in the Science Museum. Its sister ship was in a poor state having sunk in a landing accident and only one of the two S.6s was intact, the other having been wrecked in a fatal accident. Were Vickers or Supermarine seriously contemplating using one of the remaining aircraft for research purposes? It seems unlikely as they did not own the aircraft and any programme of test flying would have been of very limited value for any future aircraft designs.

Type 178 09 was a most interesting concept for a High Performance Day Bomber or Mail Carrier. This project will be described in a later chapter reviewing Supermarine's bomber projects.

Types 178 10, 178 12 and 178 14 were designs for two land fighters that will also be reviewed later in the chapter on the evolution of Supermarine's fighter family.

Finally, Type 178 11 was the Air Yacht adapted for military use. The drawings are dated February 1932, long after it was known that the performance of the aircraft was mediocre and the concept for a three-engined, open cockpit patrol flying boat had long ceased to be acceptable for the RAF.

market it was intended although it is just possible that it could have been an early project aimed to provide a replacement for the RAAF Seagull IIIs.

Type 178 03, from May 1931, was described as a Twin-engined Mail Flying Boat and powered by evaporatively cooled Kestrel engines. It was closely related to a number of flying boat projects then under development, all designs intended as potential replacements for the Southampton II. The Mail Flying Boat had a metal hull, similar to that designed for the R.4/27 biplane but with a fully enclosed cockpit. The wing design represented a major departure from the Southampton II as the central Warren girder bracing had been discarded and replaced by standard struts. These struts were canted slightly outwards and doubled as the supports for the engines, which were positioned just below the top wing. The engine nacelles and top-mounted

18

TRANSITION

Through 1929 and on into 1931 Supermarine's business transformed slowly as the Vickers work practices began to have an impact and the new team of design staff integrated into the organisation. For a short period the old and new project drawing number systems appear to have run in parallel and it is difficult to disentangle projects and note any trends.

As mentioned before, the workforce in the construction sheds had been cut by a third over the winter months into 1930 and would continue to drop. Morale was low, Vickers intervention was resented and without any significant production contracts the amount of work was limited. The Design Department continued to develop projects, some new and some

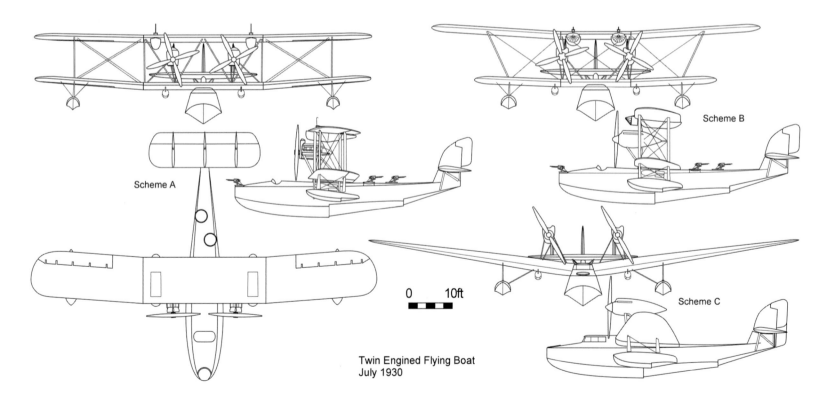

Scheme A

Scheme B

Scheme C

0   10ft

Twin Engined Flying Boat
July 1930

derived from existing designs, but these tended to be grouped within the Type 178 pigeonhole while management sought a new direction. It is interesting, therefore, to review the few projects that were allocated their own type number in this period as it implies that they were the most highly rated and most worthy of progression. However, first there are two projects under the old numbering system to consider.

SEEKING OVERSEAS CUSTOMERS

Three alternative designs for a twin-engined flying boat powered by Hispano-Suiza engines were drawn up in mid-1930, and presumably produced in response to the requirement of an overseas client. The aircraft were all similar in size to the Southampton II and they shared a new straight-sided metal hull with a side-by-side cockpit, and the tailplane, fins and rudders from the Southampton. Scheme A used the standard Southampton wings and engine mounts, and hence is little more than a Southampton II with a new hull, while Scheme B was a sesquiplane with a slightly thicker wing section, reduced span and lower overall wing area than Scheme A. Scheme C was a monoplane with straight-taper cantilever wings attached to the fuselage in the shoulder position behind an enclosed cockpit, and featured 8 degrees of dihedral to keep the tips well clear of the water. The engines for this version used much the same mounts as on two of the biplanes so they sat high above the wing. As six Southampton IIs powered by Hispano-Suiza engines were ordered by Turkey in 1932, aircraft designated Type 233 and 234, it seems quite likely that these three projects may have been proposals that actually originated prior to the Vickers takeover, hence the lack of the type number, and which were tendered to the Turks as alternatives to the Southampton.

TORPEDO BOMBER

In 1930 the Air Ministry issued specifications M.1/30 for a Torpedo-Bomber Ships Plane and S.9/30 for a Torpedo-Spotter-Reconnaissance Aircraft. Both were required to operate from carriers, carry a single torpedo and have interchangeable wheel and float undercarriage. Although the former was to carry a crew of two and the latter three, there was much in common between the requirements and in time they were merged. Aircraft of the type required by the specifications had long been the preserve of Blackburn and Fairey, both companies having produced aircraft for the carriers since the earliest

1920s. When Mitchell read S.9/30 it was obvious that the requirement to carry a single torpedo could not be met by a further variation on his amphibian flying boat theme so he had his staff start work on a radically new design. He realised that in order to break into a market dominated by others who would, more than likely, tender aircraft of similar layout and style to those they had already produced, it was going to be necessary to come up with a design that broke the mould in some way. His experience with the projects he had drawn up for the N.21/26 fighter, worthy but derivative, had proven instructive. In addition, as a result of the takeover by Vickers he now found himself in a form of internal competition, albeit healthy competition, with Pierson and Wallis at Brooklands when seeking funding and management approval, which urged him to be a little more adventurous. As a consequence, his S.9/30 aircraft was quite distinctive and completely different from those submitted by other companies.

The 'standard' design for an aircraft of this class was epitomised by the Fairey III series, a type that had been developed in the closing years of the war and subsequently upgraded and improved over many years. This aircraft was a robust, simple, single-engined biplane with no particular outstanding features yet capable of being adapted with ease to undertake a wide variety of roles, a sort of flying Model 'T' Ford. Fairey had been extremely successful with the various models, which had sold well both in Britain and overseas. Other companies pretty much followed this philosophy. Mitchell, on the other hand, stepped back, sought an alternative and came up with a design for a twin-engined biplane powered by the unusual and compact air-cooled Napier Rapier inline engine conceived by maverick engine designer Frank Halford. The Rapier was a sixteen-cylinder air-cooled engine with four inline banks of four cylinders arranged in 'H' formation driving twin crankshafts geared to the propeller shaft. The rated output was around 350hp and in Mitchell's aircraft they were installed within elegant nacelles with cantilevered mounts. The pilot sat in the nose of the elliptic section metal monocoque fuselage, well ahead of the engines, which gave him an excellent field of view. He had a fixed gun located to his left. A rear gunner sat just behind the wing trailing edge with a wide field of fire and the observer's cockpit was located behind the pilot and in line with the wing leading edge. There was a sliding hatch in the floor to be used by the observer, lying prone when acting as bomb aimer, and a port in the floor behind the gunner's cockpit to house a vertical camera. An inflatable dinghy was carried in a compartment in the rear fuselage decking. The wings were designed to fold to the rear on inboard hinges and stowed tightly against the rear fuselage, reducing the width from 45ft 6in to 17ft 6in; the span of the tailplane and just a little more than the track of the undercarriage. The fuselage was stressed for catapulting and the wide-track fixed undercarriage legs could be fitted with either wheels or floats. An obvious weakness of Mitchell's design was that the tips of the twin blade propellers were only some 6ft above the base level of the floats and about the same distance behind their noses, which would have left them very exposed to spray when operating off water.

Once again it is not clear whether Supermarine actually submitted an official tender to specification S.9/30 but it does seem unlikely as the project was never allocated an official type number, which suggests that in all likelihood it was speculative work sanctioned by Mitchell but never approved formally by McLean. Vickers worked on a submission to specification M.1/30 for which Barnes Wallis produced a new lightweight structure, a stepping stone on his way to devising the geodetic system.

The Air Ministry and Navy maintained a very conservative attitude to procurement for carrier-based aircraft at this point and the aircraft they approved for construction were all relatively conventional. They ordered prototypes from Blackburn, Handley Page and Vickers to specification M.1/30 and from Fairey and Gloster to S.9/30 before choosing to amalgamate both requirements into a new specification, S.15/33. Under this revised specification two aircraft received production contracts, both completely conventional single-engined biplanes of unremarkable performance; the Blackburn Shark and the Fairey TSR II Swordfish.

Although there is no doubt that the Navy were slower to request more innovative aircraft designs than the RAF there was rationale behind their

thinking. The resources on board an aircraft carrier for maintenance and repair was by necessity far more restricted than would be available on land and operations away from Britain only exacerbated the problem. It was therefore inevitable that solid, functional simplicity was a key requirement for their utilitarian all-purpose aircraft types. Mitchell's innovative design had a stressed skin metal fuselage at a time when the necessary skilled workers, material and tools were not yet available on the carriers. The time would come, and come quite soon, but this was perhaps a little early to make the commitment. His choice of engines was also questionable. While the inherent advantages of twin engines for an aircraft undertaking extended patrols over water made a strong case for Mitchell's aircraft, the selection of Frank Halford's unconventional engines was a rather curious decision. Not only were they viewed with a degree of scepticism by the Air Ministry, and indeed by some in the aircraft industry, they were also unnecessarily complex for a workhorse service aircraft. To service the Bristol Pegasus engine in a Fairey Swordfish meant dealing with just nine cylinders, for the two Napier Rapiers there were a total of thirty-two. The additional workload was hard to justify. In Mitchell's defence, however, it has to be noted that the Fairey Seafox biplane, ordered in small numbers a couple of years later, had both stressed skin fuselage and a Napier Rapier engine. In all it would appear that there was a negligible chance that Mitchell's aircraft would have received a contract for a prototype to be constructed, let alone a production run. It was a bold attempt to move in a new direction but flawed in detail and out of step with Navy requirements.

CIVIL FLYING BOATS

Following on from the Type 179 Giant, the next new project to commence under the Vickers project numbering convention covered two versions of a civil flying boat based on the flying surfaces of the Southampton X, both dating from October 1929. As said before, Mitchell held high hopes for the Southampton X and had notional plans for a variety of related flying boats.

The Type 180 aircraft, however, differed significantly from the Sea Hawk under Type 178 as they were notably larger and powered by four radial engines mounted in tandem pairs in a similar fashion to those proposed on the original design of the Type 179. The first variant featured a lengthened version of the hull designed for the Type 171 civil Southampton X derivative while the second had a new hull, similar to that on the Sea Hawk

0   10ft

Twin-engined Fleet Spotter to spec. S.9/30
Sept 1930

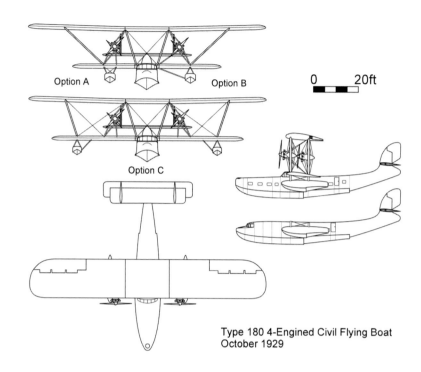

Option A   Option B

0   20ft

Option C

Type 180 4-Engined Civil Flying Boat
October 1929

MkII, with the cockpit moved to the nose. Three alternative wing float and outer wing bracing systems were investigated. They were very much from the same family, the big brothers of the Sea Hawks.

Why Supermarine chose to formalise these aircraft with a unique project number while the Sea Hawk, which had been tendered on a speculative basis and for which details had been published in the press, remained in the Type 178 pigeonhole is something of a mystery, especially as neither of the two project designs appear to have progressed much beyond basic layout.

It is quite possible that Type 180 was prepared in response to a specification issued by Imperial Airways for a large four-engined long-distance passenger flying boat to fly on the Mediterranean routes down to Egypt. This had been issued in a hurry as Mussolini was engaging in diplomatic games and they had been denied access to certain Italian ports, which meant that they required an aircraft with extended range in order to continue to serve the route effectively. The production contract for these aircraft, which numbered just three in total, was awarded to Short Bros in mid-1930 for their Kent design, an enlarged and upgraded derivative of the Calcutta flying boats then in service with the airline.

AUSTRALIAN AMPHIBIAN

The civil version of the Type 181 amphibian was discussed in an earlier chapter but this project was developed primarily to meet a requirement of the Royal Australian Air Force in early 1930 for an amphibian flying boat to replace their flight of Seagull IIIs. Mitchell was aware of the facilities available on the Royal Australian Navy's seaplane tender and the restrictions on size that this imposed so he chose to take a distinctly conservative approach and had his team design an aircraft that was very similar in style and layout to the Seagull III, differing mainly in having a metal hull which, it is assumed, was stressed for catapult launching. Both tractor and pusher versions were proposed. As the next formal project in this class of aircraft, also submitted to address the Australian requirement, was designated the Seagull V it seems quite likely that this design was known informally as the Seagull IV, although that name does not appear on the drawings. The RAAF declined the design, possibly because they considered it insufficiently advanced, but also as a consequence of the worsening financial climate that placed a tight constraint on funds. In the short term they chose instead to refurbish a number of their Seagull IIIs. Very soon after, Mitchell embarked on a new project to meet their future requirement.

CANADIAN MONOPLANE

In early 1931 Mitchell responded to a request from an unidentified Canadian customer for a general purpose aircraft capable of being fitted with either a wheel or float undercarriage. Then, as now, the myriad lakes scattered across the country provided perfect bases for seaplane operations and in a vast and mountainous territory aircraft were often the only viable means of transport for trade and communication. Mitchell's team developed two designs, Type 182 for a high-winged monoplane and Type 183, which is believed to have been for a low-winged version but for which drawings do not appear to have survived. Type 182 was to be powered by a single radial engine in a Townend ring cowl. The cockpit was fully enclosed, as befits an aircraft designed for operation in a cold environment, and the undercarriage was fixed, braced to the wings, with the wheels enclosed in spats. The aircraft was finished off with a fin and rudder of generous proportions and a tailplane mounted in the mid-fuselage position. It was similar in style to the Fokker Universal and Super Universal, aircraft that were selling well in North America at the time but beginning to appear dated. A second design, slightly

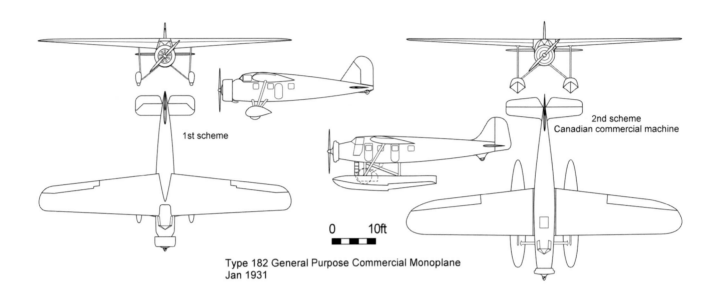

1st scheme

2nd scheme
Canadian commercial machine

0   10ft

Type 182 General Purpose Commercial Monoplane
Jan 1931

larger but with the same general layout, was drawn by William Munro but this does not seem to have been progressed.

In 1934 the Canadian aircraft designer Robert Noorduyn, who had worked for Fokker on the Universal, opened his own company in premises in Montreal. In the following year he introduced the Norseman, an aircraft with much the same layout as the Type 182. More than 900 of these aircraft were produced over the next two decades. It is therefore a great pity that Mitchell and the management team did not realise they had a potential winner on their hands and chose not to take the design further. It could have been produced with ease by Vickers' former Canadian subsidiary. However, aircraft of this type were new to Supermarine and in 1931 their Design Department was fully committed to a number of more vital projects. Further work on the project was dropped.

THE FINAL SCHNEIDER SUCCESS AND ANOTHER AIR SPEED RECORD

Before moving on to the major projects tackled by Mitchell in the 1930s we need to run briefly through the next batch of type numbers as they were all for experimental aircraft. Type 184 covered the Kestrel-powered, metal-winged Southampton II, N253. Type 185 was for

the Southampton X re-engined with Bristol Jupiter XFBMs. Types 186 and 187 covered the work undertaken for the 1931 Schneider Trophy racers S.6a and S.6b respectively.

Throughout 1930 the government, headed by Ramsay MacDonald and with the exchequer in the firm hands of Philip Snowden, stuck staunchly to their decision not to fund any further work in support of the defence of the Schneider Trophy. The economy was in freefall and their priorities lay elsewhere. The aircraft industry had no intention to fund this from their own pockets and the RAeC dithered and did essentially nothing to seek contributions from elsewhere. As the end of the year approached they started to shake off their lethargy and tried once more to gain government sponsorship but were rebuffed. The press, with the *Daily Mail* in the forefront, began to stir up popular support as it appeared increasingly likely that not only would there be no British team to defend the trophy but that the RAeC would be quite unable to host the contest for the visiting teams.

When the deadline for entries was reached at the end of the year both Italy and France declared their intention to send full teams of three aircraft and paid the deposit. This, too, had been a contentious issue as the RAeC had raised the amount significantly in order to deter speculative entries.

In January 1931 the matter came to a head when the government met representatives of the aircraft industry and the RAeC to try to resolve the impasse. Pressed hard, MacDonald conceded that the government would make service personnel available for the High Speed Flight and open facilities at Calshot if the RAeC could raise the sum of £100,000 to cover all costs. He had every expectation that they would not succeed but at the last moment the eccentric multi-millionaire widow Lady Houston, an ardent right-wing activist who held a deep loathing of MacDonald and his government, came forward and agreed to donate the entire sum. Frantic negotiations with Supermarine and Rolls-Royce led to an agreement that there was just sufficient time remaining to construct new aircraft and engines.

It was obvious to all that there was no conceivable way that an entirely new aircraft could be designed, built and tested so Mitchell's work involved overhauling and upgrading the two 1929 S.6s and constructing two new airframes. These would be near-identical to the S.6 with just localised strengthening in order to accept the modified 'R' engines that Rolls-Royce would provide, and an enlarged oil tank in the fin. In 1930 Rolls-Royce had carried out a little more development work on the 'R' engines when two extra units had been built for the water speed record contender *Miss England II*. They were confident that they could raise the power of the 'R' to around 2,300hp. Fairey would produce new propellers to handle the power.

The added weight of the new engine and greater load of fuel and oil made it necessary for Mitchell to design new floats as those fitted on the 1929 aircraft had proven to be a bit marginal for reserve buoyancy. For the refurbished aircraft Mitchell produced interim floats based on the original 1929 model. They were slightly longer with modified nose and tail sections. Water coolant radiators were fitted over the nose decking and along both sides. The two 1929 aircraft with these new floats were designated as the S.6a. Models of the floats were tested in the water tank and wind tunnel at the NPL but this was little more than a check that all was acceptable as construction work was already in hand. For the new aircraft, designated S.6b, Mitchell embarked on a completely new float design, longer still than those on the S.6a and with a refined section. In an attempt to improve handling on the water, always problematic due to the strong torque from the powerful engine, the team proposed to add small vertical extensions of the float sides down beyond the chines. Although these were only an inch or so deep it was unclear how detrimental these would prove for aerodynamic drag, but after a small amount of fine tuning an acceptable compromise was reached and construction could commence. The key feature of the new design was that the entire float above the planing bottom, with the exception of the extreme nose and tail, was skinned with radiator panels, in a similar fashion to the wings. This required very careful fabrication and installation to allow for heat expansion while at the same time ensuring that the seals

remained watertight. The integral fuel tanks were inset and insulated from the radiators.

Despite the extremely tight schedule the two S.6b aircraft were ready for testing several weeks prior to the contest. However, preparation had not gone smoothly. The first S.6a in the air, N247, the winner of the 1929 contest, developed severe rudder flutter caused by adverse vibrations from the engine and propeller and barely made it back on to the water safely. The tail of the fuselage was badly buckled and had to be rebuilt. As a precaution, mass balances were added to the rudder and ailerons of all the aircraft. The rebuilt aircraft was then lost in a fatal accident when Lieut Brinton, a Navy pilot who had just joined the High Speed Flight, stalled on take-off and plunged into the Solent. N248, the second S.6a, nearly went the same way when Flt Lieut Hope hit the wake of a ship on landing, bounced and cartwheeled on hitting the water. He survived with just a punctured eardrum but the aircraft sank. Luckily it was recovered and overhauled prior to the contest.

The initial trials with the S.6b did not go smoothly as Fairey's latest propeller made the aircraft uncontrollable on the water. The solution was

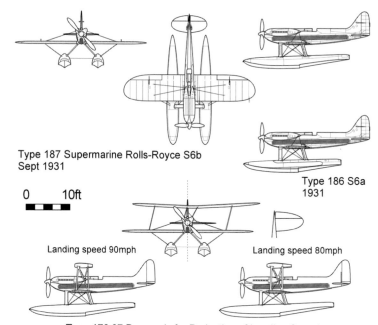

Type 187 Supermarine Rolls-Royce S6b
Sept 1931

0   10ft

Type 186 S6a
1931

Landing speed 90mph

Landing speed 80mph

Type 178 07 Proposals for Reduction of Landing Speed
Oct 1931

to use cut-down and retwisted 1929 propellers as there was insufficient time to forge new ones. Despite the increased radiator area it was not possible to run the engines at full throttle for long periods, a repeat of the problems in 1929. Otherwise, testing proceeded without a hitch.

Once again the French development programme had fallen by the wayside. The Bernard HV120 and Nieuport NiD 450 aircraft designed to compete in 1929 had both flown in 1930 but performance was way below

that of the S.6 and their Hispano-Suiza 18R engines were temperamental. Designs for new aircraft and engines had been put in hand but the pace of work was woefully slow. By early 1931 it was clear that neither Lorraine nor Renault would have viable engines ready in time and interest waned. Dewoitine had their HD410 ready and received a derated Lorraine 'Radium' engine but no flights were made. Bernard completed one HV220 airframe but the second was abandoned. Nieuport had hardly started on their NiD

← A late decision by the government to fund a British team for the 1931 Schneider Trophy contest left no time to design and develop a new racer, so Mitchell upgraded the two S.6 racers with modified floats and constructed two new airframes with a new design of float as the S.6b.

651. These were all advanced designs with the potential to be great racers and the engines were technically adventurous but the scale of the task to construct and test them had been massively underestimated. The team's entry was withdrawn.

The Italians had returned home disappointed after the 1929 contest but were not deterred and resumed their development programme only to suffer yet another fatality while preparing the Savoia-Marchetti S.65 for an attempt on the air speed record. For 1931 they once more reversed their policy and concentrated efforts on a single aircraft and engine. Fiat took the compact AS5 engine from their C.29 racer, a unit that had proven quite reliable, and mounted two nose-to-nose on a common sump to produce the AS6. Each unit of the new engine ran independently and drove one half of a contra-rotating propeller via concentric shafts. A supercharger at the rear fed both engines. In principle it appeared to be a great idea. Macchi built the sleek M.C.72 racer around this engine. Fiat, however, ran into a wealth of unforeseen problems, most especially with the supercharger and induction system, and progress was slow. They did not have an engine ready for flight testing until quite late in the spring of 1931 and once installed in the M.C.72 further problems arose and the engine could not be persuaded to run smoothly. On a flight before Fiat engineers to demonstrate the misfiring, Ten. Monti was killed when the aircraft plunged into the water. The Italians requested that the contest be postponed by six months, which was declined, and so they withdrew their entry.

Once the French and Italian competition melted away it left Britain to fly unopposed in the Schneider contest and thus to win the trophy outright. Just one aircraft flew around the course, Flt Lieut Boothman in S.6b S1595, as there seemed no reason for the others to fly once victory was secured. After the contest the second S.6b, S1596 piloted by Flt Lieut Stainforth, was sent out to raise the air speed record, which it did at 379mph, but more was to be expected. A few days later this aircraft sunk on landing when Stainforth lost control when his heel jammed under the rudder bar. He then resumed preparation using S1595 and in this aircraft went on the establish a new air speed record of 407.5mph, the first record to exceed 400mph.

Air racing had always been a high risk activity and as engine power rose and speeds increased these risks grew significantly. The years 1930 and 1931 had proven to be particularly bad with fatalities for all the nations aiming to compete for the Schneider Trophy. In truth, many people were glad that the contest had now run its course. Mitchell's S.6 aircraft were definitely among the very best seaplane racers ever built, they were appreciated by their pilots, were stable at speed and while cornering. Yet they, too, could bite back and three of the four aircraft had crashed.

19

REPLACING THE SOUTHAMPTON

The Southampton and Southampton II had proven a great success and provided the foundation for Supermarine's commercial growth through the second half of the 1920s and the backbone of the RAF's marine reconnaissance fleet. The aircraft was well liked by its crews, performed admirably in service and had no direct competition. Yet by the beginning of the 1930s they were slow, ageing, increasingly antiquated in design and would need to be replaced by a more modern type in the near future. Supermarine had begun to review options almost as soon as the Southampton II went into service and had considered both incremental improvements and a complete redesign. Under various Air Ministry contracts they had tested alternative engine types, metal wing construction, experimental wing-mounted gun positions, torpedo launching gear and, with Saunders, a new hull type. In parallel they had assessed three-engined designs, first with the Nanok and subsequently the larger Southampton X and Air Yacht, partly in response to Air Ministry requirements which, for a time, favoured the concept of three-engined flying boats. Unfortunately, none of these Supermarine aircraft had proven satisfactory. As the performance of other companies' prototypes had also been below par the Air Ministry cooled on the idea of three engines for their medium-sized flying boats and reverted to specifying twin engines for a potential Southampton II replacement. The key point here being that this was their decision to return to twin-engine aircraft and not a change of policy at Supermarine, as some authors have implied.

SCAPA

By 1930 Mitchell's ideas were beginning to focus on the development of a new twin-engined aircraft of much the same size and layout as the Southampton. The various concept drawings for these aircraft were placed within Type 178 and all were intended to be powered by two Rolls-Royce Kestrel M.S. (moderately supercharged) engines.

Two versions of the first design were included under Type 178 04. Both these aircraft had a metal hull based broadly on that of the Southampton II, which had proven to have fine hydrodynamic performance, but this was deepened and had slightly flatter sides for ease of construction. The rear fuselage retained the offset gun positions and the forward fuselage the tandem open cockpits and lowered nose gun ring. The wings were very similar to those designed for the Type 178 03 Mail Carrier with raked

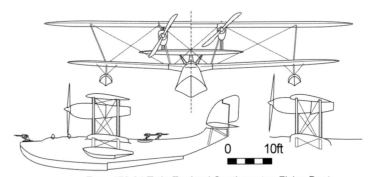

Type 178 04 Twin Engined Southampton Flying Boat
May 1930

0   10ft

inter-plane struts in the centre section that doubled as the engine mounts. One version of the aircraft showed the engines suspended on the struts, as in the Mail Carrier, while the second showed them fitted directly under the top wing. Eliminating the separate engine mount structure, which had been a feature of all Supermarine's early flying boats, helped to reduce drag, while raising the engine thrust line addressed the tendency to draw spray into the propellers. The two designs also differed slightly in wingspan. Both had Southampton-style tailplanes but with twin rather than triple fins. However, overall neither represented much more than a minimal incremental improvement on the Southampton II.

The next step in the evolution of this project was the Type 178 05, which featured a widened hull to accommodate a side-by-side cockpit, an additional gun in the tail, a cleaner second step and larger rudders, all features adopted from the Southampton X. In this design the engines were mounted directly under the top wing. Placing the engines in this position, coupled with the decision to go for single-bay bracing, necessitated the design of more robust spars and hence a thicker wing section than had been used on

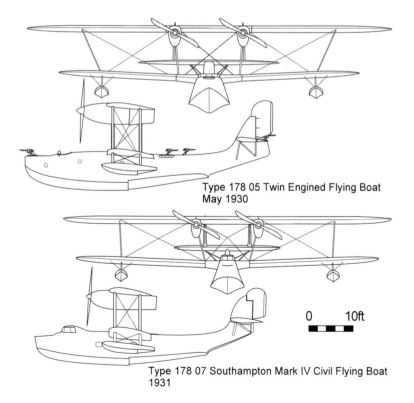

Type 178 05 Twin Engined Flying Boat
May 1930

0   10ft

Type 178 07 Southampton Mark IV Civil Flying Boat
1931

the Southampton. By July 1931 this aircraft had become a major project, allocated its own type number, Type 221, and named Southampton IV.

Type 178 07 was a civil version of the early Southampton IV design.

The Type 221 Southampton IV was developed under specification R.20/31 for a General Reconnaissance Flying Boat and a single prototype was ordered by the Air Ministry. It is said that McLean had offered this aircraft in place of the last Southampton II of the final production batch at no extra cost, part of a suite of private funding initiatives in place to stimulate the sluggish business and attract orders.

The Southampton IV was of all-metal construction with fabric covered flying surfaces. The hull reverted to the construction techniques originally developed for the Southampton II and abandoned the corrugated plating that had been a feature of the Southampton X and Air Yacht. Neither was it as slab-sided as either of these aircraft although the number of double curvature plates had been reduced. The cockpit was fully enclosed and the bow gun ring was retractable so that the position could be covered by a hatch. A small top-hinged flap panel was positioned in the extreme bow that could be opened to allow rudimentary bomb aiming or for dropping small items. The lower wing centre section spar beams were built as an integral part of two reinforced hull bulkheads, which eliminated the need for additional wing bracing struts to the lower hull sides. The tailplane was very similar to that on the Southampton II, including the bracing struts to the hull stern, but the number of fins and rudders had been reduced to two and all control activators were within the hull.

The wings were braced in single bays with the centre section struts also serving to support the engine nacelles. The wing construction was also very similar to that on the Southampton II and was built around a modified and strengthened version of Supermarine's Σ-shaped spar beams. It is interesting to note that the semi-monocoque all-metal engine nacelles with their integral engine mounts drew heavily upon experience gained from the fuselage and engine bay designs of the S.5 and S.6 racers. The radiators for the Rolls-Royce Kestrel IIIMS were placed at the rear of the nacelles, an unusual, if not unique, arrangement.

Construction proceeded quite swiftly and the Southampton IV, registered S1648, was flown for the first time in July 1932 but only transferred to the MAEE for service evaluation at the end of October after some forty test flights had been carried out by Supermarine. These tests had identified an unexpected tendency to pitch forward on the water when the rear step came in contact with the surface, a characteristic that had not been identified during tank testing, and this required rectification using parts designed originally for the planing bottom of the Southampton II. Originally, the rear step had been widened in order to minimise the possibility of the wake washing over the tailplane. This was the second time that Mitchell's hydrodynamic design staff had encountered problems with hulls that had not been noted during model tests in the Vickers tanks, the other being the Air Yacht. At the MAEE the Southampton IV was subject to thorough testing over and around the North Sea before it was despatched to Malta in November for service trials with 202 Squadron. The extended testing programme in the Mediterranean included a tour around the coast and lakes of northern Egypt in June 1933. On returning to Britain in the autumn the aircraft was renamed Scapa and a production order for twelve aircraft was received by Supermarine under specification R.19/33. This was more than a year after the first flight of the prototype, which suggests that the Air Ministry did not view the procurement as high priority.

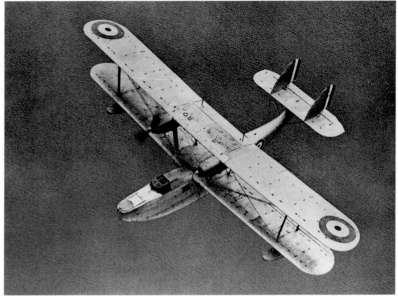

↑ The prototype Southampton IV underwent extensive trials before a production order was issued nearly a year after the first flight. Production aircraft were renamed Scapa.

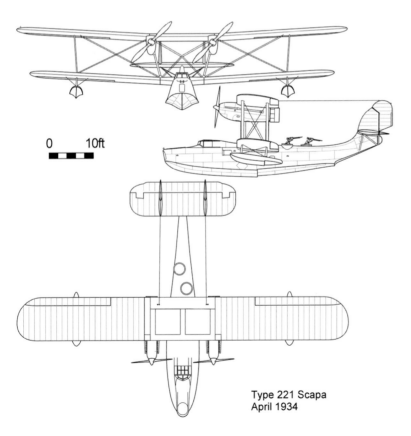

0   10ft

Type 221 Scapa
April 1934

This production contract was the first received by Supermarine for a new design by Mitchell since the Southampton in 1924, a sobering fact. The first production Scapa was delivered in 1935 and they served in the Mediterranean region based in Malta until the outbreak of the war.

The Scapa was a big improvement over the Southampton II that it was destined to replace but it was already beginning to look rather dated even as it was introduced into service. Work was already in hand for a far more technically advanced aircraft to replace it, although first Mitchell had to deal with its enlarged sibling.

STRANRAER

Even while the design of the Southampton IV was being finalised the Air Ministry issued a further specification, R.24/31, for a twin-engined General Purpose Boat-Seaplane fulfilling much the same role but slightly larger in size, which suggests that they saw the Scapa, still firmly in the same size class as the Southampton II, as something of a stopgap. The new specification called for the ability to carry a 1,000lb load over 1,000 miles and to cruise on one engine with 60 per cent fuel load. The specification drew submissions from Saunders-Roe, Shorts and Supermarine.

Mitchell's starting point, as Type 226, was in essence a Scapa powered by two Bristol Pegasus air-cooled radial engines, which was then developed further as the Type 227 featuring a new hull, slightly thinner NACA (National Advisory Committee for Aeronautics) 2412 profile wings with leading edge slats, and a tail gun. This, in turn, was modified to be powered by two Kestrels, as in the Scapa, and became Type 230. It was an alternative version of this design powered by Mitchell's favoured engine of this period, the evaporatively cooled Rolls-Royce Goshawk, which formed the basis for Supermarine's tender to specification R.24/31.

At the time the Type 230 was tendered to the Air Ministry Mitchell knew the design to be immature and that there remained a lot of detailed work to be done. This was especially needed on the complex and weighty cooling system for the evaporatively cooled Goshawk engines but also on the hull, the size of which was considered to be rather marginal to handle the specified loads. It therefore came as no particular surprise when they failed to obtain a contract for a prototype. This was issued instead to Saunders-Roe for their Bristol Pegasus-powered A.27 London biplane, a follow-on to the A.7 Severn, and Shorts for the S.18 'Knuckleduster' cantilever seagull-wing monoplane powered by Goshawks, although this was perceived very much as an experimental aircraft rather than a viable service machine. It is noteworthy that both of these aircraft were built using corrugated skins, something that had been recommended in the specification but which was not actually a requirement. The London first flew in March 1934 and twelve aircraft were ordered one year later just as the Scapa was entering service, but once again as a stopgap as specification R.3/35 was issued immediately to replace it.

Supermarine pushed ahead with the Type 230, now named the Southampton V, and the Goshawk engine gave way to the Bristol Pegasus, which was lighter and avoided the complexity of the evaporative cooling system. Mitchell widened the hull at the shoulder position, which increased the internal volume substantially for a modest increase in cross section area.

0   10ft

Type 226 Scapa dev
May 1932

Type 230 Twin engined boat seaplane
to spec. R.24/31
June 1932

↑ The Saunders-Roe London was intermediate in size between the Scapa and Stanraer and won a production contract. The hull used Saunders' patented corrugated skins and the engines were enclosed in polygonal Townend ring cowls.

↑ The strong family resemblance between the Stranraer and its immediate predecessor is clear, and as such the Stranraer was looking dated even as it entered service in 1937. It was, nevertheless, an excellent aircraft.

The widened hull provided for a roomier and lengthened cockpit and cleaner detailing around the top midships gun position, both of which helped to lower drag. The wings underwent a complete redesign. The previous single bay layout, inherited from the Scapa, was dropped in favour of twin bays, and the inherent increase in drag from the additional struts and wires was offset to some extent by changing the wing section from NACA 2412 to 2409, a reduction in thickness from 12 per cent to 9 per cent. This marked a return

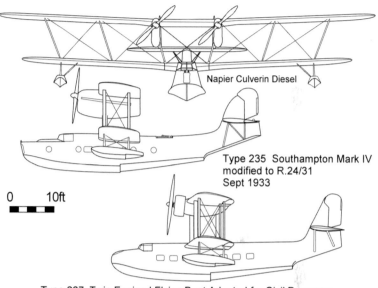

Napier Culverin Diesel

Type 235 Southampton Mark IV
modified to R.24/31
Sept 1933

0   10ft

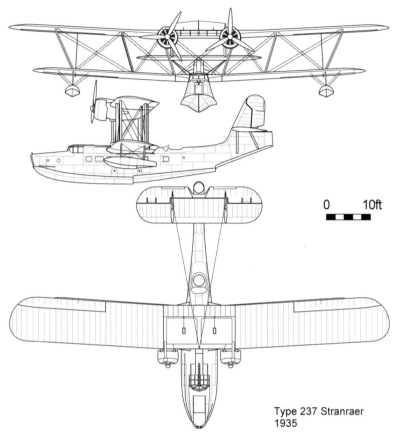

0   10ft

Type 237 Twin Engined Flying Boat Adapted for Civil Purposes
May 1935

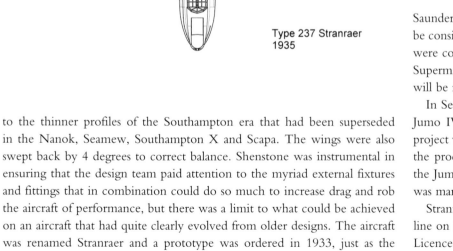

Type 237 Stranraer
1935

to the thinner profiles of the Southampton era that had been superseded in the Nanok, Seamew, Southampton X and Scapa. The wings were also swept back by 4 degrees to correct balance. Shenstone was instrumental in ensuring that the design team paid attention to the myriad external fixtures and fittings that in combination could do so much to increase drag and rob the aircraft of performance, but there was a limit to what could be achieved on an aircraft that had quite clearly evolved from older designs. The aircraft was renamed Stranraer and a prototype was ordered in 1933, just as the Southampton IV returned from its Mediterranean cruise, and flew in July 1934. Service evaluation was again leisurely and it was not until August 1935 that seventeen aircraft were ordered to supplement the concurrent order for

Saunders-Roe Londons. However, once again both it and the London can be considered as stopgaps. They were biplanes in a world where monoplanes were coming to the fore. By the time the Stranraer entered service in 1937 Supermarine were already well advanced in designing a replacement and this will be reviewed in a later chapter.

In September 1933 Mitchell investigated the possibility of fitting Junkers Jumo IV compression ignition engines to the aircraft, as Type 235. This project was intermediate in design between the original Type 230 layout and the production Stranraer. Napier had negotiated a licence to manufacture the Jumo engine in Britain, as the Culverin, but it did not find favour and was manufactured only in small numbers.

Stranraers served in British home waters but were removed from the front line on the outbreak of war, although some remained in service until 1941. Licence-built Stranraers in Canada served throughout the war.

Type 237, which dates from May 1935, was a development of the Stranraer for civil passenger service that featured a deeper hull providing accommodation for around twenty passengers.

20

SMALL AMPHIBIANS AND MISCELLANEOUS PROJECTS

SMALL AMPHIBIANS

Following close on the heels of the Type 221 Southampton IV/Scapa came the Type 223, the next attempt to provide a replacement for the Seagull III in RAAF service. After their rejection of the rather outmoded and derivative Type 181, Mitchell placed the leadership of the project to come up with a more modern design in the hands of William Munro, who had been recruited recently.

As far as is known, Munro appears to have started his career in the aviation business with Gloster Aircraft reporting to Henry Folland, where he specialised in hull and float design. Whether he learned the business of hydrodynamics at university or with a boat builder is not clear. While working at Gloster he played a key role, alongside George Dowty, in the design of the metal floats for their 1927 Gloster IV Schneider racer, the first floats both designed and built by the company. In 1928 he wrote the first of several articles on aspects of marine aircraft design and saw them published in the *Aircraft Engineer* supplement of *Flight* magazine. In late 1928 Munro left Gloster and travelled to Canada, where he was employed by Canadian Vickers. In 1929 he moved to the US to work with Tom Towle, formerly a designer at Ford's aircraft division, who had recently established Towle Aircraft Co. Inc. to build amphibian flying boats. Munro contributed to the design of the TA-2 and TA-3 twin-engined cantilever monoplane amphibians. His time with Towle was short and he returned for a brief period with Canadian Vickers before sailing for Britain in August 1930 to take up a position with Supermarine. Once back in Britain Munro resumed writing articles for *Flight* and in 1932 brought these together, along with much new material and a contribution on wing design by his colleague Beverley Shenstone, into a book, *Marine Aircraft Design*.

SEAGULL V

The RAAF specification for a replacement for their venerable Seagull IIIs, first issued in 1929 and now gathering dust on the shelf, was fairly straightforward but included one new element: the aircraft had to be capable of launch by catapult at maximum take-off weight, which was not to exceed 8,050lb. In all other respects the specification roughly paralleled that for the Seagull III as the reconnaissance/survey/communication role it was to fulfil remained largely unchanged. A tough condition for such a small craft was that it should be capable of operation in sea conditions with 6ft waves.

As a rugged multipurpose workhorse, simplicity and ease of repair and maintenance were essential so Munro and the team set out to design a metal hull in which flat sheeting would predominate and where complex curvature was minimised. The project was initiated as the Type 223 and commenced in late 1931 with wind tunnel and water tank tests carried out over the following summer. To simplify the construction of the planing bottom Supermarine took out a licence on a Saunders' patent from 1929 where the surface was built in two parts, an inner flat surfaced 'V' and an outer tapering horizontal 'ledge' at the chine, which imparted relatively clean running without the need for curvature. There was just a single step and the rear portion of the planing bottom extended to the tail. The cockpit was enclosed and there were hatches in the nose and aft of the biplane wings that could be fitted with stowable gun mounts. The single bay biplane wings had stainless steel spars and wooden ribs with fabric covering and folded to the rear. The tailplane was strut braced to the single fin. The engine was mounted as a pusher in the centre section driving a four-blade propeller and could be either a Bristol Pegasus radial engine behind an egg-shaped nacelle that held the oil tank and cooler, or a Rolls-Royce Kestrel. The engine was angled by 3 degrees to port to compensate for the slipstream yaw effect on the tail. The undercarriage consisted of a single stout oleo strut braced by radius rods to the rear and retracted by rotating outwards and upwards so that the wheels sat within wells in the lower wing. A combined water rudder and wheel was installed at the tail.

It was, of course, inevitable that a civil version of the aircraft would be considered and Mitchell established a new project in April 1932, as the Type 225. This aircraft retained most of the Type 223 structure, including the folding wings, but had a redesigned fin and rudder, which were taller and of narrower chord with the water rudder built as an extension of the main rudder. There were also small differences in the elevators and ailerons, and it

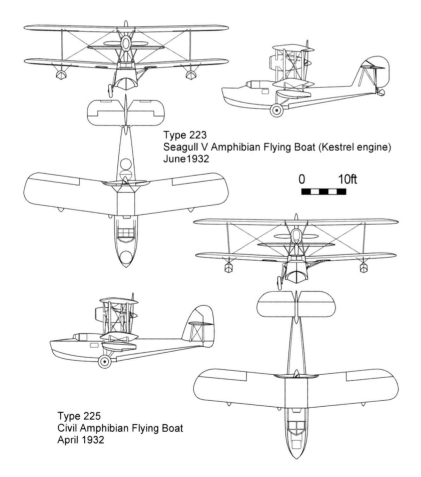

Type 223
Seagull V Amphibian Flying Boat (Kestrel engine)
June 1932

0   10ft

Type 225
Civil Amphibian Flying Boat
April 1932

is quite possible that all these may have been features shared with the earliest design of the Type 223. It was to be powered by a Rolls-Royce Kestrel. However, the stark simplicity of the aircraft did not really lend itself to civil airline duties. While the Spartan interior and 'tin can' noise levels may have been acceptable for a military or commercial freight workhorse they would have proven problematic if it were to carry paying passengers.

In late 1931 McLean authorised detailed design work and construction of the prototype Type 223, now named Seagull V, as a private venture. The Australians had been shown details and specifications for the aircraft but had not as yet placed an order. Following several sluggish years seeking orders Vickers' management had agreed to McLean's proposal to stimulate their aviation businesses by taking a more proactive approach to securing contracts by accepting a greater degree of up-front risk and providing company funding for prototypes. The Southampton IV and Seagull V prototypes were the first such moves to aid Supermarine and similar action was taken in Vickers to promote Wallis' geodetic construction system.

In 1932 the works were in a chaotic state and most projects were falling behind schedule, including the Seagull V. The aircraft, powered by a 625hp Bristol Pegasus II, flew eventually on 21 June 1933 in the hands of 'Mutt' Summers and just five days later it appeared at the SBAC show at Hendon. The amphibian was neither required nor expected to demonstrate exceptional flying characteristics yet it could, nevertheless, be rolled and looped with ease. However, the story that Summers looped it during his spirited display, much to the surprise of Mitchell, may well be apocryphal as it has proven difficult to verify. On its return to Woolston few modifications were required other than to soften the undercarriage. Company tests were completed by the end of July.

The Seagull V was evaluated at the MAEE on behalf of the RAAF, and they confirmed Supermarine's performance figures. However, in the absence of a customer specification and with no similar type in service they had no yardstick against which to judge the aircraft and hence kept their comments rather bland and singled out the performance on its undercarriage for criticism, to the annoyance of Supermarine. The RAAF by now were showing real interest and requested that it undergo catapulting trials at Farnborough, which commenced in January 1934 and were passed without any problems. Contrary to the MAEE comments, all aspects of the aircraft's performance proved quite satisfactory. The tough metal hull exhibited fine water handling characteristics even in rough conditions and it could be stalled on to the surface without sustaining damage. The undercarriage, too, could absorb a lot of punishment. The interior was basic but capacious with

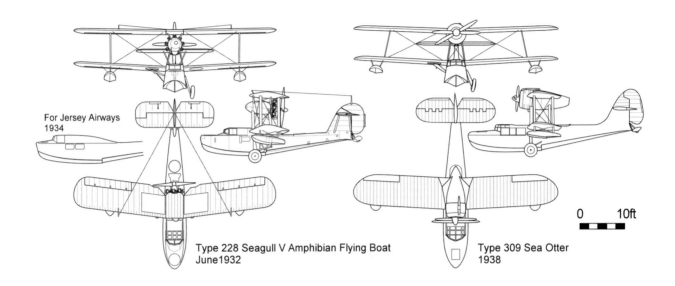

For Jersey Airways
1934

Type 228 Seagull V Amphibian Flying Boat
June 1932

Type 309 Sea Otter
1938

0   10ft

↑ Early trials of the Seagull V prototype included assessment of the catapult launch capability undertaken at the RAE in Farnborough. The aircraft passed with flying colours.

plenty of room for the three-man crew, although it proved to be tiringly noisy, the large flat metal panels amplifying the engine and water noise.

The Air Ministry issued specification 6/34 on behalf of the Australian Government in the late summer of 1934 to cover the production aircraft and the RAAF then ordered twenty-four examples. The first production aircraft, designated Type 228, was completed in mid-1935. The Type 228 was near identical to the prototype Type 223, the differences pertaining to the service equipment. Some of the machines were fitted with Handley Page slots. The Australian machines were delivered in two tranches with a hiatus in between as a result of an RAF order being given higher priority. They were deployed on the Royal Australian Navy's County and Leander-class cruisers and on the seaplane tender *Albatross*, replacing the Seagull IIIs.

In early 1934 a civilianised version of the Type 228 was drawn up and offered to Jersey Airways, a new fledgling airline working the Channel Islands routes. This featured a revised cockpit and forward cabin but was otherwise unchanged. On the drawing someone has doodled the rough layout, front view, for a parasol monoplane version with canards.

The Fleet Air Arm (FAA) had been unimpressed by the Seagull II and less than enthusiastic about any of Mitchell's possible replacements, including the Sheldrake and Seamew. As a consequence, they remained more focussed on conventional aircraft with interchangeable wheels or floats and saw no role for an aircraft of the Seagull V type. However, once the prototype had demonstrated its excellent hydrodynamic qualities, far superior to any seaplane, and ease of use with a catapult their attitude changed and a decision was made to add catapults to many of the Navy's capital ships and a modest order for twelve Seagull Vs was awarded in mid-1935. The production run was inserted into the middle of that for the Australians. These aircraft were named Type 236 Walrus, although they were virtually identical to the Seagull V apart from the installation of the more powerful 750hp Pegasus III. Further orders would follow.

The Walrus was deployed with the fleet, where it fulfilled its reconnaissance role admirably. However, it soon became apparent that in the heat of conflict the time taken to recover the aircraft after landing constituted too much of a risk to the host ship and it was soon withdrawn. The reconnaissance

→ Often unfairly described as an ugly duckling, the Seagull V/ Walrus was actually a rather clean and elegant flying boat, in a utilitarian way. It was certainly as easy on the eye as either of its larger stablemates, the Scapa and Stranraer.

role passed to carrier-based aircraft and was supplemented with radar. The Walrus did, of course, fill a crucial role as a search and rescue aircraft around the British Isles, a role at which it excelled.

It is not often that an aircraft designed for stark simplicity and ruggedness should prove to be such a capable machine both on the sea and in the air, and, while it lacked refinement, the Seagull V nevertheless had a wealth of charm and neat efficiency about it.

SEA OTTER

Notwithstanding the commercial success achieved with the Walrus, Mitchell does not appear to have been entirely satisfied with the aircraft, which had been designed to fulfil an RAAF rather than British requirement. He initiated a full redesign, despite the extremely heavy workload in the Design Department at the time, with the intention that the Type 309 should be a direct replacement for the Walrus, with almost identical dimensions and of the same layout, but with improved performance tailored more closely to the FAA's requirements.

Work on the new project commenced in late 1935 and in February 1936 Mitchell met the Air Ministry to present the project and to agree upon the specifications for the aircraft, which allowed Supermarine to complete their initial design and draw up full technical details. The Air Ministry issued specification 5/36 in April 1936 for an Improved Walrus Development for the FAA, stating that the overall dimensions and construction method were to be the same as those for the Walrus. The emphasis was on higher economical cruising speed and range; a cruising speed of 100kt for a range of 920 miles. The stalling speed was kept low at 48kt. It is also interesting to note that it mentions the possibility of fitting retractable hydroplanes in place of wing tip floats and we will come

across these later with regard to a contemporaneous large flying boat project. Two prototypes were ordered.

For some reason, Mitchell decided that the Type 309 would have its engine mounted as a tractor rather than a pusher, a somewhat curious decision as the pusher configuration made recovery of the flying boat by ship's crane much easier for the crew. The aircraft was taxied towards the hook while a crew member stood on the cabin roof to catch it and attach it to strops from the lifting points on the top wing centre section. The selected engine was Bristol's new sleeve-valve radial 796hp Perseus VI enclosed in a long NACA-style cowl and driving a two-blade propeller. Unlike on the Walrus, the nacelle was not set at an angle and the asymmetric slipsteam on the tail, which generated yaw, was offset by giving the fin and rudder an aerofoil section to produce a counter force. Structurally the Type 309 followed the philosophy of the Walrus. The hull retained the simplified planing bottom and maximised the use of flat sheets for plating but was aerodynamically cleaner around the nose. After first considering the name Stingray the Type 309 was given the name Sea Otter.

Pressure of work, and Mitchell's catastrophic decline in health, delayed finalisation of the design and the FAA's immediate requirement was met by a further order for Walruses. As a consequence, the final details of the design were completed after Mitchell's death. The first flight took place on 23 September 1938 in the hands of George Pickering. Pickering had been on the staff of the MAEE and was one of the pilots who had evaluated the Scapa

→ Mitchell undertook a thorough clean-up of the Walrus to produce an aircraft of essentially the same size but with superior performance for the Fleet Air Arm, the Sea Otter.

and Seagull V. Mitchell was impressed with his work and recommended that Supermarine should employ him to aid Summers as the company test pilot. Mitchell made him an offer and this was accepted.

The Sea Otter appears to have proven more troublesome than had the Walrus, either that or assessment was more stringent. At first the aircraft was reluctant to rise on to the step due to a lack of thrust from the propeller, which was unable to exploit the full power of the engine. As a quick solution the aircraft was fitted with two two-blade propellers set at an angle of 35 degrees to produce a workable four-blade propeller without affecting the height of the aircraft adversely, which was limited by the size of the aircraft carrier hangars. The usual series of tests dragged on well into 1939 as the project was not perceived as high priority and ironed out small problems with porpoising and spray over the nose. A three-blade Rotol constant-speed propeller was also tested. The stalling speed had been measured as 54kt, above specification, so wings increased in span by 4ft were tested on the second prototype. Catapult trials followed. The outbreak of war slowed progress further but in January Supermarine were advised that the aircraft had been selected for production. However, first the stall speed with the original wings fitted had to meet specification, which meant fitting flaps.

Supermarine's works at Woolston and Itchen were destroyed by bombing in the spring of 1940 so the production contract for 190 aircraft was issued to Blackburn, but they were forced to decline due to pressure of work on other aircraft. Work continued on the prototypes to cure cooling problems with the oil system of the Perseus until it was decided the only solution was to re-engine the aircraft with a 920hp Bristol Mercury X, which also provided a considerable increase in power. The even more powerful 965hp Mercury XXX was selected for the production aircraft, for which a contract was finally awarded to Saunders-Roe in 1942. The first production aircraft, now designated Sea Otter ABR Mk1, was completed in January 1943, a full seven years since the project had been signed off by Mitchell. Yet more service acceptance trials then took place and questions, not surprisingly, were asked whether the aircraft was actually required as the Walrus had, and was, serving with distinction. The Sea Otter entered service in the search and rescue role in November 1944, the last of the designs from Mitchell's era to do so.

TRANSPORTS

Throughout the 1920s the RAF maintained a small fleet of transport aircraft to ferry troops and cargo that could double up as bombers in an emergency.

Indeed, the Vickers Victoria and Vernon that formed the bulk of this fleet were little more than modified bombers as they used the wings and other major components of the Vimy and Virginia bomber respectively. These aircraft served primarily in the more remote areas of the Empire. By 1930 both types were aging and the Air Ministry decided to issue a specification for a new design while at the same time taking some of the later mark Virginia bombers out of service and fitting them with new capacious fuselages to become the Valentia transport. Specification C.26/31 was issued in April 1932 and called for a twin-engined, monoplane Bomber-Transport Aircraft to be used principally in tropical climates and from high altitude airfields. It was to be able to carry a variety of different loads: either twenty-four troops with full military equipment, or ten stretcher cases, or three 1,000lb aero engines, or an equivalent load in fuel, water and miscellaneous cargo. Total weight was not to exceed 18,000lb and the range with full load was to be 920 miles at 10,000ft and at a cruising speed above 95mph, a surprisingly low speed.

Mitchell's project to meet C.26/31 was Type 231 which, contrary to the requirement, he designed as a biplane using the wings, tailplane and twin Pegasus engine installation from the Type 227, the halfway step in the revision of the Scapa to meet specification R.24/31. While it was no doubt convenient to develop the Stranraer and Bomber-Transport in parallel and to share components, it is hard to understand why he would have deliberately ignored the requirement that the aircraft should be a monoplane.

The Type 231 had a monocoque Alclad fuselage of elliptical section with large side doors at the rear and a hatch in the roof aft of the enclosed cockpit for the loading of cargo using a hoist attached to the upper wing centre section. Alclad was a recent development by the Aluminium Corporation of America and comprised a Duralumin sheet coated with pure aluminium to improve corrosion resistance. The main cabin had watertight bulkheads fore and aft and the doors had seals to prevent sinking if a forced landing were made on water. The lower wing was cranked slightly at the root end in order to shorten the legs for the fixed, spatted, narrow track undercarriage.

It is not certain that the Type 231 was tendered to the Air Ministry but it is highly unlikely that it would have been selected had Supermarine done so. The elliptical section monocoque fuselage, although reasonably technically sophisticated, simply reduced the internal space while doing little to improve performance.

The designs selected to be built as prototypes were all quite different. The Armstrong Whitworth A.W.23 was a low-wing cantilever monoplane with a retractable undercarriage and rectangular section fabric-covered fuselage;

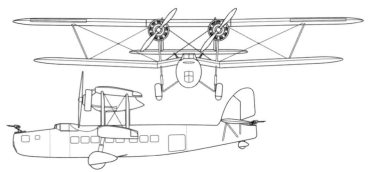

Type 231 Twin Engined Bomber Transport to spec C.26/31
Sept 1932

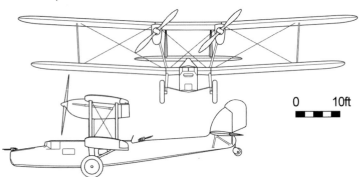

0   10ft

Type 240 Twin Engined Coastal Reconnaissance Landplane
May 1934

the Handley Page H.P.51 had a similar fuselage, a cantilever high wing with slats and slotted flaps and fixed, wide track undercarriage; while the Bristol Bombay, which won the production contract, had a high wing and undercarriage similar to the H.P.51 but a rectangular section stressed-skin fuselage. These aircraft had top speeds of between 175 and 188mph. The Type 231, based very closely on the Stranraer, would most likely have had a similar performance to the flying boat; a top speed of around 165mph.

COASTAL PATROL

Mitchell also considered options for land-based derivatives of the Scapa flying boat and conceived an aircraft to carry out a similar role for coastal reconnaissance. The RAF had not identified a need for such an aircraft so the project must have been speculative. The Type 240 dates from September 1934 and shows the Scapa with its hull replaced by a simple square section metal monocoque fuselage just 6ft deep and 4ft wide. The fixed undercarriage was designed to be jettisonable to allow forced landing in water in an emergency, and the sealed fuselage had a shallow 'V' underside for the same reason.

◄ Supermarine celebrated the armistice with this publicity calendar and artwork featuring the Baby fighter.

↓ Mitchell's large amphibian passenger flying boat for Instone Air Line would have served on routes across the Channel and into continental Europe. (Matt Painter)

The unusual SS Fighter Flying Boat was Mitchell's last attempt to interest the navy in amphibian flying boat fighters. (Matt Painter)

Air Ministry specification 9/23 for a large three-engined reconnaissance flying boat was withdrawn but Mitchell's design was a useful stepping stone on the route to the successful Southampton. (Matt Painter)

Mitchell's carrier-based fighter to N.21/26 was a conventional biplane with no outstanding features. An alternative version of the project was powered by a liquid-cooled engine.

Mitchell's potential rival to the Short Sarafand utilised the entire wing interior as a steam condenser for the engine cooling system. The wing was elliptical in plan.

The Ragazine was the Design Department's own monthly magazine. The first issue was produced in 1926.

The Type 178 High Speed Bomber design echoes the style of Mitchell's Schneider racers and hints at great things to come with the Spitfire.

Supermarine and their suppliers were proud to celebrate the success of the Schneider racers as in this advertisement by paint manufacturers Cellon.

↑ Mitchell's innovative concept for a
carrier-based reconnaissance torpedo bomber
to meet specification S.9/30 featured a metal
monocoque fuselage and twin Napier Rapier
engines.

→ The Type 232 would have undertaken
long-range patrols around the North Atlantic, a
wearing and arduous mission. (Matt Painter)

↑ This early concept by Mitchell's team to specification B.1/35 for a heavy bomber was not destined to be developed as a full project as Vickers' management preferred Vickers' Warwick design. However, several key design features were carried through to later bomber projects.

→ The Type 302, designed for Imperial Airways, would have carried up to twenty-four passengers on routes to the Mediterranean.

The Type 3.. was one of
two designs for a four-cannon
fighter submitted to the Air
Ministry. It had the potential to
be a fast and potent aircraft with
lethal firepower.

← Engine failure forces a Type 308
flying boat down in the heavy swell of
the North Atlantic and it loses one
of its retractable wing floats. A sister
aircraft guides help to the scene

British Seaplanes Triumph in the International Schneider Trophy Contests

BIRTH OF A SPITFIRE!
by GORDON BECKLES

"It's the stuck-up woman she is since Lord Beaverbrook brought down 2 Dorniers with her frying-pan."

HAVE YOU GIVEN TO A SRITFIRE FUND? Then read this book

Spitfire

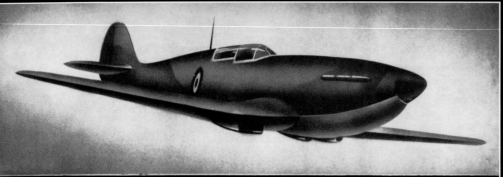

The Book of the "Spitfire"
WAR PLANES
PUBLISHED BY REAL PHOTOGRAPHS CO · COOPER'S BUILDINGS · CHURCH ST · LIVERPOOL I
No. 3 Price Is. 3d.

The success of the Spitfire in the Battle of Britain led to a range of pamphlets and books celebrating Mitchell, Supermarine and the Spitfire.

21

FIGHTERS

While a significant portion of the Design Department focussed on the Scapa, Stranraer, Seagull V and a significant number of other flying boat projects, Mitchell set about tackling a new direction for the company, drawing upon his experience building the small, metal monocoque Schneider racers. He intended to enter the market for fighters.

The big problem when recounting the evolution of Mitchell's design work on fighters is that the reader is aware in advance where the story will end and the Spitfire looms large on the horizon. Thus it is all too easy to let this colour our perception of the many ideas and decisions that led eventually to this aircraft and to imply that Mitchell was acting throughout with enviable foresight and clarity of vision. Suffice it to say that history cannot really be read backwards and extreme caution should be applied before inferences are drawn based on knowledge of later events. The Spitfire casts a long shadow but it is cast forwards and not back.

LATE 1920S BIPLANE FIGHTERS

By 1930 Supermarine were quite unusual, almost unique, amongst mainstream British aircraft constructors in not having built a single land-based fighter aircraft. There is no indication that they had responded to any Air Ministry specification or, indeed, that they had received any invitations to tender. Yet they had a fine track record in designing and building high-speed aircraft, an excellent springboard from which to get a head start in the task of developing a fighter. However, before looking at Mitchell's change of direction it is worth summarising in brief the events of the late 1920s regarding the RAF's requirements for fighters.

Immediately after the war the market for fighters for the RAF, and the FAA after its formation in 1924, had been distinctly limited, due not only to the restricted government funds available but also because the Air Ministry and forces experts had yet to define a clear role for the fighter force. There was no obvious enemy force that needed to be countered and as a consequence the Air Ministry maintained a broad, generic, defence patrol strategy and specifications for fighters were equally generic and undemanding. With Germany effectively emasculated by the terms of the Treaty of Versailles, the notional 'enemy' for planning purposes reverted to Britain's age-old adversary, France, not because there was any perceived threat but simply as they were the nearest neighbour and in the process of expanding their air force. However, the government also applied an unofficial and pragmatic 'ten year rule' whereby it was assumed that no outbreak of hostilities would occur within ten years so long as tension was not building in the region, and this assumption could be rolled forward year-on-year if the situation had not changed. By this reasoning it was not necessary to maintain a large air force but merely to ensure that aircraft technology kept pace with developments elsewhere and that the aircraft industry was in a fit state to be able to respond if the international political climate worsened. The Air Ministry worked on the basis that they should plan to defend against both night and day bomber attacks coming from France and which they assumed would be aimed mainly at London.

A common view developed immediately after the war and still prevalent at the end of the 1920s, and indeed for several years after, was that little that could be done to defend against an attack by formations of bombers, well-armed and offering mutual protection. In Britain Sir Hugh Trenchard, Chief of the Air Staff, was foremost in this belief. The RAF and the Air

Ministry, for no strong reason as there was little empirical information on which to base the view, considered the defensive effectiveness of armed bombers flying in formation to be a formidable challenge and quite capable of driving off the most concerted attack by fighters. There would be losses among the bomber force for sure, but the bulk of the aircraft would reach their target and wreak havoc. As a consequence Trenchard prioritised expenditure on the bomber force at the expense of fighters, yet it was necessary, nevertheless, to maintain a fighter force to, at the very least, harass enemy bombers. Not to do so would have been politically disastrous. For planning purposes he established two classes of fighters. First there were zone fighters, which could operate at day or night, would take off once enemy aircraft were expected and engage them on both their inbound and outbound flight within pre-assigned patrol zones. These fighters would be based on a string of airfields to the south of London. The second class were designed for the interception role, taking off as the incoming enemy were detected. They were stationed closer to the coast and were optimised for climb-rate so that they could engage the enemy as they passed overhead. These fighters would operate only in daylight and would carry less fuel. Fighting tactics for both classes of aircraft required that they should attack in formation in order to concentrate firepower. However, in practice the lack of funds limited the number of aircraft that could be purchased and the two roles became increasingly blurred throughout much of the 1920s.

The Air Ministry issued specifications through the 1920s and a smattering of prototypes had been built. Fighters of generally rather conservative design had been ordered in very small numbers from the likes of Armstrong-Whitworth, Gloster and Hawker to supplement and then replace the squadrons of late war-era types. The majority of these aircraft had wooden structures and were armed with two machine guns; the same formula as the fighters that served in the last years of the war. By 1926 these older aircraft were in dire need of replacement and the time was ripe to adopt more modern designs. Nothing had brought this fact home more conclusively than the appearance of the Fairey Fox light bomber in 1925.

Richard Fairey had been extremely impressed by the performance of the Curtiss CR-3 racers in the Schneider Trophy contest at Cowes in 1923 and had raised cash in order to negotiate the purchase of licences to manufacture the D-12 engine, Reed metal propellers and wing surface radiators. The Fox bomber, designed by Marcel Lobelle and Pandia Ralli, had a similar load and range capability to current RAF types but was developed as a private venture, funded by Fairey. He was in no doubt that it would outperform any current RAF light bomber and hence demonstrate the merits of adopting clean, uncluttered lines to produce a sleek, low drag airframe mated to the D-12 engine and metal Reed propeller. He had high hopes that substantial orders would follow. The flight tests in early January 1925 were spectacularly successful as the Fox proved to be 50mph faster than the latest RAF light bomber, which just happened to be Fairey's own Fawn. Critically, it was also faster than almost all the service fighters.

The Air Ministry response was none too rapid, the speed of the Fox only adding to the perception that fighters would not be able to provide adequate defence, but specification F.9/26 for a Day and Night Fighter was the first, and somewhat tentative, move to address the issue. This invited tenders for a metal-framed Zone Fighter aircraft with twin guns and an air-cooled engine. As there was every prospect for a substantial production contract, the specification generated a lot of interest among the aircraft constructors and several of the prototypes built for assessment were private ventures. While these prototypes were under construction, the Ministry issued specification F.20/27 for an Interceptor Fighter with a top speed greater than that required for the F.9/26 aircraft. Rate of climb was paramount: it must climb to 20,000ft in fewer than 12 minutes and have a top speed at that altitude in excess of 200mph.

Tenders for new bombers were also requested. Specification B.19/27 called for a large twin-engined night bomber with a top speed above 120mph, while single-engined light day bombers to specification B.12/26, issued in response to the arrival of the Fairey Fox, would exceed 160mph. Taken together these specifications provided some indication of the performance RAF fighters might expect to encounter from an attacking bomber force. Strategic planning envisaged that this force would be detected while still some 25 miles distant through direct observation and by the use of an array of large concrete sound mirror listening posts located along the coast. Once again industry took note of the new fighter specification and most companies submitted proposals. Supermarine was not among them, almost alone in ignoring either opportunity despite the preliminary work they had undertaken to draw up several designs to meet naval fighter specification N.21/26 at this time.

The design, building and testing of the numerous aircraft prototypes built to F.9/26 was expected to take around three years but this proved to be hard to meet and several contenders failed to be ready in time for the official tests. F.9/26 was won, eventually, by the fighter tendered by Bristol and they were awarded a production contract in 1928, but only after a partial redesign of their aircraft. This new fighter, named the Bulldog, entered service in 1929. Several of the unsuccessful prototypes were modified subsequently to meet the requirements of F.20/27, an indication of the large overlap between the two types of fighter.

F.20/27, for a higher performance machine, proved to be more demanding, as was expected, and was muddled by the partially overlapping requirements for a multi-gun fighter under F.10/27 and for a fighter mounting a 37mm COW cannon under specification F.29/27. It was further confused by the requirement for the fighter to carry two guns having been issued in error; the original intention had been for four, and by a late revision to allow the aircraft to use either water-cooled or air-cooled engines.

Construction technology was approaching a tipping point and several companies felt sufficiently confident to propose monoplane designs, although almost all had braced rather than cantilever wings which served to limit any significant step forward in performance. The majority of companies, however, followed established practice and came forward with simple evolutions of existing biplane types. This distinctly conservative response from industry resulted in a significant proportion of both monoplane and biplane aircraft types failing to meet the speed requirement of the specification, although there were several interesting innovations developed further over the coming years. Testing contenders commenced in 1929 and the Hawker Hornet, a private venture powered by a water-cooled Rolls-Royce F V12 engine, was deemed to be the winner. A modified version of this aircraft, renamed Fury, was ordered and entered service in 1931.

F.7/30 AND THE QUEST FOR INNOVATION

Discussions in the Air Ministry commenced in 1929 to formulate the specification for a Zone Fighter to replace the Bristol Bulldog, which was about to enter service. They were all too aware of the rise of a new generation of fast, monoplane, commercial aircraft then in production or under development, most notably in the USA. Aircraft such as the Lockheed Vega V, carrying six passengers and powered by a 450hp air-cooled radial, had a top speed of 165mph and it was almost inevitable that military derivatives with more powerful engines would be developed soon. Sports touring aircraft, even some larger twin-seat types, began to appear with cantilever monoplane wings and retractable undercarriage, and they often had top speeds above those of service fighters. Furthermore, after a decade of peace, tension in international relations was on the rise and first signs of an acceleration in global rearmament began to show; first in France, which

had been determined to strengthen its air defences for several years, and then in Italy under Mussolini's fascist regime. In Germany the restrictions of the Treaty of Versailles were causing problems and would soon be challenged and, in the Far East, Japan was becoming increasingly martial. Consequently, and as is common in these situations, a degree of paranoia began to emerge as people in many countries chose to believe that their neighbours and rivals had developed a lead over them. Even in the US questions were being asked and a Senate enquiry was set up in 1930 to examine the contention that they had dropped behind the European nations in regard to the development of high-speed fighters. Britain was certainly far from immune from such concerns and the need to provide some innovative thinking to the design of fighters appeared obvious. What was not obvious was how to encapsulate this within an official specification while at the same time allowing sufficient freedom of movement for the aircraft designers.

High on the list of priorities from the RAF was the provision of an enhanced field of view for the pilot as the recent annual air exercises had shown that the restricted view from service fighters hampered their engagement with the attacking bomber forces. This initiated thoughts about resurrecting the concept of pusher aircraft of the type that had formed the backbone of the RFC fighter force through much of the war, and also the merits of monoplanes. The twin requirements for a low landing speed (for safe operation at night) and a high top speed worked to pull aircraft designs in opposite directions but the Air Ministry was unwilling to include a firm requirement for flaps or slats in the specification, preferring to leave the decision whether to adopt either or both to the designers. In an attempt to square the circle they came to an agreement to allow the landing speed to rise and top speed to fall from those specified in the early draft of the next specification. There was also indecision regarding which engine type should, or could, be favoured. Although the Hawker Hornet, and the Fairey Firefly before it, had demonstrated the apparent superiority of water-cooled V12 engines over air-cooled radials, in recent evaluations the advantage was not so great and the newer generation of radial engines in drag-reducing Townend rings or cowls were already showing signs of being their equal in terms of performance and superior in terms of installed weight. Nevertheless, there was a lot of interest in recent experiments undertaken by Rolls-Royce to develop the technology of evaporative cooling, as described in a previous chapter, and in some quarters there was a desire to include the requirement for such an engine in the specification. One thing on which there was general agreement was the need to increase the firepower of future fighters in order to maximise the impact of a brief, high-speed attack on the bombers. The provision of four guns had been intended for F.20/27 but had been omitted due to an administrative error. It was certain to be included in the new specification. The standard Vickers machine gun for use in aircraft was notorious for frequent jamming and, as a consequence, it was always mounted with its breeches within reach of the pilot so that blockages could be cleared. While this was possible for twin guns, although not always easy, it would not be so for four, and there was the added complication that all four would need to be fitted with synchronisation gear to fire through the propeller disc, which reduced the total fire rate of the guns. Once again a pusher design looked to be a possible solution. One final consideration was how to encourage tenders for innovative designs rather than for more conventional types. No satisfactory formula could be agreed and this would not be included in the final draft, although in conversation with the various companies the Air Ministry definitely stressed their preference for new thinking.

These internal discussions and external consultations took place over a period of nearly eighteen months and so it was only in October 1931 that specification F.7/30 was issued to the aircraft constructors. Although the full text ensured that all options remained open, the document started: 'The aircraft is to fulfil the duties of "Single Seater Fighter" for day and night flying. A satisfactory fighting view is essential and designers should consider the advantages offered in this respect by low-wing monoplane or pusher.'

Despite the release of this specification the situation regarding the role of the RAF's fighter aircraft remained fluid. In the summer of 1931 the RAF held their annual air exercises and the intercept rate achieved by the squadrons of Bristol Bulldogs and Hawker Furys was disappointingly low. The speed differential over the fastest single-engined bombers, coupled with the limited time available to reach altitude as a result of inadequate detection-at-distance systems, combined to rekindle deep doubts within the Air Staff as to whether fighters could ever provide a meaningful level of defence. As a result, serious consideration was given to diverting a greater percentage of funds to build more bombers with which to strike back at an enemy, a policy akin to the mutually assured destruction philosophy of the Cold War era. For those who remained advocates of the fighter, and there were several in high positions, the hope was that the companies tendering to F.7/30 would read beyond the simple details of the text and come up with radical new ideas. On paper the requirements did not appear to be too daunting: a top speed in excess of 195mph at 15,000ft, a landing speed no higher than 60mph and a good field of view for the pilot.

Supermarine received a copy of the specification on 5 November 1931 but prior to this Mitchell had initiated preliminary work on new fighter designs.

McLean had agreed some time before that both Vickers and Supermarine would prepare submissions to F.7/30, Vickers through development of an existing aircraft and Supermarine with a fresh design.

Vickers had built a prototype cantilever monoplane fighter, the Type 151 Jockey, to specification F.20/27, and this had flown for the first time in 1930, too late to participate. The aircraft, developed by a team led by Joe Brewsher under the guidance of Rex Pierson, was rather simple and angular in form and constructed entirely of metal, with Duralumin frames and non-load-bearing corrugated skinning using a system invented by the French aircraft engineer Michel Wibault, for which Vickers had acquired the patent rights through a partnership deal. Vickers had considerable experience of this type of construction, firstly through production of Wibault Scouts under licence and subsequently with the Vireo fighter prototype built to specification 17/25 for an experimental carrier fighter. The Jockey was powered by a moderately supercharged 480hp Bristol Mercury IIA, an engine that had experienced teething troubles during development but which was now beginning to show considerable promise. Unfortunately, early testing of the Jockey highlighted severe vibration of the rear fuselage due to a structural weakness, and a somewhat disappointing top speed. These problems were addressed by a degree of structural redesign and by fitting spats to the wheels and a Townend ring around the engine, which had been replaced by a Bristol Jupiter VIIF giving 530hp. In this form, in January 1931, the Jockey achieved 218mph at 10,000ft. However, during further development trials in 1932 aimed at preparing the aircraft to meet the F.7/30 requirement it was destroyed after entering a flat spin.

Mitchell would have been fully aware of the design, construction and testing of the Jockey through his position on the joint design committee of Supermarine and Vickers and, as a result of all the research and development work he had undertaken on the Schneider racers, he was convinced, in all probability, that he could devise something better. Vickers, after all, were to base their submission on a design dating from 1928 and using construction techniques that even predated that. As Supermarine had never before designed and developed a land fighter Mitchell and his team were unencumbered by preconceived ideas, prior construction practices or pressure to use existing aircraft as a basis. Through their work on the Schneider racers and, to a lesser extent, flying boats they were now competent in metal wing structures and stressed skin metal construction.

It is now very clear that Mitchell's intention from the start was to tender a monoplane design, but in the very early phase of the project he hedged his bets and drew up a biplane in parallel as a back-up and reference point for comparison with the monoplane. Mitchell's second decision was to adopt the evaporatively cooled Rolls-Royce Goshawk, still called the Kestrel 'S' at this time, for both designs. He had formed a close association with the Rolls-Royce experimental department through their joint work on the Schneider Trophy racing aircraft for the 1929 and 1931 contests and obviously had a high regard for their capability. Their racing 'R' engines had never faltered in his aircraft, delivered more power than initially planned and in all respects had set a standard the competition had failed to match. When the company introduced the concept of evaporative cooling for their engines, Mitchell was most enthusiastic to incorporate this into his aircraft designs as it offered the potential for a significant reduction in both weight and drag. Hence his patents for wing leading edge condensers. Furthermore, the first experimental versions of the Kestrel 'S' had recently commenced flight testing in a Southampton II and would provide useful data. Therefore it was entirely natural that he should choose to power his fighter with one of these engines even had the Air Ministry not dropped large hints that they, too, favoured them.

The two aircraft designs started life within Type 178 as 178 10 but were split subsequently into 178 14 and 178 12 respectively. The earliest surviving layout drawings date from February 1931, after some preliminary wind tunnel tests had taken place in the Vickers' facilities and several months prior to the official release of specification F.7/30.

Mitchell's biplane fighter appears to have been conceived as a fairly conventional aircraft for the period and broadly comparable to the Hawker Fury in layout. The fuselage was constructed around cross-braced metal longerons and formers and it is believed that it was intended to be skinned, at least in part, with non-load-bearing metal panels. The cockpit was positioned quite high in order to provide the pilot with a few degrees of downward view over the nose. Two Vickers machine guns were mounted above the engine with their breeches in the cockpit. The exhaust pipes from the engine were carried back to behind the cockpit opening in order to avoid problems with glare during night operations. The metal-framed wings were of unequal span, heavily staggered and braced in single bays with 'N' struts. The leading edges of all four planes incorporated the steam condensers and hence were metal skinned while the remainder were fabric covered. The top wing was positioned ahead of the cockpit and just above the pilot's eye line in order to minimise the blind zone, while the lower wing was directly below the cockpit with trailing edge cut-outs so that the view forward and downward was reasonably unobstructed. The top wing was fitted with leading edge slats and ailerons while the lower wing housed two more Vickers guns

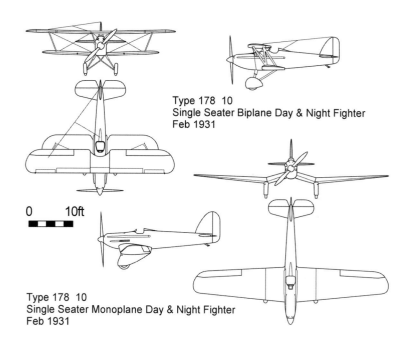

Type 178 10
Single Seater Biplane Day & Night Fighter
Feb 1931

0   10ft

Type 178 10
Single Seater Monoplane Day & Night Fighter
Feb 1931

firing outside the propeller disc, although considering the thin wing it appears doubtful that they would have fitted without substantial blisters or fairings. There was also a semi-recessed bomb rack for four 20lb bombs provided under the right wing. The undercarriage wheels had independent suspension, brakes that could be operated differentially in order to facilitate ground handling, and were enclosed in spats. In many respects this aircraft paralleled work under way at Hawker on developed versions of the Fury that would lead to their own submission to F.7/30. As Mitchell did not regard this project as his primary design it may well have been considered simply as a benchmark against which to compare the monoplane fighter.

Mitchell's monoplane Type 178 10 fighter pre-dates the issue of specification F.7/30 by at least eight months, and maybe by more than a year if the time required to test alternative layouts in the wind tunnel is taken into consideration. The first of the 1/16-scale wind tunnel models was for a low-wing cantilever monoplane with minimal dihedral, a standard tube matrix radiator below the fuselage and a conventional fixed undercarriage. This was compared with an alternative in which the wing was cranked into an inverted gull-wing shape with the wing leading edge as the steam condenser. This model also had a fixed undercarriage with the wheels and struts enclosed in large trouser fairings, which also enclosed two of the four guns. The adoption of a cranked wing with moderate dihedral on the outboard part had three benefits: it provided a natural gravity flow for the condensed coolant water down the wing to a sump located in each wheel fairing, it allowed the length of the undercarriage struts to be kept short, which reduced drag, and it provided a better forward and downward view from the cockpit, a key requirement of the specification. The fighter was to be all metal with a stressed skin rear fuselage while the wings would be constructed around a single spar and leading edge torsion box as had been conceived originally for the Type 179 Giant. This would also form the steam condenser for the engine, as in Mitchell's patent. To the rear of the spar the wing was fabric covered. Layout drawings for this project were finalised in February 1931.

Mitchell and his team were mindful of the possible adverse effect of the airflow behind the wing kink and undercarriage trouser spats on the stability of the fighter and spent much time assessing the impact of varying wing dihedral angles and incidence. However, no particular problems were noted and they were confident to proceed with finalisation of the design, which was submitted to the Air Ministry on 20 February 1932. Mitchell's design was considered to be by far the best of the submissions received, which tends to suggest either remarkable foresight by Mitchell as to the detailed requirements to be included in the specification or a fair degree of discussion between the company and the Ministry prior to the final draft.

However, it should be noted that the design did not conform completely to the specification. The landing speed exceeded the stipulated maximum by 5mph as neither flaps nor slats had been included. In the submission document it was stated that slats could be fitted if required but this could actually have proven problematic as it would have compromised part of the leading edge condenser. On the other hand, the aircraft was potentially the fastest of those tendered to the Ministry by a wide margin with an estimated top speed of 249mph, more than 50mph above the specified minimum and some 40mph faster than the Hawker Fury fighter that had just entered service. The time to climb to 15,000ft and the service ceiling also surpassed Air Ministry minimum requirements. The Air Ministry awarded a contract for a single prototype on 2 August 1932, by which date the fighter project had progressed further and had been allocated a new type number; Type 224. Mitchell was informed that he had to take steps to reduce the landing speed as, despite the wide track of the undercarriage, there was still concern that the aircraft could prove difficult to land safely at night. As a consequence, the span, and hence wing area, was increased, which raised the weight marginally and knocked 5mph off the top speed.

Throughout the autumn and winter months Mitchell worked feverishly to finalise the detailed design, no small task as a great many changes were made to all the flying surfaces and controls. In January 1933 the Type 224 was redrawn completely. The rudder and elevators were now fitted with horn balances and the wings had been swept back, from 3.5 to 5.5 degrees on the leading edge, and the trailing edges were now straight. In addition, the dihedral of the outer wing had increased from 4 to 6.5 degrees, with an associated 1.5 degree increase in the anhedral of the inner portion. Eventually the design was signed off by Mitchell and construction commenced. However, in mid-year the wing was revised again and the long span, narrow chord ailerons that had been a feature from the beginning were replaced by 'barn door' wide chord type. The reason for this late change does not appear to have been recorded.

Events now took a grim turn for Mitchell. In August 1933 he was preparing to take his annual holiday but first, as he had been experiencing abdominal pains, he arranged to have a medical check-up. His doctor was concerned and referred him to a specialist, who diagnosed rectal cancer and scheduled an immediate operation. Mitchell underwent an emergency colostomy. The period of convalescence that followed kept him away from the design office until the early spring of 1934 but he maintained routine contact from home and continued to oversee the Type 224 project. It is from this point forward that Mitchell's character becomes readily apparent, not just in his ability to continue to fulfil his role as Chief Engineer and Designer with no decline in effort or control, but also the way in which it highlights the astute choices he had made over the years as he selected staff to work within his department. Both the Drawing and Technical Offices were staffed by talented individuals working as a team and led by two thoroughly competent and experienced men, and this would reap dividends over the coming years.

The assembly of the Type 224 was complete by the end of November 1933, several weeks behind schedule, but it lacked its engine as Rolls-Royce struggled to complete the mandatory 100-hour acceptance run on the test bench. However, this was passed satisfactorily within a few days and it duly arrived on 8 December. Supermarine set about installation of the Goshawk and subsequent testing of the intricate cooling systems. Mitchell also decided to install small mid-chord flaps inboard of the ailerons at this time to supplement, or perhaps to replace, the broad brake flap positioned beneath the cockpit. The Air Ministry were not at all happy with the continuing delays and it was not until 10 February 1934 that the work was completed and the aircraft could be prepared for its first flight from Eastleigh aerodrome, where Supermarine had rented facilities. However, there were yet more delays as a consequence of problems with the steam condenser system, which prevented the attempt, and it was a further ten days before everything was ready again and the first flight finally took place in the hands of 'Mutt' Summers.

It would appear that Mitchell was already dissatisfied with the aircraft even before the first flight as he had instigated design work in the office on a series of upgrades. In the meantime, flight testing was under way

↓ The Type 224 proved to be a problematic aircraft, largely due to insurmountable problems with the engine cooling system, and its performance failed to live up to specification.

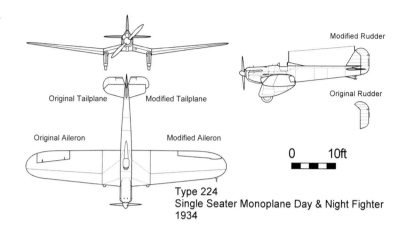

Modified Rudder

Original Rudder

Original Tailplane   Modified Tailplane

Original Aileron   Modified Aileron

0   10ft

Type 224
Single Seater Monoplane Day & Night Fighter
1934

and problems were mounting with the Rolls-Royce Goshawk engine and Mitchell's steam condenser system. Overheating was a perpetual problem and often curtailed flights. As the water sump was located below the level of the header tank the condensed water had to be pumped back up and the consequent drop in pressure at the suction end often caused the hot water to boil spontaneously, creating vapour locks within the system. This problem was not unique to the Type 224, however, as it was proving troublesome on all other Goshawk-powered aircraft with similar cooling system geometry. It was found that performance was well down on the pre-flight estimates. Top speed was 230mph and it took 9½ minutes to climb to 15,000ft, due mainly to the poor performance of the engine and cooling system, which prevented the use of full throttle. In May a series of remedial measures were suggested to address these issues. This amounted to a long and rather costly list of possible modifications to the prototype, which the Air Ministry rejected. Meanwhile, Mitchell and his team essentially started again on the design of a better fighter.

The Type 224 was a curious blend of standard and advanced features; as Supermarine stated in their submission document, 'Although different in type from existing experimental aircraft, it cannot be considered very experimental', so certainly not what the Air Ministry had hoped to hear from the designer of the current holder of the air speed record. Mindful of the specification's requirement for ease of construction and maintenance, the team's design for the fuselage was unnecessarily basic, almost crude. It was flat sided and also flat bottomed through the mid-section. The wing had been built larger than originally designed in order to meet the demanding low speed landing criteria of the specification without the need to add flaps, and this in turn required a longer rear fuselage to restore stability. The tail surfaces were relatively large in order to counter the side area of the trousered undercarriage. On the other hand, the wing structure was quite sophisticated, matching a symmetrical section NACA 0018 aerofoil for the anhedral inner part with modified RAF 34 section for the outer portion. Although it is often described as a thick wing, it was not unreasonably so. NACA 0018 has a thickness/chord ratio of 18 per cent while RAF 34 is 12.6 per cent, although this was modified to blend with the NACA profile at the gull-wing kink and then reducing to around 9 per cent the tip. This was quite reasonable for a cantilever fabric-covered wing at this time and not dissimilar to the Hawker Hurricane built a few years later. It also employed washout, that is to say variation of incidence with span, in order to ensure that the inner wing would stall before the outer and hence minimise the risk of a spin developing due to loss of aileron control. The anhedral portion of the wing housed the fuel and oil tanks, the oil cooler, ammunition boxes for the fuselage guns and the intakes for the supercharger.

There is no doubt that the Type 224 lacked aesthetic appeal, something it shared with several fighter prototypes of its era, and its performance certainly failed to match pre-flight estimates. Nevertheless, it outperformed most other F.7/30 contenders, engine cooling aside, was not an inherently bad aircraft and handled well. It was, at worst, a disappointment.

It has to be said that a significant number of Mitchell's designs produced through what could be described as the 'austerity years', 1929 to 1933 – the Southampton X, Air Yacht, possibly the Type 179 Giant, and now the Type 224 – had all proven unsuccessful for much the same reasons: a lack of design sophistication, excess structural weight and poor pre-flight estimates of performance. Some of this may well be attributed to pressure from Vickers to cut costs and some to the analysis of results from models tested in Vickers' wind tunnel having proven to be over-optimistic. Mitchell is reported to have lost faith in the use of wind tunnels at around this time despite the NPL and RAE wind tunnel research having provided sterling support for the design of his Schneider racers. Perhaps the restricted size of the Vickers facilities, compared to the far larger wind tunnel at the NPL, was inadequate. Whatever the reason, Mitchell had struggled to emulate his earlier work with the Southampton, S.5 and S.6, and was in serious need of a success.

What of the other F.7/30 contenders? They, too, had been much delayed. In addition to the Type 224, the Air Ministry had selected two others to receive funds to build a prototype, one each from Westland and Blackburn and both powered by the Rolls-Royce Goshawk. Three other companies built prototypes as private ventures: Bristol, Gloster and Hawker.

Westland had pursued the fighter market with enthusiasm, and a measure of innovation, since 1927. The strut-braced parasol monoplane Wizard II, and two low-wing, wire-braced monoplanes, the Interceptor to F.20/27 and the COW gun fighter to F.29/27, had all proven to be good performers but no better than the 'safer' biplanes against which they competed and had failed to secure production contracts. The company were also experimenting with tailless swept wing monoplane designs by Geoffrey Hill that were beginning to show promise. Westland's submission to F.7/30, the P.4, had started life as a high-wing, strut-braced monoplane but this had had to be reconfigured as a biplane in order to meet the landing speed criteria. The Goshawk engine was mounted amidships in a deep fuselage that filled the gap between the wings and drove the nose propeller via a long shaft. The engine's steam condenser sat below the fuselage. The cockpit was positioned just ahead of the top wing leading edge to provide exceptional forward and upward view, and a good view down over the nose. The view to the rear was improved by the top wing having a gull-wing inner section. The fixed wheel, independently sprung undercarriage was fitted with spats. For initial testing, in early 1934, the aircraft had an open cockpit but this was later enclosed and the fin and rudder were both increased in area. The P.4 was apparently pleasant to fly but performance was distinctly lacklustre. Reported top speed was just 185mph, which was well below the F.7/30 minimum requirement and also that of the Hawker Fury, and the location of the engine just ahead of the fabric-covered rear fuselage had a tendency to cause the fabric to catch fire.

Blackburn had limited experience building fighter aircraft as they, like Supermarine, had chosen not to tender to earlier Air Ministry specifications. They had, however, designed and built a number of light fighters targeting overseas markets in countries seeking a cheap, simple machine. The Lincock series were excellent machines with fine flying characteristics. For F.7/30 they tendered the F.3, an all-metal biplane with a monocoque fuselage. The upper wing was mounted in the mid-fuselage position with the Goshawk's radiator housed in a fairing beneath the fuselage that filled the gap down to the lower wing. The wide track fixed undercarriage was attached close under the lower wing so that ground clearance of the trailing edge was minimal. The cockpit sat over the top wing providing excellent visibility in all directions other than downwards to the sides. Taxiing trials commenced in late July 1934 and were bedevilled by the inevitable cooling problems and by instability as a result of the high centre of gravity. Tests continued through until early September, when it was noticed that the rough treatment had caused stress cracks to appear in the metal fuselage and it was never flown. With an estimated top speed of only 190mph it, too, would have failed to meet the criteria of F.7/30 anyway, and hence it was scrapped.

Bristol built two prototypes as private ventures. The Type 123 was powered by a Goshawk and resembled a Hawker Fury on steroids. The fuselage was very deep at the position of the open cockpit in order to provide a good downward view over the nose, and the pilot's eyeline was just a little below the top wing, which, due to the heavy stagger, was some distance ahead. The steam cooler was located below the fuselage and filled the gap to the lower wing. The wheels of the fixed undercarriage were fitted with large spats. There were the inevitable severe cooling problems, although the Type 123 proved to have a good top speed of around 235mph. Unfortunately, it was found to be seriously unstable laterally due to the short rear fuselage and small tail surfaces and the issue proved to be insurmountable.

The second Bristol prototype was the Type 133, a low-wing cantilever monoplane with a retractable undercarriage. It was powered by Bristol's latest version of the Mercury air-cooled radial enclosed in a long cowl. This aircraft was built entirely of metal with a stressed skin constructed of Alclad plates. The low-mounted wing featured an inverted gull-wing shape both to enhance downward visibility for the pilot and to shorten the legs for the undercarriage, which swung rearwards into small fairings from which part of the wheel protruded when retracted. The ailerons could be drooped to act as flaps. Flight testing commenced in mid-1934, during which modifications were made to the control surfaces and engine cowl, and the cockpit was fitted with an enclosed canopy. In this form top speed is said to have been measured at an impressive 260mph. The aircraft looked to be a serious contender to attract an order but unfortunately it was destroyed prior to the start of official trials after entering a flat spin.

Hawker had been experimenting with the Fury fighter in order to improve performance, first with a modified Fury II, later known as the Super or Intermediate Fury, and in mid-1933 with a further modified airframe called the High Speed Fury. From this work the company developed a private venture entry for the F.7/30 contest, the PV3, which was, in essence, a beefed up Fury fitted with new wings and a Goshawk engine. The steam cooler formed the centre section of the top wing, above the engine, and thus avoided many of the problems encountered by the other Goshawk-powered prototypes. Unlike the other contenders, all four Vickers guns were mounted in the nose and fired through the propeller disc. The aircraft flew in mid-1934 but was not submitted for competitive trials as by this point Hawker's Designer, Sydney Camm, was deep in discussions with the Air Ministry and working on a more potent monoplane fighter project.

The final F.7/30 entry of note, submitted late, came from Gloster. The Gloster fighter had started life as the SS.18, an experimental six-gun prototype built to specification F.20/27. It lost out to the Hawker Fury, in part because its Bristol Mercury engine was not yet fully developed, but the airframe had then been modified and tested with various alternative air-cooled engines before it was redesignated SS.19 and through a series of further improvements became the prototype for the Gauntlet fighter. A production order for the Gauntlet was awarded in 1933 and the fighter entered service in 1935. For F.7/30 Gloster submitted an upgraded Gauntlet, the SS.37, with new single-bay wings, Dowty internally sprung wheels on cantilever undercarriage struts and a new version of the Mercury developing 800hp. After early testing it was fitted with a cockpit canopy. In this form it had a top speed of 253mph.

It was obvious that the requirements of F.7/30 had proven unexpectedly demanding and none of the designers, both seasoned fighter designers and newcomers to the market, had felt sufficiently confident to produce a truly effective, as opposed to innovative, fighter to meet them, with the probable exception of Bristol's Type 133. The heavy emphasis on the need to provide a good field of view for the pilot and for a low landing speed had the unfortunate effect of producing somewhat freakish aircraft with indifferent performance, although looking back it is a little difficult to understand why this should have been so. Not surprisingly, none of the aircraft was deemed worthy of production and hence the Gloster SS.37, named Gladiator, was ordered as a stopgap.

Britain was not alone in struggling to define the best way forward in fighter design as technology advanced rapidly, and other nations produced a wide variety of single-seat prototypes and production aircraft. Some designers made an early commitment to cantilever monoplanes while others pushed the development of biplanes to the limit.

Among those who took the former route was Émile Dewoitine. Dewoitine, like Mitchell, had made his moves into advanced monoplane design with a seaplane racer to compete for the Schneider Trophy. His HD410 was of all-metal construction with thin profile finely tapered wings and graceful elliptical tips. It never flew as the Lorraine 'Radium' engine was completely unreliable and far below design power. While Dewoitine was working on this racer he was also developing a new monoplane fighter with which it shared several design features. The D500 was analogous to the Type 224 as it was a low-wing cantilever monoplane with a fixed spatted undercarriage and open cockpit. It was powered by a 690hp Hispano-Suiza XBrs V-12 water-cooled engine and armed with twin machine guns. It had a top speed of around 250mph and entered service with the Armée de l'Air in 1935.

Taking the alternative option was Marcel Lobelle at Fairey. In response to a requirement of the Belgian Air Force, he produced the Fantôme in 1934, perhaps the ultimate evolution of the biplane in the 1930s. The Fantôme was of conventional metal and fabric covered construction with single-bay wings with elliptical tips, a fixed, spatted undercarriage and an open cockpit. It was powered by a 925hp Hispano-Suiza 12Ycrs water-cooled V12 engine, which gave it a top speed of 270mph. There was a Hispano cannon firing through the hub and two machine guns were mounted in the fuselage. No production orders were received.

A review of foreign fighters in *Flight* magazine in 1935 listed both high and low-wing braced monoplanes, some featuring cranked wings as on the Type 224, and some with retractable undercarriages. Cantilever monoplanes, however, remained rare. There were several more standard style biplanes, although some of these, too, featured a retractable undercarriage. Both air-cooled and water-cooled engines were used and neither type appeared to have a clear edge. Top speeds of around 250mph were quoted for a few of the better aircraft, although time would show that these claims were generally a little on the optimistic side. Armament rarely exceeded four rifle-calibre machine guns but some had experimented with the installation of a single small-calibre cannon. They were a mixture of worthy and indifferent, and none was destined to become a classic. Technology needed to progress just that little further before ground-breaking fighter designs would emerge.

TYPE 300

Mitchell's team's thorough reworking of the Type 224 was given a new project number, Type 300. The initiation of this new design work can be dated to 1 March 1934, less than two weeks after the first flight of the Type 224, when Alan Clifton, head of the Technical Office, sent a series of questions to Roger Dickson, who was working as an engineer on the project. Some quick 'back of the envelope' calculations showed the weight of the fighter was split fairly evenly between engine, structure and payload, of which only the structure could be revised. Assuming the maximum saving in structural weight that could be achieved was 10 per cent, this resulted in only a 3.7 per cent reduction for the whole aircraft, which was too little to make any material improvement in performance. This indicated that addressing the overall aerodynamic cleanliness of the aircraft was the more viable way forward. Clifton asked by how much the wing area could be reduced if they were to use a higher lift NACA 2412 aerofoil section instead of RAF 34? Would there be room in this new wing for the fuel tanks and a new retractable undercarriage? By how much would the wing structure weight increase if torsional stiffness were to be maintained? And how much additional coolant water would be required as a consequence of the reduction in area of the steam coolers? Although it is not stated in this correspondence, it is implied that the gull-wing was to be eliminated and it is known that the existing wind tunnel model was modified quickly with a straight wing attached to a deepened fuselage. On receiving the answers from Dickson, which were all encouraging, Clifton gave instruction to start redesign work, allocating tasks to the key members of the team. Interesting features at this very early stage were the retractable undercarriage, the absence of flaps, the removal of corrugations from the steam cooler and the assumption that 50 per cent of the water could be allowed to boil away during flight. In addition, the wing guns were to be mounted beneath the main spar, so they were external to the wing. The question of whether the wing to the rear of the spar would be fabric or metal covered remained undecided. As part of Dickson's work he designed an undercarriage retraction mechanism that rotated the wheel and leg by 90 degrees to facilitate stowage within the wing. This system was patented jointly in the name of the company and Dickson but did not actually go on to feature in the design of the aircraft. After reviewing this initial analysis Mitchell decided to split the forward effort into two parts: a developed version of the Type 224 and a completely new design, both under Type 300.

The first approach addressed the principal shortcomings of the Type 224 and was submitted to the Air Ministry in July 1934, with cost estimates, while the aircraft itself was still undergoing company trials. This comprised a series of relatively quick modifications that could be applied directly to the prototype itself. These were an expansion of the modifications offered in May, although only the fuselage would actually be reused unchanged. The large-span cranked wing was to be discarded and replaced by a simple straight-tapered design with 4.5 degrees of dihedral and 13.5 per cent less area. Presumably this involved reusing the main components from the original outer wings. In order to maintain an acceptably low landing speed the wing was to be fitted with trailing edge split flaps inboard of the ailerons. A new retractable undercarriage was designed with the wheels retracting outwards, and the outboard guns were enclosed fully within the wings. Two schemes were considered, one with the wing guns firing through the propeller disc and the other with them placed further out to clear the disc. On the former it was necessary for the undercarriage to be mounted closer to the fuselage so the fuel tanks had to be placed mid-span beyond the wheel bays. On the latter the undercarriage was moved outboard slightly and the fuel tanks, triangular in shape, sat between the undercarriage struts. With a smaller wing and no fixed undercarriage it was now possible to reduce the size of the tail surfaces. The oil tank and cooler, previously in the anhedral inner wing, were relocated to sit below the engine, in a similar manner to the combined tank and cooler fitted on some of the Schneider racers such as the Gloster Napier IV. The sump for the condensed coolant water, a small V-shaped tank, was moved under the fuselage where it was exposed to the slipstream. The cockpit was fully enclosed beneath a tight-fitting canopy. The top speed of this reconfigured aircraft was estimated at 265mph and the design was, in almost every way, the type of aircraft that the Air Ministry

would have liked to have seen Supermarine tender to F.7/30 back at the beginning of 1932. Dowding commented as such in an internal memo. But now, more than two years later, they were not interested in the additional cost and delay and pressed Supermarine to deliver the Type 224 prototype unmodified for official testing. However, they did express interest in Mitchell continuing work on more advanced designs and the company was encouraged to explore alternative concepts. It is a measure of how rapid was the advancement in technology that an aircraft that would have been received with open arms in 1932 was considered inadequate in 1934. The team worked on.

While the F.7/30 prototypes were under construction, the Air Ministry was deep in the process of planning specifications for fighters of significantly more advanced design. It had become increasingly clear that prioritising climb rate had such a detrimental effect on top speed that the aircraft would be hard pressed to pursue and attack incoming bomber forces. The requirement for slow landing speeds, for safe operation at night, also had an impact on top speed. Opinion began to swing around to set maximum speed at altitude as the priority and to couple this with a greater number of guns in order to maximise hitting power during the brief attack runs that could be expected. The pace of development of larger aircraft could, perhaps, be seen best from the design and performance of commercial aircraft. Cantilever monoplane aircraft with retractable undercarriages and variable pitch metal propellers were becoming more common, especially in the US, with aircraft such as the Boeing 247 and Douglas DC-1 both capable of carrying ten or more passengers at speeds of up to 200mph. Both companies were working on military counterparts. On the Continent, Heinkel introduced the He 70 in 1933, ostensibly a six-passenger high-speed commercial airliner but it was obvious to most eyes it was a test prototype for a single-engined high-speed bomber. This aircraft will be reviewed later as it would prove to be rather notorious. Nowhere was the march of progress more apparent than in the line-up of aircraft entered for the 1934 MacRobertson air race from Britain to Australia. Of the thirty-two aircraft preparing to depart, no fewer than twenty-seven were monoplanes. Of these, twenty were unbraced cantilever and seventeen had retractable undercarriages. Four of the five biplanes were British.

The Air Ministry understood well enough that F.7/30 had failed to achieve the breakthrough in design and performance that had been hoped for as a consequence of inappropriately prioritised requirements coupled with tentative designs from the aircraft industry. Both sides had learned valuable lessons and on that basis the whole exercise has to be judged as somewhat successful in the way that it highlighted these shortcomings and focussed attention on the key role for future fighters. The 'ten year rule', central to military planning since the end of the war had been quietly dropped as a result of the growing belligerence of Germany after Hitler grasped power in January 1933, the growth of military forces throughout the world and the anticipated collapse of the Conference for the Reduction and Limitation of Armaments in Geneva, which all served to raise tension. In combination these concerns triggered a series of expansion plans for the British armed forces, and in particular for the RAF, that in the early phase could be met by orders for the interim Gauntlet and Gladiator fighters but which required something far more potent as soon as possible. The prospect of high-speed light bombers approaching London at speeds of 250mph, or higher, made it all too obvious that a radical rethink was required, both in terms of RAF tactics and of aircraft constructors' designs. The Air Ministry addressed the challenge on two fronts, firstly by accelerating the issue of specifications for the next generation of Zone and Interceptor Fighters, and secondly by tackling the knotty issue of how to catalyse a breakthrough in fighter design, possibly via a specification for either a specialised high-speed research aircraft or an experimental fighter. As a first move, specification F.5/34, although slightly delayed and issued to industry on 16 November 1934, called for an Interceptor Fighter to replace the Hawker Fury that required a top speed in excess of 275mph at 15,000ft, six or eight guns, an enclosed cockpit and retractable undercarriage. Six companies tendered designs but it was passed over by Supermarine as they were engaged in final negotiations with the Air Ministry regarding the next iteration of the Type 300, as we will see.

In mid-1933 Sydney Camm at Hawker Engineering had sketched out a proposal for a monoplane derivative of the Fury as the next progression in the High Speed Fury and PV3 programme. He had shown his ideas to representatives of the Air Ministry in early 1934 and they expressed an interest in funding the construction of a prototype for high-speed research. However, Hawker, mindful of the potential for lucrative production contracts, would not proceed unless this aircraft was to be considered as an experimental fighter. Mitchell's work on the Type 300 in mid-1934 mirrored Camm's approach in many respects and the Air Ministry viewed his design in much the same light. Both projects were then developed under the umbrella of the high-speed research programme as experimental fighters, quite separate from the mainstream specifications headed by the Air Staff. The key officials in the Air Ministry behind the programme were the Air Member for Supply and Research, Dowding, the Director for Technical Development, Cave-Brown-Cave, and his deputy, Buchanan. The last two

had had close association with Supermarine previously, Cave-Brown-Cave through the Far East Flight and Buchanan as a key Air Ministry representative for the Schneider Trophy research.

While development work continued on the troublesome Goshawk, Rolls-Royce had started detailed design of a completely new engine for fighters, designated PV-12, with the aim to achieve 1,000hp for production versions. This was a private venture project initiated after consultation with the main aircraft designers. The Rolls-Royce engineers' first suggestion was that the engine should be an inverted V12, prompted by representatives from the Air Ministry who saw this had the potential to improve the pilot's view over the nose, but after discussion with several aircraft companies this had been effectively vetoed by the designers, who foresaw installation problems. The PV-12 was therefore a conventional V12 in the style of the Kestrel and Goshawk but unrelated to this family of engines, which continued to be developed in parallel. It was of larger capacity, 27 litres compared to 21.25 litres, while retaining much the same external dimensions of the older engines and, like the Goshawk, it was intended to use evaporative cooling. The first engine ran on the test bench in October 1934 and after early teething troubles had been resolved it was passed for flight testing in February 1935. Mitchell and Camm designed their new experimental fighter aircraft around the Goshawk but kept a close eye on the development work under way at Rolls-Royce.

In early September 1934 Supermarine received a request from the Air Ministry for a cost estimate for a prototype experimental fighter 'generally on the lines of your proposals on Drawing 300 00, Sheet 2', as Dowding had supported the proposal to purchase an aircraft. As they had received a cost estimate for the upgraded Type 224 design this suggests that Sheet 2 showed further development of the aircraft, perhaps along the lines suggested in the question and answer memos in May between Clifton and Dickson. However, it seems probable that what they really had in mind was the more advanced reworking of the Type 300 on which Mitchell's team were now concentrating their efforts and which he had discussed with them. This new design was drawn up on 24 September 1934 as Drawing 300 00, Sheet 11 (or possibly 10, the drawing carries both numbers). Although the Type 224 lineage was still discernible, this was a completely new aircraft and shared little with the modified Type 224.

The core of the new project was a wing with a thinner higher lift NACA 2412 series aerofoil, 12 per cent thickness at the root and reducing to around 9 per cent at the tip. The thinner profile made it necessary to strengthen the spar and leading edge torsion box, achieved by increasing the root chord, and hence depth, and the gauge of the plating. The entire wing to the rear of the spar was to be skinned with load-bearing metal and the added weight, compared to fabric, offset by a small reduction in the weight of the internal rib structure. This had the added advantage of providing the smoothest possible surface. The wing plan had considerable taper with the result that the area decreased to 250sq ft, 5sq ft less than on the proposed modified Type 224 and 50sq ft less than the Type 224 itself. Landing speed was kept within acceptable limits by fitting large split rear flaps. The wing had 4.5 degrees of dihedral and retained the twist in incidence that had been carried forward from the Type 224, in this case 2.5 degrees at the root and -0.5 degrees at the tip. A further improvement was the addition of a shaped wing fillet to blend the wing into the fuselage. The wing root intersection with the fuselage was known to be a significant source both of drag and turbulence over the tail surfaces, and the advent of low-wing monoplanes with relatively thick wings at the root, compared to biplanes, had led to studies into ways to alleviate the problem. Wing fillets of various shapes had been tested and described in the aviation literature around this time, for example Heinkel had published a paper in 1933 claiming that fitting wing fillets to the He 70 had resulted in a 20mph increase in the top speed. A revised form of outward-retracting

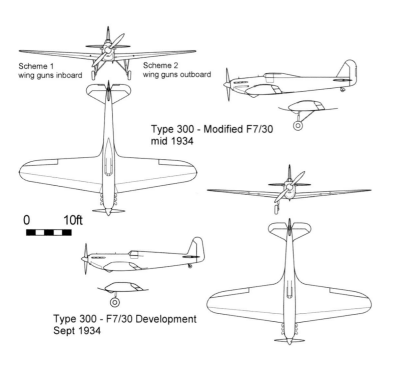

Scheme 1
wing guns inboard

Scheme 2
wing guns outboard

Type 300 - Modified F7/30
mid 1934

0   10ft

Type 300 - F7/30 Development
Sept 1934

undercarriage had been designed and all four Vickers machine guns, with 500 rounds apiece, were mounted outboard of the propeller disc and fully enclosed within the wing. It was no longer possible to fit the fuel tanks within the wing so they were moved into the fuselage between the engine and the cockpit, which required the cockpit to be moved rearwards.

The fuselage showed stylistic similarity to Mitchell's S.6 racers with the cross section reduced down to little more than the minimum necessary to enclose the engine and pilot, the fin constructed as an integral part of the structure and merged into a spine that extended back from the cockpit headrest. The nose retained the chin oil tank and cooler from the modified Type 224 and the engine thrust line was repositioned to lie parallel to the fuselage datum, in the earlier design it had been mounted at an angle of 3 degrees downwards. The tailplane and balanced rear control surfaces were all reduced slightly in size. The pilot's view over the nose was now more restricted as the cockpit was set lower relative to the engine. The top lines of the whole fuselage were essentially straight while the undersides were curved, a characteristic shared with the S.6. However, it would be wholly false to say that the fighter had been developed from the racer, although the story is appealing from the narrative perspective and often repeated, even today. The similarities are stylistic rather than structural.

This new design showed great promise and scope for a major improvement in performance over the Type 224. Consequently it was well received by the Air Ministry, who monitored Mitchell's continuing evolution of the design very closely. After an internal review of progress they issued an official 'Intention to Proceed' letter to Supermarine on 1 December, just three weeks after the Vickers Board had met to approve Mitchell's request to initiate detailed design work. Dowding at the Air Ministry had been in contact with McLean in November to agree on the future direction for the project around the time that Mitchell had received authorisation. Crucially, Dowding had agreed to give Supermarine a free hand to decide whether to proceed with the Goshawk or to switch to the new PV-12, with the air-cooled Napier Dagger held as a third possibility.

Although the latest design was a vast improvement on the Type 224, Mitchell, in characteristic style, stood back and reviewed the project as a whole. No doubt he considered the approach that Camm, a man prone to design aircraft in steady evolutionary steps from its predecessor, was likely to be taking with his project. He was also aware that the Air Staff at the Air Ministry had issued specification F.5/34 for an interceptor fighter to replace the Hawker Fury and that Pierson at Vickers was engaged upon a fighter project to meet this requirement. The Venom was all new but inspired by the Jockey. He may also have heard that Henry Folland at Gloster, a long-time specialist in fighter design and Mitchell's chief British rival when building the Schneider racers, would submit a tender. Spec. F.5/34 stipulated a minimum top speed of 275mph and it was anticipated the winning aircraft would exceed this by a substantial margin. A top speed of around 310mph was considered likely. In view of this level of competition, Mitchell made the bold decision to target 350mph. The Type 300 was updated further, as will be described shortly, and the Air Ministry drew up a brief outline specification, F.37/34 for an Experimental High Speed Single Seater Fighter, around it and a formal contract for one prototype was awarded on 3 January 1935. A similar contract was issued to Hawker for their latest design.

Over the following months, Mitchell set the team to work on an intense programme aimed at bringing the Type 300 to the peak of current structural and aerodynamic knowledge.

In the mid-1930s aircraft companies were in the process of developing fast, low-wing, cantilever monoplane aircraft for both commercial and military use, and competition was keen. Moreover, in the climate of international tension and military build-up, this competition was becoming particularly apparent for the new generation of interceptors and fighters where ultimate performance was critical. However, this was still a time of relative austerity where cost saving was high on the agenda and this constraint pressured many to compromise on their designs, even for experimental aircraft. Hawker and Gloster had both established a line of effective fighters in the 1920s and their respective Chief Designers, Camm and Folland, were prone to evolve rather than create their new aircraft, a process that provided faster and cheaper development, but which tended to restrict the introduction of new ideas. This pressure was felt more intensely by Gloster, who, in the early 1930s, struggled to achieve sales of any of their new aircraft types. Only five prototype aircraft of their own design had been built in the first three years of the decade and none had been awarded production contracts. As a result, their financial strength suffered and in 1934 they had been bought out by Hawker. Their new masters then imposed much of the Hawker system of structural fabrication on them and partially stifled design creativity.

Supermarine were in a different position entirely as they had no back-ground in fighter, or indeed small aircraft, production and hence no shop floor fabrication processes to incorporate or adapt. Although Vickers' management had driven a policy of efficiency and cost reduction into the Woolston works they did not go so far as to insist on the adoption of their construction techniques and Mitchell was able to progress with independent ideas. However, it has to be recognised that Mitchell, like his peers, frequently designed in small incremental steps. His work on small flying boats, in particular, had remained distinctly evolutionary. Mitchell's work on commercial and military projects following the takeover, including the Type 224, were quite separate from Vickers' designs but still remained fairly conservative. He was, after all, a seasoned designer who had learned his craft in a period of tight finances that imposed caution and who was now a director of the company, with all the added responsibility for stability and growth that entailed. He had, however, experienced the luxury of opportunity and funds through his work on the Schneider racing seaplanes. How bold he would be prepared to be in the development of the Type 300 remained to be seen.

Vickers Aviation, strong in the domain of bomber and large transport production, continued their programme to break into the market for monoplane fighters. By tendering to F.5/34 Pierson pursued a parallel course to Mitchell but adopted a less adventurous approach through his choice to continue development of the Vireo-Jockey lineage, albeit with significant improvements and a move away from Wibault construction. Mitchell and Pierson were thus in direct competition and there was to be little, if any, shared technology between the two lines of fighter design by the sibling companies.

It is fairly apparent now that Mitchell resolved that the revised Type 300 aircraft was to be the most advanced fighter yet conceived, as befitted an aircraft funded under the Air Ministry's experimental fighter programme, and every part was scrutinised for opportunities to introduce improvement. Considerations of ease of construction and maintenance were pushed down the priority list in a quest to achieve exceptional performance. Mitchell had chosen his team well and had confidence in their ability. They were a productive mixture of older employees, some of whom had experience of the design and construction of the Schneider racers, and younger members with new ideas and strong academic qualifications. The experience of Alfred Faddy, as Mitchell's nominated team leader, was balanced by the new ideas, academic knowledge and creativity of younger team members, such as Beverley Shenstone.

Shenstone had been employed as an expert in theoretical aerodynamics following a recommendation from Supermarine and Vickers director Air Commodore Sir John Charmier. Before being interviewed by Mitchell, Shenstone had previously sought employment with Hawker and Fairey.

During the two years he had spent working in Germany immediately after obtaining his masters degree, Shenstone had been employed at the Junkers works while in his free time he aided noted aerodynamicist and engineer

Alexander Lippisch in the construction of gliders. His involvement appears to have been largely on the theoretical side of design, judging from Mitchell's initial concern at his lack of experience with structures and manufacturing. However, he was clearly impressed by Shenstone's academic knowledge, his research into the latest ideas and techniques and his ability to observe and assimilate data from multiple sources. On this basis he was offered a position in the Technical Office.

While working in Germany Shenstone had submitted a paper to the Royal Aeronautical Society on the inter-relationship of weight and drag and seen this published in 1930, while a letter on the subject of Junkers' wing construction appeared in *Flight* magazine in March 1931. Shortly after joining Supermarine he gave a talk on gliding at the University of Southampton and a second paper on the calculation of wing twist for tapered wings was published by the Royal Aeronautical Society in 1932. When William Munro wrote his book *Marine Aircraft Design* in 1933, Shenstone contributed a chapter on wings. Mitchell was, as always, happy to support the activities of his staff outside the works.

Mitchell placed Shenstone in an interesting, indeed unique, role within Supermarine. Alongside his position as the company's aerodynamicist Mitchell decided he should take responsibility for bringing an external perspective to the Design Department. He would visit other companies and research institutes in order to garner knowledge of new ideas and technologies. This he did both as a member of delegations accompanying other representatives of the company and also on his own. For example, in early 1934 he travelled to Germany with Ernest Hives of Rolls-Royce and in the spring to the US with Rex Pierson and Trevor Westbrook. There they visited NACA, equivalent to the Aeronautical Research Committee in Britain, and several aircraft companies, including Sikorsky, Lockheed and Martin. In November he was in Paris for the Aero Salon.

In 1934 a third paper was published by the Royal Aeronautical Society in which Shenstone described a mathematical method for calculating the lift distribution for any given wing shape, as proposed by the German scientist Wolfgang Lotz in 1931. He held a strong interest in techniques to achieve clean aerodynamic form in aircraft design and had already circulated a paper among his colleagues describing the accumulative drag consequent on small imperfections, poor detailing and the external paraphernalia that so many aircraft acquired. Overall it is clear through his published works and actions that Mitchell's new recruit was instrumental in introducing a broader view on aerodynamics and a greater level of aerodynamic mathematical rigour into the Design Department, where he took an active role in perfecting the Type 300 through advice and support for his colleagues. Shenstone was an ardent champion of monoplanes and aerodynamic cleanliness although, as the title of his 1966 Royal Aeronautical Society paper, *Hindsight is Always One Hundred Percent*, makes clear, he was to acknowledge that the way forward was not always self-evident at the time as some published data was misleading and much work remained to be done.

Shenstone's views on the latest aerodynamic theories and on the high level of surface finish achieved on some US and German aircraft was reported back to Mitchell and the team, and aerodynamic cleanliness became one of the fundamental requirements for the final design of the Type 300. He also championed the use of NACA aerofoils, citing the benefits of using profiles that had been the subject of intensive, large-scale, wind tunnel evaluation.

The decision to select the PV-12 in place of the Goshawk had been made before the close of 1934 but it was assumed at first that this engine would be evaporatively cooled, so the leading edge condensers were retained. The engine exhaust pipes were recessed partly into the engine cowling and angled down diagonally to discharge below the wing. The tail surfaces were redesigned and reduced further in size. At the same time the most visually distinctive change to the aircraft took place as the decision was taken to eliminate the sweep of the spars and the simple, straight, tapered wing shape gave way to an elegant, skewed, elliptical plan. In a further bold move, the wing section was changed to yet thinner NACA high-lift profiles and this required a complete redesign of the main spar to ensure that strength was maintained. Joe Smith led the team that sought a solution to this crucial structural problem. The junction between the wing root and the fuselage came under detailed scrutiny to ensure a smooth airflow and so a new root fairing was designed with the radius of curvature increasing rearwards. Its effectiveness was tested, in a basic manner, by fabricating a crude version in sheet metal on the Type 224 and attaching wool tufts so that the airflow could be monitored with the engine running on the ground. The underside of the wing root was also sculpted carefully to achieve the optimal low drag profile and the fuselage section was modified to an elliptical form for the same reason. The final wing was a sophisticated three-dimensional surface with variable curvature, incidence and aerofoil that was totally unique.

In April 1935 Mitchell was shown a copy of the Air Staff requirement F.10/35 for an eight-gun fighter. Some of the Air Staff, surprisingly, appear to have been largely unaware of the progress under way with the experimental fighters. After discussion between both branches of the Air Ministry and Mitchell and Camm, it was agreed to modify their experimental fighters to meet F.10/35, which was then withdrawn. The two experimental

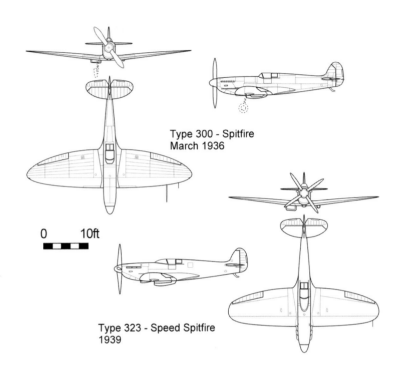

Type 300 - Spitfire
March 1936

0   10ft

Type 323 - Speed Spitfire
1939

fighters had been integrated into the mainstream fighter programme within a year.

Mitchell was able to adapt the Type 300 to accommodate eight guns and modify other aspects as required and construction commenced. The result, of course, was the Spitfire.

DESIGNING THE SPITFIRE

The development of the Spitfire lies beyond the scope of this book but the reasons for, and the timing of, some of the key design decisions are worth reviewing as they demonstrate the deep changes that had taken place within the Design Department and the evolution of a new approach to aircraft design.

When the Spitfire was rolled out in early 1936 it looked, and was, the epitome of fighter development at the time. However, and perhaps surprisingly, there was little true technological innovation in the design. Mitchell and his team had just brought together, in a highly skilful and

cohesive manner, the very best of the available structural and aerodynamic knowledge, a convergence of multiple existing technologies and research. He had, of course, achieved something comparable with his approach to the S.4 and S.5 Schneider racers many years earlier but with the Spitfire the situation was very different. This was to be a robust, versatile service fighter, built in large numbers and maintained by service personnel, not a one-off racer destined for a single race and with a life measured in weeks. The many steps that led to the Spitfire and the key design decisions that transformed the worthy, if uninspiring, Type 224, requires explanation.

Prior to the Spitfire, Mitchell's achievements as a designer had been, as we have seen, rather patchy. He had soared high with the Schneider seaplanes and the success of the Southampton, and sunk low with the Seamew, Nanok, Southampton X and Air Yacht. In this regard he was little different from most other designers of that era. In the absence of reliable wind tunnels, a paucity of published research data and so on it was difficult to achieve success with every aircraft regardless of how skilled you might be. However, moving into the 1930s the situation was improving rapidly as better test equipment became available and the volume of published information continued to grow. The opportunity was there for a skilled designer and a company willing to accept a modicum of risk to move in new directions.

Under normal circumstances, if it can be described that way, things may have turned out very differently, but for Mitchell in late 1933 life had taken a serious turn for the worst. His rectal cancer had been well advanced when detected and he had undergone major surgery as a matter of urgency. At that time there was little in the way of post-operative medical care, no radiotherapy or chemotherapy, and his surgeon was unable to say for certain whether the cancer would return. Medical science in this area was still very much in its infancy and medium- to long-term survival rates were far from high. After convalescence from the immediate effects of the surgery Mitchell returned to work and, hardly surprisingly, he was a changed man.

Mitchell's overriding priority was to ensure that his wife and son would be well provided for should the worst occur and here McLean was sympathetic and supportive. With this matter settled Mitchell was able to focus on work, as far as his condition allowed. Outwardly he does not seem to have given much sign of his medical state and even some of his closest colleagues appear to have been unaware of the nature of his illness or the precarious state of his heath. Inwardly it must have been a very different matter and his actions suggest a resolve to get things done, both at work and in his personal life, in whatever time he had remaining. Perhaps the clearest indication of this is that after fifteen years designing aircraft and flying as a passenger he set out to gain his pilot's licence. He took his first lesson on 22 December 1933 while still convalescing from his operation. In the office he embarked on a programme to refine the Type 300 as far as the technical expertise of his team could go.

The evidence suggests that Mitchell had decided the Type 300 would represent a complete change in design philosophy for Supermarine. Gone was the stark, simplified approach that had been the keynote of so many of the aircraft and projects after 1928. Now the emphasis would be placed on aerodynamic excellence at the expense of undue concerns over ease of construction or maintenance. A break with the past had to be made at some point and an experimental fighter was perhaps the ideal place to start. His vision and enthusiasm acted as a catalyst both for the team and for the Air Ministry, who were keen to see what Mitchell could produce in competition with Camm at Hawker. At no time during the redesign of the aircraft did Mitchell find himself battling against a reluctant bureaucracy, technical experts or RAF officers aiming to hold him back, despite some continuing claims to the contrary. However, this is not to say that elements of Mitchell's design were not challenged.

RAE technical advisors held the responsibility to assess all aspects of new aircraft designs from the viewpoint of safety and had been carrying out theoretical, model and full-scale experiments over many years. The phenomenon of spins, their cause, aggravating factors and methods to recover from them, was one area of particular focus. It was by now well established that wing flexure and aileron reversal were often contributory factors in the initiation of a spin, and that turbulent flow over the tailplane as it fell into the wake of the wings prevented recovery. The Vickers Jockey had been lost as the result of a flat spin in 1932 and was now the subject of a major study, and the Bristol 133 would be lost to the same cause in March 1935. There was every reason to assess new monoplane designs with care and it was obvious that both aspects of the Spitfire design would come under scrutiny.

When Mitchell's team proposed a cantilever wing of just 12 per cent thickness at the root it was only to be expected that it would draw comment. This was significantly thinner than had been attempted before and it was probably considered unlikely that Supermarine's spar design for the Type 224, the only data point available, would be acceptable to provide the necessary strength. The solution was a reversion to an aerofoil of 13 per cent thickness at the root and a novel new spar that appears to have been the inspiration of Joe Smith. A series of square tubes of decreasing section and increasing length were nested one within the other to form a composite beam, thick at the root end and thin towards the tip. Two of these beams were joined by a stout span-wise web and the D section plates that formed the leading edge of the wing. The composite structure was extremely strong.

The risk that the effectiveness of the tailplane could be compromised by falling into the turbulent wake of the low wing was very real. The extensive sculpted fillet and shaped rear fuselage went a long way to avoid this potential problem but there were still some concerns from RAE staff. After discussion these were addressed by lengthening the fuselage slightly and raising the tailplane. Mitchell and the RAE were working in close co-operation, not in conflict, and it is to the credit of both that they did not adopt a more conservative solution.

Interestingly, one of those more critical of the Spitfire design, perhaps because that was his task, was Mitchell's own deputy, Major Harold Payn. Payn was an ex-RAF pilot, engineer and test pilot, and hence extremely well qualified to comment on the capability of the aircraft as a fighter. He expressed misgivings over the forward view for the pilot, the potential stick loads resulting from the use of narrow chord ailerons and the lateral stability of the aircraft with a low wing and small dihedral. Most of these issues were resolved, or refuted, without detracting from Mitchell's overall vision for the aircraft.

In the late 1950s McLean claimed that the development of the Spitfire had been a private venture and that he had instructed the Air Ministry that under no circumstances would any of their staff be allowed to interfere with the design, but it is now well established that this is fabrication. Apart from the preliminary conceptual design work carried out through the summer and autumn of 1934, the project was never a private venture and there was extensive contact with, and input from, the Air Ministry and RAE. While it is true the Type 300 deviated from the original requirements of F.7/30, although it was at first aimed broadly at this specification, it did so while Mitchell was in close contact with the Ministry. Even during the short period in November 1934 when McLean sanctioned the detailed design work for the project he and Supermarine knew that funding for a prototype was extremely likely. The exhaustive research into Air Ministry correspondence carried out by Colin Sinnott demonstrates beyond a shadow of doubt that Air Ministry officials, representing both the technical and service side, were engaged and supportive throughout the process. There is absolutely no case to talk of 'biplane thinking' or 'perceived wisdom' among the key Ministry officials, RAE technicians or Vickers management, all of whom backed the development of the Spitfire.

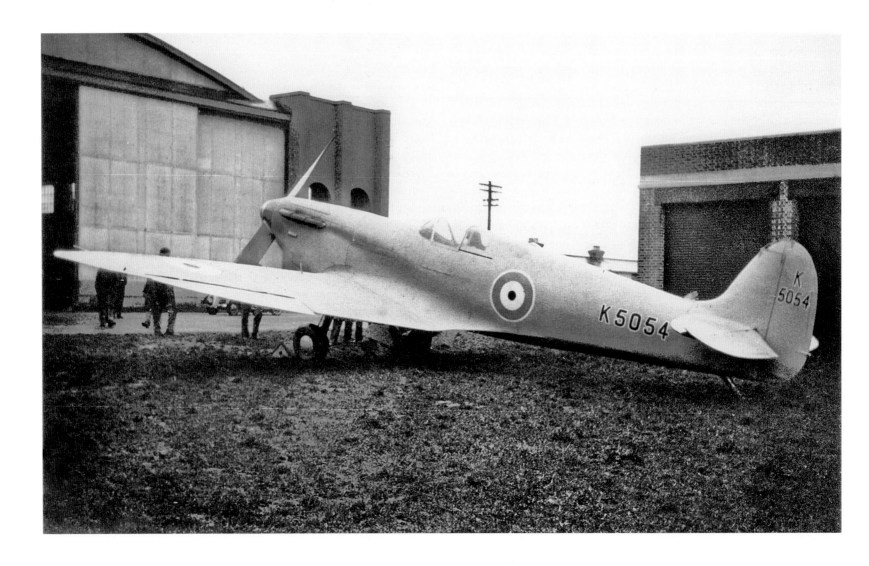

↑ The Spitfire prototype at Eastleigh aerodrome in the summer of 1936. The contoured fairing between the wing and fuselage is very evident and the exhaust staining along the fuselage serves to emphasise the clean airflow that had been achieved.

The precise sequence of events that led to the definitive Spitfire design does, however, remain rather unclear as many key Supermarine drawings and documents have been lost. Furthermore, there are a couple of issues that need to be clarified. First, Alan Clifton's notes say that Harold Smith, a talented young member of the Technical Office, carried out stress calculations on the torsion box nose for the wing of the Type 224, which was then carried over for the Type 300. Some authors have misinterpreted this and assumed that the idea to use this type of monospar construction came from Smith. However, the leading edge box doubling as the condenser for the engine cooling system had become an integral feature of Mitchell's monoplane designs when powered by evaporatively cooled engines and Mitchell had patented the idea in early 1931 based on development work for the Type 179 in 1930, some time prior to the design of the Type 224. Smith's name is absent from the patent, and it would have been standard practice for Supermarine to include it had he had been responsible for the idea. The second issue is a mistake concerning the surviving drawings for the Type 300. Supermarine drawing sets commence with general arrangement and layout drawings and, unfortunately, for the Type 300 only four in this series appear to have survived; namely 30000 Sheets 1, 11, 13H and 19.

Sheet 1, July 1934, shows suggested modifications to be made to the Type 224 aircraft including an uncranked straight-tapered wing, split flaps, and retractable undercarriage.

Sheet 11, Sept 1934, shows the redesigned aircraft with the thinner, sharply tapered wing and revised fuselage. This drawing is named Sheet 11 in the main title and Sheet 10 in the date box.

Sheet 13H shows the final configuration of the Spitfire with Merlin engine and includes the later bulged Malcolm cockpit hood introduced in 1938. The letter H implies that this was the eighth update to sheet 13; what the other seven updates may have been has remained unknown. The date on this much-revised drawing is May 1938.

Sheet 19 is a side view showing the internal arrangement of the Spitfire fuselage. The date is unreadable.

Several recent authors have referred to, or copied, an illustration from Morgan and Shacklady's excellent book, *Spitfire: The History*, which shows the September 1934 version of the Type 300 revised with an elliptical wing on swept spars, attributed to Alfred Faddy. This is captioned in the book as Drawing 30000 Sheet 11, which is obviously misleading. The accompanying text makes the true situation quite clear but tends to be overlooked: 'a representation of how this redesigned aeroplane might have appeared with a wing formed of two half ellipses …'. This makes it quite clear that it is not an actual Supermarine drawing and that the configuration is conjectural, just one possible intermediate profile between the tapered wing design and the skewed ellipse of the final aircraft, should such an intermediate wing plan ever have received serious consideration.

It is rather curious that the originator of, and reasons for, the adoption of the final skewed elliptical wing shape has become rather contentious, and articles and large sections of books have been written on the subject. Yet there really should be little mystery. The theoretical benefits of elliptical wing plans, the lowest induced drag for a given wing area, span and aerofoil, had been known for decades, and over the years wings with variations on the elliptical shape had been adopted for a small number of aircraft, typically 'one-off' racers and other specialised types. The principal reason that this style of wing, and indeed tapered wings in general, had not been more common was that aircraft builders considered the small drag benefits were more than offset by the higher cost incurred in building a wing in which every wing rib would have had a different chord and thickness. Hence, and especially for biplanes, parallel chord wings predominated. On the other hand, it had been quite common to build wings with a parallel chord main section and curved, often skewed elliptical, tips. Mitchell himself had used such wings on both his S.5 and S.6 Schneider racers. In the early concept stages of aircraft projects it was not that unusual to propose the use of an elliptical wing only for this to be dropped later on grounds of simplicity and cost. Both Mitchell's Type 179 six-engined flying boat in 1928 and Dornier's original thoughts for the Do X in 1924 started with full elliptical wings only for these to be replaced as the projects developed by tapered and constant-chord straight wings respectively.

Who precisely in the Design Department first suggested using an elliptical wing for the Type 300 will no doubt remain unknown as the recollections of those involved at the time differ. Draughtsman Fear stated that Faddy convinced Mitchell to adopt the ellipse and first drew an elliptical wing on drawing 30000 Sheet 11, but this cannot be verified from surviving drawings. Dickson wrote that an elliptical wing had featured on his drawings before he was moved off the project towards the end of 1934. Clifton said that the idea was first raised by Shenstone but, while others cited Shenstone as having made a significant contribution to the aerodynamics of the wing, none said that he actually proposed using an elliptical plan and, indeed, neither did he. Shenstone had laid out his views on wing design in the chapter he wrote for Munro's book. In the opening paragraph on wing plan forms he describes the theoretical advantages of employing an elliptical wing but follows by stating the reduction in induced drag compared to a well-designed conventional tapered wing is not that great. It would appear that the wing had many fathers.

On the other hand, the principal reason for adopting a skewed ellipse wing plan has been reported by several of the design team and is both quite logical and clear. The optimal wing loading for the aircraft had been established during the summer of 1934 and the root aerofoil profile had been selected as NACA 2412; 12 per cent thickness. When, in early December 1934, the crucial decision was taken to substitute the new PV-12 engine for

← Spitfire I P9795 from the first production batch in service with 19 Squadron, the first to receive the aircraft.

the Goshawk, which incurred an increase in weight of around 30 per cent, the centre of lift had to be shifted forward to compensate and the wing area needed to increase slightly. A logical way to achieve the forward shift was to eliminate the sweep on the main spar, which brought the added benefit of a reduction in torsion stress and simplified attachment of the ribs. The inner portion of the wing had to be sufficiently deep to provide room for the wheels to retract and to house the guns but a straight tapered wing, with the chord and thickness reducing outboard in a linear fashion, was proving to be a little restricted in internal space. The solution that resolved this problem was to change to an elliptical plan, skewed forward so the straight

spar was located at constant chord. The selected aerofoils were in the NACA 2200 series, reducing in thickness from 13 per cent at the root to 9.4 per cent at the last wing rib and just 6 per cent at the tip. It was fortuitous this elliptical design had sufficient interior space outboard to allow extra guns to be installed without major structural change when the armament for the aircraft was raised later from four to eight guns.

The decision to develop such a sophisticated wing, inevitably costly to manufacture, is the best expression of Mitchell's resolve to accept no short cut or compromise in the design of the aircraft.

ON ELLIPTICAL WINGS

The decision to change from a straight tapered to elliptical wing late in the design process has led a few to conclude that Mitchell and his team adopted that wing plan only after viewing the Heinkel He 70 at the Paris Aviation Salon in November 1934. On a superficial basis the similarity between the wings on the two aircraft can indeed be striking at some angles and on a casual glance.

The He 70 was a low-wing cantilever inverted gull-wing monoplane built as a high-speed transport for six passengers seated in cramped conditions within a sleek fuselage. It did, indeed, look uncannily like an enlarged monoplane fighter. The suggestion that the He 70 inspired the design for the Spitfire has somehow provoked near outrage in some quarters and whole chapters of books have been devoted to arguments refuting the claim. In truth this has never really been taken seriously and is quite simple to disprove, with one caveat.

The He 70's first flight predates the final Spitfire design by a clear two years, and photographs and descriptions had been published in many magazines. It drew much favourable comment when it was unveiled at the

↓ The Heinkel He 70 was an aerodynamically clean cantilever monoplane with an ellipsoid wing plan.

end of 1932 and was the fastest aircraft in its class, the holder of a number of speed-over-distance records, and would most certainly have drawn the attention and interest of all aircraft designers. The use of an elliptical wing, however, was considered neither new nor revolutionary at the time. In fact, an article describing the aircraft published in *The Aeroplane* in March 1933, shortly after it was first introduced to the press, did not even remark on the wing shape. Heinkel published an illustrated paper in December 1933 in which he described the features of the aircraft. A translation into English by NACA was made available in May 1934 and no doubt Shenstone, fluent in German, could have provided one to Mitchell *et al* earlier. One example of the He 70 made demonstration flights at Croydon, London's main airport, in the summer of 1934, and another was exhibited at the fourteenth Paris Aviation Salon in late 1934, where it was seen by Shenstone on one of his fact-finding trips. This was not in 1933, as one author asserts, as the Salon was a biennial event. It is obvious, therefore, that Mitchell and the team would have been well aware of the He 70 and its key design features some time prior to embarking on the earliest Type 300 design and well over a year before a skewed elliptical wing plan was adopted for the Spitfire.

Although there appear to have been few, if any, questions raised at the time regarding the origin of the Spitfire's wing, the suggestion of copying or inspiration arose some years later and was reinforced by remarks made by Ernst Heinkel himself in his memoirs after the war. However, even a brief comparison of the wings on the two aircraft shows that they are actually markedly different and any similarities are generic rather than specific. The wings, although both described in simple terms as elliptical, are noticeably different in plan and completely different in aerofoil profiles, twist and dihedral. There is no reason why Mitchell would have perceived the wing as something either innovative or exceptional as he had himself toyed with elliptic wings on projects several years earlier and was well aware of the theoretical advantages; papers and reports on the characteristics of various wing shapes, both theoretical and experimental, often included ellipsoids. There is, therefore, no argument at all to suggest that either he or his staff had been inspired by the He 70 and the wing was most certainly not copied.

The caveat, however, is most interesting and does not appear to have been noted before. In February 1936 the Aeronautical Research Committee published Reports and Memoranda 1709, *Experiments on a Heinkel He.70 Aeroplane in the Compressed Air Tunnel*. These tests had been requested by Rex Pierson, who had assessed a ⅛-scale model of the He 70 in the Vickers wind tunnel and had had these rerun in the 5ft tunnel at the RAE,

with similar results. Neither evaluation matched the low coefficient of drag figures claimed by Heinkel in his December 1933 article. The NPL facility was a larger and more sophisticated tunnel and the aim of the tests was simply to compare the results against those of Vickers and the RAE. The model Pierson had built was based on the simple three-view layout drawing in the German publication and hence was rudimentary and of unknown accuracy. It seems reasonable to assume the Vickers tests had taken place in 1934, followed by the RAE and NPL evaluations maybe late that year or into 1935 as published reports came out generally one year or more after the evaluations. Mitchell would have been fully aware of Pierson's project through the Joint Design Committee, indeed Pierson may have carried out the evaluation on behalf of both of them, and just confirms the obvious point that any aircraft designer would take interest in a new aircraft for which outstanding claims had been made.

When the Spitfire was revealed to the aviation press and public in the summer of 1936 there was little comment on its wing design, other than to praise its elegance. The shape was perceived as neither unusual nor especially noteworthy. Nevertheless, it has been suggested the Spitfire's wing was so revolutionary that other designers failed to recognise its merits and a long correspondence in *Flight* magazine, running from January 1936 through to early 1937, has been cited to support this theory. The argument at the root of this correspondence stemmed from a paper presented by Gustav Lachmann, Chief Designer at Handley Page, entitled *The Stalling of Tapered Wings*, which he had written primarily to promote the virtues of Handley Page's leading edge slats. Through the correspondence pages of the magazine, various writers criticised his simplistic approach, queried his data, which many considered dated, and threw doubt on his conclusions. In essence, the argument that developed centred on the application of aerodynamic theory and the reliability of measurements on aerofoils obtained in wind tunnels of various sizes and speeds. It was a wide-ranging discussion on Reynolds numbers, scale effects, aerofoil variation with span, sweep and washout, which all served to highlight the unreliability of many wind tunnels and the limitations of the mathematics of fluid flow that were becoming increasingly evident in a period of great leaps in technology and the speed of aircraft. The elliptical wing features towards the close of this prolonged argument but then only as an example of a theoretical ideal that could form the basis for a programme of high-speed research. The Spitfire, of course, was doing just that as they wrote.

THE SPITFIRE IN CONTEXT

The Spitfire was an outstanding fighter at the time it first flew and proved to be sufficiently advanced and flexible in both its aerodynamic and structural design to accept numerous modifications through the war years and thus remain in front-line service for nearly a decade. Yet, as mentioned before, Mitchell's team did not introduce any new concepts, they merely took advantage of the best elements of current technology and adopted them in the most effective way possible. There were no secrets or breakthroughs in aerodynamic theory, just scrupulous attention to detail and a determination to avoid compromise; to 'push the envelope' of cantilever monoplane design.

After all this laborious design and construction work, was the effort worthwhile? Mitchell had stretched the available technology to the limit quite deliberately and the Spitfire was one of the first aircraft destined for production to have a stressed skin wing of single spar construction, a lightweight cantilever retractable undercarriage, a minimal drag cooling system and a host of other features. The obvious comparison to be made is with the Hawker Hurricane, an aircraft built for the same experimental fighter programme and powered by the same engine. Sydney Camm had shied away from introducing more than the minimum amount of new technology into the Hurricane and elected instead to continue with the structural techniques with which his workers and RAF engineers were familiar. He was, perhaps, too focussed on mainstream fighter specifications and less on attempting something new, as the experimental programme really intended. The fuselage was built up using the same metal frame and wooden former system he had developed for the Hart and Fury biplane families, and was fabric covered. The straight-tapered wing, too, was fabric covered over twin metal beam spars joined and braced by a robust zigzag girder. The aerofoil selected by Camm was Clark YH, of 1922 vintage, modified to a slightly thicker section of 19 per cent at the root and tapering to 12.2 per cent at the tip. Clark YH was an aerofoil that had been the subject to several wind tunnel and full-scale tests over a number of years and its characteristics were very well known.

← The Hawker Hurricane was a fine aircraft and an excellent fighter. For the workmen of the late 1930s it was easy to construct and repair. It was, however, outclassed by the Spitfire.

The initial flight tests of the two prototypes were carried out by the Aeroplane and Armament Experimental Establishment (A&AEE) at Martlesham Heath under broadly comparable conditions. Both aircraft came direct from the manufacturers without any modifications, both were powered by Merlin Cs, and both carried ballast in place of the eight Browning machine guns. The Spitfire weighed 5,332lb and had a top speed of 349mph at 16,800ft. The Hurricane weighed 5,672lb and the top speed was 315mph at 16,500ft. The Hurricane could climb to medium altitudes marginally quicker than the Spitfire by virtue of its lower wing loading but fell behind at higher altitude. As fighting aircraft both excelled, providing a fine balance between stability as a gun platform and manoeuvrability for combat, but the Spitfire had a significant edge at higher speeds and altitudes as the sophisticated thin profile wing would allow the pilot to turn much tighter before the airflow broke away and induced a stall. Under full combat conditions this combination of speed, stability and control in extreme manoeuvres were precisely the attributes the pilot required. Although fighter design had focussed on the interception and destruction of bombers, fighter-versus-fighter combat was to become at least equally important. In these encounters the Spitfire's high-speed capabilities were of paramount importance.

It is also interesting to compare the Spitfire with the three aircraft built to F.5/34, which were all eight-gun fighters with radial engines: the Gloster F.5/34, the Vickers Venom and the Bristol 146. Although these prototypes were ordered in the spring of 1935, that is only a few months after the contract for the prototype Spitfire had been issued, they were all delayed as the Air Ministry shifted priority to other projects and after the Spitfire and Hurricane became the main focus concerning the forming of the backbone of the RAF's new fighter force.

The Bristol 146 can be dismissed as its performance was very poor, little better than the Gloster Gladiator biplane. Rex Pierson's Vickers Type 279 Venom continued the lineage of the Jockey, with a firm focus on simplicity, light weight and small size. Unlike its predecessor, it employed stressed metal skin for both the monocoque fuselage and the rectangular plan wing, using the RAF 34 aerofoil. It weighed in, under test conditions, at 4,156lb, considerably less than either the Spitfire or Hurricane, and was powered by a 625hp Bristol Aquila air-cooled radial engine in a NACA cowl. Top speed was 312mph and it was noted for its high rate of roll and tight turning circle. Henry Folland's Gloster F.5/34 fighter is often dismissed as just a monoplane derivative of the Gladiator but that is complete nonsense. The

← Gloster's unnamed F.5/34 contender had the potential to be a formidable fighter but was let down by a lack of engine power.

← The Vickers Venom fighter demonstrated that a small, simple aircraft had much to offer. Its chosen engine, the Bristol Aquila, needed more power.

aircraft, like the Spitfire and Venom, was all stressed skin with the twin-spar tapered wing built in one piece. Like the Spitfire, this wing used NACA 2200 series aerofoils, 18 per cent at the root tapering to 9 per cent at the tip, and was fitted with a generous fillet at the root. It was a clean and reasonably sophisticated design powered by an 840hp Bristol Mercury radial engine housed in a long cowling. The aircraft weighed 5,399lb, very close to the Spitfire, and had a top speed of 316mph. Pilots appreciated its fine field of view, its short take-off run, rapid climb and the lightness of its controls. Both the Vickers and Gloster aircraft lacked engine power compared to the Merlin engine in the Spitfire and Hurricane but nevertheless showed the potential to be capable fighters. Both were shown to be broadly comparable

in performance to the Hurricane and would have surpassed it had they been fitted with engines of similar power. The Gloster, in particular, was a more advanced design. They demonstrate quite conclusively the superiority of a smooth stressed skin for both fuselage and wing, something that Sydney Camm was slow to appreciate. Neither aircraft, however, would have been a match for the Spitfire.

While the Spitfire was the class leader by a wide margin, it was not the outlier of the group in terms of technology. Both the Gloster and Vickers aircraft had full stress-skinned structures and the Gloster's aerodynamic cleanliness was not far behind that of the Spitfire, bearing in mind that it had a radial engine. It is the Hurricane that is the odd man out as its structure and, to some extent, its aerodynamics remained rooted in late 1920s technology. The fact that it proved to be an extremely successful fighter demonstrates that in the late 1930s and earliest 1940s the old methods still had much to offer and that the Air Ministry were wise to order both the Spitfire and Hurricane in quantity, the Hurricane representing the insurance policy against failure or disappointment with the Spitfire.

TWO-SEAT FIGHTERS

Since the war the relative merits of single-seat and two-seat fighters had been the subject of debate and was far from resolved by the mid-1930s. Advocates of the two-seat fighter would point to the success of the Bristol Fighter in the closing days of the war, a versatile aircraft that had continued in RAF service for many years. Strategic planning centred on the assumption that waves of enemy bombers, flying in formation, would be engaged by squadrons of fighters, also in formation, and it was believed by many that a greater, targeted and sustained rate of fire could be achieved by a dedicated gunner working with one or more traversable guns than by a lone pilot using fixed guns for frontal attack. Not all in the Air Ministry were convinced this was the way forward but fighters in this category began to be seen as a significant part of the RAF defence planning and the force was built up in the mid-1930s when the Demon fighter variant of the Hawker Hart biplane light bomber was constructed in large numbers. However, the advent of fast monoplane single-seat fighters led, inevitably, to the desire to produce something comparable in terms of a two-seat machine. The higher speeds, well over 100mph above that of the Demon, meant a simple exposed gunner's cockpit fitted with guns on a ring mounting would not be feasible and that some form of slipstream protection or turret would be required, both to protect the gunner and to minimise drag. Some later Demons were themselves fitted with shrouds or turrets.

Specification F.9/35 was issued in May 1935 requesting tenders for a two-seat, four-gun fighter with all guns controlled by the gunner; there would be no fixed, forward-firing guns. This specification reached Supermarine around the same time that the final mock-up conference for the Spitfire was taking place. Mitchell saw the requirement as an ideal opportunity to capitalise on the design work for the Spitfire so the new project, Type 305, was conceived as a close relation using the same basic wing design matched to an enlarged fuselage. The fuel tanks were placed within the wing leading edge torsion box, formerly the space used as the

steam condensers for the early concept of an evaporatively cooled Merlin, and the oil and water radiators were repositioned from under the wings to under the nose in the chin position. The space freed up in the wings was then to be used for internal bomb racks holding four 20lb bombs on each side. Mitchell's team, believed to have been led by Harold Payn, devised an unusual arrangement for the gunner as he was to operate the four guns remotely through an electro-mechanical mechanism, one of two remote gun systems on which Supermarine were then working. He sat immediately behind the pilot in a rear-facing, spring-loaded seat that would fold away to enable him to stand to scan for targets. When standing, a front-hinged hatch opened in a low-profile transparent dome in the roof of the fuselage that acted as protection from the slipstream. The four machine guns were mounted in a shallow barbette tailwards of the gunner and had a clear field of fire across the upper hemisphere except for cut-outs to avoid the fin and propeller disc. Early design work was based on the use of Vickers guns but this was soon dropped in favour of Brownings for the tendered aircraft. The gunner had a prismatic sight to aim and a joystick control that elevated the guns and rotated both his seat platform and the barbette. Mitchell anticipated a top speed of 315mph. The design was tendered to the Air Ministry in August 1935.

Surprisingly, Vickers also worked on a design that resembled the Type 305 very closely indeed, right down to the use of a skewed elliptical wing, although this remained unofficial, was never allocated a project Type

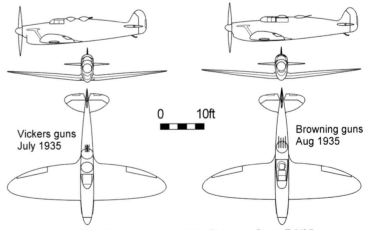

Type 305 Two Seater Day and Night Fighter to Spec. F.9/35

number and no tender was submitted to the Air Ministry. Why the company would have considered it sensible to work on two such similar designs is hard to understand, unless the key part was the turret design. Barnes Wallis was, at this point, engaged in the design of a number of turret systems.

The Air Ministry rejected the Type 305 in favour of the Hawker Hotspur, a design by Sydney Camm derived from the Hurricane, that offered comparable performance. The Hotspur featured a more conventional powered gun turret of the Boulton Paul type and this approach was favoured above the more speculative ideas in Mitchell's project. The Ministry were beginning to have misgivings at the proliferation of broadly similar turret designs and were assessing ways to standardise on a reduced number. Ironically, another consideration against ordering the Type 305 was concern that Supermarine would not be able to develop the aircraft sufficiently quickly given their work on the Spitfire, but Hawker were to suffer the very same problem with the start-up of production of the Hurricane and, hence, construction of the Hotspur prototype was delayed considerably. Consequently the Boulton Paul Defiant was ordered to fill the gap, chosen in part as that company had negotiated the rights to build the French-designed SAMM lightweight turret. In the summer of 1936, after the Type 305 submission had been rejected, Supermarine discussed their project with specialist gun turret manufacturer Nash & Thompson, who advised that they doubted the turret mounting would have proven sufficiently rigid.

The RAF experience in the early years of the Second World War showed once and for all that the two-seat fighter, although capable of engaging bombers with success, was at a distinct disadvantage when attacked by their escort of single-seat fighters, and production of the Defiant was curtailed. They did, however, find a niche role as a night fighter.

CANNON FIGHTERS

The RAF Expansion Plans continued to evolve as the international climate worsened and as technology forged ahead. In the same way that F.7/30 had looked dated even as it was issued to the aircraft industry, the armament for fighters, both in production and planned, now also appeared questionable. The option to fit cannon in place of machine guns was under serious review. The Air Ministry had experimented with the aging 37mm COW cannon in several aircraft, both fighters and larger, but none had proven entirely successful as it was both heavy and unwieldy for easy installation. By the mid-1930s a new generation of smaller, lighter cannon were under

development, of which the 20mm calibre Hispano and Oerlikon designs were among the most attractive for aircraft use, and the Air Ministry revived the idea for a cannon-armed fighter. Spec F.37/35 was issued in February 1936 for a day and night fighter armed with four cannon and capable of operating both for home defence and with field forces.

Supermarine were well aware of the ability of the Spitfire's single-spar stressed skin wing to accept alternative internal equipment and had already considered the possibility of fitting cannon armament, so they were able to respond to the Air Ministry in little more than a month with the Type 312. The layout drawings are dated April 1936. This aircraft was based heavily on the Spitfire but took account of the main criticism levelled at that design, the poor forward visibility for the pilot. Consequently, the cockpit was raised by about 6in to improve the view over the nose. The standard Spitfire wing was then adapted to carry four Oerlikon FF or G 20mm cannons, all firing outside the propeller disc, which could just be accommodated within the available space unless larger ammunition boxes were specified that would require small blisters in the wing surface. The design team believed that these were not likely to have a detrimental impact on performance.

Mitchell took the opportunity to replace the Spitfire's under-wing Meredith radiator housing with a central design located beneath the centre section and at the same time the profile of the lower nose was slimmed down. Aircraft performance was estimated to be virtually identical to that of the Spitfire I, a little below that required by the specification. The preliminary drawings were produced by Reginald Schlotel, another interesting member of the Technical Office. Schlotel had been Chief Engineer for a company building airships at the end of the 1920s and would go on to join the Ministry of Supply in the war years, where he was deeply involved in the work on early jet engines. He would advance to become their Director of Engineering, Research and Development.

In parallel with the Type 312, Mitchell's team worked on an alternative twin-engine design, Type 313, with the four cannon installed in the nose of the fuselage, not least because it was felt the Air Ministry probably favoured this approach following discussions they had held with several aircraft companies. As was so often the case, Mitchell had the team start with a blank sheet of paper so the project was completely new and independent from the Spitfire-based projects. The drawings for this aircraft, too, are dated April 1936. Great care was taken to achieve a clean aerodynamic form so the elliptical section fuselage had an elongated nose, to house the guns, and tapered to a point at the rear. The wings were a further variation on the modified elliptical theme but in this case more symmetrical in plan

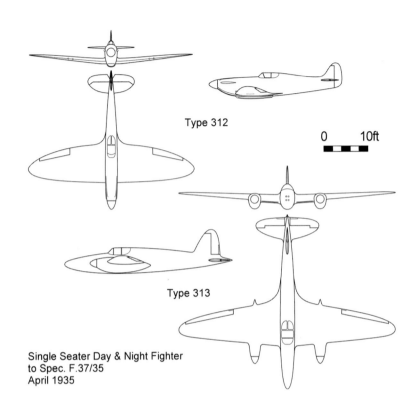

Type 312

0   10ft

Type 313

Single Seater Day & Night Fighter
to Spec. F.37/35
April 1935

than those on the Spitfire, with more gradual taper and slightly swept outer spars. The wings were mounted in the minimum drag mid-fuselage position and there were extensive fillets at the roots to blend into the fuselage. Supermarine were at pains to highlight this feature on the drawings. The tailplane and fin were also both of elliptical form. The engines were installed in nacelles under the wing and stated to be Goshawk Bs, a strange choice as Rolls-Royce had abandoned this evaporatively cooled engine in early 1935, so it may, perhaps, indicate that the intention was to use the Kestrel KV.26, a liquid-cooled engine of similar size and power that would later be renamed the Peregrine. Low-profile radiators were recessed into the mid-inner wing

with air entering through narrow slots under the lower surface and exhausting just ahead of the flaps. The main undercarriage retracted rearwards into the engine nacelles and the tail wheel into the rear fuselage.

Supermarine stressed the flexibility of the Type 313 design and some consideration was given to fitting a licence-built version of the Hispano-Suiza 12Y engine as this had been designed specifically to enable a Hispano cannon to fire through the propeller hub, thereby increasing the armament to a total of six cannon. Aeroengines Ltd had been launched in 1935 to manufacture Hispano-Suiza engines under licence for Britain and the Empire. Supermarine also suggested the airframe could be adapted to fulfil the role of a high-speed medium bomber by adding a second crew member and racks for four 500lb bombs in the fuselage behind the pilot. In this version two cannon would be retained in the nose.

By this time, the Air Ministry were all too aware of the work overload within the Supermarine works and were cautious not to award contracts that would exacerbate the situation and possibly delay work on the Spitfire. As a consequence, the Type 313 was not pursued but one prototype of the Type 312 is believed to have been ordered in December 1936 as this shared many components with the Spitfire and could be developed without too much disruption. However, they must have had second thoughts as this contract was cancelled just weeks later at the end of January 1937, which coincides with Mitchell's rapid decline in health and last days in the office, no doubt a major factor in the Ministry's decision.

The Air Ministry awarded the production contract for F.37/35 to Westland for their P.9 Whirlwind, a sophisticated but complex aircraft that was powered by twin Rolls-Royce Peregrines. However, when Rolls-Royce dropped development of this engine so they could concentrate on the Merlin the production run of the Whirlwind was curtailed.

Several other single and twin-engined, cannon-armed fighter designs were pursued in the following years by the Air Ministry, with varying results. Supermarine adapted the Spitfire wing to carry two cannon in place of the four machine guns and these were tested with success in 1939 just prior to the war. Cannon and mixed cannon and machine gun wings then entered production a couple of years later.

22

COMPETITION AND THE FOUR-ENGINED FLYING BOATS

By 1930 Supermarine were acknowledged as the class leader in Britain for medium-sized, twin-engined flying boats since securing the contract for the Southampton in 1924, but they had struggled to make any headway with larger aircraft. Short Bros and Blackburn had the edge for these flying boats, albeit their aircraft had been produced in very small numbers.

Short Bros had been forging ahead with the development of large multi-engined biplane flying boats and they had won contracts both for military application and for passenger services with Imperial Airways, a market that Supermarine had failed consistently to interest with their numerous designs. Blackburn had, for a while, appeared to be Shorts' equal but had suffered a slight setback after their large three-engined Nile monoplane, a civil version of the Sydney for service with the new co-venture Cobham-Blackburn Air Lines, had been cancelled. The airline had withered before even starting operations, having failed to receive government sanction, and the company reconsidered their commitment to producing flying boats. Nevertheless, they continued to be a potential competitor. In the last years of the 1920s Saunders had also begun to gain ground following the restructuring and refinancing of their business after the takeover by A.V. Roe and his partners. First came the three-engined Saunders A.7 Severn built to R.4/27 and subsequently the twin-engined Saunders-Roe A.27 London to R.20/31. It must have been a matter of considerable concern to Supermarine when the latter aircraft was ordered for production and took away part of the business to replace the Southampton II, most especially as this came so soon after Saunders-Roe's Cutty Sark and Cloud twin-engined monoplanes had also taken a lead for the smaller classes of flying boats.

Mitchell's failure to produce a worthy three-engined aircraft was, by any standards, a serious blow. The cancellation of the contract for the Type 179

Giant only served to rub salt into the wound. Notwithstanding Mitchell's first serious moves to diversify his range of aircraft designs, Supermarine, under Vickers control, remained a specialised manufacturer of flying boats and a significant portion of the Design Department continued to focus on these aircraft. During the period when the team were developing the Seagull V, Scapa and Stranraer several new opportunities arose to tender designs for large flying boats and Mitchell made considerable efforts to secure these potentially lucrative contracts.

In the early 1930s the Air Ministry issued specifications for both civil and military aircraft within a very short period of time and the sequence of events and timing of the initiation of projects appears slightly different depending on whether it is viewed from the perspective of Supermarine or of their competitors, and this affects the flow of the narrative. The story of Supermarine's many four-engined flying boat projects is dominated by the parallel work undertaken by Short Bros but this is the story as seen from the perspective of Mitchell and his team.

COASTAL PATROL

Under the RAF Expansion Plans and in response to the growing belligerence of Germany, with the likelihood that they would develop U-boat flotillas, there was seen to be an urgent requirement for an aircraft capable of undertaking long reconnaissance flights while carrying a substantial offensive and defensive armament. These aircraft would form the backbone of the coastal reconnaissance force, both in Britain and stationed at strategic points in the overseas territories and were destined to replace all the larger types of flying boat currently in service or in production, which were mostly Shorts Calcutta and Singapore biplanes.

In November 1933, during Mitchell's convalescence, the Air Ministry issued specification R.2/33 for a four-engined general purpose boat seaplane, a long-distance patrol aircraft with a top speed of 200mph and cruising speed of 170mph. Range was to be 1,600 miles, ceiling 15,000ft and the aircraft would need to carry 2,000lb of bombs and four defensive gun positions. In response Mitchell's team drew up no fewer than five schemes, three under Type 232, and one each as Types 238 and 239. All but the Type 238 were monoplanes.

Type 238, dating from April 1934, was a 'safe' proposal designed along the lines of a scaled-up Scapa or Stranraer. It was powered by four Bristol Perseus air-cooled radial engines mounted on the upper wing leading edge, and each lower wing had internal racks in a large bay that could hold four 100–250lb or two 500lb bombs, plus an additional four 20lb in a smaller bay. There were Lewis guns at nose and tail, the nose mounting in a turret, and further gun positions in the top and side of the rear hull. The Bristol Perseus was the world's first production aero engine to use sleeve valves and was, at this date, still unproven in service. The prototype of the engine had run on the test bench in 1932 and produced around 600hp, a little less than the conventional poppet-valve Mercury, but would be developed to deliver considerably more in the coming years.

Mitchell's favoured design under Type 232 was also drawn in April 1934. This was a large gull-winged monoplane powered by four Rolls-Royce Goshawks employing Mitchell's patented wing leading edge steam condensers. The inner wing panels had straight leading edges, reverse taper and 18 degrees of dihedral while the outer panels were straight tapered with 1.5 degrees of dihedral. Large split flaps were fitted inboard of the ailerons. The wings were strut and wire braced from the gull-wing kink down to large tapered sponson stabilisers. The Goshawks were mounted ahead of the leading edge of the inner section of the wing and their corrugated leading edge steam condensers covered the full span of the wing and around 30 per cent of the chord. The metal hull was tall with sloping flat sides for the nose and central section, while the upswept tail was curved. For the planing bottom, Mitchell introduced a knife-edge rear step for the first time since the Type 179 Giant and would stay with this feature for all future flying boats. The wing roots attached to a stub pylon on the hull's central section, with the enclosed cockpit located at its forward end. This high cockpit position gave the pilot a good view forward and to the sides but was marred by the propeller discs of the inner engines being positioned ahead of the cockpit and close on either side. The tailplane was strut-braced to the hull and fitted with twin fins and balanced rudders. Gun turrets for single Lewis guns were fitted in both the nose and tail, although a 37mm COW cannon could replace the Lewis gun in the nose. This turret was glazed with rotating and retractable panels. Additional Lewis gun mounts were included in the rear hull, one on the top under a hinged cover at the rear of the pylon and two firing through ports in the sides. The sponsons were both tapered and curved, a shape that had not proven successful in Mitchell's model tests for the Air Yacht in 1929 so presumably further evaluation using improved model support cradles in the tank had enabled Mitchell's hydrodynamic team to refine the profile. Internal bomb racks were built into the wings just outboard of the engines. These could accommodate two 450–500lb or four 100–250lb bombs plus four 20lb bombs, on each side.

Type 239, the third early design, was also drawn in April 1934 and was almost identical to the preferred Type 232 but was increased in size throughout and fitted with evaporatively cooled Rolls-Royce Merlins.

Also included under Type 232 were two closely related alternative designs dating from early 1935, a year after the main design had been drawn up. They were both based on a later civil flying boat design, the Type 302, and were to be powered by four air-cooled radial engines, the smaller of the two by Bristol Aquilas and the larger by Bristol Pegasus. The Aquila was a sleeve-valve engine of small diameter based on the technology for the Perseus and had not yet run when Supermarine drew up their flying boat project. It was to produce 600hp but would take several years of development before

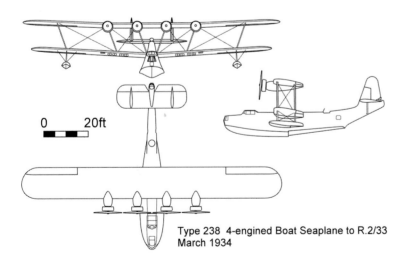

0   20ft

Type 238 4-engined Boat Seaplane to R.2/33
March 1934

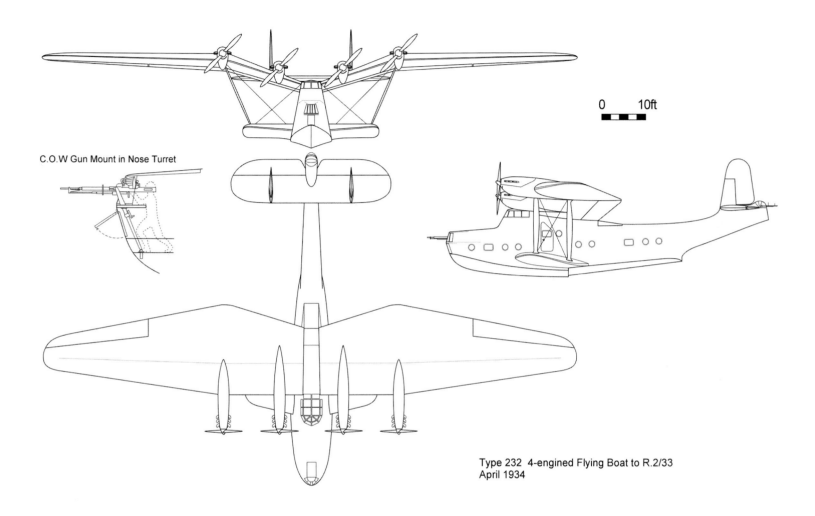

C.O.W Gun Mount in Nose Turret

0   10ft

Type 232 4-engined Flying Boat to R.2/33
April 1934

this was achieved. The Pegasus was intended to replace the aging Jupiter engine and incorporated improvements derived through the lengthy trials and development of the Mercury. Early engines produced around 700hp but in later versions this had increased to nearly 1,000hp. These flying boat projects shared a common layout, it was just the size that varied. The hull was much shallower than in Mitchell's favoured design with flat vertical sides and curved upper surface and a prominent pylon to support the wing. There was no indication of a gun position or turret in the curved bow but an open gun ring was placed in the tail and probably a second positioned beneath a hinged cover behind the wing pylon. Stabilisation on the water was by sponsons. The monoplane wing had a large constant-chord centre section on which the

engines were mounted ahead of the leading edge, braced by a single strut and wires on either side to the sponsons. The outer wing panels had asymmetric straight taper with the leading edge just a couple of degrees off being straight.

A reasonable amount of moderately detailed design work was carried out on the gull-wing Type 232 project so it does appear quite probable that Supermarine tendered to the Air Ministry, where it would have been assessed alongside submissions received from Shorts and Saunders-Roe. A third design by Blackburn, with stylistic similarity to their Sydney flying boat, may also have been tendered. At this time Short Bros were working on two closely related four-engined monoplane flying boats for Imperial Airways, which will be reviewed later, and proposed a militarised derivative for R.2/33. Saunders-Roe submitted the A.33 four-engined parasol monoplane with sponsons, incorporating a wing built by General Aircraft under Helmut Stieger's Mono-spar patents. Both aircraft were to be powered by four Bristol air-cooled radials: Pegasus in the Shorts aircraft and Perseus in the Saunders-Roe. Interestingly, Saunders-Roe had obtained a contract under specification 18/32, that is some time prior to the issue of R.2/33, to evaluate a scale version of the main components of their design by modifying a Saro Cloud with a Mono-spar wing and sponsons.

If Supermarine did indeed tender the Type 232 it obviously failed to win a contract for a prototype whereas the competing designs from Shorts and Saunders-Roe were both accepted. The Shorts design was, on paper, superior to the other two in almost all respects and proved to be so once built. This aircraft was the S.25 Sunderland, the military counterpart to the Imperial Airways Empire flying boats, or 'C' class, a highly successful aircraft capable of fulfilling a variety of roles and a design that influenced a generation of flying boats. The story of the development of the Sunderland will be covered later when reviewing the 'C' class. As the Sunderland was perceived as a relatively bold step forward, the Saunders-Roe A.33 aircraft was also ordered, possibly as an insurance against failure, but unfortunately this was also a relatively innovative design and proved to be flawed. The hull of the aircraft was kept shallow in order to minimise drag, and hence the wing had to be positioned high above the hull. There was neither a central pylon nor struts to the hull top and the wing was supported parasol-fashion by a large sloping 'N' strut on each side that attached to the balance sponsons close to the hull sides. The wing was a single structure built on the Mono-spar system where the spar carried the bending loads while torsion and drag loads were carried through a system of internal bracing wires. This was by far the largest wing of its type yet attempted. The hull was a conventional Duralumin structure that lacked Saunders' earlier corrugated skins. The A.33 was much delayed in construction and the prototype flew a whole year later than the Sunderland. On the take-off run for an early test flight it bounced badly after hitting the wake of a passing ship and the wing suffered catastrophic failure in the ensuing heavy landing. As the Sunderland had by now proven its capabilities it was not considered worthwhile repairing the A.33 to continue the tests. The prototype was scrapped and the production order cancelled.

Mitchell's enthusiasm for Rolls-Royce's evaporatively cooled engines was probably a significant contributory factor in the undoing of Supermarine's Type 232. Despite the advantage of lower drag and weight saving compared to conventional water-cooled engines, the system was proving problematic in most aircraft to which it was fitted and as the sump for the condensed coolant water was a considerable distance below the header tanks, far more so than in Mitchell's Type 224, spontaneous re-boiling in the pumps would almost certainly have occurred. Rolls-Royce would abandon the concept of evaporative cooling in early 1935. Furthermore, the Air Ministry was also showing a distinct preference for air-cooled radial engines for the majority of their larger aircraft. There were, however, other features of the aircraft design that might have proven unappealing. The wing bracing was strangely untidy, employing both struts and wires, and the gull-wing raised the centre of gravity rather high so that stability on the water may have proven to be an issue, especially as the span of the sponsons was quite low. Several large sponson-stabilised aircraft, such as the Martin M-130, were rather prone to this problem and were difficult to taxi in a crosswind. The placement of the engines well ahead of the wing leading edge and on the high-angle dihedral inner wing would no doubt have made servicing difficult. It was, overall, a rather ungainly and oddly unrefined design and Mitchell would not use this layout for any of his later flying boat projects.

IMPERIAL AIRWAYS

By 1934 Imperial Airways had been in operation for ten years. Although they were in competition with the major Continental airlines on the routes into Europe, all heavily subsidised by their respective governments, as they were themselves, the company held a virtual monopoly over the longer routes into the Empire. The government had nipped in the bud the attempt by Cobham and Blackburn to operate a rival service into the Mediterranean and Africa. The airline flew a variety of aircraft types, almost all biplanes, with the emphasis on comfort rather than speed; a genteel view of air travel that came to look increasingly archaic as the decade proceeded.

In the US, President Coolidge had established an Air Board in 1925 to recommend policy for both civil and military aviation. Their report focussed attention on the need to grow air transportation throughout the nation and so he established a five-year plan and budget to stimulate development. Part of this package was a substantial subsidy for air mail, which encouraged the design and development of a new generation of fast mail planes and passenger transport aircraft. The equivalent British aircraft of the period, and indeed most European aircraft, began to look decidedly dated, most especially when the Boeing 247 and Douglas DC-2 came into service in 1933 and 1934 respectively. The Air Ministry and Imperial Airways knew that they had to respond.

The British Government had established one of the world's first regular long-distance air mail services in 1921 to link the mandated territories of Palestine and Mesopotamia (now Iraq) to Europe via a base at Heliopolis, just outside Cairo. This service was run by the RAF using Vickers Vernon transport aircraft but in 1926 the responsibility had passed to Imperial Airways, who extended the route to India. The service was costly and subsidised heavily by the government. From the late 1920s the notion of extending this service further into the Empire, to include Australia and South Africa, began to be discussed within government, both to bind the far-flung territories together and to stimulate growth within the aircraft and airline business. This programme began to take shape in the early 1930s until it was formalised as the Empire Air Mail Scheme (EAMS) in 1934, whereby mail could be sent to any part of the Empire, excluding the Caribbean and Canada, at a fixed price. Not only did this require further huge subsidies from the government for the operation of the service but it also necessitated funding for a whole new fleet of long-distance aircraft to carry the mail. The decision was taken that the major part of this service would be handled by flying boats as the provision of landing strips along the route was seen as more costly than making use of sheltered coastal waters, major lakes and rivers.

The General Manager (technical) at Imperial Airways was Major Robert Hobart Mayo, a former RFC pilot and Ministry of Munitions aviation expert who had worked as a consultant to the air industry for many years. He was instrumental in formulating the specifications for two aircraft for the airline: one, a long-distance flying boat for the Empire routes, as mentioned above, and the other an experimental high-speed mail carrier. It is very obvious from what followed that he must have had a very close relationship with Oswald Short and his Chief Designer, Arthur Gouge.

Mayo looked first at the requirement for a dedicated mail carrier, a specialised high-speed aircraft capable of carrying mail to the outer reaches of the Empire within 24 hours. The fundamental problem was one of payload distribution; if the aircraft carried sufficient fuel to fly the long sectors along the route then the remaining capacity for mail was severely restricted. In addition, an aircraft capable of carrying this load of fuel and mail would struggle to take-off in anything other than optimal conditions and its top speed would be compromised. To resolve this conundrum Mayo, through his private consultancy, developed the concept of a two-aircraft composite, the upper component being the mail carrier, optimised for speed and long flight duration, and the lower component that carried the mail carrier on its back and functioned solely to get this aircraft into the air. He moved quickly

to patent this concept in 1932. For Imperial Airways both aircraft were to take-off and land on water; the lower component would be a monoplane flying boat while the upper would be a monoplane seaplane. The contract to build these two aircraft was accepted by Shorts, who commenced detailed design of both components as Types S.20 Maia and S.21 Mercury respectively, while the Air Ministry issued specification 13/33 to cover the work.

The second aircraft was the passenger and freight flying boat. In the early 1930s Imperial Airways operated a small number of biplane flying boats, all built by Shorts, namely the Calcutta and its enlarged successor the Kent. The Kent had a top speed of 137mph. The first thoughts for the next generation flying boat were that it should have similar range to the Kent, 450 miles, but carry a greater payload, have double the all-up weight and a cruising speed of 150mph, which implied that it would be met best by a monoplane. The draft Outline Specification for a four-engined flying boat was circulated to the various flying boat constructors in November 1933 and formalised in March 1934 but it is clear that discussions had taken place with at least some of the main aircraft companies prior to this. The specification called for an aircraft capable of carrying an 8,200lb payload, which would comprise twenty-four day passengers or sixteen night passengers, plus 6,200lb of mail and cargo. The cruising speed at 5,000ft was to be no less than 130mph and the range 500 miles against a 40mph headwind. This draft also included a requirement, later dropped, for the aircraft to be capable of being fitted with a land undercarriage, as it was thought that 7–10 per cent of its operating life may take place from land airstrips. Air-cooled engines were preferred although water-cooled were not excluded. Shorts' response was the type S.23, an aircraft that had much in common with the S.20 Maia design and a clear indication that they had been involved in quite detailed discussion with Mayo long before the specification was issued. As a result they were able to tender the S.23 to Imperial Airways at the end of June 1934 and received a contract for two prototypes in February 1935. The first flight date was specified as April 1936. Before the prototype had flown, Shorts received a production contract for twenty-eight aircraft and plans were already afoot to produce upgraded variants with higher fuel and payload capacity.

Supermarine received Imperial Airways' requirement document but chose to pass on the opportunity to tender, this occurring during the time that Mitchell was convalescing after his operation and when the Design Department was at full stretch working on the F.7/30 upgrades, Stranraer, Seagull V and Type 232. However, when a revised requirement for a similar aircraft with an extended range of 800 miles arrived at the end of 1934,

↑ Shorts' 'C' Class set a new standard for commercial flying boats in Britain.

following parliamentary approval for EAMS, Mitchell commenced work under Type 302 and, as was becoming usual practice, drew up a variety of alternative concepts.

First of all, Roger Dickson, now transferred out of the Spitfire team, was tasked with drawing up a number of long-range mail biplane schemes powered by four Bristol Perseus radial engines. All of these schemes, of which there were at least three, all dated May 1935, were broadly similar and followed the pattern established by the Scapa, Stranraer and Type 238 project. The four engines were mounted on sleek nacelles within NACA cowls ahead of the top wing. The wings were finely tapered, apart from the upper wing centre section with the engine mounts, which was parallel chord, and various single and twin bay bracing arrangements were sketched. Wing tip floats provided stability and were attached to the lower wing by aerodynamic pylons and braced with wires. The hull in each case was a steep-sided design with rounded prow and upswept tail. One version had a flared lower sector and wider planing bottom. Each had a typical Supermarine strut-braced tailplane with twin fins and rudders. They were elegant aircraft and would probably have been capable of meeting Imperial Airways' modest performance requirements. However, the primary design under Type 302 was to be a monoplane.

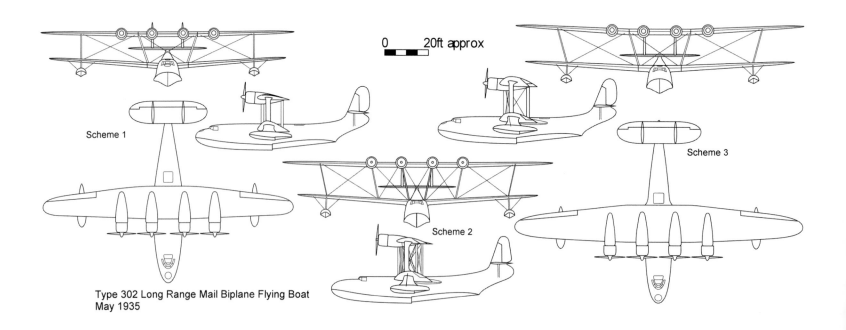

Scheme 1

Scheme 2

Scheme 3

0   20ft approx

Type 302 Long Range Mail Biplane Flying Boat
May 1935

SIKORSKY

In the summer of 1934 Sikorsky introduced the S-42 passenger flying-boat, the first of the 'Clippers' ordered by Pan American Airways. These aircraft were to operate on the airline's network of routes along the eastern seaboard of the US, around the Gulf of Mexico and down into South America. The S-42 could carry up to thirty-two passengers but generally flew with fewer as part of the payload was allocated to mail and cargo. Range with a typical load was more than 1,100 miles and the cruising speed was as high as 160mph at 12,000ft. The aircraft had a hull with vertical sides and curved roof stiffened by external stringers, and the planing bottom had a high prow and two steps. The fully enclosed cockpit was positioned well forward with a shallow vertical windscreen that gave a poor view directly forward over the curved nose but was compensated for with ample glazing to the sides. There were numerous portholes for the passengers. The monoplane wing was mounted on a short pylon on the hull roof and braced to the lower hull by twin large slanting struts on either side plus wires and supplementary minor struts. The main centre section of the span, constituting around 60 per cent of the total, was parallel chord, while the outer panels tapered sharply. Four Pratt & Whitney Hornet radial engines, delivering around 660hp apiece, were fitted within short cowls and mounted ahead of the wing leading edge. Wing balance floats were attached to the outer end of the wing centre section. The tailplane, with twin fins and rudders, was attached to a stub pylon at the rear of the hull and all were strut braced liberally. Igor Sikorsky had filed the design patent for this aircraft in October 1933.

In November 1934 Sikorsky visited Britain and presented a lecture to the Royal Aeronautical Society on the subject of long-range flying boats, which included a review of the development of the S-42 and details of its weight and performance. This attracted a great deal of interest and comment in the press. The aircraft was so attractive that in early 1936 a new company, British Marine Aircraft Ltd, was launched to build the S-42 under licence and production premises were erected on the banks of the river Hamble

→ The Sikorsky S-42 proved to be a sensation when it entered service with Pan American in 1934. Its speed and range surpassed that of any other commercial flying boat.

just a short distance down Southampton Water from Supermarine's works. Construction of the first aircraft had started by the end of the year but chronic financial problems led to the collapse of the business within weeks. Nevertheless, for a while this venture appeared to present the British flying boat constructors with a potentially formidable competitor.

MITCHELL'S VIEWS ON AIR TRANSPORT

In October 1934 Mitchell took the unusual step of expressing his views on the future development of civil aircraft in an article written for the *Daily Mirror* entitled 'What is happening now in Air Transport'.

In common with many other British aircraft designers, the contrast between the aircraft they had been requested to design for Imperial Airways and those entering service in the US was a matter of great concern to him. This had become all too apparent when Douglas and Boeing entered two of their latest airliners for the MacRobertson Air Race from Britain to Australia, carrying passengers, and had eclipsed all but the specialist de Havilland Comet long-distance racer that won the event. Mitchell attributed Britain's lethargy in building similar aircraft to official procurement policy, which prioritised safety and economy over speed. His view was that prioritising speed had not led to the other factors being sacrificed in the US aircraft. All of their key features were well understood in Britain but had yet to be put into practice. He stressed the advantages of evaporative cooling systems for aircraft and predicted that they would be used extensively in the future, just six months before Rolls-Royce would pull the plug on their development.

On the types of aircraft likely to be built in the next decade or two, Mitchell felt there was little advantage in developing types to carry more than 100 passengers except for flying boats, which he believed had a great future. He did, however, doubt that they would ever reach the size of 'a flying Queen Mary'. On performance, his view was that double the current speeds was likely but speculative comments about 1,000mph appearing in the popular press were fanciful. Flying in the stratosphere, above 30,000ft, he also thought unlikely as the cost of heating, ventilation and pressure cabins would not be viable commercially. The possibility of using catapult launching he considered to offer great advantages for mail carriers but was uncertain whether passengers would be prepared to accept it.

On safety, Mitchell saw the weather as the greatest risk, especially fog, and advocated investment in better forecasting, radio equipment and cockpit instruments, especially some form of ground proximity warning system, possibly based on the echo principle. In conclusion, he predicted that air travel would become the safest form of all in the future.

To what extent Mitchell was able to incorporate these views into his new designs for passenger-carrying flying boats would soon become apparent.

FLYING BOATS FOR IMPERIAL AIRWAYS

It has to be said that Mitchell's Type 302 design owed a great deal to the Sikorsky S-42, which it resembled to a high degree except in one detail: his primary design was fitted with sponsons. However, having said that, Mitchell later drew up an alternative version fitted with wing floats. In common with the S-42, and indeed Blackburn's earlier Sydney, the Type 302 had a pylon-mounted, strut-braced monoplane wing with parallel chord centre section and tapered outer panels. On the Type 302 the wing was braced to the sponsons by a single strut and wires on each side, while on the version with wing floats the support pylon was reduced in height, offset to port, and the wing was braced to the hull. The outer wing panels of this version were of skewed-elliptical plan. The hull of the two also differed in section; the sponson aircraft had quite straight vertical sides while on the float aircraft it was more curved. There does not appear to be any particular reason why this was so other than Mitchell's penchant for tweaks and constant revisions. In both cases the tailplane sat on an upturned rear hull, was strut braced and was fitted with twin fins and rudders. The Type 302 was to be powered by four 880hp Bristol Perseus radials. Typical range at full load was 1,000 miles and the economical cruising speed was estimated at 144mph. The aircraft cabin was configured to carry eighteen to twenty-four passengers, depending on whether sleeping accommodation was required, leaving capacity for a significant load of baggage, mail and cargo. Total payload was of the order of 18,500lb. Entry to the passenger cabin was via a door on the port side positioned over the sponson while on the float-stabilised version entry was via a door at the rear.

The Type 302 was both larger and heavier than the S-42 and could carry a slightly higher payload. Performance figures for both aircraft have to be compared with caution as one is an estimate and the other is the manufacturer's flight acceptance test results and homologated class records, but on paper the Supermarine design appears to have been slightly inferior.

One novel suggestion put forward by the design team was to develop the aircraft as an amphibian by fitting wheels to the outer end of each sponsons. The tips of the sponsons were designed to rotate downwards through 90

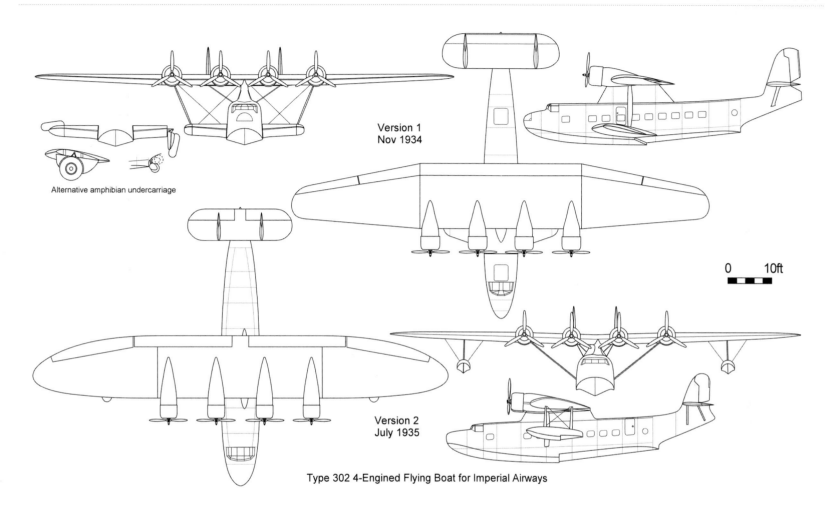

Version 1
Nov 1934

Alternative amphibian undercarriage

0   10ft

Version 2
July 1935

Type 302 4-Engined Flying Boat for Imperial Airways

degrees to lower the wheels and when retracted they lay on the upper surface exposed to the airflow, a poor arrangement that would have added considerable drag. This was an idea to address Imperial Airways' early requirement for these flying boats to be capable of having a land undercarriage fitted.

A militarised version of the Type 302 project was included under Type 232 but does not appear to have been considered as much more than an initial concept as there are no indications that any design work was carried out on the fitment of armament.

The Supermarine Type 302 was perceived to offer no compelling advantages over developed versions of Shorts' S.23 and no aircraft were ordered.

SHORTS' MONOPLANE FLYING BOATS

Shorts' S.23 represented a major step forward in flying boat design in Britain and it is worth describing its main features as they were to prove to be highly influential. The S.20 Maia, S.23 'C' class, and S.25 Sunderland were developed in parallel and shared a great many features. They are, in effect, three variations on the same design theme. Although the Mayo Composite aircraft concept was the earliest requirement to reach Shorts, followed closely by the military specification R.2/33, it was actually the Imperial Airways passenger aircraft that Arthur Gouge chose to develop first as the technical requirements for this aircraft were considered to be less exacting.

Research into hull and planing bottom design undertaken by Gouge in Shorts' own test tank facility had shown that good results could be obtained, both on the water and in the air, by using a bottom surface that was significantly narrower in relation to its length than had been common practice in the past. Adopting this new design enabled the hull itself to be made narrower at the chine and eliminated any need for an outward flare at the base of the sidewalls, thereby reducing aerodynamic drag. Gouge also intended to construct a full cantilever monoplane wing for the aircraft and hence this would require a stronger root attachment than for a strut-braced wing. This would be difficult to achieve with a simple pylon mount without incurring a large drag or weight penalty. His solution, which he thought at first might prove to be unacceptable to Imperial Airways, was to design a deep double-deck hull with the wing mounted in the shoulder position. However, his concerns proved to be groundless as Imperial Airways were delighted with the concept and he was able to move ahead with the detailed design of the aircraft. As a consequence, the S.23 was the cleanest flying boat of its generation with a full cantilever stressed skin wing, a similar cantilever tailplane and single large fin. To ensure a low landing speed, Gouge devised a flap mechanism where the flaps ran back and downwards on rails when extended, thereby providing additional wing area to increase lift. This clever design was the subject of a patent, one of several that covered the main elements of the aircraft's structure. The four Bristol Pegasus radial engines were enclosed within long NACA cowls and mounted ahead of the leading edge of the wings, and portions of the leading edge adjacent

to the engines could be hinged forward to provide platforms from which they could be serviced. The fuel tanks were located between the twin spars of the wing. Although Gouge tendered the S.23 to meet the original requirements of Imperial Airways it was a very flexible design and he was able to accommodate the extra fuel tank capacity necessary to extend the range if required. At first there was just a single tank in each wing but the number was increased progressively as the basic design evolved.

As an aside, it is interesting to note that in his patent for the extending flap system, which he submitted in January 1935, Gouge included an illustration showing the flaps installed on a wing of elliptical plan form. It would appear that the S.23 was yet another aircraft for which an elliptical wing had been proposed in the early stage of design only for it to be modified prior to construction to one with conventional straight taper over much of the span to simplify construction and reduce cost.

The S.23 formed the basis for the design of the S.25 Sunderland, Shorts' tender to R.2/33, for which Gouge was able to incorporate a number of improvements, suggested during development of that aircraft, most notably to the planing surfaces. A powered gun turret was mounted in the extended nose that could be retracted to the rear when mooring. Initially there was to be just a manual gun ring in the tail but the Air Ministry requested that a power turret be substituted after construction of the prototype was well under way. The bomb load was stored within the capacious hull and deployed on rails that ran span-wise under the wings. It was powered by four 1,010hp Bristol Perseus XXII radials.

Such was the pressing need for the aircraft, and their confidence in the design even before the S.23 had completed its test programme, that the Air Ministry placed a production order in 1936, a full year before the prototype flew.

The Sunderland flew in late 1937 but the tests were abbreviated as the added weight of the tail turret required that the wing be modified. This had been known in advance and plans were in place to add 4.5 degrees of sweep to restore balance. Flight tests resumed in mid-1938. Despite the delay the aircraft entered service in June 1938.

← The Short Sunderland marked a huge step forward in reconnaissance flying boat design for the RAF and it was a formidable aircraft with strong offensive and defensive capability.

The Sunderland was developed through five marks and served throughout the war. The last RAF aircraft were retired in 1959 but the Royal New Zealand Air Force were still using theirs throughout the 1960s. Transport versions and civilian derivatives continued in service even longer.

Gouge's flying boats, were not, however, without fault. The 'C' class suffered a series of accidents in service, almost all when landing and most attributable to pilot error. The high cockpit made judgement of height and speed difficult for pilots trained on smaller craft and the operation of the flaps was a new concept. Their structure also proved rather weak in places, especially the planing bottoms, and later models employed thicker gauge skins for the hulls and wings. Familiarity with flying boats of this type and a programme of structural improvements eliminated most problems.

TRANSATLANTIC FLYING BOATS

With the 'C' Class aircraft under construction, Imperial Airways turned their attention to the one key route not yet addressed; crossing the Atlantic. Juan Trippe, the ambitious president of Pan American Airways, had been in the forefront of the move to introduce a transatlantic air route and had urged the US Government to negotiate a deal with their British counterparts. With a fleet of Sikorsky and Martin 'Clippers' under construction he was determined to be the first to provide a commercial service over the Atlantic. Direct commercial flights from the USA to Britain or mainland Europe were beyond the capabilities of any aircraft design at that time and hence it was necessary to negotiate with Canada and the Irish Free State to provide facilities to use as intermediate bases along the way. A route between the west coast of Ireland and the east coast of Newfoundland was a distance of around 2,000 miles. A satisfactory arrangement was reached between the United Kingdom, USA, Canada and the Irish Free State in 1935 and signed as the Montreal Agreement. However, this was not the full solution as the route could be used only during the summer months as the Newfoundland coast iced up in winter. The alternative southern route was far longer and required flying to Lisbon in Portugal, across to the Azores and then to the Bahamas before continuing up along the eastern seaboard of the US. This all represented a daunting challenge and led to consideration of four alternative approaches. The first was to specify a very large aircraft capable of flying both the eastbound and westbound journeys directly, of which the westerly, into the prevailing winds, would be the more demanding. It was not at all clear at the time whether such an aircraft would be possible without incurring an unacceptable reduction in payload. The second was to consider some form of in-flight refuelling to enable an aircraft to take-off lightly loaded and then to take on fuel prior to commencing the oceanic crossing. The third was to use an accelerated launch system or catapult to aid take-off with a heavily loaded aircraft, and the fourth was a dual aircraft along the lines of Mayo's Composite Aircraft project. A fifth proposal had also been tabled at various times from the mid-1920s onwards and involved the construction of large, tethered floating runways and terminals, called Seadromes by their Canadian American inventor, Edward Armstrong, as stepping stones along the route, but this was fraught with technical issues and hence not given much serious consideration.

The transfer of fuel from aircraft to aircraft had first been carried out as a stunt during a few endurance flight attempts at airshows in the 1920s, and a small number of experimental trials had taken place with hose-based systems, but the concept had not as yet raised much interest within either the military or the airlines. In Britain the first practical system employing refuelling hoses and grappling lines was patented in 1935 by Flt Lt Richard Atcherley, a pilot who had flown in the Schneider Trophy contest in 1929, and the rights were purchased by Sir Alan Cobham, former test pilot and pioneer of long-distance flights, who had himself taken out a patent for a less advanced procedure in 1934. Cobham was in the process of establishing a business to carry out experimental development of a viable refuelling system with an eye on the opportunity to provide a service to both Imperial Airways and the RAF.

Catapult launch assistance of aircraft had been employed, on and off, for many years; indeed the Wright brothers' first flights had used such a system and it was common practice to employ elasticated cord for launching gliders. Various forms of catapults on ships were under development in the early 1930s and the German air mail service to South America used a dedicated catapult ship stationed in the mid-Atlantic to enable their moderately sized Dornier flying boats to fly the route in two legs. The Air Ministry made a proposal that a similar system could be used on the Imperial Airways routes, referred to frequently as an accelerator rather than a catapult.

While the various options for transatlantic passenger flying boats were under consideration, construction of the experimental Mayo Composite Aircraft had started in 1934 but they would not be ready for testing until the early months of 1938. The upper component, the seaplane Mercury, was not designed to carry passengers and before any form of commercial passenger-carrying version could be considered it would be necessary to prove the viability of the concept.

Mitchell worked on an aircraft capable of flying the routes in response to the Imperial Airways requirement for a Trans-Atlantic Passenger Flying Boat, which specified a range of 2,500 miles and cruising speed of 150mph against a 40mph headwind while carrying a total payload of 3,500lb. The Type 306 was designed in parallel with the Type 302, although it does seem the team put more effort into this project than they had done for the smaller aircraft. Indeed, the project appears to have been propelled with a degree of the same vigour for new techniques as had led to the Spitfire, a sure indication that Mitchell was utterly determined that his remaining time would be filled with bold ideas. Mitchell and his team reviewed the specification and routes and came to two conclusions. Firstly, the use of radial engines imposed an unacceptably high drag penalty that resulted in a requirement for a heavy fuel load and hence a protracted take-off run. Secondly, Horta in the Azores, used for the winter service, did not provide sufficient sheltered space to enable a heavily laden flying boat to take off, even if it proved possible to reduce the take-off run to less than 30 seconds.

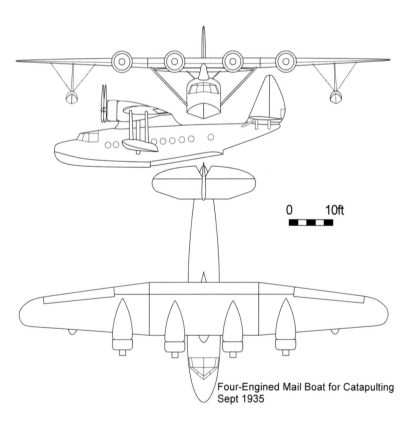

0   10ft

Four-Engined Mail Boat for Catapulting
Sept 1935

As a consequence, Mitchell proposed two versions of the Type 306, both to be powered by water-cooled engines, and two schemes for catapult-assisted take-off at Horta.

The first layout drawings under Type 306 date from August 1935 and are for a mail carrier. The first was virtually identical to the Type 302 with wing balance floats. It is likely that the design was one of several concepts for a mail flying boat considered but the preliminary drawings of this one only have survived. This second design shared its pylon-mounted monoplane wing layout with the Type 302 but had a single fin and rudder and a reduced wingspan, and consequently a high wing loading, as it was designed specifically for catapult launching. Both designs may be related to specifications issued by the Air Ministry in 1936 and which will be reviewed briefly later.

These mail plane concepts were followed by two completely new passenger-carrying designs, one powered by four Rolls-Royce Merlins and the other by four Rolls-Royce Vultures. This was a controversial decision as Imperial Airways were known to favour radial engines for their aircraft. The Vulture, just a project at this date, was to be a large 42 litre, 1,670hp engine of 'X' configuration that was, in effect, four Kestrel cylinder banks mounted at 90 degree spacing and driving a common crankshaft. It was Imperial Airways' policy to invite tenders for two designs, one fulfilling the detailed requirements of the specification and a second more speculative design to be fitted with more powerful 'next generation' engines, of which the Vulture was a good example. Mitchell, therefore, decided that both of the Type 306 aircraft designs should be tendered.

The two aircraft were similar in overall design, differing mainly in size and weight. They shared the layout with that of the Type 302 with wing floats but a lot of effort had gone into producing an aerodynamically far cleaner aircraft. The hull represented a complete rethink by the team, who appear to have taken inspiration from the development process they had used to derive the floats for the S.6 Schneider racer. For that aircraft the aerodynamic and hydrodynamic tests had both commenced using a basic shape of 'ideal' aerodynamic form, often referred to as airship shape, having the required internal volume, and the best compromise to meet the specified water and air performance was then evolved from this in incremental steps through a programme of water tank and wind tunnel testing. The hull of the Type 306 looks as if it may have undergone a similar development process as, compared to the Type 302, the nose had been lowered, there was pronounced nose-to-tail curvature in the roof contours and Supermarine's characteristic upturned tail had been discarded in favour of a pointed

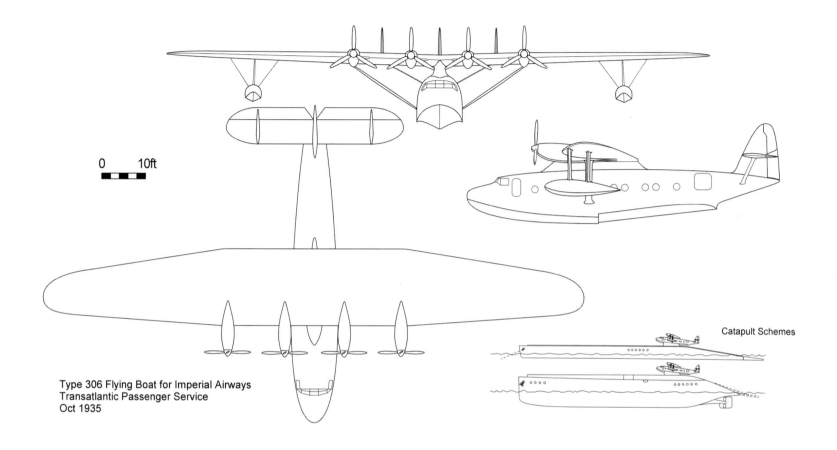

0   10ft

Type 306 Flying Boat for Imperial Airways
Transatlantic Passenger Service
Oct 1935

Catapult Schemes

termination. The wing retained the parallel chord centre section, tapered outer panels and single-strut bracing of the Type 302. There is nothing in the drawings or specifications to suggest that flaps were to be fitted although it would have been most unlikely for these not to have been included. The strut-braced tailplane was also retained but in the absence of the upturned tail there was now a large central fin to support it and two smaller fins outboard. There was no noticeable change to the main planing bottom but the wing floats were of a new low-drag design that lacked a step. In each aircraft the engines were mounted ahead of the wing leading edge and drove three-bladed, variable pitch metal propellers. The radiators were located within the wings and cooling air entered from slots in the leading edge and presumably exited below.

Mitchell's investigations suggested the optimal wing loading for the aircraft was between 30 and 31lb/sq ft, although this did raise some doubts as to whether the Merlin-engined version could meet the maximum specified take-off duration of 40 seconds in all situations. The option to fit six Merlins had been investigated but this led either to reduced stability on the water, if they were all installed as tractors, or lower efficiency and increased cabin noise if two were mounted as pushers. In addition, Mitchell remained concerned about the impact on performance that even small variations in structural weight or propeller characteristics could produce but estimated that the Merlin-engined aircraft would weigh 54,000lb loaded, cruise at 150mph and could accommodate up to twenty-four passengers. In order to ensure it would meet Imperial Airways performance requirements Mitchell proposed increasing the size and fitting it with the more powerful Vulture engine. This would weigh 71,000lb, cruise at 175mph and accommodate up to thirty-two passengers. For both versions of the aircraft the payload and cruising speed could be increased if catapult assisted take-off was employed.

Mitchell suggested two alternative catapult schemes, both using a compressed air system to accelerate the loaded aircraft to 94mph within 225ft, an acceleration force of between 1.06 and 1.33g. The key difference between the two options was basically one of cost and capability; one was mounted on a barge while the second was on a converted oil tanker that could also function as a depot and rescue ship. The barge had a shallow draft and the aircraft was taken on board via a ramp at the rear, where it engaged with a submerged trolley attached by cables to a winch, and this served as the launch platform on the catapult. The system on the ship was similar but slightly more complex due to the height of the deck above sea level.

Supermarine's tender to Imperial Airways was submitted on 10 October 1935. By this date the first two Short S.23 aircraft were already under construction and the second was being fitted with increased fuel tank capacity in order to carry out survey flights across the Atlantic.

In July 1936 a study commissioned by the Aeronautical Research Committee concluded that neither in-flight refuelling nor the Mayo Composite concept were viable for a transatlantic passenger service and supported the use of some form of take-off acceleration system. It also suggested that a wing loading of around 45lb/sq ft would be optimal, considerably higher than that suggested by Mitchell's work where catapult launching was only to be used in the restricted harbour at Horta. However, the concept of using catapults, relatively costly and as yet unproven for large aircraft, did not find favour with Imperial Airways and coupled with Mitchell's preference for water-cooled engines, the Type 306 did not appear attractive. The performance of the Merlin-engined version was acknowledged to be marginal against the specifications while the alternative involved committing to an engine that had not yet run. Indeed, when it did the Vulture was to be plagued by mechanical problems, leaving several aircraft projects stranded, and development was terminated in 1941 so that Rolls-Royce could concentrate on the Merlin and Griffon. As a consequence of these issues, and the good performance of Shorts' S.23, no orders for the Type 306 were forthcoming and Imperial Airways chose instead to commission a larger flying boat from Shorts, the S.26 'G' class. These aircraft were very similar in appearance to the earlier S.23 but were increased in all dimensions and incorporated improvements suggested from development of the Sunderland. Three S.26 aircraft were ordered by Imperial Airways to fly the Atlantic routes but war broke out before they could be introduced into service.

In 1935 Mitchell had the design team work up preliminary arrangement drawings for a military derivative of the larger, Vulture-powered, aircraft, a flying boat that would have been in the same class as the Short Sunderland. No significant changes were made to the form of the aircraft other than the installation of gun turrets in the nose and tail, and gun ports on either side and in the rear of the wing support pylon. The turrets were of unusual design and will be described later as they were carried over into one of the company's bomber projects.

Although Imperial Airways had been unenthusiastic, the Air Ministry continued to show a deal of interest in catapults or accelerators as a means to enable heavily loaded military and civil aircraft to take-off, and a requirement for this capability would be written in to a number of specifications in the mid-1930s. A Shorts project, the S.27, was ordered as a Long Range Catapulted Flying Boat under specification 35/36 at the very end of 1936. This called for a four-engined flying boat capable of carrying a 6,000lb payload, comprised of eighteen passengers, baggage, mail and freight, at a cruising speed in excess of 200mph on the Atlantic routes. Four Bristol Hercules engines were to be fitted. Shorts had carried out some wind tunnel and water tank research work on the design before the specification was cancelled. It is possible that Mitchell's Type 306 catapult mail plane designs may have been associated with early discussions with Imperial Airways and the Air Ministry regarding this requirement.

It is hard to understand why Mitchell believed that radial engines would be unable to provide the performance necessary for long-distance flying boats as neither Sikorsky nor Shorts had any such concerns regarding their aircraft. That Mitchell and his team were mistaken was further reinforced when the Glen L. Martin Company in the US introduced the M-130 four-engined Clipper flying boat at the end of 1934 destined to fly on Pan American's Pacific routes. This aircraft was powered by four 830hp Pratt & Whitney Twin Wasp radials, weighed 52,000lb fully loaded, carried up to thirty-six passengers, had a range of more than 3,000 miles and cruised at 130mph. The design was similar in many respects to both the Sikorsky S-42 and Supermarine's projects except that the wing mounting pylon was faired into a long whale-back hump. It had a single fin and was balanced on the water by sponsons, which Martin referred to as seawings. The aircraft proved to be a great success although only four were built.

Although Supermarine's close association with Rolls-Royce had reaped benefits with the S.6 and S.6b Schneider racers, and would do so again with the Spitfire, Mitchell's apparent desire to select Rolls-Royce engines for many of his new projects, regardless of the role these aircraft were designed to fulfil and the preference of customers, often placed their tenders in a weak position when in competition with others. The latest generation of Bristol radial engines, whether conventional poppet-valve or new sleeved-valve types, were light, powerful and increasingly reliable units and were more than capable of meeting the requirement of both civil and military markets. Recent developments in cowling design reduced drag down to a level at which they could compete on far better terms with liquid-cooled types. Could it be that Mitchell's outstanding success with the Southampton and his Napier and Rolls-Royce powered Schneider racers had led to him developing a slight 'blind spot' when it came to the merits of air-cooled engines and did he attribute the failure of the Nanok, Southampton X and Air Yacht to the use of this type?

Mitchell's three designs for four-engined monoplane flying boats had proven to be an eclectic mixture of the rather eccentric Type 232, somewhat derivative Type 302, and interesting Type 306, and they had the misfortune to find themselves in competition alongside the premier British flying boat designs of the 1930s, Arthur Gouge's excellent family of aircraft. There is little doubt that Mitchell had lost out to a masterly piece of design. With the S.23, Gouge had achieved much the same as Mitchell had with the Spitfire. He had created the leader of its class and set a standard that others would strive to match.

23

MORE TWIN-ENGINED FLYING BOATS

REPLACING THE STRANRAER

In the summer of 1934, shortly before the first flight of the Stranraer, Mitchell initiated a new project, Type 303, under the title R.24/31 Development. However, this appears to have been somewhat of a speculative project as it was not started in response to any specific requirement from the Air Ministry and was used as a convenient place to collect together a variety of conceptual

designs for twin-engined flying boats, of which there were at least four, all powered by Rolls-Royce Merlin engines. They are an odd collection of apparently unrelated aircraft, two biplanes and two monoplanes. The first seems to have been an upgraded version of the Type 178 03 Twin Engined Air Mail Boat project with the Rolls-Royce Kestrel engines replaced by Merlins mounted under the upper wing, in the manner of the Scapa. It had finely tapered wings with single outboard struts. There were no signs

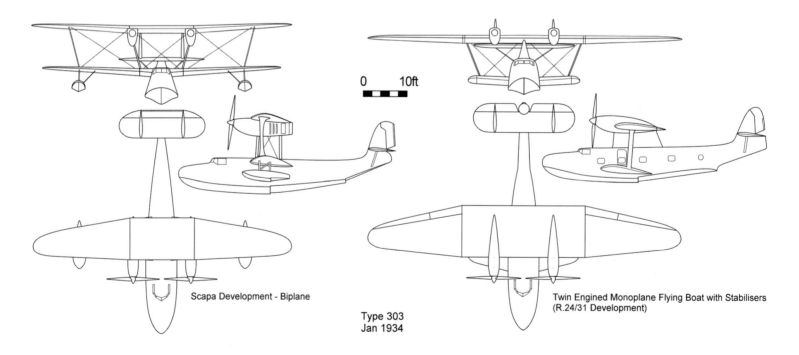

0   10ft

Scapa Development - Biplane

Twin Engined Monoplane Flying Boat with Stabilisers
(R.24/31 Development)

Type 303
Jan 1934

of armament. The second biplane was simply the Type 230 Stranraer re-engined with Merlins. The two monoplanes were essentially identical except that one was to be fitted with sponsons and the other with wing floats. They are similar to the monoplanes that had been included as a late alternative design within Type 232 to specification R.2/33, both derived from the Type 302, but scaled down slightly to be powered by two Merlins. Neither had any provision for the installation of armament. None of these designs advanced beyond the general arrangement stage.

Although the contract to produce sixteen Stranraer flying boats was welcome in the works it was readily apparent the aircraft was already an anachronism; it was for Supermarine what the Gladiator was for Gloster, the last of an illustrious line of aircraft, excellent for what it was but a stop-gap, outclassed by the newer designs then under development and on the drawing board. The leap forward in construction and aerodynamic technology that led to the Spitfire had its counterpart for larger aircraft too and Supermarine were now in real danger of being left behind in the race to build advanced flying boats. The two lucrative contracts for four-engined

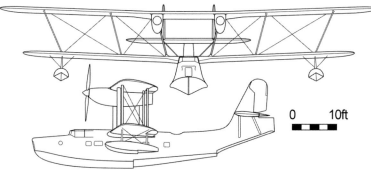

Type 303 Twin Engined Biplane Flying Boat (R.24/31 Development)
March 1934

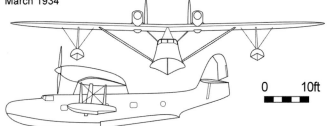

Type 303 Twin Engined Monoplane Flying Boat with Wing Floats
(R.24/31 Development)
1935

civil and military monoplane flying boats had been lost, both to Short Bros, and it must have been apparent to Mitchell that the designs he had submitted in competition with them had been demonstrably inferior. It was therefore imperative that the market for a smaller twin-engined flying boat, including the eventual replacement for the Stranraer, should not slip from their grasp. In the US a new aircraft targeting much the same market flew in the summer of 1935.

The Consolidated XP3Y-1 was an experimental patrol bomber flying boat built for the US Navy. The design dated from 1933 and the prototype flew in March 1935. This aircraft was the first of the long line of PBY flying boats and amphibians that became known later as the Catalina. The first production version, the PBY-1, entered service with the US Navy in 1936, a year before the Stranraer entered service with the RAF. The layout of the XP3Y-1 was not dissimilar to concurrent designs by Mitchell's team as the wing was mounted on a pylon above the hull and braced by twin struts on either side. The metal hull, however, was unusual in having an almost semi-circular section with an integral fin and was flush-riveted throughout. The balance floats were retractable, rotating laterally through 90 degrees to form the wing tips, under a Saunders patent that dated from 1928. It was powered by two Pratt & Whitney Twin Wasp radials producing 850hp each, compared to the Stranraer's 920hp Bristol Pegasus, and it was slightly larger overall, yet had a top speed 10mph higher and double the range. Furthermore, the aircraft was capable of carrying an ordnance load in excess of 2,000lb, which could include torpedoes, compared to the Stranraer's lighter bomb load of 1,000lb. There was a gun turret in the nose and three gun ports in the rear of the hull, one on either side and one behind the rear step of the planing bottom. It was aircraft of this capability, and better, that Supermarine needed to counter if they were to regain lost ground.

By 1935 the RAF were heavily committed to the Short Sunderland to fulfil the role of Four-engined General Purpose Boat Seaplane but the field remained open for a comparable but smaller aircraft to replace the Saro London, Supermarine Scapa and Stranraer, and which would be required within a very few years. Once more Mitchell had the team start work on yet another new base design, distinct from the styles adopted for the Type 232, 302, and 306 'families'.

↑ The Consolidated XP3Y-1 was a direct contemporary of the Stranraer. The production version entered service with the US Navy in 1936 and was ordered as a Stranraer replacement for the RAF in 1939.

HIGH-SPEED MONOPLANE FLYING BOATS

Mitchell requested that his team investigate alternative innovative layouts for a high-speed flying boat to meet the operational requirement for a Stranraer replacement and by mid-September they had drawn up at least six concepts.

The first was a fairly standard cantilever monoplane with slight gull-wing attached to the top of the hull, while the engine nacelle was mounted on a short pylon. Within this nacelle two Rolls-Royce Merlin engines drove tractor and pusher propellers. There were conventional wing floats and a single fin.

The second was similar except that the wing lacked the gull-wing form and the two Merlins, nose to tail, powered the two units of a tractor contra-rotating propeller, the driveshaft of the rear engine passing between the cylinder blocks of the front engine. This was possibly inspired by the Fiat AS6 engine installed in the Macchi M.C.72 racing seaplane that had set new air speed records in 1933 and 1934. The third was a variation modified to be fitted with sponsons and two alternative arrangements were shown, one with a cantilever gull-wing and short span sponsons, the other with the wing root attached to the engine nacelle pylon and braced by struts to longer span sponsons.

The fourth idea was for a larger aircraft powered by three Goshawks, one in a central nacelle on a stub pylon, and two in nacelles on the wing, which was of the gull-wing type again. The wing floats were designed to retract laterally into the base of the engine nacelles.

The fifth was slightly more conventional and appears to have been based on the Type 302. It was powered by four Bristol Mercury radials in two nacelles driving tractor and pusher propellers. An unusual feature was that, while the front Mercury engines were fitted with standard NACA cowls, the rear engines were enclosed completely within the nacelle. The drawings do not show how it was proposed to provide a cooling airflow for these engines.

The final layout had a taller hull, a gull-wing cantilever wing and four Mercury engines driving tractor propellers in standard nacelles on the wings. Retractable wing floats were fitted. However, none of these concept designs was chosen to be developed further and neither appear to have any bearing on later designs.

The first true project for this class of flying boat was the Type 308, a twin-engined Long Range Flying Boat drawn up in mid-1935 to Specification R.12/35. The initials of the draughtsman on the first layout drawing are R.J.M., which appears to suggest that Mitchell himself had sat at the drawing board and produced the design. This was highly unusual, he had long since delegated responsibility for drawing, checking and approving drawings to his deputies. Did Mitchell have a special interest in this project or were the Design Department so overwhelmed by work on the Spitfire, Walrus and other projects that he felt the need to step in and assist?

For the first time since the Type 179 Giant the team designed a cantilever wing for a flying boat project. It had a short straight centre section attached to an elongated support pylon on the hull and straight-tapered outer sections. The straight-sided hulls of earlier designs gave way to a new more curvaceous shape with an integral stub pylon at the rear to which the tailplane was attached. Although it retained the twin fins so typical of Supermarine designs, on this aircraft they were positioned as end-plates at the outer ends of the tailplane. It was proposed that the Type 308 should be powered by

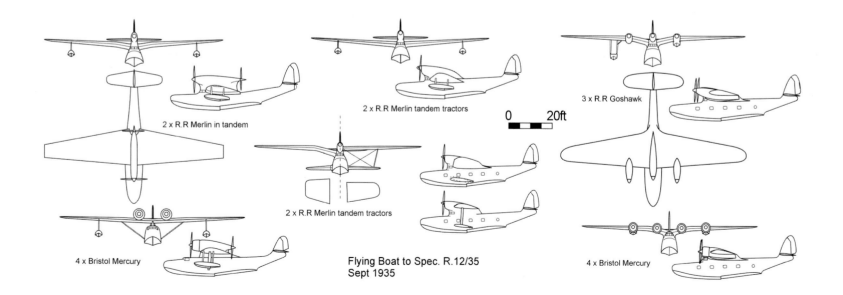

2 x R.R Merlin in tandem

2 x R.R Merlin tandem tractors

2 x R.R Merlin tandem tractors

3 x R.R Goshawk

4 x Bristol Mercury

Flying Boat to Spec. R.12/35
Sept 1935

4 x Bristol Mercury

two of Rolls-Royce's Vulture engines driving three-blade variable pitch propellers, and the radiator for them was housed within the pylon with air entering through the front and exiting through adjustable louvres on either side below the wing trailing edge. The most notable feature of the layout drawings is that they show no sign of either wing floats or sponsons. This was because the aircraft was to be fitted with a new form of retractable balance float that had been designed by Wilfred Kimber, an engineer working in the Technical Office, for which the company submitted a patent application in October 1935. These floats were akin to hydroplanes as they were of aerofoil

section and, when deployed, set at a positive angle of incidence and dihedral. When retracted they sat within recesses in the wing, matching the curvature of the under surface. Also stowed within the wings behind the single spar was the bomb load. In each wing there were two bays that could hold either 500lb or 250lb bombs, two that held 250lb bombs and a light carrier for four small bombs. The fuel was stored within the leading edge torsion box so the skin of the tank formed part of the load- bearing structure. This arrangement was patented by Mitchell in 1936, the last patent to be taken out in his name. There were three gun positions: a turret in the nose and firing positions in

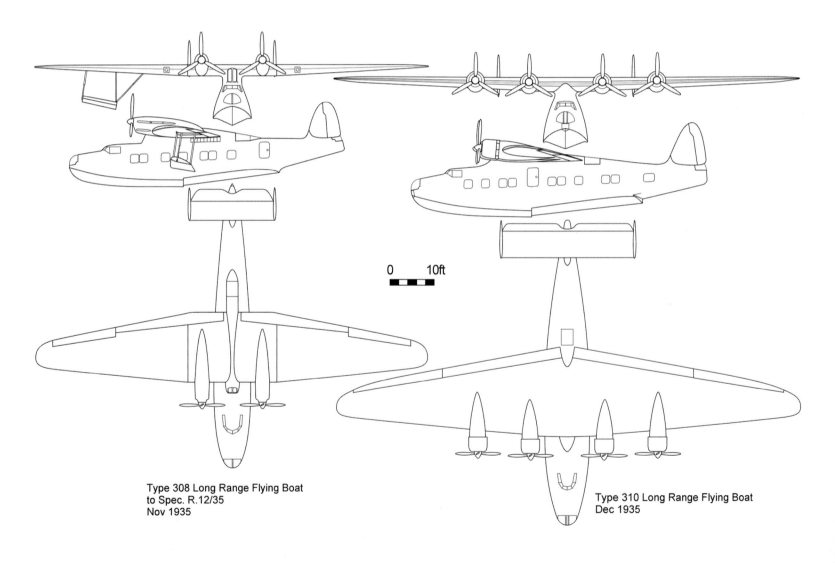

0   10ft

Type 308 Long Range Flying Boat
to Spec. R.12/35
Nov 1935

Type 310 Long Range Flying Boat
Dec 1935

the tail and the rear of the pylon. The bow turret was essentially spherical and held a single machine gun while the tail position had twin machine guns under a retractable transparent cover. The pylon gun position held a single machine gun, also under a retractable cover. Under the nose turret there was a top-hinged hatch that shielded the bomb aimer's position, a layout based on the similar fitment on the Scapa and Stranraer. Both this and the open gun positions were odd choices for a high performance aircraft. Supermarine are understood to have received a contract for the Type 308 in October 1935 but this must have been cancelled soon thereafter as a revised specification was issued in 1936.

Towards the end of the year, Mitchell used the Type 308 as the basis for a new project, the Type 310. This aircraft was very similar to the Type 308 except that it was larger and powered by four Bristol Taurus radials. The wing support pylon had been broadened and lengthened at the rear so that it blended with the side profile of the hull. Most likely this design was also aimed at R.12/35 as an insurance policy should development of the Rolls-Royce Vulture prove protracted.

For reasons that are not clear, the Air Ministry cancelled R.12/35 and replaced it with R.1/36 for a Small General Purpose Flying Boat, which specified high speed as a primary requirement. Top cruising speed was to be

in excess of 230mph and the range above 1,500 miles with full load while cruising at 200mph. Mitchell revised the Type 308, retaining the layout but with numerous detail changes, as the Type 314. There were subtle variations in the shape of the tapered wings and to the rear of the wing support pylon, an increase in the width of the upper hull and lengthened engine nacelles. The radiators for the Vulture engines were now fitted in the chin position on the nacelles and the opening tail gun position was replaced by one enclosed within a cylindrical turret. Although the design featured Kimber's retractable wing float/hydroplanes, there are conventional wing floats sketched in roughly in pencil on the layout drawings that may indicate the complex system was to have been abandoned. The Type 314 was the last flying boat project developed by the team under Mitchell's leadership.

Two other companies tendered designs to R.1/36: Blackburn with the B.20, also powered by two Rolls-Royce Vultures, and Saunders-Roe with the S.36, powered by two Bristol Hercules radials. The B.20 featured a novel retractable base section of the hull and floats that swung sideways to form the wing tips. The Air Ministry were impressed with the concept and ordered a prototype for testing but realised that development would take some time and the need for a service aircraft was pressing. Supermarine's project was considered the better of the two remaining candidates, probably

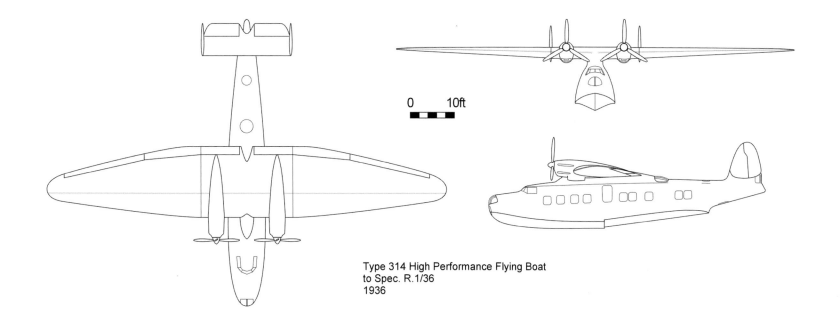

0   10ft

Type 314 High Performance Flying Boat
to Spec. R.1/36
1936

the best of the three, and was awarded the main contract, but this success was short-lived as mounting problems experienced by the company getting the Spitfire into production, which required extensive additional work from the Design Department to get data and drawings to the numerous subcontractors, led to them advising the Ministry that they would be unable to commence construction for a couple of years, so the contract was cancelled and the order transferred to Saunders-Roe. Their revised S.36 design, resembling a scaled-down Short Sunderland, was ordered off the drawing board as the need for the aircraft was now quite urgent. Unfortunately this turned out to be a serious mistake as the S.36, named Lerwick, was plagued by extremely serious handling issues both on the water and in the air, with the result that the production contract was cut short. The Stranraer and London biplanes soldiered on in service longer than intended until a replacement aircraft could be procured. The choice fell on the excellent Consolidated Model 28-5, which was named Catalina in RAF service. Although this was a rugged and capable aircraft, it is highly likely that the Supermarine Type 314 would have proven to be superior were it not for one problem: the Rolls-Royce Vulture turned out to be a flawed design prone to conrod failure, even when derated, and development was abandoned. No other engine of comparable power was available at the time and two other aircraft built to be powered by Vulture engines, both bombers, were modified extensively to be powered by four Merlins or Hercules. The Handley Page H.P.56 became the Halifax and the Avro Manchester became the Lancaster.

24

BOMBERS

BOMBERS IN THE 1920S

After the war the RAF's strategic planning centred on the bomber force, despite aerial warfare in the conflict having been dominated by observation aircraft and fighters. The development of large multi-engined bombers in the closing years, to target both military and civilian centres away from the main battlefields, had skewed thinking and a doctrine that future wars would be won or lost by the success of strategic bombing of the enemy's territory took hold throughout Europe. Sir Hugh Trenchard, the Chief of the Air Staff and architect of the RAF, was an ardent supporter of this philosophy. Raids carried out by German Gotha bombers on the English east coast and London had inflicted little serious damage but the complete inability of the small home defence fighter force and anti-aircraft guns to locate and destroy them led many to believe that large formations of such aircraft would always reach their target substantially intact, especially if they carried defensive armament. In the 1920s the French began to build a large force of bombers and it was this, as much as anything, which led to the RAF's strategic planners focusing on France as the notional future enemy. Funds to re-equip the RAF were extremely limited but the greater part was used to build a force of bombers capable of reaching Paris. These, however, were based around designs that dated from the end of the war; for the large night bombers Vickers evolved their aircraft from the Vimy, which itself remained in service until the late 1920s, and Handley Page from the 0/400. For the smaller single-engined day bombers the aircraft were upgraded versions of the de Havilland DH.4 and DH.9. Both classes of bombers were expected to fly in tight formation so their guns could be focussed on any attacking fighters. In the case of the light day bombers it was also believed their speed

would prove sufficient to make interception by fighters relatively unlikely. The more pessimistic of strategic planners fervently believed that waves of day and night bomber attacks against a major civilian and commercial centre, such as London, and carried out over a small number of days could prove decisive, forcing a quick capitulation. In essence, the only deterrent against a belligerent nation equipped with bombers was to have more bombers of your own. Similar thinking had led to the escalation in the battleship fleets prior to the First World War and in the post-Second World War era to the arsenals of nuclear weapons.

The heavy bomber force, which would fly mostly night sorties, saw limited technical development through the 1920s. Wood gave way to metal, engine power grew and defensive armament increased but the overall design philosophy changed little. The speed of these aircraft had hardly risen at all from their wartime equivalents. The faster light day bombers, however, received greater attention, not least because of the development of the Fairey Fox, a private venture design, which, as we have seen, had a performance greater than many front-line fighters. As such it was all but immune from any attack by defenders. The Air Ministry issued several specifications for single-engine and twin-engine fast bomber prototypes for evaluation.

In the annual RAF air exercises held at the very end of the 1920s and early 1930s, large-scale simulated air battles between aircraft divided into attacking and defending forces, with 'rules' and referees, several worrying conclusions began to be drawn regarding the bomber forces. Firstly, their ability to first locate and then bomb their targets accurately proved to be a lot less effective than had been assumed. Secondly, although interception rates by the fighter forces were low, as was expected, in the cases when they did manage to engage the defensive capabilities of the bombers were found to be weaker than had been believed. It was becoming clear to advocates of the fighters that it might indeed prove possible to seriously disrupt formations of bombers and hence reduce the severity of bombing. Furthermore, if approaching aircraft could be detected sufficiently early, and if defensive forces, both fighters and anti-aircraft guns, could be co-ordinated, then the tables might tip even further in their favour. Experiments with parabolic concrete sound mirrors on the south and east coasts of England and the fitment of radio in aircraft were among the first moves in this direction. Of course, this was a double-edged sword as improvements in defence against bombers from the Continent would be paralleled by similar improvements ranged against British bombers making counter-attacks. The inevitable response was to issue specifications for ever faster and more heavily armed bombers.

Air Ministry discussions in 1930 regarding future bomber types and requirements mirrored those taking place for fighters. There was a desire to stimulate the aircraft industry to come forward with new concepts embodying the latest technology but no consensus on the best manner by which to do so. To add further uncertainty, there was a very real possibility that the Disarmament Conference convened at Geneva could set limitations on the number, size or load-carrying capacity of bombers. The existing bomber force of aircraft in service or in production was of mixed vintage and capability. The Hawker Hart, the latest light bomber, had entered service in 1930. This was a very capable aircraft with sufficient range to target Paris while carrying 500lb of bombs and its top speed was not far below that of the RAFs front-line fighters. There were a small number of twin-engined Boulton Paul Sidestrand medium bombers, carrying 1,000lb of bombs at around 140mph, but the bulk of the force comprised heavy bombers primarily for night operations. The Vickers Virginia had formed the backbone of the night bomber force since 1924 and had evolved gradually through the decade by a process of incremental upgrades that resulted in ten different marks in all. Despite all of this it remained, in concept and layout, just an enlarged First World War Vickers Vimy, carrying 1,500lb of bombs, 3,000lb at a stretch, and lumbering along only a little above 100mph. Handley Page's Hyderabad, an aircraft of much the same capability, had followed a similar path of gradual improvement and the modified version was renamed Hinaidi. The prototypes of two more advanced aircraft designed to replace these aircraft, the Fairey Hendon monoplane and Handley Page Heyford biplane, both flew in the summer of 1930 but would not enter service for several years and would be essentially obsolete before doing so.

SINGLE-ENGINED BOMBERS FOR THE 1930S

Although the Hawker Hart was proving to be an excellent aircraft and would sire numerous variants over a number of years, it was acknowledged that it would need to be replaced by a more advanced machine to match the anticipated increase in performance from the latest fighters, and possibly one that could carry a higher bomb load. The Sidestrand equipped only a single squadron and the aircraft were aging. Opinions were divided as to whether this class of medium bomber was actually useful.

In 1930 the Air Ministry Supply and Research department, under Hugh Dowding, considered options to replace one or both of these aircraft and their first thoughts centred on the possibility of a twin-engined aircraft powered by either Rolls-Royce Kestrels or Buzzards. After some discussion it was felt this concept was actually rather larger than necessary and it was redefined as a single-engined aircraft powered by a new 1,000hp engine, the Griffon, recently proposed by Rolls-Royce. The Griffon, formerly the Buzzard, or 'H', Moderately Supercharged Development, can be considered in some respects as a de-rated production version of the Schneider Trophy racing 'R' engine, itself a boosted derivative of the Buzzard. The first example would run on the test bench in 1933. This experimental engine should not to be confused with the production Griffon developed during the Second World War that shared the V12 layout and cylinder size but was otherwise a completely new design.

It appears very likely the Air Ministry shared their idea for this High Speed 1,000lb Bomber with Mitchell as under project Type 178 09 his team developed a concept for a High Performance Day Bomber that matches the proposal. The schematic layout drawing is undated but based on its numbering within Type 178 is most likely from late 1931. It is referred to as Scheme 2, which implies that more than one layout had been considered. The aircraft was a large, low-wing cantilever monoplane with a retractable undercarriage and a crew of three: pilot, upper gunner, lower gunner/bomb aimer. The drawing does not specify which engine was to be fitted but the silhouette profile matches closely that of the Rolls-Royce 'R' engine from the Schneider Trophy racers, so it is fairly clear that it was intended to be powered by the new Griffon. The absence of an obvious radiator on the drawings also suggests that it may have been intended for the engine to employ evaporative cooling and to use Mitchell's leading edge steam condenser system. Mitchell was a strong advocate for this at the time. Alternatively it may be that some form of wing surface radiators were to be used, as had proven successful in the Schneider racers. The fuselage of the bomber shows distinct S.6b Schneider racer influence in the choice of an elliptical section metal monocoque fuselage, the low profile pilot's windscreen for the open cockpit and the distinct spine that ran from the pilot's headrest back to the integral fin. The fuel tanks and bomb load were fitted within a relatively thick (19 per cent) parallel chord wing centre section, a feature adopted later in other Supermarine bomber designs, and the undercarriage retracted outwards into the straight-tapered outer wings. It is not stated what bomb load would have been carried but a primary load of four 250lb bombs appears to be most likely, although, based on later bomber designs, it is probable that the four racks could have held either 250 or 500lb bombs. The aircraft design is clearly conceptual as it includes a number of features that would not have proven acceptable in a military aircraft, not least the poor view for the pilot. It is also surprisingly large, reflecting the uncertainty within the Air Ministry as to whether the aircraft was to replace the Hart as a light bomber or the Sidestrand as a medium bomber. There are no indications that Mitchell developed the scheme beyond this first basic concept.

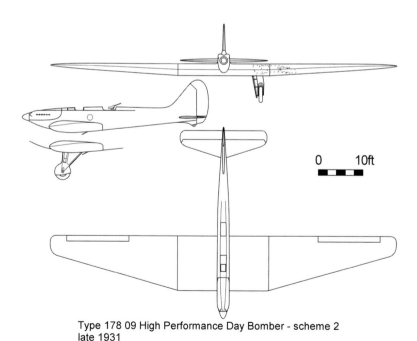

Type 178 09 High Performance Day Bomber - scheme 2
late 1931

A second drawing, with the same drawing number, shows the aircraft as a High Performance Mail Plane with the bomb bays in the wings adapted to hold 40 cubic feet of mail each.

The internal debate within the Air Ministry rumbled on for some time until eventually it was decided to specify separate Light and Medium class replacements for the Hart and Sidestrand, both with increased bomb carrying capability. In 1933 the Air Ministry issued specification P.27/32 for a Single-Engined Day Bombing Aircraft that was fulfilled, eventually, by the Fairey Battle. The larger Twin-Engined Day Bombing Aircraft was the subject of specification B.9/32 and led, in the fullness of time and after several major revisions to the specification, to the Vickers Wellington and Handley Page Hampden. These aircraft were both seriously delayed in development as a result of the uncertainty regarding aircraft structure weight limitations that could have been imposed by the Disarmament Conference and subsequently by the rise of Germany as the most likely adversary in a future war, which had a major impact on the required range for the aircraft.

B.1/35 TWIN-ENGINED HEAVY BOMBER

By 1935, after the collapse of the Disarmament Conference, some future requirements for the RAF bomber force were beginning to crystallise and in May the Air Ministry issued specification B.1/35 for a Twin-Engined Heavy Bomber capable of carrying a 2,000lb bomb load at a cruising speed of not less than 195mph over 1,500 miles. In order to ensure that the aircraft did not become unduly large and unwieldy, as had happened with a couple of earlier bomber prototypes, they chose to limit the wingspan to 100ft, a relatively arbitrary figure and, according to recent research, not related to the door size on RAF hangars as is so often reported. Although Vickers intended to tender to this specification it was agreed to allow Mitchell's team to start conceptual work on an alternative. The project leader for this preliminary design was Roger Dickson.

Dickson was almost certainly unique in the Design Department at this time as he had worked his way through the ranks having joined Supermarine as an apprentice at the age of 19 in 1925. He chose not to seek employment elsewhere on completion of his apprenticeship, as the company encouraged apprentices to do, and instead broadened his knowledge of the aircraft business through involvement in gliding. His Cloudcraft Glider Company, little more than a one-man operation, was one of just six glider manufacturers in Britain at the time. His simple training glider had proven to be a moderate success so in early 1931 Dickson designed and built his first sailplane, the Junior, but there do not appear to be any records either of its life or whether any examples were sold. However his following sailplane, the Phantom, built in mid-year, had a short but eventful life.

The Phantom was designed and built to the requirements of Percy Michelson, a keen gliding club pilot, who paid Dickson £370 for the design and construction. It was an aerodynamically very clean sailplane and among the most advanced of its era in Britain. Cloudcraft advertisements priced the Phantom at £300 for a standard model and £350 for a 'special'. As Dickson did not hold the appropriate glider pilot's licence to allow him to take the Phantom out on its first flight he asked Beverley Shenstone, who had joined Supermarine just a few months earlier, to do so on his behalf. The two, similar in age and both strong proponents of clean aerodynamics and gliding, had become close friends in the Technical Office. Unfortunately Shenstone damaged the Phantom on that first flight but it was soon repaired and then test flown by Mungo Buxton, another renowned glider pilot and friend of both Dickson and Shenstone. On 18 July Buxton took the Phantom out at Dunstable, a popular centre for gliding enthusiasts, and remained aloft for more than 4¼ hours, a British record but one that could not be ratified as the flight was neither observed officially nor did it carry the required barograph. Buxton delivered the sailplane to Mr Michelson, who intended to attempt a cross-Channel flight but this had to be cancelled after the Phantom was badly damaged by vandals. He placed the aircraft up for sale in July 1932 for £170. Dickson had closed down Cloudcraft earlier that same year but the experience he had gained with sleek, low-drag designs was carried through into the work he did at Supermarine.

Mitchell knew that Vickers would prepare a tender to B.1/35 using the Duralumin geodetic lattice structure and fabric covering that had been devised by Wallis. So he, Dickson and the rest of the team realised their project would have to be distinctively different and to draw on their recent experience integrating new technology for the Spitfire and large flying boat projects. At least four concept designs were produced, of which only Dickson's Scheme 4 appears to have survived. For this they decided upon a slender fuselage of circular section, the wing mounted in the mid position with large root fillets that blended into the fuselage shape, and a prominent single fin. The wing used Mitchell's single spar and leading edge torsion box with the spars swept back at 12 degrees. There was considerable sweep on the leading edge while the trailing edge was basically straight, both with very gentle curvature in plan. The tailplane also had a sharply swept leading edge and the elevators had large, curved aerodynamic balances, a shape mirrored by that of the fin and rudder. For the retractable undercarriage it was almost certainly intended to use Dickson's patented system that allowed the wheels to rotate through 90 degrees on the axis of the legs as the undercarriage retracted rearwards so that they would lie flat within the wing. Given the small diameter of the fuselage, the entire bomb load would have been carried within the wing to the rear of the spar.

The B.1/35 projects were required to be powered by one of the new generation of high-powered engines then under development or design, such as the Rolls-Royce Vulture, but contrary to Mitchell's usual preference for Rolls-Royce engines, for this project he selected the slim Bristol Twin-Aquila sleeve-valve radial engine fitted in long NACA cowls. This engine, presumably a twin-row design formed of two nine-cylinder Aquilas, was also just a project at the time, or maybe no more than a concept, and was never built. A smaller fourteen-cylinder, twin-row engine using Aquila cylinders went into limited production later as the Taurus and produced 1,100hp, although it was plagued by unreliability. If the assumption regarding the Twin-Aquila is correct it could have produced around 1,300hp, which would have been ideal for the bomber.

Perhaps the most innovative features were the nose and tail gun turrets. Wallis and Pierson at Vickers were concerned about the amount of drag created by conventional gun turrets and Wallis had set about designing new forms, powered by Frazer-Nash hydraulic systems, for use in the Wellington bomber. This conformed to the contours of the aircraft regardless of the elevation or traversing angle of the gun. Various designs were patented by him in 1934 and 1937. Mitchell decided that he too would investigate new designs and two of these featured in the bomber. It is also interesting that they were added to the conceptual design for a military derivative of the Type 306 transatlantic flying boat that was a major project in the Design Department at that time. The nose turret was spherical so it presented the same curvature to the airflow regardless of the position of the gun. As drawn by Dickson, the nose gun would have had a wide angle of fire in all forward directions but the gunner would have had to operate it while in the prone position due to the small diameter of the aircraft nose, which surely would have imposed a restriction on movement. The tail gun was operated remotely and the gunner sat with his head in a glazed compartment within the base of the fin beneath the rudder, while the gun was located in the extreme tail enclosed within a funnel-shaped fairing fitted to a hemispherical rotating mount. This mount provided a field of fire of about 45 degrees from centre in any direction. Presumably a rotating tail cone at the end of the finely tapered fuselage was expected to create minimal disruption to

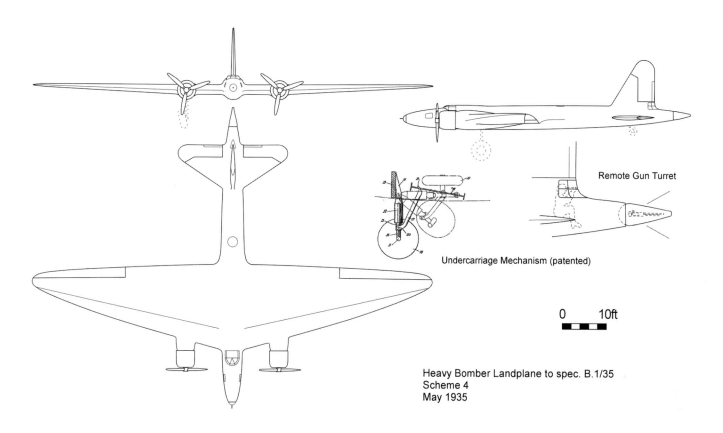

Remote Gun Turret

Undercarriage Mechanism (patented)

0   10ft

Heavy Bomber Landplane to spec. B.1/35
Scheme 4
May 1935

the airflow. A third gun position appears to have been located in the roof mid-fuselage, probably in some form of retractable mounting.

Although the project featured several interesting innovations, Mitchell did not consider it to be worthwhile to formalise as an official project type and the design lapsed, possibly also because there was no support from McLean who favoured Vickers' Warwick project. As shown in the initial concept drawings, the aircraft would certainly have proven unacceptable for service without significant modification. The fuselage was less than 6ft in external diameter at the widest point and it would have proven virtually impossible for the crew to move about the aircraft in full flight gear. The nose gunner was forced to operate in the prone position, which would have restricted his freedom of movement considerably, and the tail gunner was equally cramped in the tail, which was barely shoulder-width at the position of his seat, and he sat more than 10ft away from the guns he was controlling. The choice of engine was also unfortunate as Bristol's Twin-Aquila never left the drawing board. Substituting the smaller Taurus would not have been an option as the

aircraft would almost certainly have required more power. For comparison the Rolls-Royce Vulture, selected for the Warwick, was expected to produce in excess of 1,500hp. However, the wing design, with sharply swept leading edge and copious internal bomb storage, would become a key feature of Supermarine's next bomber project.

The B.1/35 design, although flawed, represented a radical departure from current thinking on British bomber design and mirrored the ground-breaking work under way on the Spitfire fighter. It could well have been inspired in part by aspects of US design philosophy as some work in progress had been viewed by representatives of the Air Ministry, Shenstone, Pierson and other Vickers and Supermarine personnel on visits over the Atlantic in early 1935. At the time of these visits the Boeing B-17 and XB-15 prototypes were near to completion and would fly later that year. Both had circular section, aerodynamically clean fuselages and low-drag cupolas, key features of Supermarine's design.

← The Vickers Warwick was ordered to fulfil B.1/35 but was delayed as a result of the priority of Wellington design and production.

Late in 1935 Roger Dickson left Supermarine and joined Saunders-Roe as a senior stressman. He had been unhappy at having been removed from the Spitfire team and his pay, just £4 17s 6d (£4.87) per week, was out of step with his ability. Furthermore, he had married a couple of years earlier and now had a baby son. No doubt the failure of the bold B.1/35 design to be developed as a new project was the last straw. After a couple of years at Saunders-Roe he moved to a new small company, C.W. Aircraft, as Chief Designer where he was responsible for the design of an elegant high performance, six to seven-seat civil twin-engined monoplane called the Swan. As the correspondent at *Flight* magazine commented regarding the fine aerodynamic shape of this aircraft, 'Mr R.S. Dickson … has a pronounced aversion to straight lines'. The Swan was never built as C.W. Aircraft ran into financial difficulties and the company was purchased by General Aircraft in 1938. Dickson worked on their commercial airline

projects, taking a lead role in design of the large GAL.40 airliner project, and also designed the simple Cagnet pusher primary trainer before returning to Supermarine just prior to the outbreak of the war to work in their newly formed New Project Office.

B.12/36 FOUR-ENGINED HEAVY BOMBER

Although B.1/35 was specified as a heavy bomber, strategic planning and aircraft technology were moving so fast that it was very soon to be superseded. Indeed most, if not all, of the bombers under construction to specifications issued in the early 1930s were viewed as essentially obsolete in one way or another before they had even flown. Some, such as the Vickers Wellington, underwent substantial redesign as a consequence, while others lapsed. The class of light day bomber, epitomised by the Hawker Hart, suddenly appeared all but superfluous to many in the RAF in the context of a European war with Germany. In addition, the need for such simple, light machines to protect the outer reaches of the Empire in Asia and the Far East began to look questionable. Aircraft previously perceived as heavy bombers would now be re-classified as medium bombers at best; their range was marginal and defensive armament too weak. The B.1/35 heavy bomber was viewed as inadequate within months of the specification being issued and a new requirement was formulated for an aircraft with greater payload, range and speed. There were also serious concerns regarding the teething troubles and delays being experienced by all the engine manufacturers working on the high-power engines necessary for these heavy bombers if they were to be restricted to two engines, so the new bombers were to be powered by four proven engine types.

During the short period when it had appeared possible that the Disarmament Conference may set an upper limit on the unloaded weight of bombers the Air Ministry investigated options to enable a relatively light aircraft to carry a heavy bomb load, focussing on in-flight refuelling, composite aircraft of the Mayo type and catapult take-off assistance. The latter appeared to be technically the more feasible and capable of rapid resetting to enable a number of aircraft to be launched in quick succession. Tests of various systems had been carried out by the RAE at Farnborough using a Vickers Virginia. The new specification therefore required the next generation of bombers to be stressed to allow for catapult launch under overload conditions. Specification B.12/36 was issued to industry in July 1936.

Mitchell had always known the colostomy he had undergone in 1933 did not guarantee he was free from cancer and by late 1935 he was beginning to suffer a recurrence of the abdominal pains that had been the early symptom of the disease. He was increasingly worried that the problem had returned and on the very last day of the year he wrote of his concern in his diary. By the time Supermarine received the B.12/36 document he knew that the cancer had returned and was, in all probability, incurable, yet he refused to lower his workload and threw all his effort into the bomber project.

Invitations to tender to B.12/36 were sent to the established constructors of bombers: Armstrong-Whitworth, Handley Page, Fairey, Boulton Paul and Vickers, to which Shorts were added as their recent work on four-engined cantilever monoplane flying boats had demonstrated their capability to build technically advanced large aircraft. Supermarine may have received a copy via Vickers. The specification called for a top speed in excess of 275mph

and a cruising speed above 230mph at two-thirds maximum power. The defensive armament was to be a significant step up from that carried by previous bombers: two machine guns in the nose turret, four in the tail turret and two in a retractable ventral turret. The normal bomb load was 2,000lb, made up of 250 or 500lb bombs, and with this load the take-off run had to be less than 500yd. However, the airframe was to be stressed to allow for catapult-assisted take-off at an acceleration of 2.5G up to a maximum overload of 14,000lb; 28 × 500lb bombs or 7 × 2,000lb bombs. At this maximum overload the range would be 2,000 miles. The large bomb load suggested that a portion of the bombs would most probably have to be carried within the wings.

Mitchell was aware that Vickers would, once again, tender an aircraft using Wallis' geodetic structure and draw upon their experience designing the Wellington and Warwick. The limitation of Wallis' geodetic lattice was that it made inclusion of large openings in the wing structure difficult as breaks in the stress-bearing diagonal members negated the advantages of the method. Hence, without reversion to a conventional wing structure the aircraft would have to hold the entire bomb load within the fuselage, which would, by necessity, be very large. Supermarine would not be so constrained.

It was a fairly safe bet that any design tendered by Armstrong Whitworth would resemble broadly their A.W.23 and Whitley bomber, and one by Fairey the Hendon, and indeed this would prove to be the case. Handley Page and Boulton Paul were more of an unknown quantity while it was likely that Arthur Gouge at Short Bros would not deviate far from the highly successful key structural elements of the S.23 flying boat. Supermarine had no background in the design of land-based bombers and no experience in constructing large four-engined aircraft in general. Their preliminary work on the Type 232, 302 and 306 flying boat projects provided limited material on which to draw, so the new bomber would need to be designed from scratch, although it would benefit from parallel work under way on the Type 308/310/314.

Mitchell initiated design work under Type 316 in mid-1936, around the time that the prototype Spitfire made its first flight, and incorporated some of the preliminary ideas developed for the B.1/35 concept. The wing was of similar plan, although the leading and trailing edges were straight rather than curved, but he adopted a slightly thicker NACA 2416 aerofoil at the root in order to be able to accommodate the required bomb load. As the wing structure was based once again around his single spar and leading edge torsion box, here with a sweep of 15 degrees on the spar and 20 degrees on the leading edge, there was ample space to the rear within which to install the bomb racks. The leading edge torsion box was to be used as the main fuel tanks, as developed for the Type 306, and they extended out over almost the entire span. The selection of engine type was kept open although four Rolls-Royce Merlins or Bristol Hercules were the preferred options. Alternatives considered were the Napier Dagger, Bristol Pegasus and Rolls-Royce Kestrel, while one drawing dating from September 1936 shows Rolls-Royce Vultures in the inner nacelles and Kestrels in the outer. The construction method mirrored that of the Spitfire in that the aircraft was entirely of metal and flush-riveted throughout in order to ensure the lowest possible drag.

The Type 316 had ten bomb racks in each wing, installed between adjacent ribs and extending out from the root to beyond the outer engine nacelles, and nine, in three rows of three, in the fuselage. Each rack was capable of holding either a 250 or a 500lb bomb. However, the centre row of fuselage racks and the inner two within each wing could be adapted to hold a 2,000lb bomb.

The 71ft monocoque Duralumin fuselage was reasonably large, around 8ft deep and 5.5ft wide in the centre section, but with the internal space restricted by the central bomb bay. Movement fore and aft would also have been extremely difficult with the ventral 'dustbin' gun turret retracted. The Type 316 is almost invariably portrayed as particularly compact but for comparison the fuselage was actually slightly larger than those of the Avro Lancaster and Handley Page Halifax bombers that were designed just slightly later and considered to be big. Although it was a minor requirement of the specification, the aircraft was expected to be capable of carrying troops, a legacy of all previous large bomber specifications, and seating for

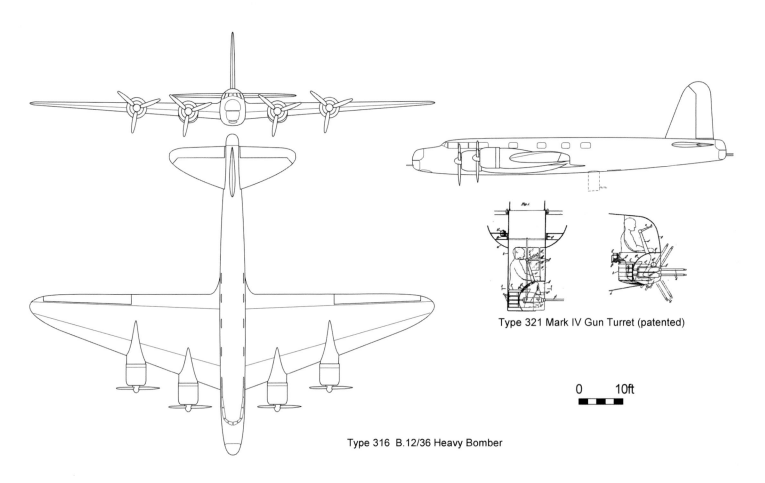

Type 321 Mark IV Gun Turret (patented)

0   10ft

Type 316 B.12/36 Heavy Bomber

twenty-six was provided, packed in extremely tightly. Wilfred Kimber was tasked with designing low-drag turrets for the aircraft and came up with a solution where the gunner sat on a swivelling seat under a fixed canopy with the guns located between his legs. The seat and lower portion of the turret rotated as one unit along with the guns, which had an arc of fire of 200 degrees laterally and 120 degrees vertically. Nose and tail turrets were identical and interchangeable. The retractable ventral turret worked in the same manner but was housed within a cylinder that retracted fully within the fuselage. These ventral guns had a full 360 degrees of freedom in rotation and from 15 degrees above to 60 degrees below horizontal, except where it was necessary to provide clearance for the wings, fuselage and tail where pitch was reduced to 5 degrees above horizontal. Both turret designs were the subject of a patent in 1937. The nose and tail turrets were allocated their own project number, Type 321, and described as the Mark IV. Which of Supermarine's earlier concept turret designs were regarded as Marks I to III is not known but the choice appears to be limited to the low profile design from the Type 305 turret fighter and the spherical nose turret and remotely operated tail 'funnel' from the Type 306 and B.1/35.

Mitchell estimated that the top speed of the Type 316 would range from 370mph for the version powered by Hercules engines down to 330mph for those fitted with Kestrels, Pegasus or Daggers. As the prototype Spitfire had reached 350mph in early tests Mitchell certainly had high hopes for his bomber, although it is a little hard to see why such high speeds would be achieved.

Somewhat bizarrely, a recent book has described the Type 316 as a delta-winged, tailless bomber, which is completely fanciful, as are suggestions that civil passenger-carrying versions were contemplated.

The Air Ministry held a Tender Design Conference in October 1936 and selected Vickers' as the best followed by those from Boulton Paul, Armstrong Whitworth, Supermarine and Shorts. The intention was that Vickers would be awarded the contract subject to the work not interfering with development and production of the Wellington and Warwick, a highly optimistic assumption even though they may well have shared many components. However, after Mitchell was interviewed by the Ministry in November the Type 316 jumped up the ranking and it was recommended that the version powered by Hercules engines should be ordered, but it does not appear to have been recorded why they had revised their opinion so dramatically. Mitchell must have made a compelling case for the aircraft, which, in characteristic Mitchell style, was undergoing a complete redesign. A design conference was then held at Woolston in January 1937 at which

it was agreed to proceed with the revised aircraft and as a result, the Air Ministry ordered two prototypes for which Supermarine received the official order in March. The Vickers design was held as a possible second option, but this was soon dropped.

Detailed design of the revised bomber began under the original Type 316 but it was renamed later as Type 317 as the work involved fundamental changes to all major parts of the aircraft. Drawings are catalogued under both Type numbers. The wings of the original Type 316 were discarded and redesigned completely with reduced sweep on the leading edge and forward sweep on the trailing edge. There was a standard linear tapered plan to the outermost nacelles and a very mild skewed-elliptical shape outboard. A thicker NACA 2218 aerofoil was now adopted from the root out to the outer nacelles, reducing to 2216 at the tip, and the span was extended by 4ft, which increased the wing area by about 10 per cent. The split flaps were increased in span at the same time. There were now nine bomb bays in each wing compared to ten on the earlier design as the outer bay had been deleted. The fuselage was both lengthened and slimmed down at the rear, and the large single fin was replaced by twin fins positioned at the tips of a redesigned tailplane. Mitchell had dropped, or had been induced to drop, development of the Mark IV turrets and to select from existing types. Judging from the revised shape of the nose, it appears he had adopted a version of the Wallis-designed and patented low-drag type as installed on the early Wellingtons. The tail and ventral turrets were to be provided by Nash & Thompson, types IV and XIX respectively. The tail turret, although modified, no longer conformed to the original tapering tail profile of the aircraft, which had to be revised.

A version of the bomber powered by Rolls-Royce Merlins was worked on in parallel and named as Type 318, but in July the Air Ministry instructed Supermarine to terminate this and to concentrate on the Type 317.

After the January design conference Mitchell's health had declined to such an extent that he was no longer able to work in the office and from February he was obliged to remain at home, keeping an interest in proceedings but within a very short while unable to contribute to the project.

By August the fuselage mock-up had been completed and was reviewed by the Air Ministry, when the only adverse comments were regarding the lack of space for the cockpit crew as there was inadequate headroom to enable the pilot to stand up. A revised design with the roof raised slightly above the line of the upper fuselage was tested in the wind tunnel but was not taken further. Detailed design then continued and in November 1938 Supermarine quoted new performance figures to the Air Ministry: a top

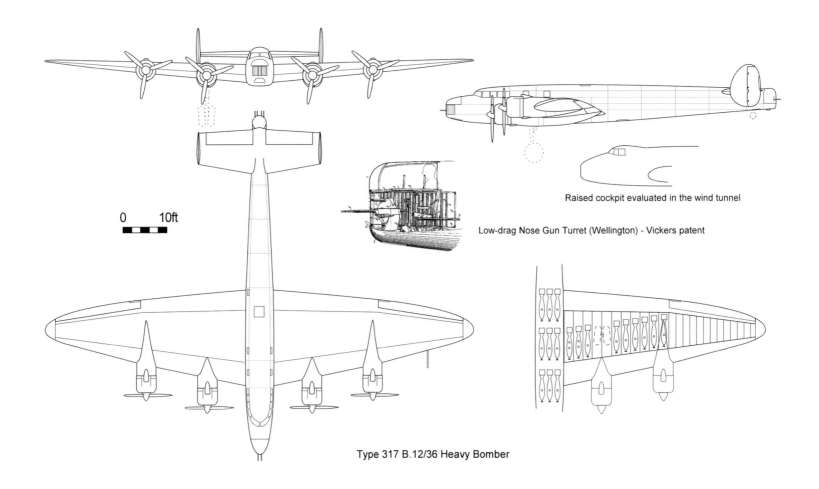

Raised cockpit evaluated in the wind tunnel

Low-drag Nose Gun Turret (Wellington) - Vickers patent

0   10ft

Type 317 B.12/36 Heavy Bomber

speed of 330mph at 17,000ft and a cruising speed of 290mph at 15,000ft. With a normal 2,000lb bomb load the range was 1,980 miles at 279mph at 15,000ft. Under overload conditions the range was 3,680 miles at 202mph carrying 8,000lb of bombs and 2,360 miles at 208mph with 14,000lb.

Although the mock-up conference had proceeded without noting any serious problems, it was obvious to the Air Ministry that Supermarine were under extreme pressure and that work on the prototypes would be delayed. Mitchell had passed away only a few weeks before and the decision on who would lead the Design Department had yet to be made, although Harold Payn had assumed the role in the short term. Furthermore, the works were in turmoil as they struggled to handle the demanding production rates insisted upon for the Spitfire. The Woolston works was still one large building

site as the construction of new workshop space had yet to be completed, and the new facility upstream, known as the Itchen works, was also in progress. The Woolston workshops were full of Stranraer and Walrus flying boat components plus the jigs and benches on the production lines for the Spitfire, so the Type 317 would have to be built at the Itchen works. The situation was so chaotic that there had been ill-tempered communication between the Air Ministry and McLean, and between McLean and Cdr Sir John Craven, the Chairman of Vickers, regarding the delays to the Spitfire programme, which had absolute priority. Vickers were unable to assist as they were also under great pressure themselves building the Wellington and Warwick and had no spare capacity, another point of friction with McLean. The Type 317 would have to wait.

The problems at Supermarine did not come as a surprise to the Air Ministry and in anticipation they had held a design conference with Short Bros in April 1937 and in July, following the death of Mitchell, they sought funding to proceed with prototypes of the Shorts design as a precaution in case of excessive delays with the Type 317. This aircraft became the Stirling and the prototype first flew in May 1939, at which point the Type 317 prototype at the Itchen works had not moved beyond initial construction work on the fuselage. In May 1940 the Itchen works were bombed by the Luftwaffe and both partially built prototypes were destroyed. However, at this late stage the aircraft was no longer viewed as essential for the RAF, who had placed orders for additional Stirlings plus Handley Page Halifax and Avro Lancasters.

It has long been questioned whether Mitchell's projected performance figures for the Type 316 could have been achieved, and it is certainly a matter of record that these estimates were reduced a number of times as the design of the Type 317 advanced. They remained, nevertheless, notably higher than for others bombers of comparable size and engine power. There is no doubt that the performance of the Stirling was way below that estimated for the Type 317, but any conclusions drawn from a comparison are limited as Gouge had designed a substantially larger aircraft from the outset and this had then proven to be over design weight. Basing the wing on that of his Empire and Sunderland flying boats seemed to be a sensible economy but abiding by the span restriction of the specification on such a large aircraft proved to be a mistake and the Stirling's operational ceiling was dangerously low. The twin-spar wings of the Stirling also limited the portion of the bomb load that could be stowed within and this was restricted to the root section inboard of the inner engines. The Type 317 was to have carried a higher proportion of its bomb load in the wings than on most rival B.12/36 designs and hence the fuselage could be designed both smaller and lighter in weight, but not dramatically so. The aerodynamic cleanliness of the Type 317, at least at the early layout phase of design with the low-drag turrets, was also superior, but these factors alone are probably not enough to explain the large difference.

↑ The Stirling was a very large aircraft, far larger than the Type 317 or the Avro Lancaster and Handley Page Halifax that were to replace it.

Later aircraft of comparable size and engine power to the Type 317, such as the Avro Lancaster, Handley Page Halifax and Boeing B-17, also failed to match the performance expected of the aircraft and, hence, this has led many to conclude that Mitchell and the team's estimates may have been distinctly optimistic throughout, and it is hard not to draw the same conclusion.

The Type 316 was the last project undertaken by Supermarine that was overseen from the start by Mitchell, but all the extensive revisions required to produce the Type 317 proceeded without his guidance.

25

SUPERMARINE AFTER MITCHELL

TURMOIL AND UNCERTAINTY IN THE WORKS

The terminal illness and untimely death of Mitchell in 1937 hit the company extremely hard. While there is no doubt that the design office was staffed with thoroughly competent people, without their leader they were, for a time, a little adrift. Major Harold Payn, Mitchell's deputy, stepped into the void but although he was a thoroughly competent engineer and very experienced pilot he lacked Mitchell's stature as a designer, so McLean assigned Rex Pierson to support Supermarine in the short term. Pierson, of course, was himself extremely busy as Vickers pushed ahead with production of the Wellington and Warwick bombers and worked on other new designs.

The Woolston works were under immense pressure as the design office strove to produce the many new drawings required for the production of the Spitfire. This was no small task as a great many components differed from those in the prototype and others required modification as a result of the continuing flight test programme undertaken by the prototype and then the first production standard machine. The Air Ministry order for 310 Spitfires had been anticipated so building work had started on a major expansion of the Woolston and Itchen sites, but this would not be completed for some time. Moreover, building 310 aircraft, even using a network of subcontractors, was a daunting task; the total output of aircraft by the company since the war had been less than a third of that figure. In combination the loss of their Chief Engineer and Designer, with his position on the Board, the turmoil caused by rebuilding the works and growing friction between Supermarine's management and the Air Ministry took its toll on staff morale. Several chose to leave in the next few years, notably Shenstone and Schlotel.

In 1938 problems at the highest level led to the dismissal of McLean. Sir Charles Craven had felt for some time that Mclean's semi-independence was cause for concern and when the delays to both the Wellington and Spitfire programmes became excessive, accompanied by constant reassurance from him despite more missed targets, he was held largely to blame and forced out. Vickers (Aviation) Ltd and Supermarine Aviation Works (Vickers) Ltd were amalgamated directly within Vickers-Armstrong Ltd. Commander James Bird was then moved aside as a result. Major Payn was also removed from his job heading the Design Department, apparently after his wife was found to have German connections and the Air Ministry refused to authorise him to work in such a sensitive position. Finally, Joe Smith was promoted to the new position of Design Manager, although still dependent on Pierson for approval of many design matters. He was only confirmed as Mitchell's direct replacement as Chief Designer in 1941.

Work on the Type 317 bomber suffered as a consequence of all this disruption and the delays were such that it would no doubt have been considered obsolete when it flew had the prototypes not been destroyed by bombing. The new projects office was established in 1938 headed by Arthur Shirvall and maintained throughout the war, but this, too, was drawn into the Spitfire programme to work on special models.

Mitchell would have been aghast at the dramatic changes that took place within Supermarine in the run-up to the war, but would most likely have been powerless to do much about it. His presence could, however, have provided a stabilising influence, a solid base of leadership that would have done much to motivate the staff. It is ironic that it was the success of the Spitfire, his finest creation, which acted as the catalyst for the forces of change.

PRE-WAR PROJECTS

Notwithstanding the strict prioritisation of work on the Spitfire within the Design Department, new opportunities still received attention in response to Air Ministry specifications. Although none of these projects involved any design input or direct ideas from Mitchell as they were all conceived well after his decline in health had forced him to leave the office, it is of interest to track in summary how Payn, Smith, Clifton and, presumably, Pierson, steered design ideas in the immediate pre-war years.

Following the production orders for Boulton Paul Defiant two-seat turret fighters to F.9/35 and Westland Whirlwind twin-engined cannon fighters to F.37/35, the Air Ministry continued to show considerable interest in variations on both themes. Specification F.11/37 invited tenders for a twin-engined turret fighter with an armament of four cannon, all in the turret. Supermarine worked on a large fighter powered by two Rolls-Royce Vultures that may have originated as a turret fighter to this specification but by the time it was allocated an official project number, Type 319, it had two fixed 20mm cannon in the nose and two in a specialised mount that enabled them to fire upwards but not traverse laterally. The idea for a fighter with upward firing guns to engage bombers in their vulnerable underside had appeared before, notably in specification F.29/27, and would do so several more times. The Type 319 had a skewed elliptical wing very similar in shape to that on the Spitfire, radiators embedded within the wings and a clean fuselage with the pilot's cockpit in the extreme nose beneath a large canopy that conformed to the profile of the fuselage. The dimensions of the aircraft, and the power available from the Vulture engines, placed the Type 319 well within the realms of several bombers of the period but with a relatively light armament and sleek aerodynamic design it would have proven very fast. It appears unlikely that this design was ever submitted as an official tender and the F.11/37 prototype contract was issued to Boulton Paul. However, as their turret design was innovative and complex they decided to construct a half-scale flying test model first. Progress was protracted so a production contract was rushed through for Bristol's Beaufighter design, an aircraft that made use of many components already in production for the Beaufort. The Beaufighter was surprisingly similar in size and power to the Type 319.

S.24/37, issued in January 1938, was for a carrier-based torpedo dive-bomber and reconnaissance aircraft for the FAA. Low landing speed was a key requirement of the specification and in order to achieve the lowest possible speed while avoiding an excessive nose-up pitch the design team devised a variable incidence mechanism for the wing, which was also fitted

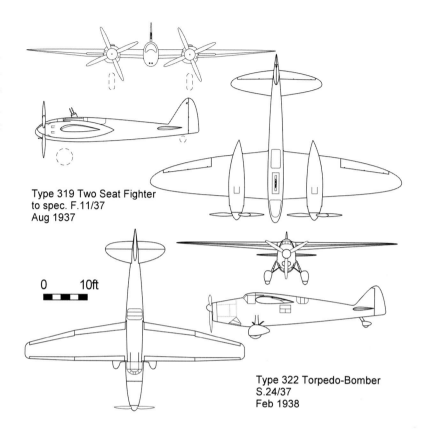

Type 319 Two Seat Fighter
to spec. F.11/37
Aug 1937

0   10ft

Type 322 Torpedo-Bomber
S.24/37
Feb 1938

with full span leading edge slots and rear slotted flaps. The Type 322 was in other regards a fairly conventional carrier-borne aircraft, stressed for catapult launch and arrestor wire retardation and with folding wings to enable stowage below decks. With the high-mounted wing and the incidence adjusting mechanism installed, and bomb stowage recessed in the lower fuselage, it was not found to be possible to fit a retractable undercarriage, so this was fixed. The aircraft was to be powered by a Rolls-Royce Exe, a new twenty-four cylinder air-cooled unit designed specifically for naval aircraft.

The Air Ministry considered the variable incidence system to be too innovative for immediate production but they ordered two experimental prototypes to assess the effectiveness of the system and to evaluate any control issues associated with its operation. These were Merlin-powered, as development of the Exe had been abandoned in 1939. The new aircraft, assigned Type 380, were constructed mainly of wood to save time and resources and first flew in 1943. It acquired the unofficial name of Dumbo, on account of the large wings reminding someone of the ears of Disney's baby elephant in the film of the same name. Supermarine's mechanism functioned as intended with no serious control problems and the system was adopted for use on a later flying boat, the Seagull ASR. A production contract for the service aircraft was issued to Fairey for the Barracuda.

The absolute air speed record had stood at 440.5mph since 1934, established by Francesco Agello flying a Macchi Castoldi M.C.72 racing seaplane. The speed record for landplanes, however, stood at 352.39mph, set by Howard Hughes flying his H-1 racer in 1935 and this was well within the capabilities of the standard Spitfire. Discussions between Supermarine and the Development and Production division of the Air Ministry resulted in agreement to modify a Spitfire to establish a new record. The forty-eighth production Spitfire was taken off the production line to be prepared for the attempt and given the new designation Type 323 Speed Spitfire. Modifications were modest and involved a reduction in span by a redesign of the wing tips, strengthened engine bearers, substitution of a sleek, contoured canopy, and enlarged radiators. Rolls-Royce undertook the construction of a dedicated racing Merlin producing 2,160hp that would drive a new fixed-pitch, four-blade propeller. The aircraft was ready by November 1938 and the team were confident that Hughes' record would be exceeded by a wide margin. However, in March 1939 the Heinkel He 100V8 raised the record to 463.9mph, which was beyond the capabilities of the Speed Spitfire. Consideration was given to removing the radiators and allowing the coolant water to boil away to gain a small increase in speed but when the Messerschmitt Me 209V1 raised the record again to 469.1mph all plans were abandoned. The aircraft was reworked to near-normal standard and served with a photo-reconnaissance unit.

It had been Air Ministry policy to issue specifications for a new aircraft around the time that the one it was due to replace was close to entering service, and the Spitfire was no exception. Specification F.18/37 was issued in January 1938 and called for a fighter capable of accepting a variety of different gun configurations, including twelve machine guns. Speed was a high priority, above 400mph at 15,000ft, and the Air Ministry wished to see full use made of the latest technical developments. It was anticipated that the aircraft would have a single engine but twin engines were not excluded. Supermarine were especially keen to compete for this lucrative contract.

With the advent of the Type 300, with its stressed skin wing, the true potential of Mitchell's single spar structure to accommodate a significant internal load had been recognised. The Spitfire wing held eight guns, retracted undercarriage and part of the radiator system while the later Type 308 flying boat and the Type 317 bomber placed the fuel in leading edge tanks and incorporated bomb bays between the ribs. The next generation of fighter designs would exploit the space still further.

Type 324 was drawn up in January 1938 as a twin-engined fighter of surprisingly small size; the fuselage length was comparable to that of the Spitfire while the wing area was only some 20 per cent greater. The wing held the fuel tanks in the leading edge, the fully internal radiators for the Merlin engines, the retracted undercarriage and large bays in the outboard section for banks of six Browning .303 machine guns and their 500-round ammunition boxes. These bays could be exchanged for other combinations of guns and ammunition. The wing plan was once again a variation on the Spitfire skewed ellipse, outboard of the engines, and in place of the Spitfire's plain split flaps there were extendable Fowler flaps on the inner section to help to keep the landing speed manageable, a potential issue given the small wing area. Additional small drag flaps were fitted at mid-chord to aid in ground strafing runs. Freed of guns and fuel the fuselage was kept very slim with the cockpit positioned well forward above the bay for the retracting nose wheel. This arrangement, unusual at the time, was selected to allow the aircraft to be flown on to the ground to eliminate any risk of ground looping and to permit the use of powerful wheel brakes, all considerations relating to the landing speed. Acknowledging pressure on Merlin engine production at this time, Supermarine also suggested an alternative version fitted with Bristol Taurus radials, which required only minimal changes to the wings, although performance was reduced slightly. In both cases the engines were counter-rotating in order to eliminate swing on take-off.

In parallel with the Type 324 the company drew up a second version of the aircraft, as Type 325, in which the engines drove pusher propellers via extension shafts. To rebalance the aircraft the wing plan had to be revised through a rearward adjustment in the skew, although the internal structure remained essentially the same. The benefit of this arrangement was that the wing was removed from the wake of the propellers and could thus operate more efficiently, which resulted in an increase in top speed of some 8mph. The downside was that the position of the propellers made escape from the cockpit in emergency potentially problematic, so the propeller shafts were fitted with brakes capable of stopping rotation within 10 seconds.

A wooden mock-up of the Type 324 was constructed at the works and the design tendered to the Air Ministry, where it received a surprisingly lukewarm reception. Although the speed of the aircraft was impressive it was not thought that the twin Merlin configuration resulted in sufficient performance advantage over a single-engined aircraft fitted with the latest

high power Rolls-Royce Vulture, Napier Sabre or similar, to justify the additional complexity. Supermarine countered with the view that servicing two twelve-cylinder engines was no more burdensome than for a twenty-four-cylinder single engine. The team continued to see merit in the Type 324 concept and carried out further work to refine the design. By August 1938 the mock-up had been modified and the revised design submitted to the Air Ministry as the Type 327 with six 20mm Hispano cannon now mounted in the wing roots. Other changes included a reduction in wingspan and a revised fin and rudder. However, these changes did not win the day, the Ministry's view on the aircraft remained unchanged and they now questioned the practicality of the compact layout of the cannon so close to

↑ The Speed Spitfire.

the fuselage-wing joint. Hawker were awarded a production contract to build Typhoon fighters.

The next new project came in response to specification R.5/39, issued in April 1939, requesting designs for a replacement for the Sunderland. This was to be a high-speed flying boat of around 45,000lb, about 15 per cent lower than the Sunderland, powered by four air-cooled engines, with a range of 2,000 miles and a cruising speed in excess of 235mph. Having failed

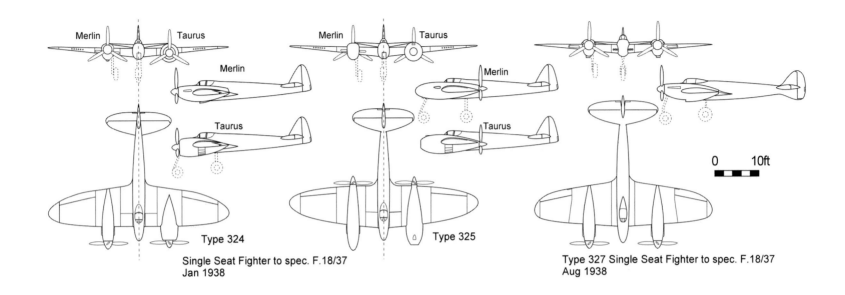

Merlin   Taurus   Merlin   Taurus

Merlin

Merlin

Taurus

Taurus

0   10ft

Type 324   Type 325

Single Seat Fighter to spec. F.18/37   Type 327 Single Seat Fighter to spec. F.18/37
Jan 1938   Aug 1938

to win a production contract for a flying boat since the Stranraer in 1935 and after the order for the prototype Type 314 was cancelled because of concerns that work on this would impact adversely on development of the Spitfire, Supermarine were determined to regain their place as a specialist in marine aircraft design. The Type 328 was thus to be, perhaps, their last opportunity to make up ground lost to Shorts. High speed was one of the key aspects of the specification so the team combined their development work on the Type 317 bomber with aspects of the design from the Type 310 and 314 flying boat projects. The aircraft was to be powered by four Bristol Hercules radials with Rolls-Royce Griffons as a possible alternative. The hull was a completely new design, moving further along the path of aerodynamic cleanliness, and was of basic elliptical section, apart from the planing surfaces, which featured a retractable step. The wing was mounted in the shoulder position and had slight gull-wing form in order to keep the propellers clear of the spray. The wing plan was a simple straight taper and the standard Supermarine single spar was without sweep. Kimber's hydroplane wing floats were modified to simplify the mechanism and they retracted into bays in the wing outboard of the engines. Eight bomb bays were positioned between the engines, the inner four capable of holding either 250 or 500lb bombs and the outer four 250lb bombs. The fuel tanks were located within the wing leading edge and extended out over two-thirds of the span. The defensive armaments comprised four 20mm cannon in a shallow inverted saucer cupola at the rear

of the wing centre section and a single cannon in a tail turret. The design was well received by the Air Ministry, who recommended that the wing area should be increased slightly, the hydroplanes replaced by retractable floats of the Saunders-Roe type and the engines repositioned slightly outboard in order to be able to fit propellers of greater diameter. An order for a prototype seemed to be likely until the rationale behind the whole requirement was reconsidered and the specification was cancelled.

The Design Department now turned their attention to fighters for the FAA, a potential market they had not pursued since Mitchell's first wheeled fighter design in 1927. Specification N.8/39, issued in June 1939, requested tenders for a two-seat fighter for use on the carriers to replace the Blackburn Skua. Primary consideration, after performance, was height and span with wings folded; both being limited to 13ft 6in in order to fit the lifts and hangars on the carriers. Supermarine's Type 333 design marked a departure from the ellipse-derived wings that had been the hallmark of all their fighter projects since the Spitfire and they proposed instead a straight-taper wing with a change in leading edge sweep just beyond half span. This offered broadly similar characteristics in a simplified structure. The wing bay holding four Browning machine guns was located just inboard of the leading edge kink and was interchangeable with one holding two 20mm cannon. In a characteristic move, Supermarine proposed two distinct versions of the Type 333, one powered by a Rolls-Royce Merlin the other by a Griffon.

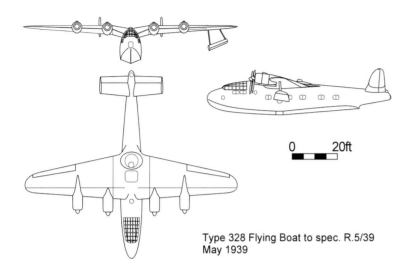

Type 328 Flying Boat to spec. R.5/39
May 1939

0 _____ 20ft

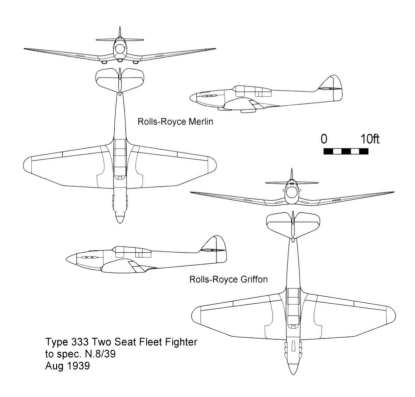

Rolls-Royce Merlin

Rolls-Royce Griffon

0 _____ 10ft

Type 333 Two Seat Fleet Fighter
to spec. N.8/39
Aug 1939

The aircraft layout remained unchanged but was scaled up to accommodate the larger engine. For the Merlin, the twin radiators and single oil cooler were housed beneath the wings and fuselage, while for the Griffon they were installed buried within the wing root section. The Air Ministry were impressed by the clean lines of the Type 333 but had reservations regarding the wing fold mechanism, as they did for several of the other tenders, and felt the tail surfaces to be a little small. After a period of internal debate the Admiralty deemed all the submissions to be unsatisfactory and the specification was withdrawn to be rewritten.

There remains Type 334 to consider. Drawings and information on this project appear to have been lost although it has been suggested that the design, and a mock-up, was produced in response to specification F.6/39 in March 1939, in which case the type number would be chronologically out of sequence with Type 333. F.6/39 was issued for a high-speed, two-seat fighter armed with four 20mm cannon with the capability to accommodate two 40mm cannon at some future date. Most companies, including Vickers, submitted twin-engined designs. This could imply that the Type 327 had undergone a further modification to meet the requirement as there was certainly a mock-up readily available. As with so many specifications in the immediate pre-war years, F.6/39 was withdrawn and rewritten the following year.

Further new project work was not abandoned completely once war was declared but most Design Department resources were put on to the many programmes to develop the Spitfire. The aircraft had proven to be so capable and versatile that the initial plans to replace it with Typhoons and Beaufighters were superseded by an expansion of production, the development of cannon-armed wings, variants optimised for high and low altitude, installation of improved Merlins and later Griffons, navalised versions for the Fleet Air Arm and unarmed photo-reconnaissance aircraft. Late in the war the wing structure was redesigned completely, although it retained the distinctive skewed elliptical plan. By the end of the war the latest types of the Spitfire were double the weight and more than 100mph faster than the Mk 1 from 1936 and they were still proving effective as dog-fighting, high-altitude interceptor fighters.

The aircraft projects developed by the design team in the two and a bit years following the death of Mitchell exhibit many of the same characteristics as those that preceded them; they show great diversity in style and tenders often included multiple variations of each type. Mitchell's approach to design had proven highly influential and the team continued in the same vein for some time after he had gone.

26

RJ, THE MAN AND THE RISE OF A LEGEND

THE LEGEND

Reginald Mitchell's reputation has been rather ill-served over the years. While he is rightly celebrated for his achievements, most especially with the Spitfire, so many distorted and erroneous stories have been told of his life and career that he has been elevated to almost mythical status, and this masks the true story of this most capable of aircraft designers. To see how the legend developed it is necessary to track Mitchell through the years as he was seen by the press and public.

Through the 1920s and 1930s aviation came to be regarded less and less as a novelty, aviators were increasingly commonplace and the companies that built aircraft became just another part of industry, the men and women who worked there as faceless as any in car or shipbuilding. British aircraft designers in this period were largely unknown to the general public, in complete contrast to many of their pre-war predecessors who were celebrities, famous as pilots, pioneers and the founders of the aircraft factories that bore their names. Reginald Mitchell was, therefore, something of an exception as his name had featured in the mainstream press on several occasions, largely as a result of Supermarine's participation in the Schneider Trophy contests and commencing after their unexpected win at Naples in 1922. The rakish S.4, record-breaker and ultimately ill-fated racer, attracted more publicity and the triple wins achieved by the S.5, S.6 and S.6b, which secured the Schneider Trophy outright for Britain, kept his name in the public eye. The Far Eastern tour by a flight of Southampton flying boats in 1927–28 was a further notable event for Supermarine that received significant press coverage.

When Mitchell's Spitfire was unveiled to the public at the RAF display at Hendon in 1936, resplendent in bright blue paint, it made headlines as the fastest fighter aircraft in the world and its aesthetic lines made it stand apart from all the other new types on show, attracting praise from all quarters. As a result, Mitchell was now as famous as any aircraft designer of the period; he may not have been exactly a household name but he was certainly better known than all his peers.

After Mitchell's death, the press published extensive obituaries, not just the aviation magazines but the mainstream newspapers including the popular titles. He was praised for his versatility and ability to listen to others before reviewing the options and making a decision. It was acknowledged that it was these strengths, in harmony with his technical ability, which had made him a great designer.

At the outbreak of war the RAF was struggling to introduce the Spitfire into front-line service in significant quantity and there was serious concern that the number of aircraft and trained pilots available would prove inadequate to repel any early attempt at invasion. Right from the outset it had been readily apparent that Supermarine's works would be incapable of handling the large production contract and tight delivery schedule, not to mention their vulnerable location to attack on the south coast, so a complex network of subcontractors and shadow production facilities had been established. This was no small matter and it was somewhat inevitable that it had stuttered into life, much to the annoyance of the Air Ministry. By the beginning of 1940 the situation was definitely coming under control but, nevertheless, when Churchill became Prime Minister in May, one of his very first acts was to establish a new Ministry of Aircraft Production, independent from the Air

Ministry. It was headed by newspaper tycoon Lord Beaverbrook, who was tasked to improve the supply of aircraft.

In April 1940 *The Aeroplane* published an article describing the design and development of the Spitfire by Mitchell, written, almost certainly, by their outspoken editor, C.G. Grey. Although much of the article is factual it does state, erroneously, that the Spitfire was built as a private venture and includes the following misleading statement:

> The case (regarding the design of the Spitfire versus that of the Type 224) was perhaps less one of trial and error than of expressing a personal inspiration at the same time that an official requirement was being met. The F.7/30 was the answer to the chief customer's demand: the Spitfire represented the designer's idea of what the customer ought to want.

The myth had begun.

It remains open to debate whether Beaverbrook actually made a material difference to production rates but he did initiate two schemes that fired up widespread enthusiasm and placed the Spitfire centrally in the public eye; firstly the 'Saucepans to Spitfire' campaign, to boost the supply of aluminium to industry, and secondly by 'The Spitfire Fund'. This initiative resurrected an idea from the First World War when similar appeals for funds had been made to the public. In this case the inspiration came partly as a result of the Nizam of Hyderabad having made a donation to equip an entire squadron of Spitfires and partly through the receipt of monetary gifts from various expatriates in the colonies and other British groups. Beaverbrook set an arbitrary price of £5,000 to buy one Spitfire, a little over half the cost of an actual aircraft, and encouraged towns, clubs and other organisations to raise money from the public; the aircraft then bearing the name of the donors. Similar funds were established for other aircraft but it was the Spitfire Fund that fired the imagination and triggered many fundraising initiatives, such as the sale of badges and of scale model Spitfires by Meccano. The fund ran until March 1941 and raised in excess of £10 million, a huge sum.

Production of the Spitfire increased significantly in the mid months of 1940 but when the Luftwaffe mounted its assault on Britain in the late summer the outcome of the battle appeared at first uncertain as the actual size of the Luftwaffe forces and the rate at which they would be able to replace lost aircraft were both unclear and estimates tended to err on the high side. However, the worst fears were not realised and it soon became apparent that the RAF had gained the upper hand and that the Spitfire was proving superior to the Luftwaffe's premier Messerschmitt Bf 109 fighters in most encounters. Losses on the British side were high but production and repair managed to keep pace and the squadrons were kept reasonably well replenished. Together, the Spitfires, Hurricanes and others imposed such heavy losses on the German aircraft that they were forced to terminate the attacks, and a possible seaborne invasion of Britain was abandoned. Churchill dubbed this encounter as the Battle of Britain and praised the RAF for saving the nation from imminent defeat.

In 1941 the Air Ministry issued a booklet, *The Battle of Britain*, which was a reasonably measured and not too inaccurate summary of the various actions that had taken place during the battle, and which stressed the role of the Hurricane and Spitfire in repelling the attacks by the Luftwaffe but made no mention of their designers. The publishers, Real Photographs, next released a slim booklet, *The Book of the 'Spitfire'*, to provide a brief history of the aircraft and of Mitchell's career. The text is riddled with errors, kindles the idea of Mitchell as the sole creator of the Spitfire, and, incidentally, suggests for the first time that the Heinkel He 70 was in part the inspiration for the fighter. The Spitfire, already held up as a symbol of British excellence, was now portrayed as the embodiment of defiance and the nation's fighting spirit, attributes shared by its designer.

The story of the Spitfire Fund campaign was celebrated in a book, *The Birth of a Spitfire*, also published in 1941. This book, by Gordon Beckles, is one of the most outrageous distortions of historical truth, placing Beaverbrook centrally in the spotlight and pouring scorn equally on the aircraft industry, the Air Ministry and prominent politicians. The account of how Mitchell came to design the aircraft based on his work on the Schneider racers is fanciful but served to bring his name once more to the fore.

In a further effort to capitalise on the success of the Spitfire and the public's enthusiasm for the aircraft, the government and RAF provided support to renowned actor Leslie Howard's project to write, direct and star in a film about the life of Reginald Mitchell and the birth of the Spitfire. Although *The First of the Few* was a privately produced and distributed film it was, in all respects, a work for the purpose of national propaganda and as a consequence the narrative takes a great deal of liberties with the truth. Even now this is not always acknowledged to be the case and it is not that unusual for scenes within the film to be quoted as factual. Nevertheless, it is a stirring fictional shell built over a sparse framework of real events. Mitchell is portrayed as a quiet, driven man of vision working alone and struggling against an indifferent government and military to ensure that Britain was armed with the ultimate fighter, an aircraft that he saw as necessary to counter the growing belligerence of Germany and Italy; written as arrogant bullies and buffoons respectively. At his moment of triumph, the first flight of the Spitfire, Mitchell dies, worn out by overwork. The film is certainly no masterpiece and the melodramatic overtones and heavy handed dialogue appear somewhat risible today, but when it appeared in British cinemas in 1942 it was a welcome and uplifting tonic to the grim and grinding toil of the war. Mitchell's fame was assured and he moved forward toward legend.

In 1944 a new fund was launched to commemorate Mitchell; the Spitfire Mitchell Memorial Fund. Among those present at the launch were Mitchell's widow, the mayors of Southampton and Stoke-on-Trent and Air Marshal Sorley, one of the champions of eight-gun fighters in the mid-1930s. The fund aimed to raise £250,000, of which £100,000 was to be used to build a youth centre in Stoke-on-Trent and the remainder to found fifteen scholarships in aeronautics, ten of which would be at University College, Southampton. An exhibition was opened in Regent Street, London, named Tribute to Genius to help raise funds. This exhibition included models of several of Mitchell's aircraft and was, perhaps, the first instance of the epithet genius having been used to describe him. Around 55,000 visitors passed through the displays during the single month that it was open. The first two scholarships were awarded in 1946 and the fund is still active today.

In the summer of 1946, a book was published to celebrate the Spitfire, dedicated to the 375 pilots of RAF Fighter Command who gave their lives in the Battle of Britain. Written by noted aviation authors John Taylor and Maurice Allward, the book, titled simply *Spitfire*, is a short history of the design, development and service career of Mitchell's fighter and is, perhaps, the first to take as its subject a study of a single aircraft type. The book repeats the statement from *The Aeroplane* in 1940 that the Spitfire was built as a private venture unrelated to any Air Ministry requirement, the inspiration of Mitchell. In 1948 Vickers celebrated the fiftieth anniversary of their aircraft business and issued a commemorative book titled *Aircraft: From Airship to Jet Propulsion*. In this they, too, wrote that the Spitfire had been developed as a private venture.

After the war, the Royal Aeronautical Society sought to recognise the achievements of important society members who had passed on by naming memorial lectures in their honour, beginning with Vickers' Designer Rex Pierson in 1952 and followed by Mitchell in 1954. The speaker at the first R.J. Mitchell Memorial Lecture, held at the aeronautics department of Southampton University, was Joe Smith who presented a paper entitled 'In Memory of Mitchell'. In his speech he outlined the career achievements of his former leader and friend, and finished with the statement: 'There is no doubt that, in order to carry on the great work which he started, more and more qualified technicians with his kind of drive and genius will be required ...' These annual lectures have continued to this day and over the years presentations have been made by other notable former Supermarine employees: Alan Clifton, Beverley Shenstone and Jack Davies.

In the post-war era there was, naturally, a lot of discussion on the conduct of the war and on the decisions that had been made in the years that led up to it. It was almost inevitable that there would be those who aimed to promote the role that they had played and to make scapegoats of others. Central to this was the portrayal of Neville Chamberlain as a weak Prime Minister lacking foresight and of Churchill as a leader of vision who had saved the nation, both views selective, skewed and simplistic. In a similar way, many in the aviation industry set out to show themselves as great innovators who had fought against a reactionary and bureaucratic Air Ministry to produce the aircraft that had helped to win the war.

As the offensive bombing campaign undertaken by the RAF against the major industrial centres of Germany was looked back on by many with some concern and distaste, because of the high number of civilian casualties, there was no great desire to highlight the key role that the bomber force had played in bringing the war to an end, and so the emphasis was placed more on the defensive actions undertaken by Fighter Command and their aircraft. The Spitfire and its creator became the focus for much attention and it helped the drama of the story that Mitchell had died at such a crucial moment. A view akin to that expressed in *The First of the Few* began to be taken as the norm and many otherwise informative aviation and history books written in the 1950s and '60s are skewed in this way. Amongst those arguing along these lines was Sir Robert McLean, who chose to accentuate this version of the story when interviewed at the end of the 1950s, promoting the idea that the Spitfire had been a private venture, a project conceived by Mitchell and nurtured by himself, with no involvement by the Air Ministry. They, he claimed, lacked vision and were holding back the development of new designs. McLean, of course, had an axe to grind having been removed from his job at the head of Vickers Aviation and Supermarine just prior to the war largely as a consequence of the big delays in bringing the Spitfire into full production, for which the Air Ministry felt he held a fair degree of responsibility. It is only in more recent years, with the release into the public domain of a great deal of government papers from the war and pre-war period, that it has been proven beyond doubt that these versions of the story are at best a gross distortion and at worst a lie. The research work undertaken by Gary Sinnot and Leo McKinstry for their respective books covering 1930s Air Ministry policies are particularly notable for having put the record straight, although the old distortions continue to reappear in some published works.

As a consequence of the significant number of skewed accounts, Mitchell was elevated to hero status, the work of his colleagues in the Design Department largely overlooked, and the true story of how the Spitfire had been conceived and developed buried under a layer of myth. A man who rightly deserved full credit for the outstanding quality of the design for the Spitfire had had his very real achievements marred by the false aura of lone genius and visionary that been attached to him.

Today Mitchell is perhaps the only aircraft designer whose name is known beyond the circles of aviation professionals and enthusiasts, and his face has appeared on stamps, commemorative medallions, collectors' plates and other souvenirs. There are statues and plaques in his home town and in several museums.

R.J. MITCHELL, THE MAN

Reginald Joseph Mitchell was known to his colleagues at Supermarine, from senior management down to the staff on the workshop floor, as RJ, and he was quite comfortable with this informal approach. So when discussing Mitchell as family man, engineer and leader of a team of design professionals it feels appropriate that here, too, he should be referred to as RJ.

Despite his fame there has been but one book written to attempt to define Reginald Mitchell the man rather than Mitchell the designer of the Spitfire, and that was the work of his son, Gordon. His book, *R.J. Mitchell, Schooldays to Spitfire*, was published in 1986, nearly fifty years after his father's death, and was revised and expanded in 1997 and again in 2001.

Gordon Mitchell, an only child, had the misfortune to lose his father while he was just a schoolboy of 16 and thus was deprived of the opportunity to know him man to man. His mother, too, he lost to cancer in 1946, breaking a further link to his father. After the war Gordon pursued a career in biology and had limited contact with the aircraft industry and those who had known his father well in the early days of Supermarine. In the 1980s, in his retirement, he began to look back on his father's career with a desire to tell the true story of his life. He sought out his father's former colleagues from the Design Department to learn more about those early years and the character of his father at work. Several, of course, had themselves passed on by then, most notably Joe Smith, while many others had only really known RJ in the last years of his life and could provide limited insight. The material he was able to gather from those still around and who had worked closely with RJ, a small number indeed, proved to be rather sketchy, anecdotal and perhaps indicative of a reticence to discuss the man rather than the legend after so many years. The book, however, is excellent although it is clear that Gordon struggled to fill out the work. Approaching half the text of the 2001 edition is composed of chapters describing the development and service life of the Spitfire, all of which occurred after the death of his father, and appendices are composed to a considerable extent of memories of the Spitfire by former pilots. At its heart, however, is a single chapter written by Gordon himself (much of the book is compiled by an editor from material provided by Gordon) that provides a wonderful insight into the relationship between a teenage son and his famous and ailing father.

Around the same time that Gordon was compiling material for his book, Eric 'Jack' Davis, who had joined Supermarine as an apprentice in 1925, had a similar idea to tell the story of the Supermarine Design Department in the early years and had also been in contact with his former colleagues. He encountered much the same problem as Gordon, a distinct lack of enthusiasm to become involved. Oliver Simmonds and Alan Clifton both declined and it was only Roger Dickson who showed any desire to help. Jack abandoned the project.

We will probably never know how RJ came to be employed by Scott-Paine or how he rose to the position of Chief Engineer and Designer by 1921. Those who would have been in a position to recall, especially Scott-Paine, Bird, Holroyd and Hargreaves, have left no record of those years. There has been a tendency in recent years to highlight how young RJ was when he assumed the role of Chief Engineer and Designer at the age of twenty-six, but in truth that was not at all unusual. Many of his peers were of similar age or younger when they took on the corresponding role in other aircraft companies; the aviation business was an opportunity for young men. Joe Smith, perhaps in the best position of all to appreciate RJ as a friend and colleague, has left us just the talk he gave at the inaugural R.J. Mitchell Memorial Lecture, which was by its nature rather formal and limited in personal detail. Alan Clifton, also close to RJ and longer-lived than many of his colleagues, contributed to Gordon Mitchell's book but he appears to have been a quiet man and uneasy with providing a personal appraisal of RJ, preferring to describe the aircraft they designed and to include in his account the whole text from the article written by RJ for *The Aeroplane* in 1929.

Notwithstanding the paucity of material, there are certain threads common to all the recollections that give a clear view on RJ's character in the office. All agree that he was a quiet, friendly man with a fine sense of humour. He was relaxed and informal in his approach to his staff. Even after 1928, when he was a director of the company and part of the joint Vickers and Supermarine strategy committee, he continued in much the same vein. Under his tenure as Chief Engineer and Designer, the Design Department expanded from fewer than a dozen up to more than fifty by the mid-1930s, yet he led, managed and mentored effectively throughout, even during the years in which his health declined. Working in the department was a positive experience for everyone but there were the occasional traumas. RJ had a volatile temper that erupted on rare occasions when he was dissatisfied with some aspect of design or behaviour. These outbursts were, thankfully, rare and short-lived, but they left a profound impression on his staff. RJ did not suffer fools gladly and if he felt that work was below par or that an idea was out of line he most certainly made his displeasure known.

Aircraft design in the 1920s and 1930s was an increasingly collaborative effort as aircraft became more complex and technology advanced. The Chief Designer remained as the final arbiter and decision maker but a prudent leader was willing to delegate and was open to ideas generated within his team to supplement his own. In these abilities RJ excelled. Several of his design team describe how it was standard practice for him to seat himself at the drawing board of one of his draughtsman, rest his elbows on the board with his head in his hands and ponder the drawing, asking questions, inviting others to join and contribute, and, most important of all, listening intently to the answers. He encouraged a dialogue to develop among the team and welcomed an open exchange of views. When dealing with a particularly difficult problem he would sit, deep in thought, for some time, and when he did so his staff soon learned to keep quiet and wait for him to speak; not to do so was to invite his wrath. As these discussions progressed it was common for him to take a soft pencil and make amendments on the drawing, leaving it to the draughtsman to interpret his pencil work and to update the drawing accordingly. Often an important decision would be made on the spot, at other times he would take time to think the matter through and would return later to give his verdict. Henry Royce is supposed to have described RJ as 'slow to decide, quick to act', which sounds to have been an astute summary of his approach to design. The downside, of course, is that finalising a design could become a protracted process if he remained dissatisfied and unsure; the Type 179 Giant and Type 224 fighter are good examples of this.

By the early 1930s the quantity of work within the department was increasing rapidly, most especially after the RAF's Expansion Plans were approved and Imperial Airways received sanction to run the Empire Airmail Scheme and to develop new routes. With Vickers' financial backing RJ was able to recruit new and experienced staff into the department, many coming from other aircraft companies who were suffering under the recession and forced to lay off staff as they lacked the financial solidity of Supermarine's owners. With a larger team in place it was now possible for RJ to assign a team leader to each new project. Those that have been well documented for projects that secured production contracts were Arthur Shirval for the Scapa, Eric Lovell-Cooper for the Stranraer, William Munro for the Seagull V and Alfred Faddy for the Spitfire. The open dialogue process continued as before but with an experienced man at the helm of each project, development of the new design proceeded more efficiently.

While we are able to draw a sketch of RJ working with his staff we are, alas, unable to see how he engaged with his managers, peers and customers. Scott-Paine, Bird, and, later, McLean were all robust characters and not averse to exerting their authority, so while RJ was in a strong position in his role he was not, even once a director, totally the master of his own destiny. With his fellow directors he would have had to argue his case for new investment, extra staff and a myriad of other issues, defend himself and his staff when things did not go smoothly, and also learn how to deal with the changing faces and characters in the Air Ministry, the RAF departments and Imperial Airways. His relationship with Rex Pierson and Barnes Wallis at Vickers, both colleagues on the joint Vickers and Supermarine management committee, remains largely unknown although his early encounter with Wallis had proven fractious and this seems to have coloured their later dealings. It is said the he was shy and uncomfortable in formal situations and when dealing with people with whom he was unfamiliar, as would often be the case, and he had a tendency to stutter, which could cause him acute embarrassment.

In his professional capacity as an engineer and aircraft designer RJ preferred to maintain a low profile. He appears to have presented papers to professional bodies just twice; once when he was awarded a silver medal by the Royal Aeronautical Society following the Schneider Trophy win in 1927 and the other at the Fifth International Air Congress in The Hague in 1930. He had only three articles published. One, in *Flight* magazine, was on the mundane subject of flying boat beaching gear, while another, in *The Aeroplane* in 1929, was about the influence on design of racing seaplanes. His third appeared in the *Daily Mirror* in the autumn of 1934 on

→ Reginald Joseph Mitchell: a formal portrait from the early 1930s.

novel or adopted subsequently by others. His early flying boats were workmanlike and had been evolved in cautious steps from the wartime designs of others, while the larger Southampton was elegant and functional rather than ground-breaking. Even his contest-winning Schneider Trophy racers incorporated little that was truly new in technology or ideas, although the diminutive semi-monocoque metal fuselage of the S.5 in 1927, with its integral, cantilever engine mount, was a remarkable tour de force for a company founded on woodworking skills, new to metallurgy, and who had only just completed their first prototype metal hull. The racers were simply very well designed for the task and as vice-free as could be hoped for with this type of aircraft. In a similar vein, the statement that RJ always favoured thin wings crops up from time to time to promote the idea that he was in the forefront of aerodynamic thinking for higher speeds, but, again, this is not supported by the evidence. His choice of aerofoil was dictated by a pragmatic engineer's view of the aircraft he was designing and there is no bias towards thinner profiles. Indeed, for the Type 179 Giant in its initial guise he had selected a particularly thick section and placed passenger accommodation within it.

Several authors, generally when writing about the genesis of the Spitfire, have implied that RJ was dismissive of wind tunnel analysis and aerodynamic experts, and it is certainly true that the Spitfire design was not subject to wind tunnel evaluation prior to construction of the prototype. RJ, unlike most of his peers, had been fortuitous to have access to the large NPL duplex wind tunnel for an extended period while working on the Schneider racing seaplanes. This programme ran from early 1926 to mid-1931. The large size of the NPL tunnel and the relatively small size of the racers enabled ¼-scale models to be evaluated, for which any scale effects would be lessened. The results of the multitude of tests appear to have matched the performance of the aircraft well enough. RJ had great respect for the RAE and NPL technicians with whom he had worked on the projects and valued the results of such work. The benefit was mutual as the staff at the NPL acknowledged how much working on the project with Mitchell, and Folland from Gloster, had extended their understanding of wind tunnel operations and limitations, and they published several reports to show how techniques and equipment were refined progressively to improve results. The quality of their assessments was and continued to be impressive.

RJ's decision to select NACA aerofoils for all his aircraft projects from the early 1930s was prompted in no small measure by the ready availability of a large body of data for these profiles from evaluations in their large variable density wind tunnels.

the subject 'What is Happening Now in Air Transport?' RJ never courted publicity and he neither gave interviews nor spoke informally to the press. It is readily apparent from numerous photographs that he was actually rather uncomfortable in public and it is rare for him to be caught smiling if there were a camera pointing in his direction. He looks especially uncomfortable in the formal photograph taken in 1933 at the time he was awarded the CBE for his services to the aircraft industry.

Despite claims by many that RJ was a great innovator there is actually little evidence in his body of work to support that view. A review of patents held by aircraft designers will show that RJ held few, certainly no more than his peers, and none were for ideas that were either particularly

In contrast, however, for design work in the Vickers era RJ was only able to use their facilities at Weybridge, which were far smaller and it would appear, a lot less sophisticated. The models evaluated for the Type 224 were $\frac{1}{16}$ scale and those for the Southampton X, Air Yacht and other larger types must have been even smaller. We can only conjecture how the results of these wind tunnel tests may have led to the over-estimation of performance for several of these aircraft but it must have coloured RJ's perception considerably. As the water tank tests on the Air Yacht and Scapa had also been misleading any scepticism that may have developed in his mind is understandable. It has to be far more likely that it was Vickers' equipment that RJ dismissed and not wind tunnels and water tanks in general. He was too experienced and professional for that.

In his contribution to Gordon Mitchell's book, Alan Clifton noted: 'Though theoretically well qualified, his outstanding characteristic was his practical outlook. His first designs were noted for reliability rather than originality', while Beverley Shenstone commented: 'Mitchell was an intensely practical man and he liked practical solutions to problems.' New ideas and solutions did not always flow freely for RJ and the transition from the era of open cockpit, wooden biplane flying boats to fully enclosed, metal cantilever monoplanes in the early 1930s proved to be especially irksome to him and he lost out first to Saunders-Roe at the smaller end of the market and then to Shorts for larger types. For a while he appears to have struggled to find a new direction while striving to design commercially competitive aircraft, and it is therefore particularly disappointing that the Type 314 flying boat, which had the makings of a class-leading aircraft, was cancelled. Similarly, despite the strong suspicion that the projected performance figures may have been optimistic, the Type 317 bomber had the potential to be a formidable aircraft for the RAF. The Spitfire therefore stands out alone as an exceptional and perhaps even somewhat unexpected success, a tribute to a designer who had regained his form. Overall it would seem that RJ is better characterised as a master craftsman rather than an innovator, a trait he shared with Henry Royce and several other great names in British engineering.

GENIUS

So, how should we assess the many claims of genius for RJ? A genius is defined as someone having extraordinary intellectual or creative powers and talent, and on that measure it could be applied equally to the Chief Designers of any of the successful aircraft companies; how could it be otherwise? Had they not had extraordinary creative powers and talent their designs would not have sold and their employing companies would have surely failed. The question is therefore: did RJ stand out amongst his peers in the 1920s and early 1930s? He was up against formidable competition: Chadwick at Avro, Gouge at Shorts, Pierson at Vickers, Folland at Gloster and Camm at Hawker, to name just five.

In terms of commercial success, Supermarine were not in the premier league during RJ's tenure. As a niche flying boat manufacturer they pursued a rather limited market and enjoyed only moderate success. Through the 1920s RJ, Scott-Paine and Bird tried long and hard to interest the British military and airlines in single and multiple-engined flying boats or amphibians but neither showed much enthusiasm.

RJ's early work was, in the main, firmly rooted in the legacy designs from the war years, the Linton Hope-hulled Channel and Baby, and he was rather slow to advance. Supermarine's aircraft were praised for their workmanship but the designs lacked refinement. The tail surfaces of the Seagull, for example, were braced by no fewer than fourteen struts. Only with the advent of the Southampton did RJ move forward and introduce a number of notable improvements and, although still lacking aerodynamic cleanliness, they were among the best of their type at the time and certainly set a new standard for British mid-sized flying boats. They provided the RAF with their first truly flexible coastal patrol aircraft capable of operation throughout the globe with minimal support, but it would be stretching the point to suggest this was a work of genius.

Then, in mid-1925 RJ stunned the British aviation fraternity when his S.4 Schneider racer was unveiled. Supermarine's racing pedigree was well established but no one was expecting RJ to produce such a radical seaplane. Notwithstanding several stylistic similarities to the Bernard V2 speed record-breaking aircraft, the S.4 was an astounding piece of work from RJ, worlds apart from his contemporaneous flying boat designs and worthy of the tag of genius. Why so little of this flair made its way into his other designs of this period is a little difficult to understand. The S.5 of 1927 was, if anything, an even more outstanding aircraft. True, the use of braced wings and floats appeared to be a retrograde step but for a world-beating racer this was soon proven to be the correct approach. Suggestions in the French and Italian press at the time that RJ had copied Mario Castoldi's Macchi M.39, with which it shared nothing more than its basic layout, are groundless both in terms of timing and of design. The S.5 was a far more advanced aircraft, in design, structure and capability. It was a better pilot's aircraft than either the S.4 or the competing biplanes from Gloster, and a superb racer. It may have been a little short on pure innovation but was very much a work of genius nevertheless. The basic design was to prove so sound that it formed the inspiration for the S.6 in 1929 and the S.6b in 1931, the latter flying with three times the engine power of the S.5 and nearly 100mph faster.

Yet at the same time these contest-dominating aircraft were being designed RJ was also working on the lacklustre Seamew and Nanok, the ponderous Southampton X and the unrefined Air Yacht. These he followed with the dithering and constant redesign of the Type 179 Giant, a project that ultimately led nowhere. It is a sobering fact that Supermarine failed to win a single production contract for any of RJ's new aircraft designs between the Southampton in 1924 and the Scapa in 1933, a full nine years kept afloat by repeat orders, replacement parts, one-off prototypes, racers and Vickers' money.

In the early 1930s Supermarine managed at last to set out on the road to commercial recovery with the development and sales of the Scapa, Stranraer and Seagull V/Walrus. The first two were the best of their class but biplanes in a world in transition to monoplanes, while the Seagull V/Walrus was a simple, rugged and effective Jack of all trades; all excellent aircraft but, again, hardly worthy of the tag of genius.

The Type 224 fighter was a radical departure for RJ, the first landplane built by the company since the diminutive Sparrow and their first completed cantilever monoplane since the unfortunate S.4, which probably goes a long way to explain why he was a little reticent to be too bold with the design. The aircraft, nevertheless, was the best of the several contenders for the F.7/30 contract and was let down more by the Goshawk engine installation than by its qualities as an aircraft. It is very clear that RJ was dissatisfied with the design even prior to the first flight as his constant fiddling with details makes readily apparent. In the light of the Spitfire that followed, the Type 224 is generally cast aside as clumsy and a total failure, but while it was lacking in many ways it was not the disaster that is often implied and was a valuable stepping stone for the design team. The other major new monoplane design project under way at the same time, the large Type 232 flying boat, was, like the Type 224, an odd blend of new ideas and conservatism and, like the fighter, it proved to be a cul-de-sac in design terms and subsequent flying boat projects took a completely different route.

It is a matter of record that the first new project undertaken by RJ after his surgery and convalescence in late 1933 was the Type 300 Spitfire. The coincidence that his finest design should emerge at this precise point in his life has led some to conclude that he must have resolved to throw all his creative efforts into the aircraft in whatever time remained to him, while others have dismissed this as groundless on the basis that the Spitfire was not his last design. The obvious problem with that view, however, is that it presumes RJ knew both how much longer he had to live and that opportunities for new aircraft on which he could work would be forthcoming. Neither, of course, would have been known to him. It is an indisputable fact that from the Type 300 Spitfire onwards there was indeed a radical change in the style of designs produced by RJ and his team; they are less conservative, feature innovative new ideas and embrace new technology. It is not at all unreasonable to conclude from this that RJ, who knew he was ailing, had indeed decided to adopt a less cautious approach to design and to encourage a more imaginative approach from his team. This, of course, proved to be spectacularly successful.

After reviewing all RJ's design work; the twenty-two aircraft types that were built and the eighty or so that did not make it off the drawing board, it is clear that while he was certainly capable of moments of genius, more frequently he chose an evolutionary and conservative path. Many of his peers, notably Pierson, Folland and Camm, did the same; it generally made commercial sense. These considerations may have led too often to RJ deciding that a more cautious approach was appropriate, but his failure to secure orders over a good number of years is a clear sign that his judgement in this regard was incorrect. Worryingly, he also showed a distinct tendency on occasion to ignore the stated preferences of his customers; for example, to offer liquid-cooled engines when air-cooled were preferred and biplanes when a monoplane was specified. As mentioned earlier, RJ, like many of his peers, struggled through the difficult transition from wooden biplanes to stressed metal skin cantilever monoplanes, which is all the more curious as his work on the Schneider racers provided him with a great deal of valuable knowledge that was not readily available to his competitors. With the benefit of hindsight it can be seen that undue conservatism tended to prevail when he was working on designs in a competitive market.

Overall it would seem that RJ's creative side was tempered by an innate pragmatism and caution that functioned as an internal governor to keep his latent inventiveness in check, and so it is particularly poignant that it was to be his critical illness that served to liberate him and ultimately released the full flow of his genius to provide the nation with the Spitfire.

APPENDIX 1
ORPHAN DESIGNS

A small number of surviving drawings do not fit within any of the Supermarine drawing number systems and also do not appear to be directly related to any known projects. They are described here for completeness.

One possible project for which neither drawings nor details are known is mentioned briefly in *The Aeroplane* in October 1919. In a short paragraph referring to the Dolphin design from the 1919 brochure the concluding remarks say that Supermarine were also working on a larger flying boat of 3,000hp. This could equate to six Rolls-Royce Condors. In the absence of even a simple layout drawing the evidence that such a concept was under consideration by Supermarine remains circumstantial, and the works were certainly not capable of assembling an aircraft of this size.

There is a badly damaged drawing of a three-engined military monoplane flying boat in the archive that lacks a date, author or drawing number. Stylistic similarity to some of the early project concept drawings for the six-engined flying boats and a hull and tailplane that are reminiscent of the Southampton X suggests that it dates from late 1928 or 1929. The engines

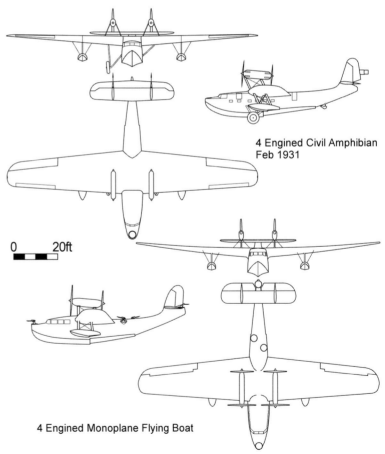

4 Engined Civil Amphibian
Feb 1931

0   20ft

4 Engined Monoplane Flying Boat

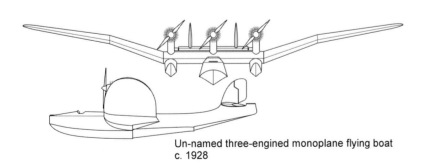

Un-named three-engined monoplane flying boat
c. 1928

are twin-row radials and hence presumably Armstrong Siddeley Panthers or Jaguars, which would have placed the aircraft in the same league as the Air Yacht and the Southampton X. Of particular note is the cranked seagull, cantilever monoplane wing with elliptical plan outer panels.

William Munro produced drawings for two flying boats that lack type numbers and which do not appear to fit neatly with any of the known Supermarine designs from the early 1930s.

The four-engined Civil Amphibian is dated February 1931. This was a large cantilever monoplane with a flat-sided hull with an upswept tail on which was mounted a typical Supermarine tailplane with twin fins. There were Flettner servos on the rudders. The undercarriage was mounted on braced oleo struts and retracted outwards with the wheels fitting into wells in the wing, as on the Seagull V, a project led by Munro. The aircraft was to be powered by four Napier Rapier air-cooled inline engines in tandem pairs in nacelles mounted above the wing.

The four-engined Monoplane Flying Boat, which is undated but from the style is likely to have been slightly later than the Civil Amphibian, was a military aircraft intermediate in size between the Stranraer and the Sunderland and, as such, not aimed at addressing any particular Air Ministry requirement at that time. The hull was similar in form to that on the Civil Amphibian but with nose, tail and staggered amidships open gun positions. The high mounted cantilever tapered wing was also similar and the engines, in tandem pairs, were Rolls-Royce Kestrels employing steam cooling.

APPENDIX 2

THE SPITFIRE'S SKEWED ELLIPTICAL WING AND NOTES ON NACA AEROFOILS

In recent years there have been a number of misleading statements made regarding the aerofoil sections and skewed elliptical plan for the Spitfire wing that would benefit from correction and clarification.

Many designers in the early 1930s were choosing to adopt aerofoils that had been developed by the NACA for which both theoretical and large-scale wind tunnel data had been published, most notably in Technical Report 460 issued in 1933. This family of aerofoils are now referred to as the four-digit series. The profile of these aerofoils are described by a series of mathematical equations with just three variables; maximum camber (M), position of maximum camber divided by ten (P) and thickness (XX), all expressed as a percentage of chord. Camber is the amount by which the mean line, the locus of mean thickness, deviates from the chord line, the aerofoil length from leading to trailing edge. The aerofoil is then characterised by the four figures MPXX. Using these equations the aerodynamicist or designer can define and optimise an aerofoil to meet their specific requirements and be reasonably confident about how that aerofoil will perform. Thus, an aerofoil designated 2213, as used for the root of the Spitfire wing, has a maximum camber of 2 per cent of chord, the position of maximum camber is at 20 per cent chord and the maximum thickness is 13 per cent of chord. The aerofoil at the tip, NACA 2209.4, is therefore a closely related section with the same camber but with thickness reduced to 9.4 per cent. The equations make calculation of the shape of each wing rib a simple process once the rate of change in thickness from root to tip has been defined.

A NACA 2200 series aerofoil is not therefore inherently of thin section as the thickness is prescribed by the designer to meet his needs. Furthermore, if, as in the case of the Spitfire, the selected aerofoils from root to tip vary only in thickness-to-chord ratio while the camber parameters remain constant there

is no complex dovetailing, blending or localised reshaping involved. There is just a smooth, and easily calculated, transition across the span. Applying this type of thickness-to-chord transition for the wing of the Spitfire was neither revolutionary nor unique; it was actually common practice for many tapered wings of the period, including both the Hawker Hurricane and Gloster F.5/34, and, indeed, the Spitfire's direct Type 300 predecessor.

As we have seen, there has been much written about the unique plan shape of the Spitfire's wing, some good, some bad. There can be no doubt that it proved to be highly effective, well in the forefront when it first flew in 1936 and still among the best nearly ten years later, but there are no secrets in its design, no mystery and, in truth, no innovations. It was all based on published information and, as such, any competent designer could have achieved the same. It is to the great credit of Mitchell, Shenstone and the others that they alone saw the benefits of bringing together several strands of aerodynamic technology within one structure at this date.

There was a detailed mathematical analysis of the Spitfire's wing shape available on the internet that provided a comparison of the lofting data, taken from original Supermarine blueprints, with ideal geometric curves. Unfortunately, it is no longer available online, but 'The Spitfire Wing – A Mathematical Model' gave a thorough description of the wing geometry. A brief summary is as follows.

The Spitfire's wing plan is not especially sophisticated; it is very close indeed to a simple skewed ellipse, neither two half ellipses nor some subtle calculated curve. In terms of the relationship between span and chord the wing is indeed elliptical; if the ribs of the wing were aligned on their chord-wise mid points an ellipse could be drawn through their ends, with just very small discrepancies of an inch or so near the tips. The Spitfire wing was constructed in two parts; the main wing built on the leading edge torsion box spar, and a wing tip that was a separate secondary structure bolted to the wing. In the main wing a nominal datum line can be established just to the rear of the spar at 27.5 per cent chord, the position that corresponds with the maximum thickness of the aerofoil. If the basic ellipse is then skewed forward so that its 27.5 per cent chord line is straightened it conforms very closely indeed to the profile of the wing as far out as the last rib. The wing tip, while still a close approximation to a skewed ellipse, is a best-fit curve from the last rib on the main wing structure around a tip defined by a circle of 9in radius, and this accounts for the small discrepancies from a true ellipse mentioned above.

The Type 224 and both the preliminary Type 300 designs had incorporated twist or washout in their straight-tapered wings with incidence of +2 degrees at the root and -0.5 degrees at the tip. This twist was carried

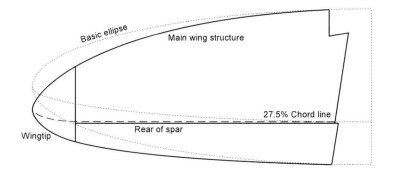

through unchanged directly on to the Spitfire and was not a late revision or optimisation specific to the elliptical wing. Furthermore, both Type 300 designs had wing dihedral of 4.5 degrees and this was originally also intended for the Spitfire. However, when Harold Payn expressed concern about stability and after consultation with Rex Pierson at Vickers it was decided to increase this to 6 degrees.

The very small deviations of the wing profile from a mathematically 'perfect' curve, and they are truly very small, are highly likely a function of the methods and limitations of the Supermarine Design Department at the time rather than some subtle adjustment of the shape based on aerodynamic theory; they are just too small to have been meaningful. Draughting was still a matter of hand-drawn curves and manual adjustment, and Mitchell was prone to making his amendments with a very soft pencil producing a thick line. Small distortions or approximations were bound to creep in from time to time. For example, when component production for the Spitfire was subcontracted out to third parties there were cases where the drawings were shown to be rather rough and occasionally inaccurate; manufactured parts would not fit together. Many later drawings are labelled 'drawing altered to suit parts as manufactured', although in these cases due allowance has to be made for the pressure of wartime work. The essence is that prior to the construction of the Spitfire Supermarine were most used to constructing rather simple flying boats in small numbers and the advent of new technology, subcontracting and quantity production was a vast leap forward. They managed to do so remarkably well, all things considered, and both further and faster than their competitors, but it is inevitable that there were more than a few approximations and short cuts along the way.

APPENDIX 3
THE DESIGN DEPARTMENT

Mitchell's Design Department underwent substantial change over the years and saw a considerable turnover of staff, reflecting the fluctuating fortunes of the company and competition from other aircraft manufacturers. It is difficult therefore to establish with certainty the exact size and composition of the department at any specific date. However, it is fortuitous that a few copies of the department's self-penned in-house magazine, *The Ragazine*, have survived from 1927–28. This magazine was still an unofficial affair at the time and they produced just a single copy each month that was loaned to members of staff for *2d* per evening. A circulation list of subscribers was pasted inside. It seems fair to assume that most of the department would have wished to subscribe. By using this list as a basis, supplemented by references to individuals in the magazine and the reminiscences of former staff members, notably Roger Dickson, the following table is a fair representation of the whole department in early 1928, just prior to the takeover by Vickers.

EARLY 1928

REGINALD J. MITCHELL
(Technical Director – Chief Engineer & Designer)

Drawing Office	Technical Office	Tracers	Boys	Clerical
Joe Smith (Chief Draughtsman)	Frank Holroyd (Assistant Chief Engineer)	Mrs Sadie Duggan		
J. Alexander	Arthur Black	Miss Barker	S. Buckle	Miss Vera Cross
H. Axtell	Alan Clifton	Miss Collett	J. Bull	(Sec. to Mitchell)
Baker	Bert Hammond	Miss Farley	W. Cox	Miss Henbery
W.E. Bourne	Wilf E. B. Hennesey	Miss A. Hiscox Jnr	Staples	(B.M.) Spencer
Bill Case	Harry Holmes	Miss E. Hiscox Snr		
Reg Caunter	Ernest (Eric) Mansbridge	Miss Jones		
William R. Conley	Pond	Mrs Laidlaw		
Eric Lovell Cooper	Oliver Simmonds	Mrs Laidman		

Drawing Office	Technical Office	Tracers	Boys	Clerical
W. Cox	Harold C. Smith	Miss Jean Leach		
Roger Dickson	H.O. (Oscar) Sommer	Miss Morgan		
Embley		Miss Frances Ommanny		
George W. Garrett		Miss Parker		
Cecil Gedge		Miss Perry		
Gross		Miss Shard		
T.H. Harris		Miss Whitfield		
Haslam				
Johnson				
Jordens				
C.V. (George) Kettlewell				
Richard Laidman				
J. Mason				
Milnthorpe				
Horace Noble				
Parkinson				
F.G. Perry				
Jack Rice				
G. Robinson				
H. Robinson				
R. Rogers				
Arthur H. Shirvall				
V.W. Steele				
Talbot				
Tong				
Harry T. Tremelling				
Walke Jnr				
Walke Snr				
Whitehead				
Young				

The department was housed on the floor above the construction workshops and directly under the roof, where it was notorious for being excessively hot in the summer and cold in the winter. In addition, the aging roof structure leaked, providing plenty of opportunities for jokes and cartoons in *The Ragazine*.

As noted in the earlier chapters, Vickers introduced substantial changes to Mitchell's department after 1928, recruiting new members from other companies and laying off a number of staff. The onset of the Depression and the cancellation of the Type 179 Giant led to further waves of redundancies before the launch of the RAF's Expansion Plans and production contract work for the Seagull V, Scapa, Stranraer and Spitfire resulted in a reversal and recruitment drive.

By 1934, when work on the Spitfire became the priority, the department had started to increase in size with most of the additional staff working in the Technical Office. Unfortunately, it does not appear to be possible at present to recreate the full staff list as only the names of the senior and key members are known with certainty. The following list is an amalgamation from various sources.

"IF YOU KNOWS OF A BETTER 'OLE" —

→ As the title suggests, *The Ragazine* contained a fair amount of humorous and satirical material. This cartoon, borrowing its caption from a famous *Punch* cartoon from the war, lampoons the less than luxurious state of the Drawing Office.

MID-1934

REGINALD J. MITCHELL
(Technical Director – Chief Engineer & Designer)

MAJ. HAROLD PAYN
(Deputy Designer & Personal Assistant)

Drawing Office	Technical Office	Tracers	Boys	Clerical
Joe Smith (Chief Draughtsman)	Alan Clifton (Head of Technical Office)	xx		
H. Axtell	Arthur Black	?	?	Miss Vera Cross
C. Blazdell	Bryant			(Sec. to Mitchell)
Bill Case	Roger Dickson			?
Reg Caunter	Harry Griffiths			
C. Childer	Bert Hammond			
William R. Conley	Wilfred Hennesey			
Eric Lovell Cooper	Harold Holmes			
W.G. Cox	R. Horrocks			
Eric John (Jack) Davis	Sammy Hughes			
Alfred Faddy	R. Kember			
J.O. Eke	Wilfred Guy Kimber			
Eric Donald (Bill) Fear	Ernest (Eric) Mansbridge			
R. J. Fenner	R. Mansfield			
Cecil Gedge	George Nicholas			
J. Harris	Jack Rice			
J. Jupp	R. M. A. Powell			
George Kettlewell	Reginald H. Schlotel			
Charles W. Labette	Beverley S. Shenstone			
Dick Laidman	Harold C. Smith			
Max Langley	H.O. (Oscar) Sommer			
William Munro	Murray White			
W. Musselwhite				
Horace Noble				
Pardoe				
Frank Parry				
Jack Rasmussen				

Drawing Office	Technical Office	Tracers	Boys	Clerical
R. Rogers				
Arthur H. Shirvall				
Tong				
Harry T. Tremelling				
T. Walker				
Probably 5–10 others				

APPENDIX 4

SUPERMARINE PROJECT LIST AND INDEX

Year	Project (single prototypes in *italics*, production aircraft in **bold**)		Chapter
1917	**Baby**	N59, 60, 61	1
1919	Single Seat Flying Boat, Type A		2
	2-engined, 3-seater flying boat, Type B		2
	Channel, Type C	Mod. AD Flying Boat	1
	3-engined triplane flying boat, 'Dolphin' Type D		2
	Sea Lion	Ex Baby N61	2
	'Shark' triplane flying boat		2
1920	Single-seat flying boat		3
	Sea King	Ex Baby N60	3
	Channel II, 4-seater		3
	Amphibian (Commercial Amphibian)		3
	Single-seat scout and bomber		3
	Single-seat ship's flying boat		3
	Amphibian flying boat for ship work		3
	Seal Mk II		3
1921	Fleet gunnery spotting amphibian		3
	Triplane torpedo carrier flying boat		3
	Swan 7-seater commercial amphibian flying boat		4
	Sea King II	Ex Sea King	3
	Single-seat fighter flying boat for ship use		3
	7-seater commercial flying boat		4

Year	Project (single prototypes in *italics*, production aircraft in **bold**)		Chapter
	Commercial amphibian flying boat for Instone		4
	School amphibian flying boat		3
	Seagull amphibian flying boat	Seagull II & III	5
	Scylla flying boat torpedo carrier	Hull only	3
1922	8-seat commercial amphibian		4
	Amphibian flying boat, school machine	Mod. Channel	-
	Bomber amphibian flying boat		5
	Twin-engined bomber amphibian		5
	4-seat commercial amphibian flying boat		4
	Twin-engined commercial flying boat	Early Swan	-
	Sea Lion II	Ex Sea King II	3
	Swan twin-engined civil amphibian flying boat		4
	Sea Eagle		4
	Amphibian flying boat for long-distance work	'Round the World'	4
	3-seat amphibian flying boat		4
1923	Amphibian flying boat service bomber type		5
	3-engined flying boat to AM spec 9/23		7
	Sheldrake amphibian flying boat service bomber type		5
	Sea Lion III	Ex Sea Lion II	6
	Sea Urchin high performance flying boat		6
	Commercial and general service amphibian flying boat	Civil Sheldrake	5
1924	**Scarab amphibian flying boat service bomber**		5
	Twin-engine flying boat converted to armed reconnaissance	Based on Swan	7
	Amphibian flying boat fleet spotter	2 designs	8
	Service type twin-engine flying boat		7
	Sparrow two-seater aeroplane	biplane	8
	Southampton		7
	Twin-engine amphibian flying boat	2 designs	8
1925	Single-seater high performance seaplane		9
	Shark twin-engine flying boat		7
	Swan MkII twin-engine amphibian flying boat		7
	Condor light bomber amphibian		8
	Southampton II		10

Year	Project (single prototypes in *italics*, production aircraft in **bold**)		Chapter
	Southampton twin-engine flying boat for civil purposes		7
1926	**Seamew**		8
	S4 seaplane		9
	Southampton development 3-engined flying boat	3 designs	7
	Solent/Nanok FBVII torpedo bomber		7
	S5 seaplane		12
	Sparrow II two-seater aeroplane	monoplane	8
	Twin-engine flying boat for civil purposes	Civil Seamew	8
	Solent 3-engined flying boat for civil purposes		-
	Single seat fleet fighter to AM spec. 21/26	3 designs	11
1927	3-engined flying boat to AM spec 4/27	biplane	13
	3-engined flying boat to AM spec 4/27 & air yacht	monoplane	13
1928	**S6 seaplane**		15
	Flying boat 6 Napier XI engines	6 designs	16
	Seamew – single Napier Lion or Bristol Jupiter engine		8
	3-engine monoplane Air Yacht		15
	3-engine monoplane flying boat		App 1
	Type 171 Southampton Mark X		15
	Type 171 civil Southampton Mark X		15
1929	Six-engined flying boat to AM spec. R.6/28		16
	Type 179 Six-engined flying boat to AM spec. 20/28	Contract cancelled	16
	Type 178 00 Sea Hawk 3-engined civil flying boat		15
	Type 180 4-engined civil flying boat		18
1930	Twin-engine flying boat – Hispano Suiza engines	3 designs	18
	Type 178 00 Sea Hawk 3-engined amphibian flying boat		17
	Twin-engined fleet spotter to AM spec. 9/30		18
	Type 178 00 3-engined civil amphibian flying boat		17
1931	Type 178 01 Civil mail carrier		17
	Type 178 02 Single-engined bomber & reconnaissance amphibian		17
	Type 181 Amphibian flying boat for the RAAF & civil		15
	4-engined civil amphibian		App 1
	4-engined monoplane flying boat		App 1
	Type 178 03 Twin-engined air mail boat		17

Year	Project (single prototypes in *italics*, production aircraft in **bold**)		Chapter
	Type 182 General purpose commercial high-wing monoplane		18
	Type 183 General purpose commercial low-wing monoplane	No information	-
	Type 184 Southampton II (R-R Kestrels and metal wings)	N253	10
	Type 185 Southampton X (mod. with Bristol Jupiters)		15
	Type 186 S6a (refurbished S6 with new floats)		18
	Type 187 S6b		18
	Type 188 Southampton X modified with cockpit canopy		15
	Type 189 Southampton II modified with Bristol Jupiters	Modified N218	10
	Type 190 Southampton II export versions; Turkey etc		-
	Type 178 04 Twin-engine Southampton flying boat		19
	Type 178 05 Twin-engine flying boat		19
	Type 178 06 Sea Hawk	Southampton Mk X	-
	Type 178 07 Southampton IV		19
	Type 178 08 Proposal to reduce landing speed	S6b	18
	Type 178 09 High performance day bomber		24
	Type 178 10 Single-seat day and night fighter (biplane and monoplane)		21
1932	Type 178 11 3-engined monoplane flying boat	Military Air Yacht	-
	Type 178 12 Single-seat biplane day and night fighter	Mod. Type 178 10	21
	Type 178 14 Single-seat monoplane day and night fighter	Mod. Type 178 10	21
	Type 221 Southampton IV	Scapa prototype	19
	Type 222 Floats for Vickers Vildebeest		-
	Type 223 Seagull V single-engine amphibian flying boat	Prototype N2	20
	Type 224 Single-seat monoplane day and night to AM spec. F.7/30		21
	Type 225 Single-engine civil amphibian flying boat	Civil Seagull V	20
	Type 226 Scapa	Production	19
	Type 227 Southampton V to AM spec. R.24/31		19
	Type 228 Seagull V	Production	20
	Type 229 Scapa with experimental stainless steel wing spars		-
	Type 230 Southampton V/Stranraer	Prototype	19
	Type 231 Twin-engine bomber transport to AM spec. C.26/31		-
	Type 232 Four-engine boat seaplane to AM spec. R.2/33		22
	Type 233 Southampton II for Turkey, Hispano-Suiza 12Nbr engines		-
1933	**Type 234 Southampton II for Turkey, Hispano-Suiza 12Nbr engines**		-

Year	Project (single prototypes in *italics*, production aircraft in **bold**)		Chapter
	Type 235 Scapa with Napier Culverin diesel engines		19
	Type 236 Walrus	Production	20
1934	**Type 237 Stranraer** (and projected civil adaptation)	Production	19
	Type 238 Biplane boat seaplane to AM spec. R.2/33		22
	Type 239 Four-engine boat seaplane to AM spec. R.2/33		22
	Type 240 Twin-engine coastal reconnaissance landplane		-
	Type 300 F.7/30 development	Projects & Spitfire I	21
	Type 301 Floats for Vickers Vincent		-
	Type 302 Four-engine flying boat for Imperial Airways		22
	Type 303 R.24/31 Scapa development	4 designs	23
1935	**Type 304 Stranraer development – Canadian Vickers production**		-
	Heavy bomber landplane to AM spec. B.1/35		24
	Type 305 Two-seater day and night fighter AM spec. F.9/35		21
	Type 306 Flying Boat for Imperial Airways transatlantic passenger service		22
	Type 307 Seagull V – Pegasus VI		-
	Type 308 Long-range flying boat to AM spec. R.12/35		23
	Type 309 Sea Otter		20
	Type 310 Long-range flying boat		23
1936	Type 311	No information	-
	Type 312 Single-seat day and night fighter to AM spec. F.37/35		21
	Type 313 Single-seat day and night fighter to AM spec. F.37/35		-
	Type 314 High performance flying boat to AM spec. R.1/36		23
	Type 315 Walrus for Argentina		-
1937	Type 316 Heavy Bomber to AM spec. B.12/36		24
	Type 317 Heavy Bomber to AM spec. B.12/36 – Hercules engines	Two prototypes	24
	Type 318 Heavy Bomber to AM spec. B.12/36 – Merlin engines		24
	Type 319 Two-seat fighter		25
	Type 320 Walrus for Turkey		-
1938	Type 321 Mark IV gun turret		24
	Type 322 Aircraft to AM spec. S.24/37		-
	Type 323 Speed Spitfire		21, 25
	Type 324 Fighter to AM spec. F.18/37		25
	Type 325 Fighter to AM spec. F.18/37		25

Year	Project (single prototypes in *italics*, production aircraft in **bold**)		Chapter
	Type 326 Walrus development - Pegasus VI		-
	Type 327 High-speed single-seat cannon gun fighter		25
1939	Type 328 Flying boat to AM spec. R.5/39		25
	Type 329 Spitfire Mk II		
	Type 330 Spitfire Mk III		
	Type 331 Spitfire Mk V		
	Type 332 Spitfire FN gun (for Estonia)		
	Type 333 Two-seat fleet fighter to AM spec. N.8/39		25

SELECTED BIBLIOGRAPHY

Andrews, C.F. & Morgan, E.B., *Supermarine Aircraft since 1914* (Putnam, 1981)

Buttler, Tony. *British Secret Projects: Fighters and Bombers 1935–1950* (Midland, 2004)

'Griff' (Harry Griffiths). *Testing Times: Memoirs of a Spitfire Boffin* (United Writers, 2001)

McKinstry, Leo. *Spitfire: Portrait of a Legend* (John Murray, 2007)

Meercoms, K.J. & Morgan, E.B. *The British Aircraft Specification File* (Air Britain, 1994)

Mitchell, Gordon. *R.J. Mitchell: Schooldays to Spitfire* (Tempus, 2002)

Morgan, Eric B. & Shacklady, Edward. *Spitfire: The History* (Key Publishing, 1993)

Pegram, Ralph. *Schneider Trophy Racing Seaplanes and Flying Boats* (Fonthill, 2012)

Price, Alfred. *The Spitfire Story* (Arms and Armour Press, 1995)

Quill, Jeffrey. *Birth of a Legend: The Spitfire* (Quiller Press, 1986)

Rance, Adrian. *Fast Boats and Flying Boats: a Biography of Hubert Scott-Paine* (Ensign Publications, 1989)

Roussel, Mike. *Spitfire's Forgotten Designer: The Career of Supermarine's Joe Smith* (The History Press, 2013)

Sinnott, Colin. *The RAF and Aircraft Design 1923–1939: Air Staff Operational Requirements* (Frank Cass, 2001)

Stoney, Barbara. *Twentieth Century Maverick: The Life of Noel Pemberton Billing* (Bank House Books, 2004)

Webb, Denis Le P. *Never a Dull Moment at Supermarine* (J&KH Publishing, 2001)

INDEX

If you enjoyed this book, you may also be interested in…

978 0 7509 6146 2